Hard Sayings

A Catholic Approach to Answering Bible Difficulties

TRENT HORN

Hard Sayings

A Catholic Approach to Answering Bible Difficulties

Published by Catholic Answers, Inc.
2020 Gillespie Way
El Cajon, California 92020
1-888-291-8000 orders
619-387-0042 fax
catholic.com

Printed in the United States of America

Cover design by Devin Schadt
Interior design by Sherry Russell

978-1-941663-74-5 hardcover
978-1-68357-073-8 paperback
978-1-941663-75-2 Kindle
978-1-941663-76-9 ePub

For Matthew

Contents

Introduction

If you could only give one book about Christianity to a non-Christian friend, what would it be? Maybe it would be a classic defense of the faith like C.S. Lewis's *Mere Christianity*? Or maybe it would be a gripping biography of a saint? Or maybe it would be the one book most Christians want with them if they were to be stranded on a desert island—the Bible.

But be careful. Although Christians think the Bible can help your faith, atheists say intensive Bible reading is a good way to *destroy* your faith. Famous magician and outspoken atheist Penn Jillette says, "[I've] read the Bible cover to cover . . . if you read the Bible or the Koran or the Torah cover to cover I believe you will emerge from that as an atheist."[1]

David Silverman, the president of American Atheists, said in the *New York Times*, "I gave a Bible to my daughter. That's how you make atheists."[2] Richard Carrier, another prominent atheist, describes his response after reading the entire Bible: "When I finished the last page, though alone in my room I declared aloud: 'Yep, I'm an atheist.'"[3]

What is it about the Bible that catapults some people into atheism?

Jillette says, "[I]t's all tribal; when you see a God that is jealous and insecure . . . it was clearly written hundreds of years after the supposed fact and full of contradictions." Carrier adds, "[T]his same cruel God orders people to be stoned to death for picking up sticks on Saturday, and commands that those who follow other religions be genocidally slaughtered." Richard Dawkins, the author of the *New York Times* bestseller *The God Delusion,* summed up many atheists' attitudes toward the Bible and its depiction of God:

> The God of the Old Testament is arguably the most unpleasant character in all fiction: jealous and proud of it; a petty, unjust, unforgiving control-freak; a vindictive, bloodthirsty

ethnic cleanser; a misogynistic, homophobic, racist, infanti-cidal, genocidal, filicidal, pestilential, megalomaniacal, sado-masochistic, capriciously malevolent bully.[4]

A jealous and cruel God. Endorsements of genocide and slav-ery. Irresolvable contradictions. When Christians are presented with these objections to the Bible many of them don't know what to say. They've been sabotaged by Sunday school lessons and homilies that ignore what Pope Benedict XVI calls "the dark passages of Scripture."[5] The goal of this book is to shine the light on these passages and equip Christians to defend the inspiration and inerrancy of God's sacred word.

Why This Book?

One reason I wrote this book is that there are no works that com-prehensively explained the Bible's tough passages from a Catholic perspective. There were some books that helped defend Scripture against general attacks on its reliability (Fr. William Most's *Free from All Error* is one example), but there were none that system-atically addressed the Bible's most infamous "tough passages."

When I would be asked in public forums to recommend books on "Bible difficulties" I usually referred the audience to books by Protestant authors, like Gleason Archer's *New Encyclo-pedia of Bible Difficulties* or Norman Geisler and Thomas Howe's *Big Book of Bible Difficulties*. These books have helpful answers, but sprinkled throughout their pages are statements that conflict with the Catholic Faith.

One example would be these authors' claim that the best way to resolve the difficulty in Jesus' command to "eat his flesh and drink his blood" (John 6:53) is to say that the passage is symbolic and not literal.[6] Indeed, to his followers this command represent-ed the original "hard saying" of Jesus. Or as John's Gospel says, "Many of his disciples, when they heard it, said, 'This is a hard saying; who can listen to it?' . . . After this many of his disciples drew back and no longer went about with him" (John 6:60, 66).

But as a Catholic it would be 1) heretical for me to denounce the Real Presence of Christ in the Eucharist and 2) an unsound approach to Scripture, since I believe that the literal view best explains this passage. Therefore, I felt it was necessary to write a book about perplexing Bible passages that would not lead Catholics into theological error. I felt called to explain the Bible's hard sayings so that today's disciples don't "draw back" and stop following Christ or believing in his sacred word.

That being said, I hope non-Catholics will examine my approach, compare it to the approach taken by authors like Archer or Geisler, and see if it is a more feasible way of defending the inspiration and inerrancy of Sacred Scripture.

The "Dark Passages" of Scripture

Pope Benedict XVI's apostolic exhortation *Verbum Domini* refers to "dark passages of Scripture," or as Benedict says, "passages in the Bible which, due to the violence and immorality they occasionally contain, prove obscure and difficult."[7] In this book I use the term "dark passages" in the sense that the Evangelical "emerging church" leader Brian McLaren uses it. He identifies the dark passages not only as those that describe violence and immorality (as Benedict references) but also those that "conflict with one another, or can't be squared with the scientific data."[8] In short, they are the apparently erroneous passages that make us question whether the Bible is the word of God.

Part I of this book addresses external difficulties, the dark passages that appear to contradict scientific or historical facts known apart from the Bible (for example, Genesis and evolution, or the historicity of the Gospels). Part II addresses internal difficulties, those passages that appear to contradict other parts of the Bible (passages that disagree on details of the same event or that describe God in very different ways). Finally, Part III addresses the passages Benedict refers to, the ones that contain "moral difficulties" that seem to endorse evils like chattel slavery or the slaughter of innocent women and children.

Keep in mind that answering every objection a critic could raise against the Bible would require a book much longer than the Bible itself. Fortunately, most of the objections critics make fall under a few common patterns, and so only a small percentage of the Bible is cited in their arguments. By reviewing these patterns and commonly cited verses you can learn to defend Scripture without having to examine each of the Bible's approximately 35,000 individual verses.

It is my hope you will see that objections to the Bible can be answered. In fact, Bible scholars have done that for centuries. Therefore, believers should not be afraid to share the good news about the love of God that is recorded in his inspired and inerrant word.

1

The Catholic View
of Scripture

Anyone who writes about the Bible does so with a particular opinion about it. An atheist might see the Bible as a collection of human writings devoid of supernatural influence. A Protestant, on the other hand, might see it as not only inspired, but the only authoritative source of Christian doctrine. In contrast to these views, I take a "Catholic approach" to Scripture. It affirms the Bible's divine inspiration but denies that Scripture is the Christian's only infallible rule of faith. I hold this view because it was the only one that made sense to me during my conversion to Christianity.

Before my conversion I was a deist, or someone who believed in a God that existed "out there" but didn't care about humanity. I didn't believe in Jesus, and I definitely didn't believe in the Bible being "the word of God." However, this changed in high school when my study of Christianity led me to accept that even if the New Testament wasn't divinely inspired, it was at least historically reliable. And because of this historical reliability, I had good reason to believe that Jesus of Nazareth rose from the dead and vindicated his claims to divinity.

These facts motivated me to become a Christian, but I still struggled with difficult questions about the Bible. Why should I believe every book found in the Bible is the inspired word of God? Even if the Bible was inspired, how do I know I'm interpreting it correctly? Worst of all, what if it's not my interpretation that's in error? What if the Bible itself contains errors?

But after I embraced the Catholic view of Scripture, my questions about the inspiration, canonicity, interpretation, and inerrancy of the Bible were answered.

The Inspiration of Scripture

Suppose the Bible does contain historical evidence of Christ's divinity. That alone doesn't prove that the Bible is *inspired*, or that every verse has God as its author. Several passages in Scripture claim to be inspired (2 Tim. 3:16) or claim they come from the Holy Spirit ("thus says the Word of the Lord"), but even if that message were stamped on every page of the Bible, it would not prove anything. After all, the Qu'ran (the holy book of Islam) and the Book of Mormon both claim to be inspired, but Christians don't believe those books have divine origins.

What evidence proves that the Bible alone is inspired and that these other holy books are not?

This question bothered me until I read Karl Keating's argument for the inspiration of Scripture in his classic work *Catholicism and Fundamentalism*. Keating says that when taken as just a reliable *human* document, the Bible shows that Christ not only rose from the dead, but that he established a Church built on the apostles (Matt. 16:18–19, Eph. 2:20). The successors of the apostles, or the popes and bishops who inherited the apostles' spiritual authority, were then able to authoritatively declare the Bible to be the word of God.

This is not a circular argument, in which an inspired Bible is used to prove the Church's authority and the Church's authority is used to prove that the Bible is inspired. Instead, as Keating says, it is a "spiral argument," in which the Bible is assumed to be a merely human document that records the creation of a divinely instituted Church.[9] This Church then had the authority to pronounce which human writings also had God as their author. St. Augustine reached a similar conclusion in the fourth century when he said, "I should not believe the gospel except as moved by the authority of the Catholic Church."[10]

This solution also had another benefit. It didn't just explain why the Bible was inspired; it explained why the particular books found in the Bible were inspired.

The Canon of Scripture

The Bible is not one book but rather a collection of seventy-three books and letters that form the canon of Scripture.[11] The word "canon" comes from a Greek word that means "rule," and it represents the Church's official list of inspired writings. In contrast to the Catholic view of the canon, Protestants claim that an authoritative Church is not needed to determine which writings are inspired. Some Protestants even say it's obvious which ancient writings belong in the Bible and which do not.

But is it really so obvious?

After all, some books of the Bible don't seem very "biblical." Ecclesiastes contains what seems to be a cynical rejection of the afterlife, the third letter of John doesn't mention the name of Jesus Christ, and the letter to Philemon doesn't teach any specific doctrine. The part of the book of Esther that Protestants consider to be inspired Scripture never even mentions God! Yet, all these writings are found in the Bible, although writings that were popular in the early Church, like the Didache or the letter of Clement (which was even read in early Church services) are not.[12]

The Protestant theologian R.C. Sproul simply believes the canon of Scripture is "a fallible list of infallible books."[13] It's fallible because, from Sproul's point of view, the Church that pronounced the canon had no real authority. But if a nonauthoritative group of Christians decided what the canon of Scripture was in the third and fourth century, then why couldn't another nonauthoritative group of Christians do the same today?

For example, in 2013, Hal Taussig, a member of the skeptical Jesus Seminar, published the findings of a "group of scholars and spiritual leaders" in a collection called *A New New Testament*. Added to the traditional New Testament were second-century apocryphal gospels like "The Gospel of Truth" as well as texts from the Dead Sea Scrolls like "The Thunder: Perfect Mind." Protestants might balk at such a collection, but what authority do they have to say someone like Taussig is wrong?

After all, 500 years ago, Martin Luther devalued the status of the letter of James because it contradicted his theology of justification by faith alone (James 2:24 says, for example, that we are *not* justified by faith alone).[14] Although that letter remained in the Bible, Luther and the other Reformers did remove the deuterocanonical books (e.g. Sirach, Tobit, 1 and 2 Maccabees, and others) from the Old Testament, and they are still absent from Protestant Bibles.[15] How can Protestants denounce a "Reformation" like Taussig's, which alters the current canon, without undermining the original Reformers' decision to change the canon that existed in the sixteenth century?

However, if the Catholic Church has divine authority from Christ and the apostles, then it alone can recognize and pronounce the canon of Scripture. It also has the authority to protect the canon from future illicit tampering. This doesn't mean the Church has a higher authority than Scripture, but rather, as the Second Vatican Council taught, that the Church

> [S]erves [the word of God], teaching only what has been handed on, listening to it devoutly, guarding it scrupulously and explaining it faithfully in accord with a divine commission and with the help of the Holy Spirit, it draws from this one deposit of faith everything which it presents for belief as divinely revealed.[16]

THE INTERPRETATION OF SCRIPTURE

Imagine if every American had the authority to decide what the U.S. Constitution means. Each person could do as he wished, saying that his actions fell under his own interpretation of "freedom of religion" or "freedom of association." What would come of this approach? Anarchy. Fortunately, America's Founding Fathers created an institution called the Supreme Court that was entrusted with interpreting the Constitution. That way, through the Court's decisions, a uniform legal code would be created that bound all citizens equally. Just as personal interpretation of the Constitution would lead to chaos for the rule of law, relying solely on one's personal interpretation of the Bible as a guide to Christian doctrine leads to chaos for the rule of faith.

The Reformers called this principle *sola scriptura* or "by Scripture alone," but Catholic apologist Patrick Madrid rightly called it a "blueprint for anarchy."[17]

In addition, unlike the Constitution, the books of the Bible were written a long time ago in languages most people don't understand and within cultural contexts that no longer exist. People who read the Bible without knowing ancient languages and ancient history risk grossly misunderstanding the biblical authors' messages. Indeed, the proliferation of Protestant denominations that teach mutually contradictory positions on important issues is evidence that such a misunderstanding has taken place on a large scale.

But if America's Founding Fathers were wise enough to foresee the dangers of individuals engaging in private *constitutional* interpretation, then wouldn't the Church's "founding fathers," or Christ and the apostles, see the danger in relegating Christian authority to private *biblical* interpretation? We read in 2 Peter 1:20 that "no prophecy of scripture is a matter of one's own interpretation," and the author later warns his readers that some passages in the Bible are "hard to understand, which the ignorant and unstable twist to their own destruction, as they do the other scriptures" (2 Pet. 3:16).

Fortunately, Christ did not leave us as orphans (John 14:18). Instead, he gave us his Church guided by the Holy Spirit, so that, unlike a fallible Supreme Court, the Church would be capable of *infallibly* teaching us the nature and meaning of Sacred Scripture. The Second Vatican Council taught that "the task of authentically interpreting the word of God, whether written or handed on, has been entrusted exclusively to the living teaching office of the Church, whose authority is exercised in the name of Jesus Christ."[18]

The problem of interpreting Scripture becomes more evident when we examine skeptical critics of the Bible. These people promote their views through inexpensive, self-published books or Internet videos that mock Scripture's alleged errors. They also scoff at the idea that special training is needed to understand the Bible. For example, Sam Warren wrote in his book *The Bible Naked*,

What qualifications do I have to write this book? I don't have a
Ph.D. after my name and I'm not a trained biblical scholar. You
don't have to be a genius to see that the Bible is full of errors, ab-
surdities, lies, contradictions, false prophecies, immorality, etc.[19]

Ruth Hurmence Green wrote in her *Born Again Skeptic's
Guide to the Bible*,

I accepted a "call" to put into writing my personal observation
and considerations born of an unsophisticated examination of
the scriptures. The result is the Bible as I saw it, and, since I
feel that theology should require no "expert" interpreters, I
believe my impression is admissible.[20]

Most critics of the Bible would say that if God wanted us
to know his message, then he would have made it impossible
to misunderstand. But why should we believe that anyone is
capable of understanding what every part of the Bible means?
Dan Barker, the co-president of the Freedom From Religion
Foundation, put it this way: "An omnipotent, omniscient deity
should have made his all-important message unmistakably clear
to everyone, everywhere, at all times."[21]

I agree with Barker that God should provide an opportunity
for all people to be saved since 1 Timothy 2:4 says God wants all
to be saved. But that is not the same thing as saying that the Bible should be easily understood by anyone who reads it. Perhaps
God has given people a way to know him outside of the written
word? For example, St. Paul taught that God could make his
moral demands known in the hearts of those who never received
written revelation (Rom. 2:14–16). The Church likewise teaches
that salvation is possible for those who, through no fault of their
own, don't know Christ or his Church.[22]

In fact, the idea that universal knowledge of God's saving
plan should come in the form of universal understanding of the
Bible is a distinctly Protestant one. It grew out of the Reformation's rejection of the Catholic Church's authority to preach the

gospel and be "the pillar and foundation of truth" (1 Tim. 3:15). In place of Christ's Church, the Reformers held up the Bible as the sole rule of faith and highest authority for all Christians, a doctrine that later came to be known as *sola scriptura*. According to Protestant historian Alister McGrath,

> Luther demanded that all Christians should be able to read the Bible for themselves. The agenda here was both political and theological. Lay access to the Bible was about power as much as it was about encouraging personal spirituality. Pressure for the Bible to be placed in the hands of the ordinary person was an implicit demand for the emancipation of the laity from clerical domination.[23]

In order for the Bible to be every Christian's ultimate authority it had to be clear enough for any Christian to understand. This gave rise to the Protestant doctrine of the clearness or *perspicuity* of Scripture. Luther wrote in *The Bondage of the Will* that "they who deny the all-clearness and all-plainness of the scriptures, leave us nothing else but darkness."[24]

But the idea that Scripture is clear to anyone who reads it is demonstrably false. This is true even if Scripture's "clearness" is restricted only to truths that are necessary for salvation (a position advocated by later Reformers).[25] After all, as we've noted, numerous Protestant denominations disagree over what the Bible teaches, and on crucial issues, like the validity of infant baptism, the Real Presence of Christ in the Eucharist, or whether believers can lose their salvation.

Catholics agree that these essential truths are indeed found in Scripture, but it doesn't follow that anyone who reads Scripture will be able to glean these truths from the sacred text.[26] This is why St. Vincent of Lerins said in the fifth century, "It is very necessary, on account of so great intricacies of such various error, that the rule for the right understanding of the prophets and apostles should be framed in accordance with the standard of Ecclesiastical and Catholic interpretation."[27]

Certainly, God has given us his word in Sacred Scripture, but the fullness of God's word is found only in his Son, Jesus Christ. That is because Christ is the Word incarnate (John 1:14) and he represents the one utterance in whom God expresses himself completely (CCC 102). Quoting the *Catechism of the Catholic Church*, Pope Benedict XVI wrote,

> [T]he Christian faith is not a "religion of the book": Christianity is the "religion of the word of God," not of "a written and mute word, but of the incarnate and living Word." Consequently the Scripture is to be proclaimed, heard, read, received and experienced as the word of God, in the stream of the apostolic Tradition from which it is inseparable.[28]

Of course, much more could be said (and has been said) in defense of the claim that the Catholic Church is the authoritative custodian of God's word.[29] My point is simply that there are good reasons for listening to the Catholic Church's pronouncements on Scripture, which I will routinely cite in this book in order to explain the Bible's dark passages.

THE INERRANCY OF SCRIPTURE

Before I explain the Bible's difficult passages, I want to be clear that because the Bible is *inspired* (God is the author of Sacred Scripture), it follows that the Bible must be *inerrant,* or free from error. This means that God prevented the human authors of Scripture from asserting something false in the original biblical texts. Allegations of error in Scripture cannot be explained away as the inevitable by-product of the Bible's human authors. As St. Basil the Great said in the fourth century, "What is the distinctive mark of faith? Full and unhesitating certainty that the words inspired by God are true."[30]

Since before and after Basil's time, the Church has uniformly taught that Scripture is without error. Pope Leo XIII wrote in his 1893 encyclical *Providentissimus Deus,*

[I]nspiration not only is essentially incompatible with error, but excludes and rejects it as absolutely and necessarily as it is impossible that God himself, the supreme Truth, can utter that which is not true. This is the ancient and unchanging faith of the Church, solemnly defined in the Councils of Florence and of Trent, and finally confirmed and more expressly formulated by the Council of the Vatican.[31]

But what it means for the Bible to be inerrant is not as simple as that. The Pontifical Biblical Commission said that

If it is taken in its absolute sense, this term [inerrancy] would suggest that there can be no error of any kind in the Bible. But with the progressive discoveries in the field of history, philology, and the natural sciences, and because of the application to biblical research of the historical-critical method, exegetes have had to recognize that not everything in the Bible is expressed in accordance with the demands of the contemporary sciences, because the biblical writers reflect the limits of their own personal knowledge, in addition to those of their time and culture. The Second Vatican Council had to confront this problem in the preparation of the dogmatic constitution *Dei Verbum*.[32]

Dei Verbum, the Council's "Dogmatic Constitution on Divine Revelation," taught,

[S]ince everything asserted by the inspired authors or sacred writers must be held to be asserted by the Holy Spirit, it follows that the books of Scripture must be acknowledged as teaching solidly, faithfully and without error that truth which God wanted put into sacred writings for the sake of salvation.[33]

The last clause, "for the sake of salvation," is debated among some theologians. The traditional view is that this clause refers to God's *purpose* in putting inerrant truth into the sacred writings, that it was done "for the sake of [our] salvation." Another school of thought holds that it refers to *which truths* in Scripture God protected from error, that Scripture's inerrancy is restricted only to what is "for the sake of [our] salvation." Other statements in the Bible not related to our salvation, especially those concerning scientific and historical facts, could be in error. Although some Catholic theologians and scholars endorse this latter view, it is not the historic view of inerrancy and there are good reasons to be skeptical of it.[34]

Nearly twenty years before the Second Vatican Council, Pope Pius XII condemned the actions of those who "ventured to restrict the truth of Sacred Scripture solely to matters of faith and morals," and also said that Pope Leo XIII had "justly and rightly condemned these errors" in *Providentissimus Deus*.[35] *Dei Verbum* itself says that the human authors of Scripture were "true authors, consigned to writing everything and *only those things which he* [God] *wanted* [emphasis added]."[36]

This statement applies not just to truths given to us for the sake of our salvation, but to everything written in the Bible. To say that the Bible contains errors is to say that God wanted to inscribe errors into the biblical text, which would contradict his perfection and undermine our ability to trust the revelation he gave us.

The Nature of Assertion

Does the traditional interpretation of *Dei Verbum* mean that everything written in the Bible is without error? No, because *Dei Verbum* makes a crucial distinction between what is *written* in Scripture and what is *asserted* in Scripture. As it says, "everything asserted by the inspired authors or sacred writers must be held to be asserted by the Holy Spirit."[37] If I say, "It's raining cats and dogs outside" or "I have a million things to do today," the average listener will know that I am asserting a message that differs from what my words literally mean.

Of course, although it may be easy for modern English speakers to understand a fellow English speaker's assertions, understanding statements made in other languages and cultural contexts becomes more difficult. For example, the German phrase *Jemanden einen*

Bären aufbinden literally means, "to tie a bear onto someone," but it's just an expression. It means to humorously dupe someone into believing something that's false. It's equivalent to the American idiom "to pull someone's leg."

One simple way of determining the meaning of a foreign text is to consult a native speaker who understands the context behind the language of the text. But we don't have access to anyone who understands the biblical texts in this way. Sure, there are scholars who know ancient Greek and Hebrew, but none of them learned those languages in the contexts of the ancient Near East (ANE) where they were originally used. Instead, we have to infer Scripture's context by investigating literary and archaeological artifacts that date from when it was written. Pope Pius XII recognized this difficulty in 1943 when he wrote in the encyclical *Divino Afflante Spiritu*,

> What is the literal sense of a passage is not always as obvious in the speeches and writings of the ancient authors of the East, as it is in the works of our own time. For what they wished to express is not to be determined by the rules of grammar and philology alone, nor solely by the context; the interpreter must, as it were, go back wholly in spirit to those remote centuries of the East and with the aid of history, archaeology, ethnology, and other sciences, accurately determine what modes of writing, so to speak, the authors of that ancient period would be likely to use, and in fact did use. For the ancient peoples of the East, in order to express their ideas, did not always employ those forms or kinds of speech which we use today; but rather those used by the men of their times and countries. What those exactly were the commentator cannot determine as it were in advance, but only after a careful examination of the ancient literature of the East.[38]

THE SENSE OF SCRIPTURE

In order to understand and explain what *appear* to be errors in the Bible, we have to consult a variety of sources and disciplines in order to recover what the Bible's human authors originally asserted. As *Dei Verbum* says, "The interpreter must investigate what meaning the sacred writer *intended to express and actually expressed* [emphasis added] in particular circumstances by using contemporary literary forms in accordance with the situation of his own time and culture."[39]

For example, the *Catechism* tells us that there are two different senses of Scripture: the literal sense conveyed by the words of Scripture and the spiritual sense conveyed by the realities and events within those words (115–118). If we don't understand both senses we risk misunderstanding the author's meaning. Take Matthew 2:15's assertion that the infant Jesus' departure from Egypt fulfilled Hosea 11:1's prophecy, in which God says, "out of Egypt have I called my Son."

Critics like Steve Wells who say this passage in Hosea "is a reference to the Hebrew Exodus from Egypt and has nothing to do with Jesus" are right—and wrong.[40] The prophecy is literally about Israel, and Matthew knows this, but the prophecy was also spiritually fulfilled in Jesus. Matthew shows us that God, in his Providence, used the Exodus as a "type" or "precursor" to model his future call, which brought his only-begotten Son out of Egypt and into Nazareth as an infant.

But how do we know that the biblical author was using a figure of speech and that he did not intend his words to be understood in a literal or scientific way? Discerning the meaning of sacred texts is not an easy task and has served as a source of theological differences among Christians for centuries. But to paraphrase law professor Hadley Arkes, an absence of consensus is not an absence of truth.[41]

Just because there is debate over a text's meaning, it does not follow that the text has no meaning or that it is in error. It only means that there is a difficulty in discovering the original meaning or that we aren't sure how to understand the text. The remainder of this book will outline the ways we can discover the true meaning of biblical texts, and, in the process, refute the charge that all apparent errors in the Bible are labeled "metaphors" to avoid confronting genuine difficulties with what the text is saying.

Finally, because human beings evaluate evidence in different ways, competent authorities may arrive at different possible solutions for various difficult passages. When that happens, I will present a few of the most promising solutions and leave it to the reader to decide what he thinks is the most plausible one. Although the Church has taught that certain conclusions about the Bible are opposed to the Faith (for example, that it is not divinely inspired), the teaching office of the Catholic Church (also called the Magisterium) has not explained the meaning of every passage in Scripture. Instead, as Pope Benedict XVI said,

> The correct interpretation of these [difficult] passages requires a degree of expertise, acquired through a training that interprets the texts in their historical-literary context and within the Christian perspective which has as its ultimate hermeneutical key "the Gospel and the new commandment of Jesus Christ brought about in the paschal mystery." I encourage scholars and pastors to help all the faithful to approach these passages through an interpretation which enables their meaning to emerge in the light of the mystery of Christ.[42]

Catholic Scripture scholar Brant Pitre wrote, "The doctrine of inerrancy does *not* mean that there are no *apparent* errors, *apparent* contradictions, or other serious difficulties littered throughout the Scriptures."[43] In the following chapters I'll discuss the most prominent cases that fall under the three categories I described earlier: apparent external, internal, and moral errors in Scripture. I will also explain some of my own rules for Bible reading that will help you understand and explain these difficulties to others.

Part I

External Difficulties

2

Unscientific Nonsense?

The Claim: A modern person cannot trust what is written in
a two-thousand-year-old book whose authors were illiterate shepherds
who thought the earth was flat.

Before we examine passages that allegedly contradict well-established scientific or historical facts, we should address some generic smears made against the Bible's trustworthiness.

One smear is that you cannot trust something that was written thousands of years ago. Although, do you trust your schoolteacher when she says Hannibal crossed the Alps with a pack of elephants? Do you trust your museum guide when he says "King Tut" began to rule when he was nine years old? How do you know these people are correct? Ultimately, their sources for these facts are documents that were written thousands of years ago.[44]

Just because a historical record was made a long time ago does not mean it is unreliable. In fact, when a writer is closer in time to an ancient event—and as a result his writings are very old—we have *more* reason to trust his account. That's because he is more likely to have access to the original sources that describe the event in question, or may even be the original source.

Another smear is that you can't trust something that was written by illiterate, "Bronze Age" goatherds. Indeed, the advocacy group American Atheists calls the Bible "a barbaric and Bronze Age book."[45] But just because someone wrote during the Bronze Age (that is, between 3300–1200 B.C.) does not mean he was unintelligent or untrustworthy. The late Bronze Age Amarna letters, for example, have provided historians with valuable information about ancient Egypt's eighteenth dynasty and aren't dismissed as useless relics.

Also, most of the Old Testament was not written during the Bronze Age. It was written during the Iron Age (1200–500 B.C.), and the New Testament was written even later, during the classical period (500 B.C.–A.D. 500). If a skeptic dismisses the Bible because it was written during this time, then to be consistent he must dismiss all ancient historians, including those who describe events no one doubts (like Tacitus's account of the great fire of Rome in A.D. 64).

But weren't the writers of the Bible different from ancient Greek and Roman historians? Weren't they illiterate desert wanderers? Well, they certainly weren't illiterate, because they *wrote books*.[46] It's true that books like Genesis record the actions of nomadic people who might have been illiterate, but those nomads did not write the Bible. Instead, their recollections of past events were passed down through oral tradition and were eventually preserved in the writings of later scribes.[47]

Another smear is that, age aside, the Bible describes things like worldwide floods, virgins giving birth, and men rising from the dead. and you can't trust a book that posits such impossible things. When it comes to the Bible and miracles there are three kinds of objections skeptics make:

1. The Bible contains falsehoods because it describes miracles, and miracles can't happen.
2. The Bible contains falsehoods because the miracles it describes are no different than the miracles found in other religions that Christians regard as legendary or fictional.
3. The Bible contains falsehoods because it describes miracles that should have left nonbiblical evidence.

Objection number one reveals a philosophical assumption that needs to be challenged. Yes, a human woman can't conceive a child without the sexual cooperation of a man; and yes, dead people don't naturally come back to life. These events are impossible only if *natural* forces are operating. But there is no reason to think that *God* can't cause a virgin to conceive and bear a child, or that *God* can't bring the dead back to life. If God can create an entire universe out of nothing, then he would have no difficulty in performing a miracle.

Miracles are only impossible if God does not exist, so the critic has to prove that there is no God before he can prove that miracles are impossible.[48] If he can't do that, then he has no grounds to impose upon the biblical texts what Pope Benedict XVI called "a secularized hermeneutic." This is an interpretive framework that denies even the possibility of miracles, or, as Benedict wrote, "According to this hermeneutic, whenever a divine element seems present, it has to be explained in some other way, reducing everything to the human element. This leads to interpretations that deny the historicity of the divine elements."[49]

Extreme versions of this hermeneutic lead to denying even the historicity of providential events (that is, events involving nonmiraculous perfect timing). Consider retired Episcopalian Bishop John Shelby Spong's reaction to the story of John the Baptist leaping in his mother's womb during Mary's visit (Luke 1:41). Spong wrote, "Surely no one would seriously argue that this story was literal history!"[50] But it is common for pregnant women to feel the movement of their unborn children, so Spong's skepticism is completely unwarranted.

Like the first objection's philosophical assumption, objection two reveals a historical assumption that needs to be challenged— the assumption that the quality of evidence for the miracles of the Bible is the same as the quality of evidence for miracles in ancient, nonbiblical works that are considered sacred in other religions. But this simply isn't true.

Consider the Resurrection of Jesus Christ.[51] Our earliest surviving source for this miracle is Paul, a convert to Christianity from Pharisaic Judaism. He wrote within twenty years of this event, and his writings contain creeds that can be dated to within a few years of the Crucifixion. These writings attest to an early belief in Christ's physical, post-Resurrection appearances to the apostles.

The appearance stories aren't legends; Paul was acquainted with the people who saw the risen Jesus (Gal. 1:18–19) and could confirm that they did see him.[52] Paul himself converted to Christianity because of such an appearance while he traveled to Damascus (Acts 9:1–19). The Gospels also provide multiple, independent corroboration of things like the discovery of Jesus' empty tomb. This fact dispels the theory that the disciples hallucinated Christ's appearances since visiting Jesus' occupied tomb would have quickly disabused them of the notion that he'd risen from the dead. Therefore, the best explanation for these minimal facts of history is that Jesus really rose from the dead.[53]

Now, compare the evidence for Christ's Resurrection to the evidence for miracles associated with other ancient wonder-workers like Buddha, Muhammad, or Apollonius of Tyana. The Qu'ran does not record Muhammad performing miracles, and the earliest sources about Buddha say he refused to perform miracles.[54] Both men are described as performing miracles only in legends written long after their deaths.[55]

The first-century wonder-worker Apollonius of Tyana (who skeptical scholars often compare to Jesus) was said to have appeared alive again to his followers after his death. However, this account comes from only one source—*The Life of Apollonius* by Philostratus. It was written over a hundred years after Apollonius died, for the express purpose of commissioning a Roman temple in his honor.[56] This stands in sharp contrast to the accounts of Christ's Resurrection that we find in the letters of Paul, the Gospels, and the Church Fathers.

Unlike the stories of other ancient wonder-workers, the Christian accounts were written relatively soon after the events they describe and are preserved in multiple sources. Moreover, the account of Apollonius was written to promote a state-sanctioned religion, while the accounts of the Resurrection were proclaimed for evangelistic purposes, in the face of martyrdom for doing so.[57] Antony Flew, who was at one time one of the most famous atheists in the Western world, even admitted that

"The evidence for the resurrection is better than for claimed miracles in any other religion. It's outstandingly different in quality and quantity."[58]

But what about the other miracles in the Bible that do not have the same kind of evidence as Christ's Resurrection, like miracles recorded in an older source like the Old Testament? Is it inconsistent for Christians to believe in those miracles recorded in the Bible but not in miracles in other religions? No, because if the evidence for Jesus' Resurrection is better than other miracles, then we have good reason to believe that Christ is the risen God. If we believe that, then we have good reason to believe Christ's teaching that he would establish a Church that would never perish but would always have his authority (Matt. 16:18–19, Luke 10:16, Eph. 3:20–21, 1 Tim. 3:15). We would then have good reason to trust this Church when it affirms that miracle accounts in the whole of Scripture are without error.

But my aim in this book is not to prove that every miracle or event described in the Bible can be verified with the tools available to modern historians. Instead, it is to show that certain events described in the Bible do not contradict scientific or historical facts. In other words, I am not trying to prove these events happened. I am instead answering the arguments of critics who say they did *not* happen. Disproving these arguments does not prove the historicity of these events, but it is an essential part of defending their historical nature.

This is actually the substance of objection number three, which says that there are events described in the Bible, like Noah's Flood or the widespread darkness during Christ's Crucifixion, that nonbiblical authors should have recorded. Since they did not, it follows that they never occurred. But in these cases, the critic has misunderstood either the genre of the text he's critiquing or the description of the miracle found in those texts. As a result, he expects there to be earth-shattering evidence for an event that wasn't earth-shattering in the first place. I'll discuss some of those specific events in the next few chapters.

The Meaning of Inspiration

When Christians say the Bible is inspired, or that it is the word of God, that phrase can be misunderstood. Some people think the Bible is the word of God because God penned every word in it and used some kind of heavenly parcel delivery service to send it down to earth. But Jews and Christians have always known that the parts of the Bible that came directly from God, such as the Ten Commandments God wrote on the tablets at Mount Sinai, are few and far between. Instead, it was human beings who picked up pens and wrote the Bible's original manuscripts.

A more common mistake is to believe that although human beings wrote the physical words found in the Bible, they were only the *mechanical* authors of Scripture. According to this view, none of the Bible's texts came from the human authors' minds, but from God's mind alone. The human authors either recorded the revelation God audibly gave them or God took control of their bodies and wrote his revelation through them. As Protestant author Jasper James Ray put it, "The very words of the Bible were given to the authors, and not just the ideas they convey. The writers were not left to choose the words."[59]

This brings us to our first rule for reading the Bible: *The Bible's human authors were not divine stenographers.* The idea that the human authors of Scripture recorded what God said just as a stenographer records courtroom testimony is common in certain kinds of biblical fundamentalism, which, according to the Pontifical Biblical Commission, "seeks to escape any closeness of the divine and the human . . . for this reason, it tends to treat the biblical text as if it had been dictated word for word by the Spirit. It fails to recognize that the word of God has been formulated in language and expression conditioned by various periods."[60]

But this "dictation theory" of inspiration doesn't make sense of passages like 1 Corinthians 1:14–16, in which Paul wrote, "I am thankful that I baptized none of you except Crispus and Gaius; lest any one should say that you were baptized in my name. (I did baptize also the household of Stephanas. Beyond that, I do not know whether I baptized any one else.)" Paul didn't write down whatever God told him because God would have known who Paul baptized. Instead, Paul used his own ideas and own words to write to the Christians in Corinth. That being said, God is still the author of Scripture even if the Bible's human authors used their own words and ideas when they wrote the Bible. According to *Dei Verbum*,

> The books of both the Old and New Testaments in their entirety, with all their parts, are sacred and canonical because written under the inspiration of the Holy Spirit, they have God as their author and have been handed on as such to the Church herself. In composing the sacred books, God chose men and while employed by him they made use of their powers and abilities, so that with him acting in them and through them, they, as true authors, consigned to writing everything and only those things which he wanted."[61]

Another way to understand the inspiration of Scripture is to compare it to the Incarnation. When God the Son became incarnate as Jesus of Nazareth, he remained a divine person with a divine nature; but in becoming man, God the Son acquired an additional human nature. Christ's humanity did not affect his divine nature, but neither was Christ's humanity "swallowed up" in his divinity. Christ was and still is fully God and fully man.

During his earthly ministry, Christ was the eternal and omnipotent God, but as a man he possessed human limitations that do not belong to the divine nature. For example, he would thirst (John 19:28), grow tired (John 4:6), and even weep (John 11:35). The Second Vatican Council taught that Christ "has truly been made one of us, like us in all things except sin."[62]

Just as Christ is God's Word that became flesh and dwelt among us (John 1:14), Scripture is God's word made into written characters that dwells among us.[63] *Dei Verbum* taught, "For the words of God, expressed in human language, have been made like human discourse, just as the word of the eternal Father, when he took to himself the flesh of human weakness, was in every way made like men."[64] Pope St. John Paul II agreed and said in an address to the Pontifical Biblical Commission, "After the heavenly glorification of the humanity of the Word made flesh, it is again due to written words that his stay among us is attested to in an abiding way."[65]

This analogy also illustrates a similarity between people of the first century who rejected Christ's divinity because all they saw was his humanity, and people of the twenty-first century who reject the Bible because all they see are the limits of its human authors. As Scott Hahn says, "To put it bluntly, the written word of God strikes many as too human to be divine. Unnumbered intellectuals throughout history have thus faced the scandal of the Bible and chosen to reject it. In this way too the inspired Word treads the path of the incarnate Word and mirrors its mystery."[66]

Christ's human nature did not contradict his divinity and the human words of Scripture do not contradict God's authorship of it, even though their finite nature limits what God can communicate through them. This is unavoidable, because any way an infinite being would choose to reveal himself to finite creatures would involve some limiting of the divine. For instance, God allowed the human authors of Scripture to retain their own way of speaking about the world. He did this even if that way of speaking does not correspond to our modern, scientific descriptions of the natural world.

The Language of Appearances

Our second rule for reading Scripture is: *The Bible's human authors were not writing scientific textbooks.* Pope Leo XIII said of the ancient authors of Scripture that "they did not seek to penetrate the secrets of nature, but rather described and dealt with things in more or less figurative language, or in terms which were commonly used at the time, and which in many instances are in daily use at this day, even by the most eminent men of science."[67]

Just like ancient people who spoke of "the sun [that] goeth forth in his might" (Judg. 5:31, KJV), we describe what we observe with expressions that are useful. After all, we too speak of the sun "rising" and "setting" even though the sun does not move in an orbit that "rises" over the earth. Or, we speak of a pregnant woman's "water breaking" even though it is the thin lining of the amniotic sac that breaks and not the fluid itself.[68] We call this "the language of appearances" because it describes the world as it appears to our senses. These descriptions are true, but they are not literal in nature.

Therefore, when skeptics mock scriptural passages that describe human beings "thinking in their hearts" (for example, Esther 6:6), they demonstrate an unwillingness to allow the text to be as flexible as modern expressions.[69] With this attitude, one could say that skeptics who talk about being "heartbroken" over a failed relationship don't understand basic biology, since feelings of sadness come from chemical interactions in the brain, not the heart.

If a skeptic can talk about a broken heart using the language of appearances, then the authors of the Bible should be allowed to speak to us using the same kind of language. Even if the sacred authors believed that the heart was the seat of intellectual activity (a view common until the seventeenth century), their text is not making a scientific assertion about the human body.[70] Instead, it is describing the world in a way that most people (ancient or modern) perceive it.[71]

Another example of this kind of description, which is also called "phenomenological language," is Genesis 1:6, in which the sacred author depicts God saying, "Let there be a firmament in the midst of the waters, and let it separate the waters from the waters." The Hebrew word *raqiya* that is translated "firmament" is derived from a verb that means "to hammer out" or "to make firm." Some scholars have proposed that the ancient authors believed that the sky, or the firmament, was a dome above which sat the waters that rained down upon the earth. But this may just be a way of describing how the sky *appears*, not how it actually *is.* After all, even ancient people knew that it wasn't the sky that brought rain, but the rain clouds in the sky.

In any case, St. Thomas Aquinas recognized in the thirteenth century that Genesis' literal description of the firmament may not be literal because "Moses was speaking to ignorant people, and that out of condescension to their weakness he put before them only such things as are apparent to sense." Thomas also said that if a physical theory about the world that comes from an interpretation of Scripture "can be shown to be false by solid reasons, [then] it cannot be held to be the sense of Holy Scripture."[72] While commenting on this passage, Scott Hahn and Curtis Mitch said it does not constitute infallible divine revelation about the physical world because "The Church, following the wisdom of St. Augustine, maintains that the Bible does not contain any properly scientific teaching about the nature of the physical universe."[73]

As we already saw in our discussion of *Dei Verbum*, Scripture is free from error in what the ancient authors *asserted*, not in what they *wrote*. The author of the book of Genesis did not understand some of the scientific truths we know today (just as we don't understand scientific truths humans will come to learn in the future). But any lack of knowledge on the part of the ancient author would not constitute an error in his text.

That's because these texts are not asserting a scientific description of the world. They are instead asserting a *popular* description of the world for the purpose of helping the readers and hearers of God's word to understand his saving plan for humanity. The ancient author's purpose was not to help his audience pass biology or geography tests.

But why didn't God just reveal to the human authors of Scripture the understanding of the natural world we now possess? Questions like this one remind me of St. Augustine's reply to critics in his own day. He said to them, "One does not read in the Gospel that the Lord said: 'I will send you the [Holy Spirit] who will teach you about the course of the sun and moon.' For he willed to make them Christians, not mathematicians."[74]

One could just as easily ask in A.D. 4000 why God didn't explain to ignorant people from A.D. 2000 how the natural world functions. The answer is that God had no need to do that. He had already given the people of that period in history (as well as in earlier periods) the information they needed for what is most important in life: coming to know him and his offer of glorious, eternal life. As Pope St. John Paul II said,

> The Bible itself speaks to us of the origin of the universe and its make-up, not in order to provide us with a scientific treatise, but in order to state the correct relationships of man with God and with the universe. Sacred Scripture wishes simply to declare that the world was created by God, and in order to teach this truth it expresses itself in the terms of the cosmology in use at the time of the writer.[75]

3

Darwin Refutes Genesis?

*The Claim: The world was not, as the first chapter of Genesis says,
created six thousand years ago over the course of six 24-hour days.
Instead, science has proven that life slowly evolved over billions of years.
Any attempt to reinterpret Genesis is just an accommodation of new
knowledge that exposes the Bible's scientific errors.*

When it comes to proving the Bible contradicts science, many
people point to the first chapter of Genesis. Michael Shermer,
the editor of *Skeptic* magazine, wrote, "Young-Earth Creationists, for example, believe that the world was created around
6,000 years ago, about the same time that the Babylonians invented beer. These claims cannot both be correct, and anyone
who thinks the former is right has relegated all of science (along
with brains) to the dumpster of life."[76]

We've already seen how the Bible can be without error even
if it contains descriptions of the natural world that are not scientific in nature. But the Bible's authors never assert, much less
say, what the age of the universe or the earth is. Christians who
believe the Creation is only a few thousand years old (Shermer's
"Young-Earth Creationists") come to that conclusion by counting up the years included in the genealogies of the Old Testament. The most famous attempt to date the Creation in this
way comes from the seventeenth-century Anglican Archbishop
James Ussher. He said the world was created in the year 4004
B.C. on the night before Sunday, October 23.[77]

However, the genealogies in the Bible cannot be used to date
the age of the universe because they were not meant to be exact
chronicles of history. In some cases generations were omitted in
order to make a symbolic point. In other cases the ages themselves may be symbolic and not literal (see chapters 5 and 11

for more about those issues). The genealogies in Scripture were primarily focused on showing how different people were related to one another, not how long ago they lived.

In contrast to Ussher's exactness, the Catholic Church does not teach that either the Earth or the physical universe is of any particular age.[78] The First Vatican Council only requires Catholics to believe that "the world and all things which are contained in it, both spiritual and material, as regards their whole substance, have been produced by God from nothing."[79]

A LESSON FROM A VACATION

According to Young-Earth Creationists, the book of Genesis says that God created the world in six 24-hour days. According to the theory of evolution, life evolved over billions of years through a slow and gradual process.[80] Doesn't it follow then that Genesis contradicts modern biology?

You may be surprised to learn that long before Darwin's theory of evolution was published in 1859, critics of the Church attacked the Creation account in Genesis. In the second century, the pagan critic Celsus mocked Genesis for describing the existence of "days" before the creation of the sun, which is of course the astronomical body we use to measure days. He wrote, "By far the most silly thing is the distribution of the creation of the world over certain days, before days existed: for, as the heaven was not yet created, nor the foundation of the earth yet laid, nor the sun yet revolving, how could there be days?"[81]

In the fourth century, a group of heretics called the Manichees challenged the authority of Scripture and said, "How had God already divided earlier between day and night, if this is done by the heavenly bodies now on the fourth day?"[82] Any reader, ancient or modern, should be puzzled by the fact that Genesis 1:3 describes how God created "light" on the first day, but created the sun, the thing that makes the light, on the fourth day. How do we explain this odd sequence of events?

Imagine you're trying to recount what happened on a recent

family vacation. How would you tell the story? You could present it in *chronological* order and talk about the long drive to the beach, the mix-up checking into the hotel, the visit to grandma, then lounging on the beach, getting lost downtown, and stopping at a cheesy tourist trap on the way home.

Or, you could present it in *topical* order. You could first tell someone about your favorite parts of the trip—going to the beach, seeing grandma, stopping at the tourist trap. Then, you might follow this with a description of your least favorite parts of the trip—the boring drive, the mix-up at the hotel, and getting lost in an unfamiliar place. Both approaches would be valid ways of retelling the story, even though one of them, the topical method, seems inaccurate if the listener assumed you were telling the story in chronological order.

The early Church Fathers and ecclesial writers understood this distinction and responded to their critics accordingly. The third century ecclesial writer Origen said in his response to the pagan critic Celsus,

> Now who is there, pray, possessed of understanding, that will regard the statement as appropriate, that the first day, and the second, and the third, in which also both evening and morning are mentioned, existed without sun, and moon, and stars—the first day even without a sky? . . . I do not suppose that anyone doubts that these things figuratively indicate certain mysteries, the history having taken place in appearance, and not literally.[83]

St. Augustine responded to the Manichees in a similar fashion. He said that the fourth day of Creation symbolically demonstrates how God gave the sun and moon authority to rule over the kingdoms created during the first three days. Augustine went on to say that he believed God created the world instantly: "the sacred writer was able to separate in the time of his narrative what God did not separate in time in his creative act."[84] He even proposed the idea that God could have planted within

Creation "dormant seeds" that would grow and take different forms over time—not unlike the change that occurs in living species through the process of evolution.[85]

THE FRAMEWORK VIEW

It is understandable that some people read Genesis as a literal description of God creating the world in six 24-hour days; that view was held by many of the Church Fathers. But there is an alternative way of reading Genesis that has come to be called "the framework interpretation." This is the view that the six days of Creation do not consist of a literal, chronological description of events, but instead represent the human author's nonliteral, topical way of describing how God created the world.[86]

In the first three days God creates the realms where specific creatures will reside—the sky, the waters, the land and vegetation. He fills those realms in the next three days, creating the lights in the sky, birds and fish, and land animals. This interpretation explains passages like Genesis 1:14–18, which describes God creating the sun on the fourth day even though he already created the realm where the sun (or the light) will reside on the first day.

Augustine said that the author of Genesis described the Creation as occurring in six days because, according to Greek mathematicians, six is a perfect number. A perfect number is one that can be reached by taking the numbers it can be divided into and adding them together. Six is the lowest perfect number (1+2+3 = 6); 28 and 496 are the next perfect numbers. According to Augustine, six represents how the world is perfected through the act of Creation.[87] The *Catechism* says, "Scripture presents the work of the Creator symbolically as a succession of six days of divine 'work,' concluded by the 'rest' of the seventh day" (337). Jesus himself even says this "rest" is symbolic because God, who sustains all of existence, has been working since the Creation (John 5:17).

The Catholic Church allows a person to believe the earth is only six thousand years old and was created in six days, but it does not require this belief. If someone believes that this contradicts how the world really is, then he is not obligated to believe it. A Catholic does not have to believe that God inspired the sacred writers to deliberately fashion a literal history of the world that is not literally true. The Church instead teaches that faith and the findings of modern science do not contradict one another. The *Catechism* says that these findings

> have splendidly enriched our knowledge of the age and dimensions of the cosmos, the development of life-forms and the appearance of man. These discoveries invite us to even greater admiration for the greatness of the Creator, prompting us to give him thanks for all his works and for the understanding and wisdom he gives to scholars and researchers (283).

Finally, the fact that a nonliteral interpretation of Genesis was proposed 1,400 years before Darwin shows that the current view is not a desperate attempt to explain away Genesis in light of the findings of evolutionary biology. Indeed, shortly after Darwin published his theory, Cardinal John Henry Newman remarked in a letter to a friend that "Mr. Darwin's theory need not then to be atheistical, be it true or not; it may simply be suggesting a larger idea of Divine Prescience [Foreknowledge] and Skill."[88]

DEATH AND THE FALL

One objection to the view that Genesis represents a symbolic framework and not a literal retelling of the Creation is the claim that the Bible teaches that death came into the world when Adam and Eve sinned. St. Paul wrote in Romans 5:12, "Therefore as sin came into the world through one man and death through sin, and so death spread to all men because all men sinned," and in 1 Corinthians 15:21, "For as by a man came death, by a man has come also the resurrection of the dead."

If death came into existence at the fall of man, then it would have been impossible for life-forms to grow, evolve, and die for millions of years before human beings came to exist through the evolutionary process. But this objection is overcome if we understand that Paul is talking about *human* death entering the world through the fall, not death in general.

According to Genesis 1:29, God gave man "every green plant to eat." This doesn't mean that mankind and animals *only* ate green plants, but even if it did, that would still involve death. Plants and fruits are living organisms that die when they are cut off from their roots and stems. Even if man only ate leaves or berries, his digestive system would kill the living materials in those foods. It is simply not true that death came to be through the fall of man. St. Thomas Aquinas even said,

> The nature of animals was not changed by man's sin, as if those whose nature now it is to devour the flesh of others, would then have lived on herbs, as the lion and falcon . . . thus there would have been a natural antipathy between some animals.[89]

According to Thomas, not only would plants have died when humans invented salad, animals would have died at the hands of carnivores using the predatory abilities God gave them. Even if man never sinned, the shark would still have its rows of razor-sharp teeth, the alligator would still have its powerful jaws, and the snake would have its deadly venom. It would be strange if God created these predators with the ability to efficiently kill other animals but then expected the animals only to use their abilities on defenseless plants.

One last argument is that a good God would not create a world that contained the natural evil and suffering that is present in the evolutionary process. The *Catechism* addresses this objection as follows:

> But why did God not create a world so perfect that no evil could exist in it? With infinite power God could always create something better. But with infinite wisdom and goodness God freely willed to create a world "in a state of journeying"

towards its ultimate perfection. In God's plan this process of becoming involves the appearance of certain beings and the disappearance of others, the existence of the more perfect alongside the less perfect, both constructive and destructive forces of nature. With physical good there exists also physical evil as long as Creation has not reached perfection (310).[90]

The most sensible interpretation of the biblical evidence is that Adam and Eve's disobedience in the Garden of Eden forfeited the grace God originally gave them. These graces would have protected our first parents from the effects of disease and death as they lived in friendship with God their Creator. But because of their fall from grace, those protections were lost and could not be passed on to future descendants. As the *Catechism* put it, "the consequence explicitly foretold for this disobedience will come true: man will 'return to the ground,' for out of it he was taken. Death makes its entrance into human history" (400).

THE QUESTION OF GENRE

This discussion about Genesis brings us to Bible-reading rule number three: *The Bible contains many different literary styles*. Although some books of the Bible are written in genres that literally narrate historical events (such as the description of Jesus' ministry in the Gospels), it is an error to think that every book of the Bible, not to mention every part of every book, was composed in that style.

The Bible is a collection of many different books that exhibit a variety of literary styles. According to the Pontifical Biblical Commission, "In the Bible, we find different literary genres in use in that cultural area: poetry, prophecy, narrative, eschatological sayings, parables, hymns, confessions of faith, etc., each of which has its own way of presenting the truth."[91]

Some of these genres are strictly historical, and others are poetic and use fictional elements to communicate their message to the reader. These may include the story of Jonah being swallowed by a "great fish" (Jon. 1:17), Job's endurance of suffering (Job 1–2), and Jesus' story about the prodigal son (Luke 15:11-32). In one of his Wednesday audiences, Pope St. John Paul II described other Old Testament books that fit this genre: "The Books of Tobit, Judith, and Esther, although dealing with the history of the Chosen People, have the character of allegorical and moral narrative rather than history properly so called."[92]

Catholic apologist Karl Keating explained what this kind of literature is when he wrote of the story of Jonah: "The most common interpretation nowadays, and one that is held by indubitably orthodox exegetes, is that the story of the prophet being swallowed and then disgorged by a 'great fish' is merely didactic fiction, a grand tale told to establish a religious point."[93]

When it comes to the book of Job, conservative New Testament scholar Craig Blomberg accepts a similar explanation. He wrote that it's possible that the story of Job was a poetic retelling of events that happened to an actual man, but he says it's also possible the entire story is fiction. According to Blomberg, Job is a "spectacular contribution to scripture," and "not a shred of it changes even if the entire book is parabolic rather than historical! The Jewish philosopher Maimonides recognized this as long ago as the twelfth century."[94]

Even if Jonah, Job, Tobit, and the prodigal son did not exist as historical individuals, the beneficial truths found in these stories (that we should have faith in God even when we suffer, that every man is your neighbor, and so on) are not diminished in any way by their having fictional protagonists.

It's true that Jesus said, "For as Jonah was three days and three nights in the belly of the whale, so will the Son of man be three days and three nights in the heart of the earth" (Matt. 12:40), but this does not mean that Jonah had to exist as a real person in order for Jesus to have meant what he said. Blomberg said that this kind of description is no more problematic than a Christian saying our trials in life will be as great as the trials Frodo faces when he returns the Ring to Mordor. The fact that *The Lord of the Rings* is fiction doesn't make the comparison any less true.

Of course, a critic might object that if Job and Jonah did not exist, then maybe Jesus and Peter never existed either. Maybe the entire Bible is didactic fiction. But that leap in logic is as unwarranted as saying that because a library contains books of fiction, it follows that every book in a library is fiction. Like any piece of literature, we can examine the genre of a particular scriptural passage and see what kind of message it communicates. When we do that, we find that categorizing Jesus' life or his Resurrection as "helpful fictions" does not make sense of the biblical data.

The story of Job teaches patience and the story of Jonah teaches obedience, but a fictional story about Jesus dying and coming back to glorious, immortal life would not teach people anything (except the nonsensical idea asserted by some liberal scholars that we should "have faith in faith").[95] The nonexistence of Job or Jonah would not make those stories any less valuable, but Paul and other early Christians clearly taught that "If Christ has not been raised, your faith is futile and you are still in your sins" (1 Cor. 15:17). Simply put, if Christ didn't really rise from the dead then there is no point in being a Christian.

In fact, N.T. Wright has shown in his massive treatment of the Resurrection that an actual resurrection from the dead is the most plausible explanation for why first-century Jews came to believe that Jesus rose in the first place.[96] At that time, the most Jesus' disciples could hope for was that their leader had spiritually ascended to be with God. To them, a physical resurrection from the dead could only take place at the end of the world. This belief is encapsulated in Martha's response to Jesus' reassuring words that her dead brother Lazarus "will rise again" (John 11:23). Martha said, "I know he will rise again in the resurrection *of the last day* [emphasis added]" (John 11:24).

Jesus, of course, brought Lazarus back to life, but there is no evidence that Lazarus lived forever after that miracle. Lazarus was not resurrected to immortal life, but *resuscitated,* or brought back to a normal, mortal existence. He probably died at some point just as all humans die unless they are assumed alive into heaven (like Enoch or Elijah). But Jesus' disciples embraced the unheard-of notion that someone could be resurrected before the end of the world. The reason they believed in something so countercultural was that they had a real encounter with Jesus, the resurrected Son of God.

True Myths

We've seen that the books of the Bible include literal histories (the accounts of Christ's life), poetry (the Psalms), and nonhistorical narratives used for teaching purposes (parables). When it comes to the stories found in the first chapters of Genesis, however, we are not limited to saying that they are either literal history or poetic fictions. They could instead be nonliteral accounts of actual historical events. In a 2007 address in Italy, Pope Benedict XVI said,

> [T]here are so many scientific proofs in favor of evolution which appears to be a reality we can see and which enriches our knowledge of life and being as such. But on the other, the doctrine of evolution does not answer every query, especially the great philosophical question: where does everything come from? And how did everything start which ultimately led to man? I believe this is of the utmost importance.[97]

The Catholic Church teaches that the first eleven chapters of Genesis contain historical truths that answer these basic questions (that is, God created everything and made humans in his image in order to know and adore him as the one, true God). But those chapters, in the words of Pope Pius XII, in "simple and metaphorical language adapted to the mentality of a people but little cultured, both state the principal truths which are fundamental for our salvation, and also give a popular description of the origin of the human race and the chosen people."[98]

Think about how a parent might explain to his child that babies "come from a seed daddies give to mommies that grow inside the mommy's tummy." That's a true explanation, but it shouldn't be taken literally since it was accommodated for a child's level of understanding. Likewise, the stories in Genesis are true but consist of nonliteral language that comes down (or condescends) to the level of understanding found in the audience that first heard these stories. Pope St. John Paul II even referred to the Creation stories in Genesis as "myths," but he was also adamant that they were not mere fictions:

> [T]he language in question is a mythical one. In this case, the term "myth" does not designate a fabulous content, but merely an archaic way of expressing a deeper content. Without any difficulty we discover that content, under the layer of the ancient narrative. It is really marvelous as regards the qualities and the condensation of the truths contained in it.[99]

The *Catechism* says, "The account of the fall in Genesis 3 uses figurative language but affirms a primeval event, a deed that took place at the beginning of the history of man" (CCC 390). So, for example, Genesis 3's language about talking snakes and eating forbidden fruit may be a figurative way of describing our first parents' sin. In *Dominum et Vivificantem*, John Paul II wrote,

> According to the book of Genesis, "the tree of the knowledge of good and evil" was to express and constantly remind man of the "limit" impassable for a created being . . . The words of the enticement, that is to say the temptation, *as formulated in the sacred text* [emphasis added], are an inducement to transgress this prohibition—that is to say, to go beyond that "limit."[100]

The Catholic Church has infallibly taught that God created the world from nothing by his own free choice and that he made man's immortal soul in his image.[101] The Church has not, however, taught about the precise method God used to create the world or how old the Creation itself is. Since a Catholic is free to form his own opinion on those questions, the critic cannot say that our Faith asserts a scientifically inaccurate description of the world.

4

Bronze Age Ignorance?

The Claim: The Bible is supposedly the word of God, but the biblical
God knows nothing about disease, genetics, or animal classification.
Maybe the God of the Bible should go back to high school.

As we've already seen, God allowed the biblical authors to describe the world as it appears, and not as modern science catego-
rizes it. But when we take a closer look at some of these alleged
errors in Scripture, we find that it is actually the critics who, in
their zeal to disprove the Bible, have overlooked some errors of
their own.

BUNNIES, BATS, AND BUGS

To modern people, "chewing the cud" refers to rumination, or
to the process of partially digesting food in the stomach and then
regurgitating it into the mouth as "cud," where it is chewed and
swallowed again. Leviticus 11:5–6 says that because the badger
and the hare "chew the cud," and do not have cloven hoofs like
cattle, they are unclean and therefore can't be eaten. But Dennis
McKinsey points out in his *Encyclopedia of Biblical Errancy* that
"Hares never have and never will chew the cud. They are not
ruminants like cattle."[102]

McKinsey is correct that hares do not ruminate, but they do
engage in a similar behavior called *refection*, the eating of its own
droppings in order to absorb nutrients it didn't get the first time
around. (Don't try this at home to see if it works.)

The author of Leviticus is saying that, apart from cattle, the
Israelites were not allowed to eat animals whose diet consisted of
food they had already digested. Rabbits are listed with animals
that "chew the cud" because rumination is similar to refection,

not because the author was classifying hares as ruminants. In fact, Carl Linnaeus, the eighteenth-century pioneer of modern biological classification systems, listed hares as ruminants in some editions of his work *Systema Naturae*.[103]

Another alleged error is found in Leviticus 11:13–19, which lists birds that could not be eaten. In the *The Skeptic's Annotated Bible,* Steve Wells wrote that according to Leviticus 11:19, "Bats are birds to the biblical God."[104] We know today that bats are mammals because, unlike birds, they lack feathers and nurse their young with milk. Is Leviticus in error because it refers to bats as birds? The word in Leviticus 11:13 translated as "bird," *oph*, is defined in Hebrew lexicons as "flying creature."[105] Modern translators use the word "bird" instead of "flying creature" because every other animal on the list besides bats is a kind of bird. There is no scientific error in listing bats as "flying creatures" because bats are indeed creatures that can fly. If anything, the placement of bats at the end of the list is evidence that the ancient author knew bats differed from other flying animals.

Finally, Leviticus 11:20 says, "All winged insects that go upon all fours are an abomination to you." In response, former minister turned atheist Farrell Till wrote, "What educated person today doesn't know that insects have six legs? We have to wonder why God, who so routinely gave scientific insights to his inspired writers, couldn't at least have opened the eyes of his earthly messenger in this case and had him count the legs on a grasshopper."[106]

The problem with Till's response is that the Biblical writers were aware that insects had six legs (Hebrew children would have counted the legs of insects just like modern children do). Leviticus 11:21 even describes the legs besides the four a grasshopper "goes on" as "the legs above its feet." These were the larger hind legs the grasshopper uses for jumping.

But why does the grasshopper go "on all fours"? Because for the Israelites, and modern people as well, there was no expression for "going on all sixes" for insects, or "all eights" for spiders, or "all hundreds" for millipedes. The phrase "go upon all fours" was simply an idiom that referred to any creature that did not walk upright on two legs, so there is no error in this text.

These examples only show that the biblical author's way of describing ruminants, birds, and insects differed from how we describe these creatures today. They are not proof of error, since the human authors never assert that these statements represent modern taxonomy (the science of classifying animals). They are popular descriptions of animals listed in ancient dietary restrictions and should be read in that context.

JACOB, CATTLE, AND GENETICS

The latter half of the book of Genesis includes an account of how Jacob fled from the wrath of his stepbrother Esau and settled with his uncle Laban. Unfortunately, Laban was not an honest person and routinely deceived Jacob for his own ends. In one instance, Laban promised Jacob that he could keep any spotted or speckled goats as well as any black lambs he tended (Gen. 30:34). However, after making this promise, Laban removed the sheep, the goats with spots and speckles, and the lambs with black coats and put them in his own herds (Gen. 30:35). This should have resulted in Jacob not being able to produce these kinds of animals through natural breeding processes. But Genesis 30:37–39 tells us,

> Jacob took fresh rods of poplar and almond and plane, and peeled white streaks in them, exposing the white of the rods. He set the rods which he had peeled in front of the flocks in the runnels, that is, the watering troughs, where the flocks came to drink. And since they bred when they came to drink, the flocks bred in front of the rods and so the flocks brought forth striped, speckled, and spotted.

By having the cattle mate in front of the spotted rods, their offspring were born with white spots and speckles. In his book *Biblical Nonsense,* Jason Long wrote, "As someone with a thorough background in human physiology, I hold the opinion that

this is easily the single most embarrassing error contained between the Bible's covers. Peeled branches have absolutely no effect on an organism's appearance; DNA does."[107]

But if we read further in Genesis we discover that it was God
who miraculously intervened to counter Laban's unfairness, not
wood with magical power over genetics. Under divine influence, animals that had particular color markings were induced
to mate with one another. According to Hahn and Mitch,

> Ancient herdsmen believed that visual stimuli could affect the
> offspring of breeding animals . . . Building on the previous
> narrative, which emphasizes the human element of Jacob's
> cleverness (Gen. 30:25–43), the story is retold to stress the
> divine element, stating that God is ultimately responsible for
> Jacob's protection and prosperity during his years in Paddan-
> aram (Gen. 31:5, 7, 9).[108]

This story only proves that God's will is not thwarted by
anything, including scheming uncles, common superstitious
practices, or the laws of genetic inheritance. God can always
intervene with a miracle to rescue his chosen people, and he can
manifest that miracle any way he chooses—including through
common cultural practices of the people to whom he has revealed himself.

SUBSTANDARD HEALTH CARE?

Some atheists say the Bible is unscientific because it encourages
"faith healing" or praying for the sick instead of treating them
with medicine. These critics then try to disparage religion as a
whole by citing tragic stories of "Bible-believing" parents who
chose to pray for their very sick children instead of taking them
to a hospital. But as heartbreaking as these stories are, they only
tell us about the danger of specific individuals' beliefs. They tell
us nothing about religion itself, since the vast majority of religious believers see faith and medicine as compatible.

This viewpoint is supported in the Bible.

Ezekiel 47:12 describes leaves that can be used for healing, and in Jeremiah 8:22 the Lord rhetorically proposes that his people are ill because "there is no physician" in the land of Gilead. In Colossians 4:14 Paul calls Luke "the beloved physician," and in Mark 2:17 Jesus said that "Those who are well have no need of a physician, but those who are sick." The Bible certainly says we should pray and ask God for all kinds of help, including when we are sick. But the Bible never says we must *only* pray in the face of illness.[109] We read in the book of Sirach,

> When you are sick do not be negligent, but pray to the Lord, and he will heal you . . . And give the physician his place, for the Lord created him; let him not leave you, for there is need of him. There is a time when success lies in the hands of physicians, for they too will pray to the Lord, that he should grant them success in diagnosis and in healing, for the sake of preserving life (Sir. 38:9, 12–14).

Other critics claim that the Bible contradicts modern medical knowledge. Their prime example is the elaborate purification ritual given to victims of what the Bible calls leprosy (also known as Hansen's disease) that is described in Leviticus 14.[110] Wells summarized the ritual this way:

> God's law for lepers: Get two birds. Kill one. Dip the live bird in the blood of the dead one. Sprinkle the blood on the leper seven times, and then let the blood-soaked bird fly away. Next find a lamb and kill it. Wipe some of its blood on the patient's right ear, thumb, and big toe. Sprinkle seven times . . . [then] sprinkle the house with blood 7 times. That's all there is to it.[111]

Of course, Wells is being facetious. He and critics like him think this ritual is nonsense and can't cure anyone of a disease like leprosy. But Wells is mistaken, because this ritual was not

intended to physically heal anyone. It was performed to make
the leper ceremonially clean *after* his disease was cured and to
welcome him back into the community. To see why that is, read
Leviticus 14:2–4 carefully:

> This shall be the law of the leper for the day of his cleansing.
> He shall be brought to the priest; and the priest shall go out of
> the camp, and the priest shall make an examination. *Then, if
> the leprous disease is healed in the leper* [emphasis added], the priest
> shall command them to take for him who is to be cleansed two
> living clean birds and cedarwood and scarlet stuff and hyssop . . .

The Israelites believed that bodily fluid was sacred (Lev.
17:14), so they purified anyone who lost fluid through wounds or
sores, which often occurs with leprosy. The priest inspected the
leper to see if the disease had been healed, and *only then* would
the ritual described in the ensuing verses be performed. Thus, in
the Gospels, after Jesus heals a leper, he tells him, "Go and show
yourself to the priest, and make an offering for your cleansing,
as Moses commanded" (Luke 5:14). *The Catholic Commentary on
Holy Scripture* describes how the symbolism of this ritual helped
the Israelites understand larger spiritual truths:

> The symbolism of this ceremony is obvious. The sprinkling
> cleanses; the blood, and the water from a spring, not from a
> cistern, symbolize the new life which is being imparted to a
> person hitherto regarded as dead [i.e., separated from the com-
> munity]; the setting of the bird free represents release from
> confinement and reinstatement in civil rights; the cedar is not-
> ed for its soundness and medicinal powers; the hyssop . . . was
> selected for its cleansing properties; the scarlet color of the band
> represents the blood of a new life.[112]

Sometimes allegations of biblical medical malfeasance are the
result of the critic not reading the text carefully. This is evident
in the following comments from Jason Long:

The author of the first letter to Timothy advises his reader to drink wine instead of water (5:23). While researchers in the medical profession currently believe that alcohol is beneficial in moderation, consuming enough wine to remain hydrated for the rest of Timothy's life would certainly destroy his liver after a very brief period.[113]

My only response to this argument is to say that it's baffling why Long would interpret Paul's advice that Timothy "No longer drink only water, but use a little wine for the sake of your stomach and your frequent ailments" to mean that Timothy should drink only wine in the future. The Fundamentalist tendency to read into a text what a person wants to see can be found even among nonreligious fundamentalists—including some atheists who are hell-bent on discrediting the Bible.

DEMONIC NONSENSE?

What about the Bible's description of healings performed by the "casting out of demons"? Shouldn't modern people view these accounts as failures to diagnose mental illness and not as descriptions of demonic forces?

Today, as in the ancient world, there are reports of demonic possession. While some of these are the result of mental illness, we can't say that all of them are. We would only be justified in saying that if we assume that there are no such beings as demons, or that such demons aren't capable of possessing people. Neither of these statements has been proven to be true.

Demons may exist and may be able to harm humans, but science can't test or locate these extremely intelligent, malevolent, and most important, *immaterial* entities. Science is limited to observing and describing the physical world. Anything that may lie beyond that world is unapproachable from a scientific perspective.[114] If God exists and created angelic beings who later disobeyed him and now serve the devil, then it is possible cases of demonic possession, including accounts found in Scripture, are real.

We shouldn't immediately dismiss ancient accounts of demonic possession especially since they have been recorded throughout history, even to the present day.[115] Now, this is not to say that all accounts of demonic possession are genuine. In fact, the Church has issued guidelines for how modern exorcists should distinguish between cases of actual demonic possession and cases that involve only natural mental illness.[116] For example, the former can be identified by symptoms such as the victim speaking a language he supposedly does not know, or the victim possessing superhuman strength.

Since science can neither prove nor disprove the existence of demons, and since demonic possession is possible, it is not true that reports of demonic possession in the Bible contradict modern medical knowledge.

A MATH BLUNDER?

The first book of Kings describes how Solomon selects Hiram to create a large bronze basin of water for the new temple. It says Hiram "made the molten sea; it was round, ten cubits from brim to brim [a cubit is about 18 inches in length], and five cubits high, and a line of thirty cubits measured its circumference." (7:23). But skeptics say this is wrong, because if the diameter of the basin was 10 cubits, then the circumference should be about 31.4 cubits, not 30 cubits. This means that the Bible teaches that pi (the ratio of the circumference of a circle to its diameter) is 3 instead of the correct value of approximately 3.14.[117]

But the book of Kings is neither a mathematics textbook nor an architecture manual. The ancient writers would have had no qualms referring to the circumference of Solomon's basin as being 30 cubits in length even if it was 31 cubits in length. This is like the way we might say a Boeing 747 jet airliner can hold 63,000 gallons of fuel even though it can actually hold 63,705 gallons.[118]

This passage is not trying to teach us what the value of pi is; it's recording how a real object was created and giving us the approximate size of that object. Calculating the circumference of a circle in a math problem is easy because the circle is composed of a line that has no width. Solomon's basin, in contrast, would have had thick sides in order to maintain its structural integrity. 1 Kings 7:26 says, "Its thickness was a handbreadth; and its brim was made like the brim of a cup, like the flower of a lily; it held two thousand baths."

This means that the basin had a rim that was greater in circumference than the basin's interior. According to 1 Kings 7:23, if the basin was 10 cubits from "brim to brim" (which would include the thick edge fashioned like a lily that was a handbreadth wide), then the diameter of the basin may have been closer to 9.6 cubits. If it were, then the circumference of the basin below the ornate lily rim would have been 30 cubits in length, just as the Bible describes it.

THE BIBLE AND SCIENCE

When critics claim the Bible is "unscientific," they are correct in the sense that the Bible does not present itself as a scientific description of the world. The Bible's human authors, under the inspiration of the Holy Spirit, weren't offering descriptions of the world in order to impart technical, scientific knowledge to human beings. Their discussions of subjects were primarily used to communicate important truths about God, humanity, Creation, and our ultimate salvation. As Cardinal Caesar Baronius is supposed to have said back in the sixteenth century, "The Bible teaches us how to go to heaven, not how the heavens go."

5

Legendary Biblical Creatures?

The Claim: The Bible describes fantastic, mythical beings—
men who lived to be nearly a thousand years old, giants who
walked the earth, and creatures like unicorns and dragons.
This shows that the Bible is just a book of myths and can't be
trusted to inform us about the historical past.

The fifth and eleventh chapters of the book of Genesis describe
the descendants of Adam, who apparently lived for centuries.
These include Adam's son Seth, who lived to be 920, and Me-
thuselah, who lived to be a whopping 969 years old, making
him the oldest person in the Bible. But don't these long ages
contradict what we know about the average human life span?
They certainly are above average. Being omnipotent, God could
have caused these people to live this long, but there is reason to
believe these ages are symbolic and not literal.

In ancient Mesopotamia it was a common practice to ascribe
greatness to someone by inflating his life span.[119] This is evident
in an ancient list of the kings of Sumer (a region in what is now
modern-day Iraq) that describes rulers who allegedly lived for tens
of thousands of years. The earliest king on this list to be confirmed
as having an actual historical existence is Enmebaragesi, who was
recorded to have lived for 900 years. Another historically verifiable
king, Aga of Kish, was recorded to have lived for 625 years.[120]

Since historians don't discount the existence of these kings
despite their inflated life spans, we should not discount the
trustworthiness of the Bible just because it describes people with
similar life spans. These descriptions may be nonliteral ways of
ascribing greatness to someone, or, as Scott Hahn and Curtis
Mitch say, "this may be simply a literary technique used to assert
the remarkable age of the human race itself."[121]

The Nephilim

According to Genesis 6:4, by the time of Noah there came a group of individuals called the Nephilim, who "were on the earth in those days, and also afterward, when the sons of God came in to the daughters of men, and they bore children to them. These were the mighty men that were of old, the men of renown."

Critics say this passage is mythological because it describes sexual unions between angels (sons of God) and humans (daughters of men) that resulted in the birth of the mysterious Nephilim. But the text never says the "sons of God" are angels. Indeed, what makes angels different from humans is that they do not have physical bodies, and so they can't sexually reproduce.[122] But if that's true, then who were the sons of God and their offspring, the Nephilim?

One interpretation of the Nephilim, which Christian theologians like St. Augustine and some Jewish rabbis in the first few centuries after Christ held, is that they were the righteous descendants of Adam's good son, Seth (or the Sethites).[123] The Sethites, who obeyed God's commands, were God's "sons," but they later lost their righteous standing by marrying the worldly and immoral descendants of Cain (or the "Kenites," who Genesis 6:4 calls "the daughters of men"). The children of these mixed marriages became very powerful and corrupt rulers, the Nephilim.

Another interpretation, which the Jewish historian Josephus as well as early Church Fathers like Justin Martyr favored, holds that the Nephilim were gigantic offspring that came from angels mating with humans.[124] How this occurred would be a mystery, but we can't rule out the possibility that fallen angels could have manipulated matter in order to cause pregnancies in human women. Either way, the Church has not officially defined the nature of the Nephilim, so a Catholic is free to accept the theory that best explains the text and its relation to other truths of the Faith.

The Bible's other descriptions of giants can be explained by the human authors' use of exaggeration for rhetorical effect, or hyperbole. For example, in Numbers 13:33, a group of scouts sent into Canaan reported back to Moses that in comparison to the land's inhabitants, "we seemed to ourselves like grasshoppers, and so we seemed to them."[125] This doesn't mean that the inhabitants of Canaan were 500-foot-tall monsters. It just means they were larger than the Israelites, which is quite plausible since ethnic groups can vary in height. Even today men in Scandinavian countries are on average seven to eight inches taller than men in Southeast Asia.[126] If you belonged to a basketball team and the opposing team was, on average, a foot taller than your team, you might say it was difficult playing against such "giants," without meaning that the other team climbed down from a beanstalk.

Mything in Action?

Even if the Bible's references to giants are hyperbolic, what about the Bible's references to supposedly mythical creatures? Bible critic Jason Long wrote, "The cockatrice, unicorn, and dragon are examples of mythical creatures in the Bible that fail to leave any reliable evidence for their existence."[127] Don't these legendary animals prove the whole Bible is a collection of legends?

No, because in most cases the Bible is affirming the existence of real animals. It is only the work of later translators, not the Bible's original authors, that refers to unicorns or dragons. This is especially prevalent in the King James Version of the Bible. This translation is well known among lay people for its eloquent seventeeth-century English (including its use of the pronouns "thee" and "thou"), but it is also known among scholars for its inaccurate rendering of several scriptural passages.

It is in this translation that we find the majority of references to mythical biblical animals. This is unfortunate, because ever since Steve Wells used this translation for his popular *Skeptic's Annotated Bible,* critics often use the King James Bible as their standard for arguing against the Bible.

Unicorns

A unicorn is a horse with a long horn protruding from its forehead. Medieval literature described it as possessing medicinal or even magical powers. In the KJV, the unicorn is depicted as a symbol of strength and wild power. Numbers 23:22 says, "God brought [the Israelites] out of Egypt; he hath as it were the strength of an unicorn." In Job 39:9–10, God points out Job's human limits and says, "Will the unicorn be willing to serve thee, or abide by thy crib? Canst thou bind the unicorn with his band in the furrow?"

The Hebrew word the KJV translates as "unicorn" is *re'em*, which modern scholars have identified with an auroch, or a large, horned cow that is now extinct. The ancient Assyrians also referred to these animals by a similar name, *rimu*.[128] So how did the Hebrew word *re'em* become "unicorn" in the King James Version?

The translators of the Septuagint, the ancient Greek translation of the Old Testament, used the Greek word *monoceros* (literally "one horn") in place of the Hebrew word *re'em*. In the fifth century, St. Jerome translated the Septuagint into the Latin Vulgate and used the Latin equivalent of "monoceros," or *unicornis*. Eventually, this word became "unicorn" in English.

But why did the Septuagint translators use a word that literally meant "one horn" instead of something like "wild ox"? One theory is that they may have been thinking of another animal that also fits the description found in passages like Numbers 23:22. The first-century Roman naturalist Pliny the Elder described a real animal from India called a *monoceros:*

> [It] has the head of the stag, the feet of the elephant, and the tail of the boar, while the rest of the body is like that of the horse; it makes a deep lowing noise, and has a single black horn, which projects from the middle of its forehead, two cubits in length. This animal, it is said, cannot be taken alive.[129]

Today, in northern India, there is a very strong animal with feet like an elephant, a large body, and one horn that protrudes from its head. If we allow some leeway in Pliny's description (which is necessary in ancient descriptions of unique creatures), we can identify this creature as the modern Indian rhinoceros.

Indeed, *monoceros* means "one horn" and rhinoceros means "nose horn" (*rinoceros*). A rhinoceros would make sense in these biblical passages because, unlike unicorns, they are known for being very strong beasts that can't be domesticated. In order to remain faithful to the original language, and to avoid confusion with the medieval concept of a unicorn, most modern translations of the Bible render the Hebrew word in these passages as "wild ox" and not "unicorn" or "one horn."

THE COCKATRICE

This creature is mentioned several times in the KJV's translations of the books of the prophets. Jeremiah 8:17 reads, "For, behold, I will send serpents, cockatrices, among you, which will not be charmed, and they shall bite you, saith the Lord." Isaiah 11:8 says, "And the sucking child shall play on the hole of the asp, and the weaned child shall put his hand on the cockatrice' den." Long wrote, "The prophet Isaiah informs us that a cockatrice, a mythical creature able to kill its victim with a casual glance, will arise from a serpent (Isa. 14:29). What tangible evidence do we have to believe that a creature with this incredible ability has ever existed?"[130]

However, Long is mistaken. Isaiah never mentions the cockatrice, nor does he describe this creature as having supernatural powers. Like the King James Bible in whose pages it is found, the cockatrice is a product of medieval European imagination and would have been unknown to prophets like Jeremiah or Isaiah. According to English scholar Laurence Breiner, "The cockatrice, which no one ever saw, was born by accident toward the end of the twelfth century and died in the middle of the seventeenth."[131]

Although allusions to the creature can be traced back to Pliny the Elder, the dissident Catholic John Wycliffe first used the term "cockatrice" in 1382 in his popular translation of the Bible. It was later used in the 1535 Coverdale Bible, which may have been the source for the King James Version's use of this word.

Although Isaiah and Jeremiah would have been unaware of the cockatrice, they would have known what a *tsepha'* was. This is the Hebrew word used in passages like Isaiah 11:8, and it simply means "poisonous serpent."[132] Today, most modern translations use the word "adder" in these passages.

Other biblical creatures that could fall under the category of "mythical snakes" are the so-called fiery serpents found in passages like Numbers 21:6. This verse says, "the Lord sent fiery serpents among the people, and they bit the people, so that many sons of Israel died." What in the world is a fiery serpent? The Hebrew phrase is *hasseraphim hannekhasim* and, according to one commentary, the fire probably refers not to the snake itself but to "the burning sensation and pain brought about by the lethal injection of venom through the serpents' fangs."[133]

Before we continue, I should point out that these examples of "mythical creatures" help illustrate Bible reading rule number four: *Check the original language.* Remember, the Bible was not written in seventeenth-century English. The Old Testament was written in ancient Hebrew (along with some Aramaic and Greek) and the New Testament in ancient Greek. (The Old Testament was later translated into the Greek Septuagint.) This refutes objections raised by atheists like David Mills, who said of passages that seem to describe mythical animals, "in the newer, modern-language translations of the Bible, these ridiculous passages of Scripture have been dishonestly excised, rewritten or edited beyond recognition from their original translation in the King James."[134]

However, Mills is erroneously treating the King James Version as if it were the original text of the Bible.[135] The truth is that newer translations of the Bible are better than the King James because they use earlier manuscripts that better capture the sense of the Bible's original text. But even these Bibles represent the opinions of modern translators. This is why when we confront a Scripture passage that is difficult, we must examine what the inspired author originally said in Hebrew or Greek. By doing this, we sometimes see that the words the original author used make more sense than a word a later translator chose, especially if the translation is an older one, like the King James.

SATYRS

In the King James Version, Isaiah 13:21 says of the mighty city of Babylon, "wild beasts of the desert shall lie there; and their houses shall be full of doleful creatures; and owls shall dwell there, and satyrs shall dance there." In Roman mythology, a satyr was a creature that resembled a human but had horns and the legs of a goat. In earlier Greek mythology, satyrs were depicted as having animal tails and horns, but human legs. The King James translator probably used the English word "satyr" because the Hebrew word is the similar-sounding *sa'iyr*. But the Hebrew word does not refer to the Roman or even to the Greek concept of the satyr.

Although it generally means "devil," *sa'iyr* is often used to refer to actual goats or even just to hairy things, such as Jacob's hairy brother Esau (Gen. 27:11). A rendition of the passage that makes more sense to modern readers would be the New American Standard Bible's translation, which reads, "their houses will be full of owls; Ostriches also will live there, and shaggy goats will frolic there."[136]

The closest the word *sa'iyr* comes to referring to something like a Roman satyr would be in Leviticus 17:7, which prohibits sacrifices to "goat-idols" (NIV). But the word's use in this context doesn't mean that the human writers affirmed that a creature resembling the mythological satyr actually existed. The author was referring to idols shaped like goats, since most ancient idols were crafted in the form of known animals.

DRAGONS

In some parts of the Bible the word "dragon" is used metaphorically to refer to the devil (Rev. 20:2), or even to humans like the Pharaoh of Egypt (Ezek. 29:3). But in other passages the word

dragon appears to refer to an actual animal. In the King James
Version, Jeremiah 10:22 says, "Behold, the noise of the bruit is
come, and a great commotion out of the north country, to make
the cities of Judah desolate, and a den of dragons." Psalm 91:13 of
the King James says, "Thou shalt tread upon the lion and adder:
the young lion and the dragon shalt thou trample under feet."

In these passages, the Hebrew word that is translated as
"dragon" is *tannin*, which can mean "serpent" or "dragon." The
word *tannin* comes from the root word *tan*, which means "jackal."[137] Modern translations usually render the text based on the
root word because it better fits the context of these passages.
Consider the Revised Standard Version's rendering of Jeremiah
10:22: "Behold, it comes!—a great commotion out of the north
country to make the cities of Judah a desolation, a lair of jackals." If an ancient city were destroyed we would expect scaveng-
ing animals like jackals to inhabit it and feast on the dead bodies
left amidst the desolation.

In other instances, the word "dragon" seems to refer to a
mythical creature and not a real animal like a jackal. Psalm 74:13
says of God, "You divided the sea by your might; you broke the
heads of the dragons on the waters." But this does not mean the
Bible endorses the existence of dragons, as will be made clear in
our discussion of a creature called "Leviathan."

LEVIATHAN

In Job 41, God demonstrates his power to Job by contrasting it
with man's inability to tame one of God's creatures. God says,
"Can you draw out Leviathan with a fishhook, or press down
his tongue with a cord? . . . Can you fill his skin with harpoons,
or his head with fishing spears? . . . Upon earth there is not his
like, a creature without fear."

What is the Leviathan?

Asking what the Leviathan is like asking what the "beast"
is—the word can refer to different kinds of animals depending
on the context in which it is used. In some contexts Leviathan

appears to refer to a whale, as in Psalm 104:25–26: " Yonder is the sea, great and wide, which teems with things innumerable, living things both small and great. There go the ships, and Leviathan which you formed to sport in it."

In other contexts it clearly refers to a kind of mythical animal. Job 41:19–21 says of Leviathan, "Out of his mouth go flaming torches; sparks of fire leap forth. Out of his nostrils comes forth smoke, as from a boiling pot and burning rushes. His breath kindles coals, and a flame comes forth from his mouth." Psalm 74:14 tells us that God in the primeval world "crushed the heads of Leviathan; you gave him as food for the creatures of the wilderness," but Isaiah 27:1 says that at the end of time "the Lord with his hard and great and strong sword will punish Leviathan the fleeing serpent, Leviathan the twisting serpent, and he will slay the dragon that is in the sea."

How can God be the one who destroyed Leviathan at the beginning of Creation and also be the one who will destroy him at the end of time?

It seems that the Hebrew authors were poetically comparing Yahweh to a well known fictional entity called Leviathan in order to demonstrate God's power and sovereignty. Bible scholar Mark Smith observed that while other cultures made beasts like Leviathan equal and threatening to their gods, the Hebrews described these creatures as God's pets. God has complete control over them, reflecting the Jewish view that God has complete control over everything.[138] In his book *The Bible Among the Myths*, John Oswalt argued that the writers of Scripture were using "a self-conscious appropriation of the language of myth for historical and literary purposes, not mythical ones."[139]

This literary device does not mean that the author was asserting that Leviathan was a real animal. Like *The Lord of the Rings* example cited earlier, comparing Yahweh to a fictional entity is no more problematic than modern Christians comparing Jesus to Superman. Even saying that God would destroy a creature like Leviathan does not assert its real existence. It may simply have been a way of asserting Yahweh's omnipotence and showing peo-

ple who thought these creatures were real—such as the followers
of the Canaanite deity Baal, for whom Leviathan was an enemy—
that these beasts did not threaten the God of Israel.

The Bible's depiction of fantastic dragon creatures and Leviathan may have also come about when ancient people like
the Israelites discovered dinosaur fossils.[140] All they would have
known from examining these unearthed bones was that they
came from huge beasts with big teeth. There is nothing problematic in the human authors of the Bible communicating this
message in their writings: "whatever these huge animals were,
and no matter when they lived, our God (Yahweh) is stronger
than them."

6

The Mythical Patriarchs?

The Claim: Bible scholars once thought that Abraham, Isaac, Jacob, Joseph, and Moses really existed, but we now know they were myths created by the ancient Israelites. The Bible is neither inspired nor is it historically reliable.

Genesis 12–50 describes the story of Israel's patriarchs, the men who first answered God's call to be the "founding fathers" of his chosen people. It describes them as a nomadic family that migrated from Mesopotamia (what is now modern-day Iraq) to Palestine before finally settling in the land of Egypt. The patriarchs included Abraham, to whom God revealed the covenant sign of circumcision; his son, Isaac, who came to be known as "the son of the promise": and Isaac's son Jacob, who was later renamed Israel. Jacob's twelve sons became the ancestors of the twelve tribes of Israel.

The existence of Israel as a distinct group of people is attested to not only in the Bible, but also in a slab of granite called the Merneptah Stele that has been dated to 1208 B.C. It contains a text describing the Egyptian pharaoh Merneptah's victories in the region and includes this boast, "Israel is laid waste and his seed is not."

Even a moderate scholar like William Dever admits that unlike many Egyptian names that only refer to a place, "the name Israel is followed by a different sign: 'man + woman + three strokes,' which refers to peoples in contrast to nation-states or their capitals—in other words, to an ethnic group."[141] Since ethnic groups are often named after people they came from, this stele provides early evidence for the existence of a person named Israel from whom the ethnic group "Israel" originated.[142]

Now, it is true there is no ancient, nonbiblical evidence that *directly* refers to individuals like Abraham, Isaac, or Jacob. But as Egyptologist James K. Hoffmeier observed, "We should not expect people living such a [nomadic] lifestyle between 3,500 and 4,000 years ago to have left any archaeological evidence of their existence, and ancient texts from urban centers are unlikely to specifically document their presence."[143] But even without direct corroboration, there are details within the patriarch narratives that indirectly confirm their authenticity.

First, these narratives include many embarrassing details that would have been omitted by an Israelite who simply invented the stories. These include the use of deception by all three patriarchs (Gen. 12:10–13; 20:1–2; 26:7; 27:18–27); Abraham having sexual relations with his maidservant, Hagar (Gen. 16:4); Abraham violating later Mosaic Law by being married to his half sister (Gen. 20:12); and Jacob's sons engaging in sex with prostitutes and selling their own brother into slavery (Gen. 37:12–36; 38:18).

Second, the patriarchs' status as lowly outsiders in the land of Canaan makes the story less likely to be a myth. Later Israelites would have been tempted to ground their right to settle in Canaan on their ancestors' origins there and would not be expected to fabricate the migratory nature of their forefathers. Finally, the tools and customs described in the narratives fit well in the historical period when the patriarchs were supposed to have lived, the middle to late Bronze Age (2000–1200 B.C.).[144]

Absurd Anachronisms?

Some critics argue, however, that the patriarch narratives are not historically accurate because they contain anachronisms, or historical errors about the past made by a much later writer. For example, a history of the Revolutionary War that included aerial bombings would be anachronistic because airplanes weren't invented until the twentieth century and weren't used in combat until World War I. If a historian included such a detail in his account of the Revolutionary War, we would question his ability to accurately record any other detail from that time period.

When it comes to Genesis, critics say similar anachronisms exist, and so we can't trust the stories about the patriarchs.[145]

One example is the patriarch's use of camels (Gen. 12:14–16; 24:63; 30:43; 37:25), which they claim is anachronistic because camels were not domesticated until the tenth century B.C., and the patriarchs lived long before that time.[146]

It's true that camel bones discovered in Israel have been dated to the tenth century B.C., but this does not prove that camels were not domesticated in Israel before that point. The remains of nearly all animals used for human purposes during the second millennium B.C. have not survived to the present day. The discovery of domestic animal bones from one century does not preclude their existence in an earlier century.

Moreover, there is evidence from ancient cave drawings and pottery illustrations that camels were domesticated during the time of the patriarchs and even earlier. Camel petroglyphs near Aswan and Gezireh in Upper Egypt, for example, have been dated to the third millennium B.C.[147] In his study on the domestication of the camel, Martin Heide concluded that the use of the word "camel" in the patriarch narratives "may refer, at least in some places, to the Bactrian camel," or a camel with two humps that migrated from the mountainous areas of Iran.[148]

Another alleged error is Abraham and Isaac's contact with the Philistines (Gen. 21:34; 26:1), who critics say did not exist during the lifetimes of the patriarchs. But according to scholars David Jobling and Catherine Rose, "Rabbinic sources insist that the Philistines of Judges and Samuel were different people altogether from the Philistines of Genesis."[149] This is especially likely since the Philistines described in Genesis were not a major military power nor were they as belligerent as the Philistines described in later books like Samuel.

One explanation for this is that during the time of the united monarchy (when Israel was united under King Saul, David, or Solomon), the name "Philistine" may have been a reference to "non-Israelites" in general and not to a distinct people such as the group described in Genesis.[150] The Philistines in Genesis may actually have been emigrants from what is now modern-day Greece. In fact, a stone tablet called the Phaistos Disc testifies to the existence of a seafaring group of people that originated on the island of Crete in the year 1700 B.C., which was near the time and place Abraham lived.[151]

It could be the case that the author or a later editor of Genesis used a name that was familiar to his readers in order to illustrate for them where these ancient people settled. In doing so, he probably did not intend to identify these people with the Philistines who attacked the fledging nation of Israel several centuries later. This would be similar to modern historians describing the people who interacted with Jesus in the first century as "Palestinians" even though the term "Palestinian" did not become prominent until the twentieth century, and the two groups are not politically or socially related to one another.[152]

JOSEPH'S PLIGHT IN EGYPT

Genesis 39–50 describes Jacob's beloved son Joseph being sold into slavery by his jealous brothers. The slave traders Joseph was sold to brought him into Egypt, where he was purchased as a servant for an Egyptian official named Potiphar. After Joseph refused the romantic advances of Potiphar's wife, she lied and accused him of attempting to rape her, which led to Joseph being imprisoned.

Fortunately, his ability to interpret dreams was called upon when the pharaoh was confused about a dream involving healthy and sick cows. Joseph correctly interpreted the pharaoh's dream as a warning of an impending famine and, as a result, the nation of Egypt was able to store up enough food to survive. In reward for his service, Joseph was promoted to the role of vizier, or what me might call today a chancellor. Through this position, he was able to turn the tables on his brothers, who didn't recognize him when they came to Egypt in search of food. Joseph later secured his family's relocation to Egypt and set in motion the Israelites dwelling there as a people and a future nation.

There are several pieces of evidence that count in favor of the plausibility of this story's core elements. First, the Egyptian king

Khety Nebkaure described in his "Instructions to Merikare" how to deal with Semitic invaders along the Nile Delta who were searching for food during the mid- to late second millennium B.C.[153] This fits well with Genesis' description of Jacob's family traveling to Egypt during that time in search of food during a widespread famine.

Second, the price that Joseph was sold into slavery for—twenty shekels—was the accurate price for a slave during the second millennium B.C. If a later writer had invented the story he would have probably said Joseph was sold at the value of a slave in his own time, or thirty shekels.[154] Similarly, Joseph was said to have died at the age of 110, which was the ideal life span for ancient Egyptians. If a later Hebrew author wanted to communicate that Joseph lived a full life, he might have chosen an ideal Jewish life span of seventy or eighty years.[155] This provides evidence that this story came from an early oral account from Egypt and did not have a fictional origin in Israel.

Finally, foreigners could ascend to positions of power and authority in ancient Egypt. After the death of Pharaoh Seti II in 1194 B.C., a Syrian-born official was elevated to chancellor over the whole land. Under the fifteenth-century Pharaoh Hatshepsut, a man with a Semitic name served as her vizier.[156] Therefore, there is no historical difficulty in asserting that Joseph's interventions led to the Israelites dwelling in Egypt, where their descendants would eventually be enslaved. This brings us to a figure in Judaism who is held in even higher esteem than the patriarchs, but whose existence scholars also question.

MOSES

In the beginning of the book of Exodus we read about a certain Levite man and woman in Egypt who gave birth to a son and hid him from the Egyptian authorities. They did this because the pharaoh had recently ordered the death of all newborn male Hebrews in order to prevent the slave population from growing too large and uncontrollable. When they could no longer hide him, the boy's parents had his sister place the child in a basket among some reeds along a riverbank. As she watched from a distance, his sister saw the daughter of the pharaoh come to the river to bathe, where she discovered the child. The pharaoh's daughter named the child Moses, which means, "I drew him out of the water."

Some critics contend that this story is an imitation of an earlier myth about a hero of the ancient Akkadians named Sargon.[157] One version describes Sargon recounting his own birth story:

> My mother was a vestal, my father I knew not . . . [My mother] laid me in a vessel made of reeds, closed my door with pitch, and dropped me down into the river, which did not drown me. The river carried me to Akki, the water carrier. Akki, the water carrier, lifted me up in the kindness of his heart, Akki, the water carrier, raised me as his own son.[158]

Although the story has some superficial similarities to the Moses account, there are also significant differences that point to them having independent origins. First, the structure and themes in the narratives differ substantially. Moses is calmly set in the river in order to be found, and the narrative makes no mention of his traveling down the river. Sargon's story, on the other hand, gives no explanation for why he is placed in the river, which is surprising since this would be quite an unusual thing for a mother to do with her child.

The most probable reason is that Sargon's mother wanted to dispose of him, either by death or disappearance, in order to retain her position as a virgin priestess. After all, giving birth to a child would probably have cast doubt on the virgin part of her job description. Sargon even ironically reflects upon this when he says that his mother's actions did not drown him. This is quite different from the benevolent act of placing Moses amidst shoreline reeds to save him, as described in the Exodus story.

The Exodus account also utilizes Egyptian vocabulary, which would not be expected if the story had been borrowed from the Akkadians and then crudely set in Egypt. For example, the name Moses definitely shares a root with the Egyptian word *mse,* which means "to give birth." It was prominent in the name of several pharaohs, including Thutmose and Ramesses. Also, the Hebrew word for river in the Exodus account is not the usual Hebrew word *nahar,* but the word *ye'or,* which is a transliteration of the Egyptian word for the Nile.[159]

In fact, the Sargon story may have borrowed from the Moses story when it was written in the late eighth century B.C. to honor the Assyrian king Sargon II. If this is correct it would place the story's composition several centuries after the composition of the sources used in the book of Exodus, thus eliminating it as a source for the Moses story.

THE EXODUS

Critics often argue that the exodus is not historical because there is no evidence that the Israelites dwelled in Egypt, the plagues that afflicted Egypt during the exodus are mythical, and there is nothing in the historical or archaeological record to corroborate the Bible's account of a mass exodus of Israelites out of Egypt.

In regards to the Israelites dwelling in Egypt, not all Egyptian sources have survived to the present day, so this detail may have been lost or glossed over in Egyptian histories. However, the biblical account fits the Egyptian context and doesn't appear to be a fabrication produced by later Israelites. For example, Egyptologists have discovered the presence of Semitic names in Egyptian records from the time of the Exodus. They have also found descriptions of forced laborers making bricks in order to meet quotas as well as failures to meet those quotas because of a lack of straw—details that can all be be found in the book of Exodus (Exod. 5:7–14).[160] The famed Egyptologist Sir Alan Gardiner, who was generally dismissive of the historicity of the Old Testament, said "that Israel was in Egypt under one form or another no historian could possibly doubt."[161]

What about the plagues? Exodus 7–12 depicts the plagues in this order—water turns to blood, infestation of frogs, infestation of gnats, infestation of flies, disease, skin boils, hail, infestation of locusts, darkness, and the death of every firstborn male. Far from being unexpected miracles, many of the plagues represent natural hazards that still exist in Egypt to this day, such as infestations of locusts or disease.[162] These natural occurrences would have taken on a supernatural quality to the Egyptians primarily because of their severity and close proximity to one another.

What about the lack of Egyptian sources describing the Hebrew slaves leaving Egypt? It's true these sources have not been discovered yet, and it's possible that none exist. One reason is that the Israelites settled in Goshen (Gen. 45:10), which lies in the eastern part of the Nile Delta. The annual flooding of the Nile into this region would have regularly covered areas with new topsoil, thus making artifacts and documents difficult or impossible to recover.

This argument also assumes that ancient historians, like those associated with the Egyptian royal court, would have meticulously and objectively recorded events the way modern historians do. But what we know about Egyptian history should make us question that assumption. Historians of antiquity usually focused on recording what was useful to the people who paid for their services. That means they often glossed over the failures of their employers.

For example, both the Egyptians and the Hittites recorded the battle of Kadesh as a major victory, but only one side of the battle could have been victorious![163] Even more intriguing is that the commander of the Egyptian forces during this battle was Pharaoh Ramesses II, who some scholars believe was the pharaoh during the Exodus.[164] If Ramesses's battle with the Hittites was wildly exaggerated in order to hide his failure, couldn't his dealings with the Israelites also have been omitted in order to hide his failure with them as well?

THE WANDERING AND CONQUEST NARRATIVES

After the Israelites fled Egypt, the remainder of the Pentateuch (the first five books of the Bible) describes how the fledging nation of Israel wandered in the desert of Sinai for forty years before finally entering the promised land of Canaan. The books of Joshua and Judges pick up where the Pentateuch leaves off and describe Israel's military campaigns against the Canaanites and Israel's subsequent occupation of Canaan.

As with the Exodus, critics have attacked these stories both for lacking evidence that confirms their authenticity and for contradicting the history that secular sources seem to establish. Paul Tobin said of the "wilderness wandering stories,"

> We are also told this one-million-plus nation wandered for forty years in the wilderness in Sinai (Josh. 5:6). Surely more than a million people wandering around for forty years would have left some traces for archaeologists to find. Yet not a single piece of archaeological evidence has been found . . . the main details of the Exodus (Moses, the forty-year trek in Sinai, and the locations the Israelites went through) must all be pieces of historical fiction.[165]

There are two points that Tobin does not consider in his argument. First, even when past groups were known to exist in large numbers, that did not guarantee they left behind in the archaeological record abundant evidence of their existence. For example, in the nineteenth century, there were once billions of passenger pigeons in North America, but due to overhunting they went extinct by World War I.[166] In spite of their huge numbers and having lived for tens of thousands of years, only about 100 fossil specimens have ever been found.[167] Should we expect to find more evidence for a much smaller group of people who lived over thirty centuries ago?

Second, the Israelite's nomadic lifestyle makes it even more difficult to locate traces of their existence. They probably carried water in animal skins rather than in pottery and dwelled in tents instead of houses. These objects were well suited for nomadic migration, but not for enduring the centuries before later archeologists could find them. Israel Finkelstein, an archaeologist Tobin cites who is very skeptical of the historicity of the events described in the Old Testament, even admits, "Nomadic societies do not establish permanent houses, and the constant migration permits them to move only minimal belongings. Moreover, their limited resources do not facilitate the creation of a flourishing material culture that could leave rich archaeological finds."[168]

What makes finding this evidence even more improbable is that the descriptions of the number of Israelites that wandered in the wilderness as well as how long they wandered may not be literal. Regarding the length of time, the number forty is often used symbolically in Scripture to separate time periods or epochs.[169] Therefore, this may refer to an indeterminate amount of time the Israelites wandered, not an exact amount of time.

When it comes to the number of Israelites who wandered, however, this is a more curious detail. Both the book of Exodus and the census in Numbers 1 seem to attest that "the people of Israel journeyed from Ram'eses to Succoth, about six hundred thousand men on foot, besides women and children" (Exod. 12:37). The latter detail would probably have raised the total number of Israelites to over a million.

Critics have a point that this number of people would probably have left behind some archaeological evidence of their activities. Even if they didn't, such a sizable group should have been able to leave Egypt at will, as it was larger than any army at that time. Given these factors, it's possible that the numbers recorded in these texts are either exaggerated based on the literary genre of the time, or they are mistranslations.

The latter suggestion is plausible because the Hebrew word in these passages that is translated as thousand, *elep*, can also mean "clan" or "military unit." For example, Gideon speaks of his *elep* (or clan) being the weakest in Israel (Judg. 6:15), and David presented a gift to the commander of Israel's *elep* (1 Sam. 17:18). So, rather than 600,000 "men on foot" leaving Egypt, there may have been just 600 families or 600 groups of fighting men who left.[170]

Extra Exaggeration

Exaggeration was common among cultures in the ancient near east. One text from Ugarit (an ancient city that lies on the coast of modern Syria) says, "Let your strong army be numerous, three hundred ten thousands, conscripts without number, soldiers beyond counting."[171] But given that at Kadesh the Egyptian and Hittite forces each possessed about 20,000 soldiers, and the U.S. military today only has about 2.3 million active, and reserve duty soldiers, we can safely say that this description of a 3-million-man ancient army is hyperbolic.[172]

For the ancients, a number like three million was essentially the same as being "without number," "beyond counting," or just "really big." The Israelites' use of hyperbole in this case is akin to another nonliteral Hebrew refrain that asserted the greatness of Israel's monarchs: "Saul has slain his thousands, and David his tens of thousands" (1 Sam. 18:7). Either way, the post-Exodus wandering narratives are only talking about a people numbering in the hundreds or thousands, not millions. It would be far more difficult to find with the archaeological record evidence of such a small number of people. But what about the conquest narratives in the book of Joshua? Paul Tobin wrote,

> One of the most memorable stories in the Bible is that of the conquest of Jericho by Joshua and the Israelites (Joshua 6:1–21) . . . Unfortunately, archaeological digs led by Kathleen Kenyon in the 1950s showed that in the period most likely for this event (1550 to 1200 BCE), Jericho was either uninhabited or a small village with just a few huts. There was certainly no fortified wall that could have dramatically came tumbling down![173]

But we must not think of Jericho as it is often pictured in Sunday school illustrations, or as a large castle-like structure. It was a city whose walls consisted of tall, earthen embankments layered with stone. Egyptologist Kenneth Kitchen wrote, "The town was always small, an appendage to its spring and oasis, and its value (for eastern newcomers) largely symbolic as an eastern gateway into Canaan."[174] He noted that Kenyon did find some remains of Jericho, but she did not take into account the devastating effects of centuries worth of erosion on Jericho's eastern slope. "[A]ll of this has long, long since gone," Kitchen said. "We will never find 'Joshua's Jericho' for that very simple reason."[175]

A Lesson from the Hittites

Finally, we must expose a hidden assumption in the critics' arguments. It forms the basis of our fifth rule for reading the Bible: *The Bible is allowed to be a sole witness to history.* Some people will say, "Even if the accounts of the patriarchs, or the exodus, or the Israelites in Canaan are not anachronistic, that doesn't prove those accounts describe real events in history. They could just be pieces of historical fiction." But when people say this they are assuming that unless a historical event described in the Bible is also described in a nonbiblical work, then the event either never happened or we have no way of knowing if it did happen.

This way of approaching Scripture, what some call a "hermeneutic of suspicion," treats the historical accounts in the Bible as being "guilty until proven innocent." If a justification is given for this assumption, it's usually that the Bible describes miracles, and that makes its historical accounts unreliable. But other ancient historians like Josephus, Tacitus, Suetonius, and Herodotus also record miracles, and their knowledge of the ancient world isn't deemed "suspect" unless someone else corroborates their assertions. In fact, these writers represent our only knowledge of many ancient historical episodes.

Another point to remember is that critics who rejected the Bible because it was the only witness to something have been proven wrong before. We've already discussed the Hittites who fought with Ramesses II at Kadesh, but it may surprise you to know that prior to the late nineteenth century, the Bible was the only source that attested to the existence of the Hittites (Gen. 50:13, Deut. 20:17, 1 Sam. 26:5). Since no other works or artifacts corroborated their existence, modern critics said this was yet another example of the Bible getting ancient history wrong.[176]

But in 1880, an expert in Assyrian culture named Archibald Henry Sayce delivered a lecture in England demonstrating that hieroglyphics found in Turkey and Syria showed that the Hittites had indeed existed at one time. Then in the early twentieth century, thousands of stone tablets were discovered in that region, and after Bedřich Hrozný translated them in 1915 a new historical science called Hittitology, or the study of Hittite culture, was born.[177]

Because of the incomplete nature of the ancient historical record, it's not implausible that an event like the Exodus could have occurred with only the Israelites successfully passing on the story through their oral and written tradition. The fact that the Israelites were the sole witnesses to this event (like the Christians who were the sole witness to several New Testament events we'll discuss in the next chapter) does not prove that it did not happen.

7

Bungled History?

*The Claim: The Bible is full of descriptions of events that
contradict what we know from the secular study of ancient history.
The adventures of the prophet Daniel and even the birth of Christ
are two prominent examples of these historical inaccuracies.*

The book of Daniel describes the visions of the prophet Daniel
as well as his interactions with the kings of Babylon and Persia.
This included his interpretation of their dreams, his refusal to
worship their pagan deities, and the persecution he suffered for
worshipping the true God (including the well-known story of
his being thrown into a den of lions). One of the book's major
themes is that just as God delivered his prophets from their enemies (including miraculously protecting Daniel from the lions),
God will deliver Israel from her enemies.

Critics of the Bible, however, have long accused the book of
Daniel of being filled with glaring, historical inaccuracies. One
critic said, "Daniel may have survived meat-hungry lions, but
fact-hungry historians have ripped him into shreds."[178]

DANIEL IN THE SKEPTIC'S DEN

What exactly have these historians "ripped into shreds"? First, they
argue that Daniel 1:1 is wrong when it says that during the third
year of the reign of the Judean king Jehoiakim, the Babylonian
king Nebuchadnezzar besieged the city of Jerusalem. They say that
Nebuchadnezzar did not become king of Babylon until the fourth
year of Jehoiakim's reign. Moreover, the Babylonian siege of Jerusalem took place in 597 B.C., after Jehoiakim was already dead.

They also say that Daniel 5:1–2 is wrong when it describes
Belshazzar as a king and son of Nebuchadnezzar. According

to *The Skeptic's Annotated Bible*, "It was Nabonidus, and not Belshazzar, who was the last of the Babylonian kings. Belshazzar was the son and viceroy of Nabonidus. But he was not a king, and was not the son (or any other relation) of Nebuchadnezzar."[179] Many modern critics add that the ruler who came after Belshazzar's demise, Darius the Mede, is a fictional character who is not documented in any nonbiblical sources.

NEBUCHADNEZZAR AND BABYLON

Before we begin, it must be recognized that dating systems in the ancient world were more complicated and tended to be more local than the standardized dating systems we use today. So it could be the case that the Bible arrives at allegedly contradictory dates for events because the sources behind those dates used different systems of reckoning time—such as the Jewish calendar versus the Babylonian calendar. This presents us with several ways of understanding the chronology of Old Testament events like those found in the book of Daniel.

Regarding the reign of Nebuchadnezzar, secular historians agree that he ascended to the throne of Babylon in the fall of 605 B.C. However, in the ancient Near East, the length of a king's reign depended on whether one included his accession year. This was the few months of the king's reign, such as September through December (on our modern calendar), that took place before the start of the first full year he reigned.

Daniel may have included the accession year as a distinct year within Nebuchadnezzar's reign, and, as a result, said Nebuchadnezzar's reign began during the third year of Jehoiakim's rule. Other sources, like Jeremiah 25:1, may not have counted the accession year, and so they would have said Nebuchadnezzar became king of Babylon one year later, or during the fourth year of Jehoiakim's reign.[180] Since the same time span is being counted in two different ways, there is no contradiction.

When it comes to the siege of Jerusalem, it may be the case that there was a military conflict in Jerusalem eight years before the more famous siege of 597 B.C. In fact, Babylonian sources tell us that after Nebuchadnezzar's victory against the Egyptian forces at the battle of Cardemish (a city on the border between present-day Turkey and Syria), Nebuchadnezzar marched victoriously through the regions of Syria and Palestine.[181]

According to 2 Kings 23:34, Egypt controlled the kingdom of Judah; the pharaoh had even appointed Jehoiakim as the nation's ruler. It would not be surprising then for Nebuchadnezzar to make a show of force at Judah's capital city of Jerusalem after his victory at Cardemish, especially since Judah was a vassal state under Egyptian authority. Indeed, Daniel 1:2 says that only some of the vessels in the Jerusalem temple were plundered, not all of them, as happened in the siege of 597 B.C. A Babylonian priest named Berosus also confirms that Nebuchadnezzar took Jewish prisoners with him to Babylon in 605 B.C., where he secured the throne after the death of the previous king, Nabopolassar.[182]

All these details fit the description in Daniel 1 of some kind of military conflict at Jerusalem during the third year of Jehoiakim's reign. This conflict ended in the taking of goods and human prisoners to Babylon, including the prophet Daniel, who was taken into captivity in that region.[183]

Nebuchadnezzar and Belshazzar

According to the fifth chapter of the book of Daniel, when Nebuchadnezzar's successor Belshazzar ruled Babylon, he sacrilegiously used vessels stolen from the Jerusalem temple for one of his private banquets. As a result of this, a mysterious hand wrote on the wall of the banquet hall in a language that only Daniel was able to interpret. The message said that the days of Belshazzar's kingdom were numbered and coming to an end. (This is the most likely origin of the phrase "the writing is on the wall.")

Just as they did with the Hittites, modern scholars once doubted Belshazzar's existence because it was only recorded in the Bible. But like their assumptions about the Hittites, their view of Belshazzar was disproven when extrabiblical artifacts bearing his name were discovered. According to one clay tablet called the Nabonidus Chronicle, Belshazzar's father, Nabonidus, would often leave his kingdom under the authority of his son for years at a time in order to pursue the worship of other gods.[184] Another ancient tablet refers to this son's name: "Belshazzar, the eldest son, my offspring."[185] About his reign as king, Scott Hahn and Curtis Mitch say,

> Belshazzar did in fact exercise royal authority in his father's absence. The situation is presupposed in Daniel for Belshazzar can only offer to make the interpreter of the writing "third ruler" in the kingdom [see Daniel 5:7, 16, 29]. In other words, the highest position available at that time was under the king (Nabonidus) and his deputy regent (Belshazzar).[186]

Even if Belshazzar had royal authority, how could he be the son of Nebuchadnezzar (Dan. 5:2) when archaeological finds say Nabonidus was Belshazzar's father? One possibility is that these two men could have been "father" and "son" within a Jewish context that allowed a grandfather to be referred to as a father (see chapter 10 for more on this usage). This is possible if Belshazzar's mother was Nitocris, the daughter of Nebuchadnezzar.

We know from the Bible that a king's mother often served as the "great lady" and held a prominent place above the king's wives. That's because the king may have had many wives as a result of marriages he made in order to secure political alliances. For example, David's son Solomon had 700 wives, but his mother, Bathsheba, had a special title, as the *gebirah* or the king's mother (1 Kings 2:19). The king's mother worked to maintain political stability in the kingdom as well as within the royal dynasty.

John Goldingay wrote that the use of the word "queen" in Daniel 5:10 "suggests not a mere consort but a political figure, presumably the queen mother, often a significant political figure in an ancient court."[187] The ancient Greek historian Herodotus also tells us that Nitocris's son ruled Babylon when Cyrus the Great attacked the city, which of course took place at the same time that Belshazzar held a position of authority in Babylon.[188]

Another possibility is that royal successors in the ancient world could be described as having a symbolic father/son relationship. Nebuchadnezzar was Belshazzar's "father" in the sense that he reigned before him and provided his heir with a kingdom. Either way, Daniel's description of Nebuchadnezzar as a father to Belshazzar is a plausible one given their royal and possible biological relationships.

DARIUS THE MEDE

Darius the Mede, Belshazzar's successor, may be another name for Cyrus the Great, who captured Babylon in 540 B.C. Andrew Steinmann, a scholar who's written extensively on biblical chronology, opts for this approach. That's because Cyrus's mother was a Median princess, Herodotus tells us that Cyrus was not his original name, and Daniel 6:28 can be translated "the reign of Darius *that is* the reign of Cyrus the Great." He wrote,

> By tying the names *Darius* (the Mede) and *Cyrus* (the Persian) together, Daniel makes the point that Babylon fell to "the Medes and the Persians" (Dan. 5:28) in fulfillment of the prophecies that Babylon would fall to the Medes (Isa. 13:17; Jer. 51:11, 28) in conjunction with the Persians (Isa. 21:2).[189]

For those who hold that Daniel 6:28 distinguishes Darius from Cyrus, another proposal is that "Darius the Mede" refers to one of Cyrus's generals.[190] Both the Nabonidus Chronicle and the Greek historian Xenophon say that one of Cyrus's generals died from old age shortly after the capture of Babylon. This person, who is usually identified as Gobryas, had previously governed Gutium, a region of Mesopotamia that bordered Media. Thus, he would have been a "Mede."[191]

This also explains the reference in Daniel 5:31 to Darius having "received the kingdom, being about sixty-two years old." Cyrus would have given this acquired territory to the elderly Gobyras as a reward for his years of faithful service. Also, if

Gobyras/Darius died shortly after the invasion of Babylon, his short tenure in office would explain why other historical records (of which there are few) do not mention him.

The burden of proof falls on the critic who asserts that the Bible contains errors. As rule number five tells us, just because biblical history does not always match nonbiblical history, it does not follow that the Bible is automatically in error. After all, nonbiblical historians made and continue to make mistakes. In addition, biblical and nonbiblical sources could be using different ways to describe certain times or names, thus creating an apparent contradiction between the sources and not an actual one.

An Issue of Genre

These ambiguities in the field of ancient history show that critics do not have an open-and-shut case that the book of Daniel is the product of a mistaken writer of history. But what if Daniel and other authors of Scripture weren't trying to write historical accounts at all? For example, in response to Cardinal Franz König's suggestion that Daniel's text represents errors in the Bible, Fr. William Most said,

> It is idle, therefore, to charge them with historical error. The author [of Daniel] simply did not mean to *assert* that he was writing history. He was not. He was writing a different genre, the edifying narrative. So the "problem" Cardinal König thought insoluble turns out to be no problem at all.[192]

One approach to the difficulties surrounding the history of Israel up to the coming of Christ, including objections to the historicity of the patriarchs, the exodus, the conquest of Canaan, and the events in Daniel, is to say these accounts are not of the same genre as modern histories. This would mean that not every detail recorded in them should be viewed in a literal, historical framework.

To understand this approach, consider an argument against the historicity of the patriarchs based on incredulity rather than a supposed anachronism. Some critics find it completely implausible that Abraham and Isaac would both need to dupe a king in love with their wife by identifying her as a sister instead (see Gen. 20:1–6 and 26:1–33, as well as the similar story in Gen. 12:10–20 involving Abram and pharaoh).

We should not immediately dismiss these stories just because they share common features. Similar events can happen to fathers and sons; the first and last deaths in the construction of the Hoover Dam, for example, were a father and son who died exactly thirteen years apart.[193] It's also possible that Abraham and Isaac may have encountered two different kings who shared the same name (a common practice among royal dynasties both in the past and the present). This obviates the critic's objection that a king would fall for the same trick twice. Besides, if Isaac knew the trick had worked for his father, then he'd be more likely to use the same survival strategy for himself.

But it may also be the case that some of the descriptions of the patriarchs are part of a literary genre that is not literal in nature. This genre, akin to didactic fiction, would include stories about these historical figures that were meant to teach a valuable lesson and not record historical details. According to the Pontifical Biblical Commission,

> There are different ways of writing history, which is not always an objective chronicle; lyric poetry does not express what is found in an epic poem, and so forth. This is valid also for the literature of the ancient Near East and the Hellenistic world . . . The narrative of Genesis 1–11, the traditions dealing with the patriarchs and the conquest of the land of Israel, the stories of the kings down to the Maccabean revolt certainly contain truths, but they do not intend to propose a historical chronicle of the people of Israel.[194]

Certain facets of these stories whose historicity is doubted may not recall actual historical events. In the case of the Egyptian plagues, for example, the author may have used these stories to symbolically communicate God's judgment against the Egyptians.[195] However, just because some narratives in the Old Testament contain nonhistorical stories designed to teach valuable lessons does not mean the protagonists in these stories did not exist. The tale about George Washington chopping down a cherry tree is apocryphal, but George Washington still existed.

Granted, Washington and Abraham lived in very different historical contexts, of which the former provides us with more historical evidence than the latter. But the point is that both figures demonstrate how a writer can affirm someone's historical existence without asserting the historical nature of every story about that person. The Pontifical Biblical Commission says that, for the Israelites who composed the final versions of the stories about people like the patriarchs,

> [t]he interpretation of the concrete facts, the sense which emerges from their interpretation in the "today" of the rereading, count[ed] more than the facts themselves. Indeed, it is only with time that the meaning of a historical period which lasted for centuries can be understood and written down in the form of a theological account or a hymnic poem.[196]

Keep in mind that this is one possible way to read these stories. We must always search out the sacred author's intended meaning and not rush to a nonliteral interpretation just because we worry about the consequences of accepting a literal interpretation of the text. But on the other hand, we must not be afraid to admit that the sacred author, far removed in time and culture from the present day, may have intended to communicate a message that is very different from what we apprehend upon a casual reading of his text.

Luke's "Missing" Census

The late Bible scholar Fr. Raymond Brown said the following in his landmark 700-page commentary on the stories related to Christ's birth:

[C]lose analysis of the infancy narratives makes it unlikely that either account is completely historical. Matthew's account contains a number of extraordinary or miraculous public events that, were they factual, should have left some traces in Jewish records or elsewhere in the [New Testament] . . . Luke's reference to a general census of the Empire under Augustus which affected Palestine before the death of Herod the Great is almost certainly wrong.[197]

Is it possible that Luke did not intend to write history but chose to fashion a nonhistorical account of Jesus' life? It's possible, but unlikely. Luke stresses at the beginning of his work that he is communicating a carefully chronicled history. In his book *Jesus of Nazareth: The Infancy Narratives,* Pope Benedict XVI wrote,

[W]hat Matthew and Luke set out to do each in his own way, was not to tell "stories" but to write history, real history that had actually happened, admittedly interpreted and understood in the context of the word of God. Hence the aim was not to produce an exhaustive account, but a record of what seemed important for the nascent faith community in the light of the word. The infancy narratives are interpreted history, condensed and written down in accordance with the interpretation.[198]

Let's now examine those elements of the nativity story that Fr. Brown and other critics consider unbelievable, starting with the issues surrounding the census described in Luke's Gospel. Luke 2:1–4 says,

In those days a decree went out from Caesar Augustus that all the world should be enrolled. This was the first enrollment, when Quirinius was governor of Syria. And all went to be enrolled, each to his own city. And Joseph also went up from Galilee, from the city of Nazareth, to Judea, to the city of David, which is called Bethlehem, because he was of the house and lineage of David.

According to critics this is wrong on several accounts. They say no such empire wide census ever took place, and even if it had, Joseph would not have been required to travel to his place of ancestry. Although a census was taken in A.D. 6, it was limited to Judea, in order to inaugurate the beginning of direct Roman rule in that region.

Did Luke simply bungle this detail about Jesus' life? That shouldn't be our first assumption, because in all other respects Luke is a careful historian. When it comes to Herod the Great's son Herod Antipas, Luke correctly describes his family drama (Luke 3:19), and the offices he and his family held (Luke 3:1), and even demonstrates knowledge of Herod's lower-level servants (Luke 8:3).

One plausible explanation is that Luke was not describing an empire-wide census for tax purposes but a registration that took place before the A.D. 6 census. The King James Version renders the latter part of Luke 2:1 this way: "there went out a decree from Caesar Augustus that all the world should be taxed." But a better translation of the word that is rendered "taxed," *apographesthai*, is "registered."[199] What kind of registration could Luke have been talking about?

The Jewish historian Josephus tells us that during Herod's reign, "all the people of the Jews gave assurance of their goodwill to Caesar, and to the king's government."[200] These "loyalty oaths" were not uncommon and could be the kind of civil registration to which Luke referred. In fact, Augustus described such an oath, composed some time before his death. He said, "[When I was] in my thirteenth consulship [2 B.C.], the senate and Equestrian order and Roman People as a whole called me father of my country, and voted that this should be inscribed on the porch of my house."[201]

On a side note, don't be confused by the conclusion that Christ was born during a year marked with a B.C. suffix. About 500 years after Christ's birth, a monk named Dionysius Exiguus created the B.C./A.D. dating system. B.C. stands for "Before Christ," and A.D. stands for *Anno Domini*, a Latin phrase that means "in the year of our Lord." Modern scholarship has shown, however, that Dionysius's calculations were incorrect and, as a result, nineteenth- and twentieth-century scholars tended to date Christ's birth to the year 4 B.C.

But before Dionysius's dating system, Christians referenced time using events like an emperor's reign or even the Olympic games. Even today the liturgy of the Midnight Mass at Christmas recounts how Christ was born during "the 194th Olympiad, the 752nd year from the foundation of the city of Rome, the 42nd year of the reign of Octavian Augustus." Using those references, several Church Fathers and ecclesial writers, including Irenaeus, Clement of Alexandria, Tertullian, Origen, and the early Church historian Eusebius say that Christ was born during the years 2–3 B.C.[202] This makes the details about the enrollment in Luke's Gospel much more plausible since it would correspond with the mandated loyalty oaths to Caesar that occurred during this time period.

The only problem with this response is that Christ was born before the death of Herod the Great, which most scholars say occurred in the year 4 B.C. But new scholarship has emerged that places Herod's death closer to 1 B.C., thus allowing for Christ to be born one to two years before that event.[203]

The Quirinius Conundrum

Even if we reconcile the census with Christ's birth there is still a problem. Luke 2:2 says, "This was the first enrollment, when Quirinius was governor of Syria." But according to Josephus, Quirinius did not become governor of Syria until the year A.D. 6, or long after the events of the Nativity were supposed to have taken place.[204]

But the Greek word *hegemon*, translated as "governor" in this passage, can simply mean "leader." It could refer to a general who oversaw a province, called a *legate* in Latin. Or it could refer to a lower administrative position like a procurator or a prefect. Luke uses *hegemoneuontos* to describe Pilate's position, even though Pilate was a procurator or prefect, and not a legate (Judea was not placed under the rule of a legate until after the destruction of the Temple in A.D. 70).

Josephus says that Varus was the governor who ruled over Syria until the death of Herod the Great, but does not mention what Quirinius was doing during this time.[205] Tacitus, however, says that Quirinius conducted a military campaign in nearby Galatia, which leaves open the possibility that Quirinius had a leadership role of some kind in Syria during the birth of Christ.[206]

Or, Luke may have referred to an event that happened before Quirinius was governor in A.D. 6. Luke knew about the census that took place that year because in Acts 5:37 he correctly associates it with the rebellion of Judas the Galilean. The fact that Luke 2:2 says this was the first enrollment under Quirinius may be Luke's way of acknowledging that the census affecting Christ took place before the more well-known census in A.D. 6 when Quirinius was the official governor of Syria. Historical Jesus scholar and former Anglican bishop of Durham N.T. Wright agrees:

> [M]ost translations of Luke 2.2 read "this was the first [*protos*] census, when Quirinius was governor of Syria," or something like that. But in the Greek of the time, as the standard major Greek lexicons point out, the word *protos* came sometimes to be used to mean 'before,' when followed (as this is) by the genitive case. A good example is in John 1.15, where John the Baptist says of Jesus "he was *before me*," with the Greek being again *protos* followed by the genitive of "me." I suggest, therefore, that actually the most natural reading of the verse is: "This census took place *before the time* when Quirinius was governor of Syria."[207]

HEROD'S MISSING MASSACRE

Matthew 2:12 tells us that the Magi were warned in a dream not to return to Herod the Great after visiting Jesus and his family, and so they departed for their country by another way. Herod, upon realizing their failure to report to him, subsequently ordered all the male children in Bethlehem under the age of two to be executed (Matt. 2:16). Atheist C.J. Werleman wrote of this story,

> [T]here is no record of King Herod or any Roman ruler ever giving such an infanticidal statute. In fact, the ancient historian Josephus, who extensively recorded Herod's crimes, does not mention this baby murdering, which would undoubtedly have been Herod's greatest crime by far.[208]

Now, it's true that no one but Matthew records Herod's slaughter of the Holy Innocents. But that is not a sufficient reason to say that Matthew created the story out of his own imagination. Such an act of cruelty perfectly corresponds with Herod's paranoid and merciless character. Josephus records that Herod was quick to execute anyone he perceived to threaten his rule, including his wife and children.[209] Two Jewish scholars have made the case that Herod suffered from "Paranoid Personality Disorder," and Caesar Augustus even said that it was safer to be Herod's pig than his son![210]

In addition, first-century Bethlehem was a small village that would have included, at most, a dozen males under the age of two.[211] Josephus, if he even knew about the massacre, probably did not think an isolated event like the killings at Bethlehem needed to be recorded, especially since infanticide in the Roman Empire was not a moral abomination as it is in our modern Western world.

Herod's massacre would also not have been the first historical event Josephus failed to record. We know from Suetonius and from the book of Acts that the Emperor Claudius expelled the Jews from Rome in A.D. 49, but neither Josephus nor the second century Roman historian Tacitus record this event (Acts 18).[212] Josephus also failed to record Pontius Pilate's decision to install blasphemous golden shields in Jerusalem, which drove the Jews to petition the emperor for their removal. The Alexandrian phi-

losopher Philo was the only person to record this event.[213] This is
further evidence of why rule five—*the Bible is allowed to be the sole
witness to history*—is correct. Sometimes historians choose not to
record an event, and their reasons cannot always be determined.

In the nineteenth century Pope Leo XIII noted the double
standard in critics for whom "a profane book or ancient document is accepted without hesitation, whilst the Scripture, if they
only find in it a suspicion of error, is set down with the slightest
possible discussion as quite untrustworthy."[214]

It is far beyond the scope of this book to defend the historicity
of every event described in the Bible.[215] But we can explain why
certain events that critics claim contradict the historical record
actually do not. As we've seen, ancient nonbiblical testimony
can be wrong or incomplete, and even if it contradicts or fails
to complement the Bible, that testimony does not prove that the
Bible is in error.

8

Over-the-Top Miracles?

The Claim: From a worldwide flood to the sun standing still for a day, to risen saints invading Jerusalem, the lack of nonbiblical evidence for these extraordinary stories proves they never happened.

According to popular interpretations of Genesis 6–8, when God saw how evil mankind had become he decided to flood the entire earth in order to rid it of human wickedness. Fortunately, life was able to continue because God commanded Noah to build an ark to save his family as well as two of every kind of animal. One hundred fifty days after the Flood began, the waters retreated and Noah, his family, and the animals left the ark. He then offered a sacrifice to God, who made a covenant with Noah and promised that such a catastrophic flood would never happen again.

The main complaint critics have about this story is that there is no evidence the whole earth was ever inundated by a flood.[216] They say it is more likely that the Genesis account is a retelling of an earlier Babylonian myth called the Epic of Gilgamesh. In that story, a council of gods floods the earth and selects one man, Utnapishtim, to gather animals aboard a boat shaped like a cube. After surviving the flood, Utnapishtim releases a bird to find land and offers a sacrifice to the gods, just the way Noah did.

How should we understand the biblical flood story?

First, similar accounts of a massive flood in the ancient Near East should serve to *corroborate* the Genesis account, not contradict it. Geologists have discovered that melting glaciers near the Black Sea could have caused the collapse of giant ice dams about seven thousand years ago. Such an event would have triggered sudden, massive flooding across a wide area, which would have served as the basis for all the flood accounts in the region.[217]

But how could the collapse of something like an ice dam cause the worldwide flood described in Genesis 6–8? It couldn't, but we shouldn't assume the author of Genesis was asserting that a global flood took place.

Modern readers may interpret passages in Genesis that describe water covering "the earth" as meaning that the entire planet was inundated. But a resident of ancient Mesopotamia may have only understood the "the earth" to mean "the land" or the region he knew. In fact, the Hebrew word for "earth" used in this passage, *eretz*, can also mean "land," as in Genesis 41:57, where it says that "all the *eretz* came to Egypt to buy grain" when a famine struck the region. Of course, this doesn't mean that everyone on the planet went to Egypt to buy grain, just those people who inhabited the region the author was referring to went there.

The author of Genesis may also have used popular storytelling devices found in other flood narratives in order to show how the God of the Israelites was superior to pagan deities. For example, in the Epic of Gilgamesh the gods are afraid of the flood and flee to higher ground, but in the Genesis story God is in complete control of the disaster and is unaffected by it.[218]

The Epic of Gilgamesh also seems to have been derived from an even older story called the Epic of Atrahasis. In this story, a pantheon of gods flood the earth because human beings had become too numerous and noisy. The author of the Genesis account may even have been purposefully subverting this anti-life attitude in his own narrative in which God commands that Adam and Eve "be fruitful and multiply." God's decision to send the flood in judgment of sin instead of as a population control measure would be a further subversion of this theme.[219]

Pope Pius XII acknowledged in his encyclical *Humani Generis* that "If, however, the ancient sacred writers have taken anything from popular narrations (and this may be conceded), it must never be forgotten that they did so with the help of divine inspiration, through which they were rendered immune from any error in selecting and evaluating those documents."[220]

Just as the Creation story communicated spiritual truths about God and the significance of humanity through figurative language, the story of Noah's Flood in Genesis 6–8 (as well as the Tower of Babel in Genesis 11) uses similar language to communicate truths about God's attitude toward sin and redemption.[221] Just because the author chose to model his stories after existing narratives and literary conventions does not disprove the message he was communicating: that it was the true God and not any of his pagan competitors who intervened to save the survivors of the Flood that devastated the land.

DARKNESS OVER THE WHOLE EARTH

One kind of miracle described in several parts of the Bible is supernatural darkness. It might be confined to one area (for example, the areas not inhabited by the Hebrews during the seventh plague in Egypt) or it might have affected "the whole earth," as some interpretations of Christ's Crucifixion claim. But if these episodes of darkness really did happen, then why didn't any other culture record such monumental disruptions of the natural order?

Let's begin with the darkness at the Crucifixion. Mark says that when Christ died, "there was darkness over the whole land until the ninth hour" (Mark 15:33). Luke says the same thing but adds the detail that "the sun's light failed," in Greek, "*tou heliou eklipontos*" (Luke 23:45). You might recognize the word *eklipontos* as being similar to the word *we* use to describe the sun's light failing—an eclipse.

But these passages do not necessarily refer to a solar eclipse or a complete cessation of the sun shining upon the earth. In fact, early Christians knew that a solar eclipse could not have occurred at the Crucifixion because Jesus died during Passover. Passover takes place according to the Jewish lunar calendar; it always occurs during a full moon, and solar eclipses can only happen during a new moon.[222]

As we saw with the words used to describe Noah's flood, Mark 15:33 only says the "land" (in Greek, *ge*) became darkened, not

the entire world. It's possible that the darkness came in the form
of thunder clouds or even a spring dust storm, both common to
the region even to the present day. St. Thomas Aquinas mentions
Origen's theory that heavy clouds obscuring the sun caused the
darkness at the Crucifixion.[223]

A weather phenomenon may also explain the darkness that be-
fell the Egyptians for three days (Exod. 10:21–23). Having lived in
the desert for many years, I know firsthand the fear and confusion
sandstorms can bring. They can send thick clouds of dust high
into the sky that block out almost all sunlight. Exodus 10:21–23
even says that the darkness could be "felt" and that it prevented the
Egyptians from leaving their homes, while the Israelites were unaffected. This seems to imply that a windy dust storm reduced visibility and prevented movement and the use of torches to navigate
through the darkness. A localized dust storm would also explain
why some areas of Egypt, such as where the Israelites dwelled, had
light and visibility while others were shrouded in thick dust.

But as we've already seen regarding to the Egyptian plagues,
the particular literary genre found in these texts may be a nonliteral one. Such a reading of the text may also explain Joshua
10:12–14, which says that the Lord stopped the sun in the sky so
that the Israelites could defeat the Amorites in battle. Although
Joshua could be describing a miracle in which the Lord provided
sunlight without stopping the earth's rotation, this might also
be a literary way of describing how God aided the Israelites,
one that parallels other ancient battle accounts. Richard Nelson
writes in his commentary on Joshua,

> Habakkuk 3:11 suggests that sun and moon were understood
> as part of Yahweh's heavenly host, who engage in battle as
> cosmic powers (Judg. 5:20). From this perspective the contri-
> bution of sun and moon would not be extended daylight, but
> active participation in the battle.[224]

Other commentators have proposed that the language of the
sun standing still could be hyperbolic and simply means that God

helped the Israelites accomplish more than a normal army could accomplish in a day.[225] The text could also refer to praying for favorable omens in the positions of the sun and moon, which would have encouraged the Israelites or frightened the Canaanites.[226] Joshua 10:13 says this story can be found in the book of Jashar, which has been lost and now exists only in secondary references. If the book of Jashar was a collection of poems and songs, as some scholars believe, then its author may not have intended to record the stopping of the sun as a strictly historical event.[227]

The Mysterious Star

Another astronomical event critics say is unlikely or impossible is the star of Bethlehem recorded in Matthew's Gospel. In Matthew 2:1–6, the Magi tell Herod that they have seen the star of the newborn King of the Jews and have come to bid him homage. Herod sends them to find the child and, according to Matthew 2:9, "When they had heard the king they went their way; and behold, the star which they had seen in the East went before them, till it came to rest over the place where the child was."

But isn't it scientifically inaccurate to say that the star "went before them" in order to lead them on their way and that it "came to rest" over the house where Jesus was? Perhaps it would be if the text was describing the natural motion of stars, but the passage could instead be describing the miraculous appearance of a light in the sky. If that were the case, then the passage would not be unscientific since science must be agnostic toward miracles.

However, the passage could also be describing a natural event as is evident in the following details. First, the Magi asked Herod, "Where is he who has been born king of the Jews?" (Matt. 2:1–6). If they were following the star to the site of Jesus' birth, then such a request would be unnecessary.[228] Second, Matthew 2:10 literally said in Greek that they "rejoiced with exceedingly great joy" upon seeing the star. The Magi's unexpected joy would be expected if the star's appearance wasn't necessary for their journey but was instead a joyful surprise that confirmed where they were.

Finally, within the context of the story, the Greek words used in these passages can have a non-miraculous meaning. In Matthew 2:9, the word translated as "went before," *proegen*, is also used in Matthew 21:9 to describe the crowds going before Jesus as he entered Jerusalem. The crowds didn't physically lead Jesus into Jerusalem but merely went in the direction he was going. In a similar way, the Magi's star may have providentially moved at the normal rate in the night sky without actively "leading them" toward their destination.[229] Regardless of which interpretation is correct, neither demonstrates a scientific inaccuracy in the biblical text.

MATTHEW'S RAISED SAINTS

After describing the darkness following Jesus' death and the curtain in the temple being torn in two, Matthew 27:52–53 says, "the tombs also were opened, and many bodies of the saints who had fallen asleep were raised, and coming out of the tombs after his resurrection they went into the holy city and appeared to many." This short description has led to some rather colorful polemics from critics who say that Matthew is describing an implausible "invasion" of risen saints in Jerusalem.[230]

The main thrust of one critic's argument is that neither Josephus nor any other New Testament writer recorded this spectacular event. He then concludes it never happened and was merely an invention on Matthew's part. But why should we believe that other sources would have recorded this episode?

Most critics assume that the description of "many" raised saints implies a veritable army of the recently deceased that other writers could not have missed. But the text never says how many there were. Could it have been a dozen? A handful? If you saw the starting lineup of the 1923 New York Yankees walk into Yankee Stadium, you'd probably say that "many" raised baseball players were there (it doesn't take *that many* to get one's attention!). That's assuming, of course, that you are a baseball aficionado who could recognize these men.

Matthew's saints may not have been recognized by most of the small population in Jerusalem who saw them, which would explain why the other evangelists did not report this episode. They simply may not have had access to the source or person who described this event to Matthew. And since Josephus tells us hardly anything about the events surrounding Jesus' Crucifixion, why should we expect him to have known about this event? There is nothing implausible in Matthew being the only evangelist to have preserved this account, or, if he wrote his Gospel first, being the only one who thought this story would be beneficial to his audience.

Some ask, though, "If this was a historical event, then where did these people go?" It may be the case that God raised the saints to *mortal* life in the same manner that Jesus raised Lazarus, and so simply they died again. Or, the saints may not have died but were assumed into heaven. If this were the case, then there would have been even less time for other people to observe this miracle, which explains why other sources do not record it.

It could also be the case that Matthew used apocalyptic imagery to convey just how earth shattering the death of Jesus really was. The Pontifical Biblical Commission proposes this view and says that most of the phenomena in the Gospels following the death of Christ may not be literal in nature. For example, the earthquake described in Matthew 27:51–54 was not a "force [that] could be measured according to the grades of a specific scale." Instead, this detail seeks "to awaken and direct the attention of his readers toward God, highlighting the most important fact about the death and resurrection of Jesus: their relationship with the saving power of God."[231]

However, I am inclined to hold the view that this event was as historical as the Crucifixion Matthew describes before it, even if modern historians may not be able to use the historical-critical method to demonstrate its historicity. As N.T. Wright wrote,

> [I]t is better to remain puzzled than to settle for either a difficult argument for probable historicity or a cheap and cheerful

rationalistic dismissal of the possibility. Some stories are so odd
that they may just have happened. This may be one of them,
but in historical terms there is no way of finding out."[232]

The End of the World

If there's one event you wouldn't want to fabricate, it's the end of
the world. After all, there's no event that's easier to disprove. But
what are we to make, then, of critics who say Jesus was wrong
when he said the world would end within his own lifetime?
Didn't Jesus tell people standing in front of him that they would
see the coming of the kingdom of God before they died (Mark
9:1)? Or that *his* generation would not pass away until the end
of the world took place (Matt. 24:34)? If Jesus was wrong about
this, then how could he be God incarnate? How could the Bible
be God's word if it contains this glaring error?

Known as the problem of the Second Coming or the delayed
Parousia, this is only a problem if Jesus was teaching that the
end of the *physical world* would take place within the lifetime of
his followers (say, within eighty or ninety years at the most). It's
possible that Jesus's graphic language was not talking about the
end of *the* world, but the end of *a* world. In fact, the devastation Jesus predicted in Matthew 24:2 *would* come to pass forty
years later during the Roman siege of Jerusalem that resulted
in the destruction of the Jewish temple. His prediction of coming again, then, may have referred to his coming in judgment
against the city. Fr. William Most explained,

> The *coming* is best understood within the common Scriptural
> concept of *visitation,* God intervening to help, to save, to pun-
> ish. The intervention of Jesus, His coming, probably refers
> to the wars of A.D. 66–70 and the fall of Jerusalem, which
> put an end to the Jewish persecutions before the disciples ran
> out of places in which to preach. In the city's destruction,
> Jesus "visited Jerusalem," as we gather from chapter 24 of
> Matthew. Further, in view of the fact that Scripture often

utilizes multiple fulfillments of prophecies (and Matthew 24 is a specially good instance), this saying may also have another fulfillment at the end-time.[233]

A similar interpretation of Mark 9:1 says Jesus' statement that "there are some standing here who will not taste death before they see the Son of man coming in his kingdom" refers to the disciples who would see him come in glory during his Transfiguration. This occurred six days after this teaching and is described in the very next verses of Mark's Gospel. Pope Benedict XVI commented about Mark 9:1 in *Jesus of Nazareth*:

> If we learn to understand the content of the transfiguration story in these terms—as the irruption and inauguration of the messianic age—then we are also able to grasp the obscure statement that Mark's gospel inserts between Peter's confession and the teaching on discipleship, on one hand, and the account of the transfiguration, on the other.[234]

We should treat this "hard saying" of Jesus the same way we should treat his other unclear sayings. If Jesus is the Son of God, and he vindicated that claim by rising from the dead, then there must be a better explanation for why he uttered these words than "Jesus was wrong."

It turns out that in order to answer the question "What did Jesus mean?" we have to answer the even more fundamental question Jesus posed to his disciples: "Who do you say that I am?" (Matt. 16:15). If we believe that Jesus was who he said he was, then we should give him the benefit of the doubt when he teaches us truths that we don't always understand the first time we hear them.

What We've Learned

In Part I we reviewed several rules for reading the Bible that help us see why difficulties in the biblical text do not show the

Bible is in error. We must take into account the freedom of the human authors of Scripture to write in their own words, as well as their freedom to use popular descriptions of the world instead of scientific ones. We learned that sometimes a text only seems to be in error because we have misunderstood how it should be translated or even the genre it's written in. Finally, we should not dismiss the historicity of a biblical story just because ancient nonbiblical evidence does not confirm it.

But even if the Bible didn't contradict facts established outside of it, it would not exonerate the Bible from the charge of being uninspired. What about the supposedly hundreds of passages in the Bible that contradict one another? We'll examine objections related to those kinds of passages next.

Part II

Internal Difficulties

9

"1001 Bible Contradictions"?

*The Claim: From Genesis to Revelation, it's easy to find passages
in the Bible that contradict one another. The Bible can't be the Word of
God if it is riddled from beginning to end with contradictions.*

Several years ago I flew into Los Angeles for an evangelism event
hosted at a university four hours away from the airport. I finished
the rest of the journey by train to spare the organizers having to
pick me up. After I arrived on campus, a student asked how I got
there and I said, "I took a train." Later at dinner, another student
asked me the same question and I said, "Oh, I flew into LAX."
Did I contradict myself by not saying I flew on a plane and rode
on a train? Of course not, because I never said that I *only* flew on
a plane or that I *only* rode on a train. I revealed one detail in one
conversation and another detail in another conversation.

So what does this have to do with the Bible?

Critics often claim that differences among certain Bible passages are evidence of contradictions that disprove the Bible's divine origin. One website boasts of a list that contains "1001
Bible Contradictions."[235] But like the differing details of my trip,
these are only apparent contradictions, not real ones.

Ancient versions of this argument can be found as far back as
the writings of third-century pagans, but modern versions owe a
debt to William Henry Burr. In 1860, Burr published a pamphlet
called *Self-Contradictions of the Bible* that contained 144 entries. Although modern lists have added more contradictions, they follow
Burr in simply listing the verses with little commentary, thinking
that the difficulties are self-evident and irresolvable.

Since it would take a large encyclopedia to go through every
alleged contradiction critics put forward, let's look at the common patterns that lie behind them instead.

READ IT IN CONTEXT

The Protestant scholar D.A. Carson once said, "A text without a context is a pretext for a prooftext."[236] Carson was referring to the practice of isolating Bible verses from their original context in order to use them to support a doctrine that the verses don't actually support. But it's not just Christians who are guilty of taking Bible verses out of context. Atheists and other critics of the Bible often do this in order to produce contradictions. Here are some examples of ignoring the sixth rule of Bible reading: *Read it in context!*

Is it wrong to drink alcohol? John 2:3–10 and 1 Timothy 5:23 promote drinking wine, but Numbers 6:3 and Proverbs 20:1 condemn drinking alcohol.[237]

Proverbs 20:1 only condemns being led astray by wine and beer, not drinking alcohol in general. Likewise, the prohibition in Numbers 6:3 only applied to Israelites who had taken a Nazarite vow, not all people or even all Israelites. Since Jesus' first miracle involved turning water into wine and the *Catechism* only warns of abusing alcohol, it follows that the responsible drinking of alcohol is not a sin (John 2:1–12; CCC 2290).[238]

Should we pray and do good deeds in public? 1 Timothy 2:8 and Matthew 5:16 say we should, but Matthew 6:1–6 says we should pray and give alms in secret.[239]

The *Catechism* says that Christians should practice "almsgiving, prayer and fasting, directing them to the 'Father who sees in secret,' and not from a desire to 'be seen by men'"(CCC 1969). This is because our intentions are, as the *Catechism* says, "essential to the moral evaluation of an action . . . an added bad intention (such as vainglory) makes an act evil that, in and of itself, can be good (such as almsgiving)" (CCC 1753).

In Matthew 5:16, Jesus says, "Let your light so shine before men, that they may see your good works and give glory to your Father who is in heaven." The point of our works is to glorify God, not ourselves. Jesus' command in Matthew 6:1–6 prohibits publicly praying and doing good deeds in order to receive praise from other people. Jesus was not condemning prayer or almsgiving done out of a genuine desire to please God—even if other people see us pray or perform good deeds.

Is God peaceful or warlike? Exodus 15:3 says the Lord is a "man of war" but Romans 15:33 says the Lord is "the God of peace."[240]

Exodus 15 is a poetic expression of Israel's gratitude to God for rescuing them from the Egyptians. It does not contradict Paul's supplication for "the God of peace" to be with the Church in Rome. That's because violence, even war, can be necessary to secure peace in a fallen world.

For example, when he was accused of "disturbing the peace" with his boycotts, Martin Luther King Jr. said, "True peace is not merely the absence of tension: it is the presence of justice."[241] This is why the *Catechism* does not absolutely forbid war and lists the requirements that must be met for a conflict to be considered a "just war" (CCC 2309).[242] There is no contradiction in describing God having both a desire for peace as well as a special care for those who secure justice through armed conflict.

Should we answer a fool according to his folly? Proverbs 26:4 says, "Answer not a fool according to his folly, lest you be like him yourself," but Proverbs 26:5 says, "Answer a fool according to his folly, lest he be wise in his own eyes."[243]

At this point the critic should take a step back from his diligent hunt for contradictions and ask himself, "Was the author of Proverbs really so obtuse that he wrote two contradictory verses right next to each other? Or was the author using this apparent contradiction in order to teach us a lesson?" Specifically, if you do not answer a fool, then he will think he is smarter than he actually is and plunge deeper into his harmful ignorance. But if you do answer a fool, then you risk looking like a fool yourself as you argue with him over his inane beliefs. The author of Proverbs may have wanted his readers to avoid this dilemma by either avoiding fools in general or by using wisdom to discern when it is worthwhile to engage a fool in conversation.

FIND THE CONTEXT

We've seen how understanding the context surrounding a passage can often explain an apparent contradiction with another passage in Scripture. But for some alleged contradictions we have to dig a little deeper to find the context. Consider, for example, the death of Saul during the battle of Gilboa.

1 Samuel 31:4 says that Saul, realizing he would soon die from a mortal wound or be captured by the enemy, told his armor-bearer, "Draw your sword, and thrust me through with it, lest these uncircumcised come and thrust me through, and make sport of me." Feeling that this was not part of his job description, the armor-bearer refused. The verse then says that, "Saul took his own sword, and fell upon it." But in the beginning of 2 Samuel, David meets an Amalekite who says he fulfilled Saul's request to be killed. The soldier says, "I stood beside him, and slew him, because I was sure that he could not live after he had fallen; and I took the crown which was on his head and the armlet which was on his arm, and I have brought them here to my lord" (2 Sam. 1:10).

Did Saul kill himself, or did an Amalekite help him take his own life?[244]

Even though the accounts seem contradictory, there actually is no contradiction. That's because the ancient Israelite hearing this story would have remembered this important rule: "Never trust an Amalekite" (they were a warring tribe that had viciously attacked the Israelites ever since they left Egypt).[245] The Amalekite was lying about how he found Saul in order to gain favor with the new king.[246] David saw through the deception and so he had the Amalekite executed.[247] Furthermore, the Amalekite's testimony is never portrayed as being a reliable record of what happened.[248]

This brings us to rule number seven: *Consult a reliable commentary.* Commentaries help readers understand details about a passage's original language, its cultural and literary context, and other details that might be missed in a casual reading of the text. My favorite such resource is *A Catholic Commentary on Holy Scripture,* which is very thorough and orthodox in its interpretations. Among newer commentaries, I recommend Scott Hahn and Curtis Mitch's

Ignatius Catholic Study Bible, which is just as orthodox and also contains great teaching notes on biblical theology.[249]

Finally, regardless of what commentary you use, remember that they are not all equal. Some express anti-Christian or even antireligious attitudes, and the opinions expressed even in Catholic commentaries do not necessarily represent Catholic teaching. If you are in doubt about what a commentary says, consult a source that presents what the Church teaches concerning certain passages, such as the *Catechism*.

READ IT AS A WHOLE

In his book *Godless*, Dan Barker cites 1 Peter 2:13–14, which says, "Be subject for the Lord's sake to every human institution, whether it be to the emperor as supreme or to governors." He then cites an apparently contradictory verse in Acts 5:29, which describes Peter and the other apostles saying, "We must obey God rather than men." Has Peter contradicted himself in saying that we should obey the authorities and not obey them?

In Acts 5:29, Peter is saying we should not obey civil authorities if by doing so we disobey God. In Peter's case, obeying the authorities would have meant not preaching the gospel, which violated Jesus' command to preach the gospel to all nations (Matt. 28:19). 1 Peter 2 reinforces this message by teaching Christians to obey both the civil authorities and God, remembering of course that the latter is our ultimate authority. 1 Peter 2:16–17 says, "Live as free men, yet without using your freedom as a pretext for evil; but live as servants of God. Honor all men. Love the brotherhood. Fear God. Honor the emperor" (notice that we fear God before we honor the emperor).

This brings us to the eighth rule for reading the Bible: *Evaluate Scripture against the whole of divine revelation.*

Sometimes atheists and biblical fundamentalists make the same error—they assume that a command found in one passage of Scripture applies to all people at all times, regardless of what the rest of the Bible or the Church teaches. Atheists make this error, for example, when they say that statements about obeying authorities found in 1 Peter 2 or Romans 13 mean Christians must practice unconditional obedience to any civil authority. They ask, "Should Christians in Nazi Germany have unconditionally obeyed Hitler?"[250]

Of course not, but these passages never speak of absolute or unconditional obedience to civil authorities. Christians should not have obeyed Hitler or any evil ruler because that violates the natural moral law, scriptural commands to protect the innocent (such as Prov. 24:11 and Isa. 1:17), as well as what the Church teaches. The *Catechism* says that "If rulers were to enact unjust laws or take measures contrary to the moral order, such arrangements would not be binding in conscience" (CCC 1903).

When all of divine revelation is examined, we learn that Christians should promote the common good, which usually (but not always) includes obeying civil authorities. This principle of interpreting Scripture against the whole of divine revelation is known as "the analogy of faith" (CCC 114). According to *Dei Verbum*, "[S]erious attention must be given to the content and unity of the whole of Scripture if the meaning of the sacred texts is to be correctly worked out. The living tradition of the whole Church must be taken into account along with the harmony which exists between elements of the faith."[251]

Since God is the author of all revelation, one passage of Scripture cannot contradict another passage of Scripture, what the Church teaches, or the natural moral law. If we believe that a contradiction does exist among these sources of revelation, then ultimately it is we who are in error—not God's revelation.

A GOD OF CONFUSION?

Here's another example where knowledge of a verse's context deflates a critic's objection. Dan Barker writes in *Godless*,

> Paul said, "God is not the author of confusion" (1 Cor. 14:33), yet never has a book produced more confusion than the bible!

There are hundreds of denominations and sects, all using the "inspired Scriptures" to prove their conflicting doctrines . . . The problem is not with human limitations. The problem is the bible itself."[252]

In 1 Corinthians 14 Paul is describing how the members of the Church in Corinth spoke in tongues. This is a gift of the Holy Spirit that allows a person to speak a language others cannot comprehend (1 Cor. 14:2). Paul acknowledges this is a gift of the Spirit (1 Cor. 12:10), but he warned the Corinthians that if they all spoke in tongues at the same time, non-Christians would think they were out of their minds (1 Cor. 14:23). So, Paul proposed a plan for them. He said, "For you can all prophesy one by one, so that all may learn and all be encouraged; and the spirits of prophets are subject to prophets. For God is not a God of confusion but of peace" (1 Cor. 14:32–33).

Does 1 Corinthians 14:33 teach that God would never allow people to become confused over the Bible? Not at all! 2 Peter 3:16 even says that some passages in Scripture are "hard to understand" and that the ignorant twist them to their own destruction. The Greek word in this passage translated "confusion," *akatastasia,* goes far beyond meaning simple misunderstanding; its meaning is closer to "disorder," "upheaval," or even "anarchy."[253]

Paul is only saying that the liturgy should not be unintelligible because the God of peace does not want our worship of him to be chaotic. He is not saying that everyone will agree on what the Bible means, and in fact, (as we saw in chapter 1) the idea that the whole of Scripture can be easily understood by anyone who reads it is not a Catholic notion. God has given us his Word in Sacred Scripture, but he has also given us a collective understanding of the Word in the form of Sacred Tradition, as well as a Church that safeguards his Word and protects believers from erroneous interpretations.

Remember that even if we examine a verse's context and still can't resolve an apparent contradiction, that doesn't mean that the Bible is unreliable or uninspired. It only shows that we don't know how to explain the apparent contradiction! As St. Augustine once wrote,

> The authority of these books has come down to us from the apostles through the successions of bishops and the extension of the Church, and, from a position of lofty supremacy, claims the submission of every faithful and pious mind. If we are perplexed by an apparent contradiction in Scripture, it is not allowable to say, The author of this book is mistaken; but either the manuscript is faulty, or the translation is wrong, or you have not understood.[254]

As we proceed in our investigation we will find that many of Augustine's explanations for difficult passages in Scripture, like faulty manuscripts, faulty translations, or faulty understanding, have proven to be correct.

10

Gospels That Can't Agree?

The Claim: There are dozens of instances where the Gospels disagree with one another about facts related to Jesus' birth, life, death, and Resurrection. This proves that the Gospels, along with the rest of the New Testament, are uninspired, untrustworthy documents.

Christians have always known that the four canonical Gospels describe the same major events in Christ's life, but in different ways. For example, consider what God says at Jesus' baptism. In Mark 1:11 and Luke 3:22, God says, "You are my beloved Son; with you I am well pleased." But in Matthew 3:17 God says, "This is my beloved Son, with whom I am well pleased." So which is it? Did God say, "*You* are my beloved son" or "*This* is my beloved son?"

The apocryphal second-century Gospel of the Ebionites proposed a novel answer to this question. In this account, written over a century after the events it purports to describe, the Father speaks three times—presumably to account for what Matthew, Mark, and Luke record. But this seems implausible given that none of the canonical Gospels—or the ones the Church recognizes to be inspired—describe the Father speaking more than once. Besides, would the Father really need to repeat himself to the crowd, or to Jesus, when both could hear what he said the first time?[255]

A better explanation for passages like these is that they differ only in what they *say*, not in what they *assert*. This brings us to rule nine: *Differing descriptions do not equal contradictions.* A true contradiction in Scripture can only occur when two statements taken together *assert* that both "X" and "not X" are true at the same time and in the same circumstance. Nonidentical descriptions are not necessarily contradictions, because the author may not have asserted the literal truth of every detail in his account. This is understandable given the nature of ancient historical writing.

How to Write History

The second-century Roman author Lucian of Samosata said that the historian "must sacrifice to no God but Truth" and that "Facts are not to be collected at haphazard, but with careful, laborious, repeated investigation."[256] This parallels the prologue of Luke's Gospel, in which the evangelist describes gathering sources in order to create his historical record of what Jesus said and did.[257] Both Luke and Lucian were committed to accurately recording the past, but Lucian also wrote, "the historian's spirit should not be without a touch of the poetical."[258]

Consider, for example, how ancient historians recorded speeches that were given decades or centuries earlier. According to Lucian, speeches "should suit the character both of the speaker and of the occasion . . . but in these cases you have the counsel's right of showing your eloquence."[259] In other words, historians can compose speeches with words that were never actually spoken as long as the words they choose are something the person would have said. Thucydides, one of ancient Greece's most important historians, put it this way:

> With reference to the speeches in this history, some were delivered before the war began, others while it was going on; some I heard myself, others I got from various quarters; it was in all cases difficult to carry them word for word in one's memory, so my habit has been to make the speakers say what was in my opinion demanded of them by the various occasions, of course adhering as closely as possible to the general sense of what they really said.[260]

Historiography scholar Jonas Grethlein corroborates this: "It is widely agreed that most speeches in ancient historiography do not reproduce *verba ipissima* [what was originally said]."[261]

As long as the meaning of the speaker was preserved, an ancient historian was free to use words that differed from what the speaker might actually have said. We even do this today when we paraphrase speeches given at formal events. After all, when we are asked, "What did the speaker say?" we give a summary with some quotation—not an hour-long recitation!

What is true of ancient historians is also true of the authors of the Gospels. They were concerned with recording history, but their style of historical writing was not the same as the histories we are familiar with today. According to New Testament scholar Craig Keener,

> It is anachronistic to assume that ancient and modern histories would share all the same generic features (such as the way speeches should be composed) simply because we employ the same term today to describe both . . . Ancient historians sometimes fleshed out scenes and speeches to produce a coherent narrative in a way that their contemporaries expected but that modern academic historians would not consider acceptable when writing for their own peers.[262]

This is why when we read the Gospels we must distinguish between truths the evangelists were asserting and details they provided to accompany those assertions. The latter could vary in accordance with the standards of ancient historical writing without compromising the truths the author wanted to express to his audience.

EFFECTS ON THE GOSPELS

Let's return to the example of Jesus' baptism. All three evangelists agree that at this event God publicly revealed himself to be the Father of Jesus. Matthew, Mark, and Luke only differ in the words they used to describe that revelation. Matthew chose to emphasize how this message affected the crowd, whereas Mark and Luke emphasized how the message affected Jesus. There is no contradiction, because all three writers are asserting the same truth—that Jesus is God's Son—but they do so in different ways.

The same can be said of the cock crowing before Peter's denial. Each evangelist records this detail differently (possibly because they used different sources), but they all assert the same truth—that the cock's crow coincided with Peter's denial of Jesus. In fact, sometimes these differences reveal more about the author of a story than the story he was describing.

For example, think about how Mark describes the hemorrhaging woman who Jesus healed. He says she "suffered much under many physicians, and had spent all that she had, and was no better but rather grew worse" (Mark 5:26). Luke, "the beloved physician" (Col. 4:14), on the other hand, may not have wanted to unduly criticize his peers, so he simply said the woman "spent all her living upon physicians and could not be healed by any one" (Luke 8:43). Both statements assert the same thing—the best human medicine could not help this woman. They simply describe this fact differently.

Another example is the Roman centurion who asked Jesus to heal his beloved servant. Matthew 8:5 says the centurion came forward to request Jesus' help, but Luke 7:1–6 says the centurion sent friends and Jewish elders to make that request. So who requested Jesus' help, the centurion or his friends and allies? There is no contradiction because Matthew and Luke assert the same thing: the centurion requested Jesus' help. Luke adds the detail about the emissaries he sent while Matthew credits the petition directly to the centurion.[263] This is reminiscent of John 19:1 and its report that "Pilate took Jesus and scourged him." Of course, Pilate didn't actually flog Jesus; some of his soldiers did.[264]

Such variations in details also resolves the allegation of contradictions among the Resurrection narratives. As Bart Ehrman put it, "All four Gospels agree that on the third day after Jesus' crucifixion and burial, Mary Magdalene went to the tomb and found it empty. But on virtually every detail they disagree."[265] Ehrman goes on to say that the Gospels do not agree on who went to the tomb, how many angels the women saw there, whether the stone was rolled away when they got there, what the angel told them, or what the women did after they left.

But many of these details can be harmonized when we understand that the Gospel authors were not trying to provide an account written according to modern standards of historiography. For example, when John says, "Mary Magdalene went to the tomb and saw that the stone had been removed from the entrance" (John 20:1), he wasn't saying that Mary Magdalene was the *only* woman who went to the tomb (though the Gospels do agree that she was among the several women who went). John was simply focusing on Mary Magdalene and her later response to the disciples.

The other variants can be explained as the product of a culture that allowed variation in the details of their narratives. According to the Pontifical Biblical Commission,

> The four accounts of the visit to the tomb, with their differences, make a historical harmonization rather difficult, but these very divergences constitute for us a true stimulus to understand them more properly . . . they testify to God and to the decisive intervention of his saving power in the resurrection of Jesus. This result [is] . . . on the one hand, free from the constraint of having to see in every detail of the narrative—not only of the Easter accounts, but of the whole gospels—a precise record . . . on the other hand, it compels us to remain open and attentive to the theological meaning of both the differences and the details of the account.[266]

THEOLOGY MEETS HISTORY

The concept of theological import also applies to cases in which the Gospels seem to contradict accounts in the Old Testament. Consider when Mark describes Jesus speaking to the Pharisees about the Sabbath law. In this encounter, Jesus justifies his disciples picking grain on the Sabbath by comparing it to the time "when Abiathar was high priest" and David took the sacred bread of the Presence for his men to eat (Mark 2:26). But according to critics, 1 Samuel 21:1 says Ahimelech was high priest when David took the bread—not his son, Abiathar.

How can this apparent contradiction be reconciled?

One way is to recognize that Mark 2:26 can be translated "in the days of Abiathar the high priest" or "concerning Abiathar the high priest," instead of "when Abiathar was high priest." This would mean that the reference to Abiathar only gives us the approximate time period being described, or the location in the ancient scrolls of the book of Samuel, where this event is recorded, so there is no contradiction.[267] Other solutions have also been presented for this difficulty; one of them says that Jesus was asserting a theological rather than historical point through this detail.[268] According to Hahn and Mitch in their commentary on Mark,

> Abiathar is infamous in Old Testament history as the last high priest of his line, who was banished from Jerusalem and the priesthood for opposing Solomon, the son of David and the heir of his kingdom (1 Kings 2:26–27). He thus represents the end of an old order that passes away with the coming of David's royal successor . . . The Pharisees, then, represent an old order of covenant leadership that is about to expire, and if they persist in their opposition to Jesus, the new heir of the Davidic kingdom, they will meet the same disastrous fate that befell Abiathar.[269]

Literary Style

Ancient historians were not only free to vary the details of an event; they were free to rearrange the order of the events they described. For example, Suetonius wrote in his biography of Caesar Augustus, "Having given as it were a summary of his life, I shall now take up its various phases one by one, not in chronological order, but by categories, to make the account clearer and more intelligible."[270] Something similar can be seen in the second-century writings of

Papias, who served as the bishop of Heirapolis (a region in what is now modern Turkey). He wrote of Mark,

> Mark having become the interpreter of Peter, wrote down accurately whatsoever he remembered. It was not, however, in exact order that he related the sayings or deeds of Christ. For he neither heard the Lord nor accompanied him. But afterwards, as I said, he accompanied Peter, who accommodated his instructions to the necessities [of his hearers], but with no intention of giving a regular narrative of the Lord's sayings.[271]

Just as the author of Genesis provided us with a topical rather than a strictly chronological account of the Creation, Mark appears to have done the same with Jesus' ministry. Origen also came to this conclusion and said he would not condemn the Gospel authors who "speak of a thing which happened in a certain place, as if it had happened in another, or of what took place at a certain time, as if it had taken place at another time, and to introduce into what was spoken in a certain way some changes of their own."[272] St. Augustine likewise said, "in the case of those incidents with regard to the question of order, whether it were this or that, detracted nothing from evangelical authority and truth."[273]

This understanding of Scripture's order resolves difficulties like the one found in John and Mark's descriptions of Jesus meeting Peter. John describes Andrew introducing Peter to Jesus (John 1:40–42), but Mark tells us that Jesus met Peter and Andrew when they were fishing and said to the pair, "Follow me and I will make you become fishers of men" (Mark 1:17). However, the accounts aren't contradictory because Mark's narrative simply omits the episode in John that describes what happened when Jesus and Peter first met.

Modern readers assume that Mark 1:16–18 is talking about the first time Jesus and Peter met, but notice in the text that Mark says, "[Jesus] saw Simon and Andrew," not "[Jesus] saw two fisherman called Simon and Andrew," or something similar. The passage makes sense if we assume that the three men already knew each other. It also explains Peter and Andrew's hasty decision to follow Jesus. In fact, Mark introduces other people in his narrative, like John the Baptist, and even important concepts like "the Gospel," with little or no explanation. His audience may already have been familiar with these details, and so they were omitted from Mark's Gospel for the sake of narrative simplicity.[274]

This difference in narrative style also explains certain alleged discrepancies between the synoptic Gospels (the name given to Matthew, Mark, and Luke, because they are similar in what they record) and John's Gospel. One example that critics often cite relates to what happened after Jesus' baptism. The synoptic Gospels say that Jesus was driven into the wilderness to be tempted by Satan, but John's Gospel does not record the temptation and trials Jesus faced there. John says instead that on the next day Jesus saw John the Baptist (John 1:29), and after that he began to gather disciples.

Ehrman considers this to be a clear contradiction. He wrote, "Mark especially is quite clear about the matter for he states, after telling of the baptism, that Jesus left 'immediately' for the wilderness."[275] But anyone who has studied the Gospels knows that Mark uses the word "immediately" (the Greek *euthys*) for dramatic effect. He was concerned with portraying Jesus as a man of action, ready to inaugurate the coming of God's kingdom. Mark's Gospel, therefore, emphasizes Jesus' deeds and miracles through "action words" that convey an urgency in Jesus' mission.

This can be seen in the fact that the word *euthys* is used in Matthew, Luke, John, and Acts combined only ten times, Mark uses the word forty-seven times! In addition, an astonishing sixty percent of the verses in Mark's Gospel begin a sentence with the word "and" (*kai*).[276] Mark was concerned with drawing his audience into the excitement of how Jesus did this, *and* this, *and* this, and *immediately* afterward how he did *this* as well!

Just as Papias tells us, Mark did not intend to describe a precise, chronological account of Jesus' ministry, so it is not fair to accuse him or the other evangelists of contradicting a modern narrative framework they never intended to use in their writings.

The same is true of expecting the evangelists to use modern methods of citing sources. For example, Cardinal König claimed at the Second Vatican Council that Matthew 27:9–10 attributes a prophecy to Jeremiah that was actually from Zechariah, and so the text was in error. But Fr. Most correctly observed, "Matthew was putting together passages from Jeremiah and Zechariah, chiefly Jeremiah 32:6–15 and Zechariah 11:13. As to the fact that Matthew puts the name Jeremiah on the combined text, it was a rabbinic practice to use the name of the best-known author in such combined texts."[277]

DID THEY HEAR THE VOICE?

Rule four showed us that some Bible difficulties can be resolved by checking the passage's original language. This approach also resolves apparent contradictions, one of the most famous being a discrepancy in Paul's conversion story. Acts 9 describes how Paul (known then as Saul) was on his way to Damascus to arrest Christians when Jesus appeared to him in the form of a blinding light and a voice that said, "Saul, Saul, why do you persecute me?" (v. 4) Acts 9:7 then says, "The men who were traveling with him stood speechless, hearing the voice but seeing no one." But when Paul recounts his conversion in a later public address he says, "Now those who were with me saw the light but did not hear the voice of the one who was speaking to me" (Acts 22:9).

Did Paul's companions hear the voice or not?

Although this may seem like a contradiction, it exists only because the English word "hear" can have different meanings based on how the word is used. For example, imagine you are in a bustling airport and a muffled voice over the intercom seems to say something about your flight. A companion travelling with you might ask, "Did you hear that?" He doesn't mean, "Did you recognize that a voice was speaking?" Instead, he means, "Did you *understand* what the voice was saying?"

A similar example can be found in John 12, when the Father speaks to Jesus. Verse 29 says, "The crowd standing by heard it and said that it had thundered. Others said, 'An angel has spoken to him.' Notice that everyone in the crowd would have *heard* the sound of the Father speaking, but not everyone would have *understood* the Father's message. As Jesus says, "Hearing they do not hear, nor do they understand" (Matt. 13:13).

Returning to our alleged contradiction, Luke records Paul using the Greek word *akouo,* which means "hear" (from which we get the English word "acoustic"), and the Greek word *phone,* whose meaning includes both the broader notion of "sound" and the narrower notion of a "voice." Paul probably did not use these specific words in his public address because Luke says Paul spoke to the crowd in a Hebrew dialect (Acts 22:2), but Luke was preserving Paul's meaning with these words in his Greek manuscript. Luke can do this without contradiction because *akouo* can mean both "audibly recognize" (as in, "Don't shout, I heard you the first time"), or it can mean "understand" ("Do you hear what I'm saying?").

Therefore, there is no contradiction in saying that the men heard a sound (Acts 9:7), but they did not understand what it was or what the voice in the sound was saying (Acts 22:9).

INCOMPLETE IS NOT INACCURATE

The literary and narrative variations we see in the New Testament also help us understand rule ten: *Incomplete is not inaccurate.* It may be the case that the sacred author omitted some details about an event that were not pertinent to his literary aims.[278] For example, did two criminals mock Jesus on the cross (Mark 15:27–32), or did only one mock him (Luke 23:39–43)? It could be the case that both criminals mocked Jesus initially but only Luke recorded the story of the criminal who admonished the other man for berating Jesus, and who then repented.[279] Just because the evangelists did not record *everything* the criminals did does not mean that their descriptions of some of what they did were in error.

Or consider the accounts of Jesus' birth that are found in Matthew's and Luke's Gospels. According to critics, Matthew 2:1–23 tells us that Mary and Joseph lived in Bethlehem, where Mary gave birth to Jesus and the couple received the Magi. Later, the family fled to Egypt, and after Herod's death they returned to Judea and settled in Nazareth. But according to Luke 2:1–7, Joseph and Mary already lived in Nazareth. They went to Bethlehem to enroll in a census, whereupon Jesus was born in a manger. The family later returned to Nazareth without traveling to Egypt.

Are these accounts at odds with one another?

They would be if they purported to be an exhaustive description of everything the Holy Family did. But just because some details are omitted from either Matthew's or Luke's account does not mean that the accounts aren't accurate in what they do describe. This objection also assumes that the events in Matthew's Gospel take place immediately after Jesus was born. But Matthew 2:1 says, "[W]hen Jesus was born in Bethlehem of Judea in the days of Herod the king, behold, wise men from the East came to Jerusalem." In other words, Matthew never says that the Magi were present at Jesus' birth. He only says that "in the days of Herod the king" the Magi came to Jerusalem, not Bethlehem.

Also, after the Magi failed to return to Herod after visiting Jesus, Herod ordered all of Bethlehem's male children under the age of two to be killed. If the Magi had gone only six miles from Jerusalem to visit the newborn Jesus in Bethlehem and failed to return after a few days, then why would Herod need to kill *toddlers*? This implies that much more time had passed between Jesus' birth and the Magi failing to return to Herod, thus motivating Herod's plan to kill any child that could be the young king, who, by the time of the issuance of this decree, might have been two years old.

This additional period of time allows us to construct a timeline that makes sense of both accounts.

1. Joseph and Mary live as a betrothed couple in Nazareth when the angel Gabriel visits Mary (Luke 1:26–38).
2. The Holy Family travels to Bethlehem, where Mary gives birth to Jesus (Luke 2:1–20).
3. Jesus is circumcised (Luke 2:21) and then presented in the Jerusalem temple (Luke 2:22–38).
4. Luke tells us that the Holy Family returns to Nazareth after the presentation in the Temple (Luke 2:39) and not, as Matthew says, after the flight to Egypt and the death of Herod (Matt. 2:19–23). This is the most contested difference between the narratives, but there are two options that explain it. One the one hand, Luke may be "compressing" his narrative and only describing the final return to Nazareth in order to signify that this was Jesus' hometown. He would then be consciously omitting a brief residence in Bethlehem where the Holy Family encountered the Magi, as well as the later flight to Egypt. On the other hand, Luke could be describing an immediate return to Nazareth after the presentation that did not preclude a later, temporary trip to Bethlehem. Luke 2:41 even says that Jesus' parents made a pilgrimage every year to Jerusalem, so they may have stayed in Bethlehem with extended family during those visits and it was under those circumstances that they encountered the Magi.
5. Sometime after the birth of Jesus, possibly as long as two years later, the Magi visit Herod and the Holy Family (Matt. 2:1–12). The Holy Family were either permanently residing in Bethlehem after Christ's birth (until they fled to Egypt and then later settled in Nazareth) or they were temporarily residing there while they were away from their home in Nazareth.
6. The Magi leave and do not report back to Herod, which motivates the king to slaughter the young male children of Bethlehem in order to ensure the child's destruction. Fortunately, Joseph is warned in a dream to flee to Egypt in order to avoid the massacre (Matt. 2:13–18). This comports with ancient evidence of a large Jewish population living in northern Egypt during this time.[280]

7. Joseph returns from Egypt after the death of Herod the Great and chooses to live in Nazareth rather than Bethlehem, in order to avoid Herod's brother Archelaus (Matt. 2:19–23). Since Matthew did not describe the initial journey to Bethlehem, he informs the reader about Joseph's decision to move to "a city called Nazareth." This does not mean that Joseph had never lived in Nazareth. It only means that the readers of Matthew's Gospel might have been unfamiliar with the city and needed it explained.

How Did He Die?

Another example in which the rule "incomplete is not inaccurate" should be heeded involves the death of Judas Iscariot.[281] According to Matthew 27:3–10, Judas threw the thirty pieces of silver he was given to betray Jesus on the temple floor. But rather than contaminate the temple treasury with blood money, the priests bought a field with it, and Judas hung himself on a tree. However, Acts 1:18–20 says Judas bought the field himself and died by falling headlong off a cliff, which caused his bowels to gush out on the rocks below. Which account is correct? Matthew or Acts?

Matthew is probably correct that it was the priests who bought the field. If that's true, then Acts 1:18 would be a case of Peter making a pun about Judas indirectly buying the field. Peter essentially said, "Judas might have gotten a lot of silver, but his wickedness only bought him the field upon which he died." This is equivalent to saying that a criminal who tries to funnel stolen money through a charity but fails to retrieve the money only managed in his wickedness to "buy himself a new soup kitchen."

But how did Judas die? It's important to remember that Acts never says that Judas killed himself by jumping off a cliff. It only says that he fell off a cliff and that his gut burst open. Typically, when people fall from great heights their organs stay inside their bodies, so this detail in Acts is peculiar. But outside Jerusalem there are trees situated on the edges of steep cliffs. It's possible that Judas hung himself on one of those trees and then fell later, after the rope broke from his weight, causing his decomposing body to rupture on impact. Or the Jews may have cut Judas down since they would never have touched a dead body (Num. 19:11), but would normally have let it fall and dealt with the mess later. Therefore, there is no inherent contradiction between Matthew's and Act's descriptions of Judas's death.

No doubt some will see this as a desperate harmonization, and it's possible that there is some other explanation that would help us better understand the texts in question.[282] Such a solution could be one we least expect, as is seen in an example offered by New Testament scholars Paul Eddy and Greg Boyd. They cite the 1881 lynching of Frank and Jack McDonald:

> One account claimed that the boys were hung from a railroad crossing, while the other claimed they were strung up on a pine tree. The accounts seemed hopelessly contradictory until [two historians] discovered old photographs that showed the bodies hanging *at different times from both places.* As macabre as it is, the McDonald boys apparently had first been hung from a railroad crossing, then taken down, dragged to a pine tree, and *hoisted up again.* Sometimes reality is stranger—and more gruesome—than fiction.[283]

Ancient Biography and Ancient History

It is a fallacy to say the Gospels must either be chronologically ordered and detail rich accounts of the life of Christ, or they must be fictional, theological treatises. Instead, the closest literary genre that describes the Gospels is *bioi*, or ancient biography.[284] According to Richard Burridge ancient biography, "was a flexible genre having strong relationships with history, encomium and rhetoric, moral philosophy and the concern for character."[285] The purpose of *bioi* was to recount stories of important people for the purpose of edifying readers, not merely to recount historical facts in the life of a certain person.

Burridge goes on to say, "[T]rying to decode the Gospels through the genre of modern biography, when the author encoded his message in the genre of ancient [biography], will lead to another nonsense—blaming the text for not containing modern predilections which it was never meant to contain."[286] This includes blaming Mark for not describing Jesus' infancy, blaming John for not describing events like the Last Supper, or blaming the evangelists as a whole for not conforming to our expectations of a modern biography or newspaper article.

The differences among the Gospel accounts are also typical of ancient Roman historical writing. For example, there are three contradictory ancient accounts of what Emperor Nero did during the Great Fire of Rome in A.D. 64. Some say he metaphorically "fiddled while Rome burned," but others say he had nothing to do with the fire.[287] Since scholars rarely doubt the accuracy of nonbiblical ancient Roman history in spite of these contradictions, they should give the same benefit of the doubt to the Gospels and not hastily write them off as unhistorical contradictions just because they differ in the details they record. As we've seen, a contradiction can involve only differing *assertions*, not differing *details* that accompany those assertions.

11

Contradictory Names and Numbers?

*The Claim: Good luck keeping track of who did what,
where they did it, and how many people or things were
involved in the Bible's many contradictory stories.*

With hundreds if not thousands of different people listed in the
Bible, it's not surprising that critics find apparent contradictions
in descriptions of them all. Here are two examples made popular
in atheist books and websites:

- Who was Moses' father-in-law? Exodus 2:18–21 says it was
  Reuel, Exodus 3:1 and 18:1 say it was Jethro, and Judges 4:11
  says it was Hobab.[288]
- Who were the twelve apostles? Some lists include an apostle
  named Thaddeus (Matt. 10:2–4, Mark 3:16–19) while others
  include a second Judas, the son of James (Luke 6:14–16).[289]

How do we explain these apparent contradictions? Here we
don't need a rule but a common sense principle—a person or
place can have more than one name.[290] For example, when I
was younger my siblings and I would refer to our cousin Phillip
by his middle name, Michael. This means we might tell a story
about cousin Michael that my parents told about their nephew
Phillip, all without contradiction.

When it comes to the differing lists of the apostles, it was
probably the case that the mysterious twelfth apostle was named
both Judas and Thaddeus (just as Simon was also called Peter).
Matthew and Mark may have referred to him as Thaddeus so as
to not confuse him with the Judas who betrayed Jesus. A similar
explanation exists for the identity of Moses' father-in-law.

Exodus 18:1 refers to Jethro as Moses' father-in-law, but the name Jethro appears to be a title on par with "your excellency."[291] This title could then belong to either Hobab or Reuel. Numbers 10:29 describes Moses speaking to "Hobab the son of Reuel the Mid'ianite, Moses' father-in-law." In this case the term "father-in-law" could refer to Reuel or to Hobab without any contradiction. If it refers to Reuel, then the Hebrew description for Hobab in Judges 4:11 would mean "brother-in-law" instead of "father-in-law." If Jethro refers to Hobab, however, then that would simply make Reuel Moses' grandfather-in-law. Both explanations are plausible given the ambiguities present in the Hebrew text.[292]

Of People and Places

The fact that a person can be known by more than one name is also true of groups of people. For example, a critic might ask, "After Jacob's son Joseph was sold into slavery, which group of people brought him to Egypt? Was it the Ishmaelites as Genesis 39:1 says, or was it the Midianites as Genesis 37:36 says?"[293] The answer is, it was both.

It could be that the Midianites bought Joseph from his brothers, then sold him to the Ishmaelites, who brought Joseph into Egypt. Or it could be that the terms "Midianites" and "Ishmaelites" referred to the same group of desert nomads. In Judges 8:22, the Israelites tell Gideon that he has saved them from the "hand of Midian," but in verse 24 Gideon refers to the Midianites as Ishmaelites.

Not only can a person or a group of people be known by two different names, so can a location. Where I grew up in Arizona there is a mountain that used to be called "Squaw Peak." Since the word "squaw" is offensive to Native Americans, it was renamed "Piestewa Peak" in honor of a fallen Native American servicewoman. The fact that a mountain can have two names helps us resolve two other alleged contradictions in Scripture. Specifically, did Moses receive the Ten Commandments at Mount Sinai (Exod. 34:4) or at Mount Horeb (1 Kings 8:9)? And did Aaron die on Mount Hor (Num. 33:38) or at Moserah (Deut. 10:6)?[294]

In both cases we are referring to locations known by different names. Sinai and Horeb could both refer to the mountain where Moses received the Ten Commandments, or one name may refer to the mountain while the other refers to the desert surrounding it.[295] Indeed, James Hoffmeier tells us that the name Horeb means "a dry wasteland and devastation—and is cognate with the Akkadian *hurbu* and *huribtu,* which mean 'desert.'"[296] Just as Sinai was probably a location within Horeb, where Moses received the Ten Commandments, Mosera was probably a location on or around Mount Hor, where Aaron died.

We must be careful, however, not to stretch this rule too far and miss more obvious explanations. For example, some critics ask, "Where did Moses get water from a rock? Was it the wilderness of Sin in Rephidim (Exod. 17:1–7) or the wilderness of Zin in Kadesh (Num. 20:1–8)?"[297] Sin and Zin are two separate places, not one place known by two names. The error belongs to the critic who failed to notice that these accounts describe two separate events.

The first account of the events in the wilderness of Sin records how Moses faithfully followed God's command to strike a rock and produce water. The account about the desert of Zin, however, records how Moses disobeyed God's command to *speak* to the rock and decided to strike it instead. As a result of this particular act of public disobedience (as well as for taking credit for the miracle), God punished Moses by not allowing him to enter the promised land (Num. 20:7–13).

LIKE FATHER, LIKE SON

Richard Dawkins thinks that the Bible's numerous genealogies are fertile ground for finding contradictions. He wrote, "Why don't [fundamentalists] notice those glaring contradictions? . . . Shouldn't a literalist worry about the fact that Matthew traces Joseph's descendants from King David via twenty-eight intermediate generations, while Luke has forty-one generations?"[298]

The problem for Dawkins is that the genealogies in Matthew and Luke do not intend to record every father-son pair going back a thousand years from Jesus to David. The Hebrew word for son, or *ben*, is very flexible and can mean grandson or even great-grandson. This is why Jesus could be called the "son" of David even though David lived long before Jesus did (Matt. 15:22; 20:30).

The reason Matthew describes twenty-eight generations between David and Jesus is because Matthew divided his entire genealogy into three parts, each containing fourteen generations. Matthew tells us, "all the generations from Abraham to David are fourteen generations; and from David to the deportation to Babylon, fourteen generations; and from the deportation to Babylon to the Messiah, fourteen generations" (Matt. 1:17). The three Hebrew letters that make up David's name also have a numerical value that adds up to fourteen.[299] This means Matthew was probably creating a mnemonic device to help his readers understand that Jesus is descended from David.[300]

In the twenty-first century, with our seemingly endless supply of paper and digital hard-drive space, we are obsessed with recording every single detail of past events. But ancient people, who had little access to paper and primarily transmitted their accounts through oral tradition, didn't feel the need to be exact in their details. The Bible's genealogies show us that the sacred authors had no qualms about compressing generations or leaving some out in order to make a literary point.

Some critics will say, however, that it's not just completeness that is at issue in the Bible's genealogies. In *The Case Against Christianity,* Michael Martin wrote, "[T]heir genealogies are very different and cannot both be correct . . . Luke says the father of Joseph is Heli (Luke 3:23) but Matthew maintains that his father is Jacob (Matt. 1:16)." I remember reading one critic who wryly observed of this discrepancy, that either God approves of same-sex marriage or this is a clear contradiction.

One way to resolve this contradiction, which was made popular by the Church Father Eusebius, is to propose that Joseph was the product of a Levirate marriage. This means he was the biological son of one man who later died (Jacob), and the legal son of the man (Heli) who remarried his mother, who tradition gives the name "Estha."[301] Eusebius also notes that Matthew uses the term "begot" in his genealogy whereas Luke describes people as being "of" a father, thus allowing for both physical and legal descendants in his genealogy.

CHRONOLOGICAL CONTRADICTIONS?

Along with who, what, and where, another source of supposed contradictions in Scripture is *when* events happened. Consider the following examples:

- Was Jacob named Israel after he won his wrestling match in Genesis 32:25 or when God appeared to him in Genesis 35:9?[302]
- Did Jesus chase the money-changers out of the temple at the beginning of his ministry, as John 2:11–25 says, or at the end, as the synoptic Gospels describe?[303]
- After his Resurrection, did Jesus go to Galilee, as Mark 16:7 and Matthew 28:16 report? Or did he meet the disciples in Jerusalem, commission them, and then ascend into heaven, in accordance with Luke 24:36–53?[304]
- After his conversion, did Paul immediately go into Arabia for three years, as he recounts in Galatians 1:16–18? Or did he immediately go to Jerusalem after a short stay in Damascus, as is described in Acts 9:20–26?[305]

Since the evangelists were not necessarily focused on creating chronological accounts, we should not expect their writings to always be in the same order. When it comes to driving the money-changers out of the temple, John may be describing this event without asserting precisely when it happened. This is all the more evident given that he does not include time cues like, "and such-and-such days later this happened" or even, "and then this happened" in his account. John just includes the story at the beginning of his Gospel, possibly in order to set the tone for the rest of his narrative.[306]

But sometimes critics erroneously assume an event could not have happened more than once, and so multiple accounts of it must be contradictory. After all, it could be the case that Jesus cleansed the temple at the beginning *and* at the end of his ministry.[307] The first time would have earned Jesus the reputation as a rabble-rouser and the second time would have sealed his fate in the eyes of the Jewish leaders, who were now convinced he was a danger to Israel's existence (John 11:50). Similarly, Jacob may have been named Israel more than once. Catholic apologist Jimmy Akin notes that in the ancient world, a person or place "could receive a name for one reason on an initial occasion and then receive the same name for another reason on a second occasion. The latter naming presumably was seen as in some way fulfilling or confirming the initial naming—i.e., it was doubly appropriate that this person be called by this name."[308]

When it comes to chronological contradictions, we should also be mindful of a literary device called telescoping. Just as a telescope can make celestial bodies appear closer than they actually are, literary telescoping makes events within a narrative appear closer together in time. Luke employs this device frequently in both his Gospel and its sequel, the book of Acts.[309]

Notice that in both Acts 9 and Luke 24, where critics say Luke offers contradictory testimony of what Jesus did after his Resurrection and what Paul did after his conversion, time cues like, "and after such-and-such days this happened" are absent. In their place are more generic phrases like, "And then he did this." But in other parts of his writings Luke meticulously records time cues (see Luke 2:46; 9:28 and Acts 17:2; 20:6; 21:4). One explanation for their absence in Acts 9:20–26 and Luke 24:36–53 is that Luke eschewed chronological ordering so that he could maintain the flow of his narrative. He just wanted to describe what happened, not necessarily when it happened, so a contradiction only arises if we impose a chronological framework that may not be appropriate.[310]

Do You Have the Time?

We have to remember that context is important when analyzing claims of chronological contradiction. We cannot project our modern, atomic-clock Gregorian calendar way of reckoning time on ancient writings. Just as two road signs may differ based on how they reckon distance (for example one sign may use miles and another uses kilometers), two passages in Scripture may differ based on how they reckon time. So, for example, claims that Mark and John contradict one another on the day (Mark 14:12, John 19:31) and the time (Mark 15:25, John 19:14) when Jesus was crucified must be evaluated against ancient, alternative ways of calculating time.

In the case of the day on which Jesus was crucified, Mark says Jesus was crucified one day *after* the day of preparation for Passover, whereas John says Jesus was crucified *on* the day of preparation for Passover. However, both are probably referring to the same day in different ways. According to Mark, Jesus was crucified on Friday, the day after the traditional day of preparation for the Passover being observed that year, on Thursday. John was probably referring to a different group of Jews such as the Sadducees, who celebrated the Passover that year one day later (on Saturday). This means that the day of preparation for them was Friday, so it would be appropriate for John to say that Jesus was crucified on the day of preparation for their Passover.[311]

When it comes to the time of day of the Crucifixion, Mark 15:25 says, "It was the third hour when they crucified [Jesus]," but John 19:14 says, "It was about the sixth hour" when, before the Crucifixion, Pilate said to the crowd, "Here is your King!" The synoptic Gospels all agree that Jesus died on the ninth hour, or at three o'clock (which is why Divine Mercy chaplets are traditionally prayed at that hour). But how can these passages be reconciled with John's testimony, which seems to put the condemnation later than the Crucifixion?

It could be the case that John referred to a condemnation that occurred between nine and noon and felt it was closer to the sixth hour, whereas Mark referred to the Crucifixion taking place between the same time period and felt it was closer to the third hour. According to Craig Blomberg,

> In a world with no more sophisticated a time-keeping device than a sundial, writers did not refer to the hours of the day with nearly the precision that we do . . . If Pilate's verdict and the start of Jesus' crucifixion occurred somewhere roughly equidistant between 9:00am and noon, one writer could very easily have 'rounded up' and the other 'rounded down' especially when John explicitly uses the qualifying word 'about" (in Greek *hos* or 'as').[312]

As should be clear by now, describing something in a *different* way is not the same as describing it in a *contradictory* way.

COPYIST ERRORS

One time when I was working as a videographer, I showed a video to a client and was horrified at what I saw. The video played back with the audio and video out of sync, like a bad kung-fu movie. Fortunately, he accepted my explanation that the original video I created for him was without any flaws. Instead, what we were watching was a defective copy from a duplicator I never used again.

Just as this flawed copy did not prove that there was an error in my original work, a flawed copy of the Bible does not prove that the original text was in error. The Church teaches that Scripture is free from error, but that protection only extends to the original manuscripts that were penned by the Bible's human authors. Pope Leo XIII said in 1893, "It is true, no doubt, that copyists have made mistakes in the text of the Bible; this question, when it arises, should be carefully considered on its merits."[313]

According to Brant Pitre, "[T]he Catholic doctrine of inerrancy does *not* mean that subsequent manuscripts of sacred Scripture are somehow preserved from any textual errors, omissions, or alterations."[314] We can call this rule number eleven: *Only the original texts are inspired, not their copies.* Does this mean that the biblical text we possess today is just an uninspired copy of the original? No. It means that the original text preserved in the copies we currently possess is inspired. What's the difference?

Through the science of textual criticism we can reconstruct the Bible's original text to an extremely high degree of accuracy. According to Brooke Westcott and Fenton Hort, whose nineteenth-century compilation of original Greek manuscripts is still used by New Testament scholars, variants in the text only affect .001 percent of the New Testament and none of them call into question important doctrines of the Faith (see also Appendix).[315] In other words, we can be fairly certain what the original text of the Bible said, so demonstrable copying errors are not the inspired word of God.

For example, no sincere Christian would follow the rendering of Exodus 20:14 that is found in Robert Barker and Martin Lucas's 1631 printing of the King James Bible. It infamously said, "Thou shalt commit adultery." This Bible is now called "the wicked Bible" and, because most copies were destroyed shortly after printing, only a few highly valuable specimens exist today in museum collections.

Since the work of professional copyists (or scribes) was a long and arduous process, mistakes sometimes slipped into the biblical text. Here's one example that critics frequently cite as a contradiction:[316] 1 Kings 4:26 says, "Solomon also had *forty* thousand stalls of horses for his chariots, and twelve thousand horsemen," but 2 Chronicles 9:25 says, "Solomon had *four* thousand stalls for horses and chariots, and twelve thousand horsemen." Which is it—four thousand stalls or forty thousand?

It's probably not forty thousand, because in the ancient world that would have been a gigantic stable, even for a king like Solomon.[317] The forty thousand in 1 Kings 4:26 probably made its way into the manuscript because in Hebrew the word for "four" is spelled with the Hebrew letters "aleph-resh-bet-ayin-heh," and the word for "forty" is spelled "aleph-resh-bet-ayin-*yodh-mem*" A copyist simply added the wrong ending to the word and transformed "four" into "forty."

Copyist errors can also contribute to apparent inconsisten-
cies in people's names. For example, according to Genesis 11:12,
Arpachshad (the son of Noah's son Shem) was thirty-five when
he became the father of Salah. But in his book *The Cure for
Fundamentalism: Why the Bible Cannot Be the Word of God,* Steve
McRoberts wrote, "According to Luke, Salah's father was not
Arpachshad at all, but one Cainan; and, in fact, Cainan's father
was Arpachshad! If the Bible can't get physical facts straight,
how can we trust what it has to say about spiritual matters?"[318]

As we've seen, it could be the case that both men were a father of some kind to Salah, Cainan being his father and Arpachshad his grandfather. But another explanation is that a copyist
simply duplicated the name of Cainan, an especially plausible
explanation since another Cainan appears in the very next verse.
So the writer may have erroneously copied it copied it (see, it
can happen to anyone!).

"Ditto" and "Uh-Oh"

Two other common copyist errors in biblical text are dittographs
and haplographs. A dittograph occurs when a scribe accidentally
duplicated what was already in the text (hence the word "ditto,"
which is slang for "again"). This can be seen in one of the earliest
manuscripts of Leviticus 20:10. It reads, "and a man who commits adultery with the wife of a man who commits adultery with
the wife of his neighbor should be put to death."[319] It would be
strange if God condemned adultery only when a man cheats on
his wife with a woman whose husband is *also* cheating on her with
another woman. Rather than leave the text in this puzzling state,
most Bibles simply omit the erroneously repeated phrase.

In a dittograph, a copyist erroneously said "ditto" and copied
something he was not supposed to copy, but in a haplograph, he
should say "uh-oh," because he forgot to copy something. For
example, 2 Kings 24:8 says that Jehoiachin (also called Jeconiah)
was *eighteen* years old when he became king of Judah, but the
later book of 2 Chronicles says Jehoiachin was *eight* years old

when he began to reign (2 Chron. 36:9). How old was Jehoiachin when he began to reign?[320]

It could be the case that Jehoiachin was a "co-regent" with
his father at the age of eight and only became the sole ruler of
the kingdom ten years later. This would not be unprecedented
given that forty years earlier Josiah began to reign at the age
of eight (2 Chron. 34:1), and other kings like Uzziah granted
royal authority to their sons before the end of their reigns (2
Chron. 26:1).

However, this may also be a copyist error as Ezekiel 19:5–9
refers to Jehoiachin killing and ravaging strongholds (or in some
translations "widows"), and 2 Chronicles 36:9 says he did evil in
the Lord's sight—things you would not expect from an eight-
year-old. Therefore, a copyist probably incorrectly changed
"eighteen" to "eight" in a haplography; he forgot to copy the
Hebrew word for ten in the word for "eighteen." What remained
was just the word for "eight," and thus the king was turned into
an elementary school student with the stroke of a pen.

Here are some other common alleged contradictions that are
most likely copyist errors:

- Was Ahaziah twenty-two (2 Kings 8:26) or forty-two (2
  Chron. 22:2) when he began to reign?[321] The answer is twen-
  ty-two, since the alternative would make him older than his
  father.
- Did Baasha die during the twenty-sixth year of the reign of
  Asa (1 Kings 16:6–8) or the thirty-sixth (2 Chron. 16:1)?[322]
  According to C.F. Keil and F. Delitzsch's commentary, both
  numbers are probably copyist errors, and the true number of
  years is sixteen.[323]
- Did David kill Goliath (1 Sam. 17:50), or was it Elhanan (2
  Sam. 21:19)?[324] David killed Goliath whereas Elhanan killed
  Goliath's brother, as is correctly recorded in 1 Chronicles
  20:5: "Elha'nan the son of Ja'ir slew Lahmi the brother of
  Goliath the Gittite." A copyist error in 2 Samuel had Elhanan
  killing Goliath instead of Goliath's brother.[325]

Finally, the number of items may differ between various accounts if the human authors gave us approximations. This is probably the case with the casualties of the plague God sent against the Israelites when they worshipped Baal-Peor in Shittim. Numbers 25:9 says, "those that died by the plague were twenty-four thousand," but Paul writes in 1 Corinthians 10:8, "We must not indulge in immorality as some of them did, and twenty-three thousand fell in a single day." Did twenty-four thousand or twenty-three thousand die from the plague?[326]

It's possible that twenty-three thousand died in one day and the remaining thousand died later, but it's more likely that these figures are estimates. After all, what are the odds that the exact number of the dead would be a round, easy-to-remember number like twenty-four thousand? Karl Keating wrote, "These verses . . . are both approximations. When police estimate a crowd at fifteen thousand, they may well mean anywhere from ten thousand to twenty thousand—the order of magnitude is correct, and that's all that's needed."[327]

EXPLANATIONS, NOT ESCAPE HATCHES

Critics often fume over this response to allegations of Bible contradictions. Dennis McKinsey calls it "the 'copyist' defense" and Dan Barker calls it a "convenient assumption."[328] Even an academic critic like Hector Avalos says translations that correct for copyist errors are "mere suppositions" that "lie" to readers.[329] These critics say the very idea is a desperate attempt to rescue the original text from the charge of being in error. But this is a double standard, since the translators of nonbiblical ancient works often report the existence of copyist errors and are not accused of covering up an error in the original manuscript.

For example, Josephus's *Jewish War* says there were thirty-seven towers in the fortress of Masada, but archaeologists have only found twenty-seven. Magen Broshi, former Curator of the Shrine of the Book at the Israel Archaeological Museum in Jerusalem, says this discrepancy in the text "may possibly be the fault of a copyist."[330] Tacitus said in his account of the life of his father-in-law Julius Agricola that Agricola was fifty-six when he died. But the dates Tacitus gives of Agricola's birth and death only accounts for fifty-four years. One commenter concedes that "copyists must probably have written by mistake LVI [56] instead of LIV [54]."[331]

If you encounter an alleged contradiction in numbers or names in the Bible, explain to the critic that it may be a copyist error or an approximation—not evidence that the Holy Spirit inspired an error into the sacred text. You can also tell him that copyist errors are fairly easy to spot and that just as we don't discount the testimony of other ancient works that contain copyist errors (like Tacitus and Josephus), we should not discount the Bible because it contains similar errors.

The Burden of Proof

When it comes to allegations of contradictions in the Bible, remember rule number twelve: *The burden of proof is on the critic, not the believer.* A critic might say that because I can't prove exactly how certain verses fit together with an explanation all rational people accept, then it follows they are contradictory. But that is illogical.

Imagine a trial in which the prosecutor said that because the defense attorney could not prove *exactly* where the accused was during a murder, it follows that the accused was guilty of the murder. The defense would correctly respond that it is the prosecutor's job to prove guilt, because he is the one accusing the defendant of committing the crime. All the defense has to do is offer a reasonable alternative explanation of the evidence the prosecutor presents. He does not need to prove his client is innocent (though that is very effective at refuting charges of guilt). He only has to show that the evidence does not prove the defendant's guilt.

Similarly, it is the critic's burden to prove there is a contradiction in the Bible because he is the one accusing the text of being contradictory. All the believer has to do is offer one or more reasonable explanations of how the passages could be reconciled, thereby showing that the critic's evidence is not conclusive.

12

Conflicting Advice?

The Claim: Don't bother relying on "the Good Book" to tell you how to live. Are we saved by faith or by works? Will those who love God be happy or suffer? Is there an afterlife or is death the end? The Bible's contradictory answers to these important questions make it a useless source of wisdom.

Gill and Corinne Keith are Protestant ministers who publish a special edition of the Bible called *Your Personalized Bible*. According to their website,

> Your Personalized Bible series of Bibles has your name personalized into the text in over 5,000 places in the New Testament with Psalms & Proverbs, 7,000 places in the complete Old and New Testaments. Personalizations include: first name, last name and spouse's name (if married).[332]

In this Bible, John 3:16 becomes, "For God so loved *Trent* that he gave his one and only Son," and the title of Paul's letter to the Romans becomes, "Paul's Letter to *Trent Horn* and to the Romans." When Christ explains to the Pharisees why divorce is wrong he quotes this famous passage in Genesis: "For this cause *Laura* shall leave her father and mother, and shall join to *Trent*; and *Laura* and *Trent* shall become one flesh" (I'm sure the Pharisees were a bit confused by that response).

It's laudable to encourage Bible reading, but it's unwise to make people think the words of the Bible were written specifically for them. After all, Paul wasn't writing to the Romans and Trent Horn—he only had the Christian community in Rome on his mind. Granted, what he taught the Roman Christians is the inspired word of God, and so its truth is still relevant for me, but Paul did not have *me* in mind when he wrote this letter.

If someone reads the Bible thinking God wrote it just for them, they might become frustrated with passages that seem unhelpful or even contradictory. However, when these passages are read in their proper context, the modern reader can appreciate both their literal sense as well as the way God uses these words to teach believers in all times and all places.[333]

General Truths

One way to resolve allegations of contradiction is to understand that Scripture usually speaks in a *general* rather than an *absolute* sense. This explains the following alleged contradictions:

- Does wisdom make us happy? Proverbs 3:13 says it does, but Ecclesiastes 1:18 says it causes us sorrow.[334]
- Do the wicked live long? Proverbs 10:27 says the years of a wicked man's life will be short, but Job 21:7 says he will have a long and prosperous life.[335]
- Will bad things happen to good people? Proverbs 12:21 says no evil will befall the righteous, but Habakkuk 1:13 says the wicked man devours he who is more righteous.[336]

When it comes to the wisdom literature of the Bible, or books like Proverbs, Psalms, Sirach, and Ecclesiastes, we must remember that we are dealing with poetry and prose, not technical instruction manuals. These books must be examined in light of their original context, their intended audiences, and the message each author was asserting through his text.

For example, one of the themes in the book of Proverbs is that happiness comes from wisdom, and the beginning of wisdom is a healthy respect for God, that is, fear of the Lord (Prov. 1:7). The wise man will usually lead a happy life because he respects God's will and does not give in to destructive habits like alcohol abuse, pride, or promiscuity. One of the lessons of Ecclesiastes, on the other hand, is that as we become wiser we stop being blissfully ignorant. We see more clearly both the positive and the negative aspects of life, as well as our own shortcomings. This doesn't mean we shouldn't pursue wisdom. It only means that the pursuit isn't easy. When it comes to wise living, Proverbs and Ecclesiastes are both true when each book is read in its appropriate context.

Proverbs 10:27 and 12:21 are also both true in a general sense. The wicked man's life is often cut short by his evil deeds, and the wise man tends to live well because of his prudent choices. But these passages are not true in an absolute sense. Bad things still happen to good people (Habakkuk's point) and good things still happen to bad people (Job's point). As Peter Kreeft writes in his textbook on logic,

> Proverbs often seem to contradict each other when they do not, if they refer to different situations. They are not as universal as they seem, and two non-universal propositions do not contradict each other. "Out of sight, out of mind" is true of weak relationships, "absence makes the heart grow fonder" is true of strong ones.[337]

In short, the wisdom literature is not a collection of universal axioms. It is a collection of prose that teaches us, through various themes and writing styles, how to find happiness by living as God intended. We're not guaranteed happy lives, but by living holy lives we can find meaning even in suffering. As my favorite verse in the Bible says, "Accept whatever happens to you; in periods of humiliation be patient. For in fire gold is tested, and the chosen, in the crucible of humiliation. Trust in God, and he will help you; make your ways straight and hope in him." (Sir. 2:4–6, NAB).

A MILLION EXAGGERATIONS

Along with speaking generally, Scripture also speaks hyperbolically. Hyperbole is a literary device that allows the writer to use exaggerated or grandiose language to make a point. When a person has "a million things to do today," he is being hyperbolic. Such an observation should go without saying, but understanding this literary convention refutes several claims that the Bible is "nonsense."

For example, did *all* of Judea and Jerusalem go out to be baptized by John (Mark 1:5)? Did the *entire world* really go after Jesus (John 12:19)? Did Jesus say the mustard seed is the smallest of every seed *on earth* (Mark 4:31)? If we think Jesus was giving a botany lesson or Mark was giving us crowd statistics, then we miss the points the sacred authors were making. Specifically, that there were large numbers of people following John and, just as the tiny mustard seed can grow into a large tree, a person with a small amount of faith can grow an abundant spiritual life from it.

The Bible also uses hyperbole to underscore the significance of certain events. For example, Numbers 11:31 says, "There went forth a wind from the Lord, and it brought quails from the sea, and let them fall beside the camp, about a day's journey on this side and a day's journey on the other side, round about the camp, and about two cubits above the face of the earth." Steve Wells claims that if there were quails two cubits high (about six feet) thirty kilometers in each direction (a day's journey), there would have been three trillion quail.[338]

Of course there weren't that many quail, but the ancient historian Pliny the Elder did describe flocks of quails so large they could land on boats and sink them.[339] Therefore, it's not unreasonable to believe God caused a large flock of quail to land near the Israelite camp. The author of Numbers was just using exaggerated language to say that a lot of quail appeared, not that trillions of them actually surrounded the Israelite camp.[340]

Critics like Wells often ignore hyperbole in the Bible in order to strain a contradiction out of the sacred text. Here's another example: "Is anyone righteous? There are many Bible passages that say a certain person was righteous (Gen. 6:9, Prov. 9:9, Luke 2:25), but Ecclesiastes 7:20 says, 'there is not a righteous man on earth who does good and never sins.' Romans 3:10 also says, 'as it is written: None is righteous, no, not one.'"[341]

However, Ecclesiastes and Romans are describing the general sinfulness of humanity, not the complete lack of any righteous people anywhere. We know this because Ecclesiastes 7:15 speaks of the righteous and Romans 3:10 quotes Psalm 14, which says in its fifth verse, "God is with the generation of the righteous." These passages only teach that no group of people is righteous in and of themselves. Whether it's the godless Gentiles described in Psalm 14, or the Jews that Ecclesiastes cynically refers to, Paul's point in Romans 3:10 is that all people stand in need of Christ's salvific work on the cross.[342] According to the Navarre Bible commentary,

> These words should not be taken as referring to absolutely everyone. We do know that, in addition to the sacred human nature of Jesus, the Blessed Virgin was exempted from the stain of all sin, even venial sin . . . and also that even before Christ there were just and devout people like Noah, Abraham, Moses etc., who received divine grace and were enabled to do good works by virtue of the future merits of Christ.[343]

FINAL DESTINATION

Fr. Raymond Brown claimed that the Bible contained errors not just in matters related to history or science, but in faith and morals as well. He wrote, "[C]ritical investigation points to religious limitations and even errors. For instance, many recognize that Job 14:13–22 and Sirach 14:16–17; 17:22–23; 38:21 deny an afterlife."[344] Other passages that might be added to this denial include Psalms 115:17 ("The dead do not praise the Lord, nor do any that go down into silence") and Ecclesiastes 9:5 ("For the living know that they will die, but the dead know nothing").

When it comes to the Bible's view of the afterlife, it's important to remember that just because truths about the afterlife were revealed to God's people in a gradual way does not mean that they were revealed in a contradictory way. These passages represent the way death appeared to the human authors of Scripture at different times in salvation history. In Ecclesiastes, for example, the author is expressing the cynical repercussions of a naturalist worldview. He is saying that from human reason alone all looks hopeless and the dead seem to be gone. Indeed, before Christ's death on the cross the fate of the dead was a gloomy one. Fr. William Most wrote of the passages Fr. Brown cited,

> But—and this is of capital importance—conditions in the afterlife were radically different in the day of Job from what they are today. Why? Jesus had not yet died. Heaven, the vision of God, was not open, even to the just who had paid in full the debt of their sins. Theologians commonly speak of this state as the Limbo of the Fathers. Job was quite right. In Sheol there is no knowledge of what goes on on earth. Since there is no such knowledge, "he feels no pain for anything but his own body, makes no lament, save for his own life." But those words do imply consciousness in Sheol . . . Job denies a return to present conditions and he does not seem to know of a *glorious* resurrection.[345]

The passages in the Old Testament that speak of the dead not returning to life are true because there is no natural return for the dead to this mortal, present life. Moreover, at that time in salvation history, those who died went down to Sheol, where they unknowingly awaited the descent of Christ, which Peter refers to when he describes how Jesus "preached to the spirits in prison" (1 Pet. 3:19). As the *Catechism* says, "It is precisely these holy souls, who awaited their Savior in Abraham's bosom, whom Christ the Lord delivered when he descended into hell" (CCC 633). Pope Benedict also informs us that "Israel's archaic understanding of Sheol is what, if anything, would link her to the nations. That understanding simply illustrates a stage of awareness found in all cultures at a certain point in their development. As yet, Israel's faith in Yahweh had not unfolded in all its inner consistency."[346]

What we observe in the Old Testament on the issue of the afterlife, then, is just another example of God's progressive revelation of supernatural realities (CCC 992).

WHAT MUST I DO TO BE SAVED?

In Acts 16:30 the Philippian jailer asks Paul and Silas one of life's most important questions: "What must I do to be saved?" Many Protestants take Paul's answer, "Believe in the Lord Jesus," as proof that one only needs to make an act of faith in order to be saved (what the Protestant Reformers called *sola fide*, or salvation by faith alone). Through this act of faith, God declares the sinner to be righteous (he doesn't make him righteous) and, according to some Protestants, nothing can undo this declaration—not even the sinner rejecting God in the future. This means that one's salvation can never be lost.[347]

Critics, however, object to this view and say it doesn't makes sense of passages that describe our salvation requiring good works (Phil. 2:12; James 2:24), baptism (John 3:5, 1 Pet. 3:21), eating Christ's flesh (John 6:53–57), or preserving in faith (1 Cor. 9:27, Gal. 5:2–4), While Protestants try to interpret these verses according to their theologies, atheists just think the Bible contradicts itself and view this as more evidence of its fallible authorship. Steve Wells even lists 189 contradictory ways he thinks the Bible teaches us how to be saved.[348]

But the main problem with objections like this one is that it assumes that the Bible is one book written by God as an instruction manual for getting to heaven. If that were its purpose, then God would have been better off writing a short leaflet and miraculously distributing it all over the world (along with the ability to read, which is a skill most people in human history have lacked).

Instead, the Bible's purpose is to be a repository of God's revelation and a witness to his actions in salvation history. This includes the different times God revealed to his people how to be saved from their sins—a revelation that differed based on the particular circumstances affecting God's people. For example, God did not expect Noah to follow the Law given to Moses, nor did he expect the ancient Israelites to put their faith in Christ. Reading the Bible as if every one of its instructions for salvation applies equally to everyone today leads to an erroneous understanding of the biblical texts.

In addition, throughout Christian history it was assumed that Christ's Church would teach people how to be saved—not the Bible alone. Consider the encounter Philip had with a eunuch associated with the queen of Ethiopia. Acts 8:30–31 says, "Philip ran to him, and heard him reading Isaiah the prophet, and asked, 'Do you understand what you are reading?' And he said, 'How can I, unless some one guides me?' And he invited Philip to come up and sit with him." The pair then discussed to whom the "suffering servant" passage in Isaiah 53 referred. The text continues, "Then Philip opened his mouth, and beginning with this scripture he told him the good news of Jesus. And as they went along the road they came to some water, and the eunuch said, 'See, here is water! What is to prevent my being baptized?' And he commanded the chariot to stop, and they both went down into the water, Philip and the eunuch, and he baptized him" (Acts 8:35–38).

Just as Philip was able to help the eunuch overcome his ignorance of Scripture and attain a saving knowledge of Jesus Christ, the Church helps people overcome modern misinformation about the Bible and attain salvation through grace. The *Catechism*, quoting the Second Vatican Council, says, "The bishops, successors of the apostles, receive from the Lord . . . the mission of teaching all peoples, and of preaching the Gospel to every creature, so that all men may attain salvation through faith, Baptism and the observance of the Commandments" (CCC 2068).

How to Get to Heaven

Despite their abundance, Wells's biblical ways of being saved can be divided into four categories: having faith, being predestined to salvation, doing good works, and "other," which are usually just examples of Wells misreading the text.[349] It's true that the Protestant position of *sola fide* may not adequately explain how these different passages form a cohesive plan of salvation, but Catholic theology does explain the biblical data.

First, before the beginning of time, God knew who would and would not freely accept his offer of grace and salvation. The

Catechism says, "To God, all moments of time are present in their immediacy. When therefore he establishes his eternal plan of "predestination," he includes in it each person's free response to his grace" (CCC 600). God has given all people sufficient grace to seek him because God desires that all men be saved (1 Tim. 2:4). However, not everyone will respond to that grace, which is evident in Jesus' refrain, "Many are called but few are chosen" (Matt. 22:14).

Those who will respond to God's grace are brought to initial salvation through baptism (John 3:5, 1 Pet. 3:21). This washes away original sin and makes us children of God capable of receiving God's grace through the sacraments (Rom. 8:15; Titus 3:5, 2 Pet. 1:4). Notice that when Philip shared the gospel, the eunuch did not respond by "accepting Jesus Christ as his personal Lord and Savior." The eunuch instead asked to be baptized (Acts 8:36). Similarly, after Paul told the Philippian jailer, "Believe in the Lord Jesus, and you will be saved, you and your household" (Acts 16:30), the text goes on to say the jailer "was baptized at once, with all his family" (Acts 16:33).

Since most people are baptized as infants they must later make a conscious act of faith by putting their trust in Christ for their salvation (Rom. 10:9). After they have made this act of faith, they receive the body and blood of Christ (who is our new Passover lamb, who takes away the sins of the world).[350] Through the sacrament of the Eucharist, Catholics receive the sacrifice of Christ's body in a nonbloody form that gives them the grace necessary for attaining eternal life (John 6:53–57; 1 Cor. 11:23–34). Catholics also confess their post-baptismal sins to priests who possess the apostle's authority to release people from their sins by being channels of God's sanctifying grace (John 20:23).

Finally, as James 2:24 says, "a man is justified by works and not by faith alone." As children of God, our good works do not earn our salvation because God's grace is the reason we are capable of performing and desiring salvific works in the first place (Eph. 2:8–9). That doesn't negate the fact that we were "created in Christ Jesus for good works, which God prepared beforehand, that we should walk in them" (Eph. 2:10). Even though they can't earn our salvation, our good works do please God. As a result God freely rewards his children with eternal life for performing the good works he prepared for them (Rom. 2:6–11; Gal. 6:8).[351]

But salvation isn't a one-time event; it's a process. So in order to be saved we must not choose later on in the process to abandon God by renouncing our faith (Matt. 10:22) or by committing a grave sin (1 John 5:17). Such deliberate, evil acts reject the grace God has given us (Matt. 25:31–46) and cause us to fall and be cut off from God (Rom. 11:22). If we do commit such a sin, then we must confess it and seek reconciliation with God before death (John 20:23, James 5:16) or else our salvation will be lost (1 Cor. 9:27, Heb. 6:4–6).

Fortunately, God has given us his Church, which provides for us the "ministry of reconciliation" (2 Cor. 5:18). For those who choose reconciliation with God, they know that "anyone [who] is in Christ, he is a new creation; the old has passed away, behold, the new has come" (2 Cor. 5:17).

13

An All-Too-Human God?

The Claim: Far from being a perfect deity, the biblical God is all too human in his emotional weaknesses and physical limitations. He is merely a cosmic version of a Bronze-Age dictator.

The ancient Greek philosopher Xenophanes claimed that the gods of his time, like Zeus or Poseidon, were myths because they were modeled after the appearances and moral weaknesses of human beings. In fact, he claimed this was true for all mythic gods:

Ethiopians say that their gods are snub-nosed and black . . . Thracians that they are pale and red-haired . . . But if cows, horses and lions had hands or could paint and sculpture with their hands like humans, then the horses would represent the gods as horses and bullocks as bullocks, and they would create bodies in the same way as their own bodies.[352]

Modern critics of religion say Christians have done the same thing with the God of the Bible. They point to biblical descriptions of God's emotions or his physical body as proof that the Bible is not a revelation from God but a fabrication from man. The nineteenth-century philosopher Ludwig Feuerbach put it this way: "God did not, as the Bible says, make man in his image; on the contrary man . . . made God in his image."[353]

Now, this argument might have serious weight if the Bible represented our only way of knowing God. But that is not the case. The First Vatican Council dogmatically decreed, "God, the source and end of all things, can be known with certainty from the consideration of created things, by the natural power of human reason."[354] Since reason can tell us what God is like, it becomes our guide when trying to understand the Bible's different descriptions of God.

Thinking About God

The *Catechism* says, "Since our knowledge of God is limited, our language about him is equally so. We can name God only by taking creatures as our starting point, and in accordance with our limited human ways of knowing and thinking" (CCC 40). We take creatures as our starting point but not as our conclusion, because God is not a creature.

Contrary to some popular descriptions, God is not an all-powerful "super being" who peers into the cosmic fishbowl he created for his human pets. God isn't even *a* being at all. He is instead, as St. Thomas Aquinas described him, *ipsum esse*, or the sheer act of being.[355] God is just pure actuality, so he exists without limit, flaw, or deficiency of any kind.

In the *Summa Theologica,* Thomas shows that God must be *ipsum esse* because an unchanging, infinite, immaterial, and eternal Creator is the only explanation for why a changing, finite, material, and temporal universe exists.[356] While everything in the universe changes and depends on something else to exist, God is existence itself. Therefore, God depends on nothing to exist and is able to explain the existence of all finite beings. This is similar to how a locomotive on a train is able to pull all the other cars without itself being pulled by anything.

Since God created all of reality, this means God is not limited by reality. As a result, God is necessary (not limited by existence), immaterial (not limited by space), and eternal (not limited by time). Although popular descriptions of God help us talk about him, they are always metaphorical in some sense. For example, God doesn't "think" or "decide" to do anything because he exists in a perfect, timeless moment where all truth is immediately known to him. "Thinking," "deciding," and even "reacting" are functions of creatures, not of *ipsum esse.* God doesn't have a divided mind or an intellect the way we do. Instead, God *is* intellect, God *is* wisdom, and God *is* goodness because God contains all perfections in one undivided act of being.[357]

The *Catechism* quotes Thomas saying, "In God, power, essence, will, intellect, wisdom, and justice are all identical. Nothing therefore can be in God's power which could not be in his just will or his wise intellect" (CCC 271). It also tells us,

> Our language is using human modes of expression; nevertheless it really does attain to God himself, though unable to express him in his infinite simplicity. Likewise, we must recall that "between Creator and creature no similitude can be expressed without implying an even greater dissimilitude"; and that "concerning God, we cannot grasp what he is, but only what he is not, and how other beings stand in relation to him" (CCC 43).

If this is difficult to grasp, don't worry. Theology is a science (Thomas called it the "queen of the sciences"), and all sciences have complicated elements that teachers gradually explain to beginners. Theologians, or the experts who study God and his revelation, also use conceptual frameworks from earlier scholars in order to explain complex truths about the divine. These include frameworks from other theologians and even from nonreligious scholars. One example of the latter would be mathematical concepts of infinity that help us better understand a God who exists without limit.

Keep in mind that this progressively refined understanding of theology doesn't mean that what the Bible teaches us about God is false. It only means that just as the Bible is not a science textbook and so it does not contain a modern, scientific description of the world, the Bible is not a theology or philosophy textbook so it does not contain a modern, philosophical description of God. Instead, the Bible contains popular descriptions of both the world and God. These descriptions help people approach God, but they can also handicap our understanding of God if they are taken too literally.

DIVINE CONDESCENSION

I once heard biblical scholar Tim Gray give the following analogy about God and his relationship to human beings on a Catholic radio show.[358] He told the audience to imagine glancing over a fence and seeing their neighbor dressed as a pirate and swinging a sword and yelling into the air. At first, you might think your neighbor had lost his mind, but when you looked closer you saw that he was playing with his five-year-old son. Suddenly, the context shows you that your neighbor isn't crazy. He is just taking on a role in order to connect with his son's particular level of development.

The Bible's descriptions of God must be understood in a similar way. They are not literal descriptions of what God is like but examples of God stooping down to our finite level so that we can better understand him. They are examples of what theologians call *divine condescension*. For example, in his divine nature God does not speak, think, or exist in any visible form. But when he interacts with humans, God accommodates our weaknesses by having a physical form and speaking in sentences. This brings us to Bible-reading rule thirteen: *When the Bible talks about God, it does so in a nonliteral way.* The *Catechism* tells us,

> God transcends all creatures. We must therefore continually purify our language of everything in it that is limited, image-bound or imperfect, if we are not to confuse our image of God—"the inexpressible, the incomprehensible, the invisible, the ungraspable"—with our human representations. Our human words always fall short of the mystery of God (CCC 42).

Popular descriptions of God, be they modern or biblical, must be understood in light of God's unlimited and wholly unique nature that we can know from reason alone. But why wouldn't God reveal himself all at once to the Israelites as both *ipsum esse* and the Holy Trinity? Why use anthropomorphic language that could be misunderstood? Thomas tells us, "Man acquires a share of this learning, not indeed all at once, but by little and little, according to the mode of his nature."[359]

Both individuals and mankind as a whole require layered conceptual frameworks in order to understand deeper aspects of reality. We see this in the natural sciences, where modern thinkers build on what previous thinkers have discovered (for example, Stephen Hawking's work builds on Einstein, who built on Newton, who built on Aristotle, and so on). Similarly, theological truths are built up over time based on what Thomas calls "the mode of the receiver."

It was simply the case that anthropomorphic descriptions (which included caveats about the uniqueness of God to keep them from being taken too literally) were best suited for the Bronze Age "mode" of the people in the Old Testament. As Benedict XVI said, "Biblical revelation is deeply rooted in history. God's plan is manifested progressively and it is accomplished slowly, in successive stages and despite human resistance. God chose a people and patiently worked to guide and educate them"[360]

WHY PERFECT-BEING THEOLOGY?

Some critics claim that interpreting passages about God in light of so-called "perfect being theology" is deceptive.[361] They say that referring to God's imperfections in Scripture as "nonliteral figures of speech" is just a way to rescue these uninspired descriptions of the divine. For example, religion professor Mark Roncace says that rather than approach Scripture with preconceived beliefs about God, "Shouldn't we, instead, read the Bible first, and then draw conclusions about the character of God, rather than determining what we think about God and then forcing the Bible to fit those ideas?"[362]

No, we shouldn't do that, because our preconceptions about God (like his being necessary, infinite, simple, and perfect) are not faith-based assumptions. They are instead the conclusions of logical arguments that show what human reason reveals about God. Besides, the concept of divine condescension was not invented recently in order to answer post-Enlightenment critics of the Bible. St. John Chrysostom said in the fourth century that God had to accommodate even the weaknesses of the angels who surrounded his throne:

They did not see the pure light [of God] itself nor the pure essence itself. What they saw was a condescension accommodated to their nature. What is this condescension? God condescends whenever he is not seen as he is, but in the way one incapable of beholding him is able to look upon him. In this way God reveals himself by accommodating what he reveals to the weakness of vision of those who behold him.[363]

DON'T GET SO EMOTIONAL

Valerie Tarico is a psychologist and atheist whose writings are very critical of Christianity. In her essay "God's Emotions" in the anthology *The End of Christianity*, she argues that emotions are a nonrational "evolved functional feedback response" found in higher-order animals. Therefore, the Bible's depictions of God having emotions like anger or regret reveal that ignorant nomads who "only had a superficial idea of what these words mean" wrote the Bible. According to Tarico, "It is a testament to our narcissism as a species that so few humans are embarrassed to assign divinity the attributes of a male alpha primate."[364]

Now, Tarico is correct that God does not have emotions in the sense that he has immediate, affective responses to stimuli. Nothing can change or surprise the infinite act of being, so of course God lacks emotions.[365] This doesn't mean, however, that God is an impersonal force of nature. It just means that although God has qualities we see in persons, God himself is not a person in the same way humans are persons (similar to how God is not *a* being but just is *being*).[366]

God does not belong to the genus *persona* or to any genus. Every genus, or every different kind of being, exists because God is pure being itself and sustains them. When we speak of God as a person, including when we speak of him as a Trinity of three persons, we use the term "person" in an analogous way since it roughly describes God even though it doesn't communicate his unique, infinite nature.[367]

For example, the persons you and I know have intellects and loving qualities, but God *is* "intellect" or he *is* "love" (1 John 4:8). God is not a person or being who embodies these attributes; he is the perfect exemplification of them. This is similar to the fact that God doesn't have "goodness" or "being" but simply is "Goodness" or "Being" itself. If this is hard to grasp, remember what God said about himself through the prophet Isaiah: "My thoughts are not your thoughts, neither are your ways my ways. For as the heavens are higher than the earth, so are my ways higher than your ways and my thoughts than your thoughts" (Isa. 55:8–9).

When the Bible describes God as having emotions like anger, regret, or pleasure, we understand that these are metaphors that describe how human beings relate to God—not how God relates to us.[368] Saying God is angry at our sin or pleased with our obedience doesn't mean God is reacting to something we did. It means we did something to alienate ourselves from God or to draw us closer to him. Pope Benedict XVI put it this way:

> The wrath of God is a way of saying that I have been living in a way that is contrary to the love that is God . . . "The punishment of God" is in fact an expression for having missed the right road and then experiencing the consequences that follow from taking the wrong track and wandering away from the right way of living.[369]

The Bible's descriptions of God's emotions also represent how ancient people conceived of God in light of their cultural context. In places like the ancient Near East, deities were often compared to human kings, and the best kings were those who were strong and swiftly punished anyone who threatened the populace, whether foreign invaders or domestic rebels.

Just as the Bible contains ancient, popular descriptions of the world that should not to be equated with modern scientific descriptions of it (for example, descriptions of the firmament), the Bible also contains ancient, popular descriptions of God that are true if they are not treated like modern theological or philosophical descriptions of God.

Not Mere Metaphors

Tarico emphatically objects to the idea that the Bible's descriptions of God's emotions are not literal. She says, "A metaphor about something as deep as the human relationship to ultimate reality needs to be deeply accurate . . . but the Biblical descriptions of God have this backwards." They are backward, according to Tarico, because emotions are just physiological responses to weakness or stress. Saying God became angry or pleased with others would indicate that God was imperfect.

But remember that these descriptions of God are not obscure or "mere" metaphors. They are expressions, albeit in an indirect way, of real truths about God that ancient people understood despite their ignorance of the physiological causes of emotions. Though they lacked Tarico's training in psychology, ancient people still knew that "being angry at someone" meant you had a negative relationship with that person, and "being pleased with someone" meant you had a positive relationship. These are not naïve or improper ways of describing how finite, sinful humans might stand in relation to God.

People who say that the God of the Bible has "all-too human needs or desires," like Tarico's fellow contributor to *The End of Christianity,* Jaco Gerike, fail to grasp this metaphorical understanding of God's emotions.[370] Sometimes they even fail to grasp the literal truth behind these nonliteral descriptions. For example, Gerike says that God is "narcissistic and egotistic" because he prescribes in detail how to worship him.[371] Of course, it's egotistical for creatures to demand to be worshipped because they are not infinite in value like God. God, however, has a right to our worship because he is "that which no greater can be thought." Worship means we give someone his "worth-ship," and so a being of infinite worth has a right to our unconditional obedience and adoration.[372]

God Is Spirit

Along with having emotions, another way God comes down to our level is by taking on a physical form. This can be a form that represents his power and mysterious nature, like the burning bush of Exodus 3, or even a humanlike appearance, such as when Moses saw God's "back" (Exod. 33:23). Exodus 33:11 even says that Moses spoke with God, "face-to-face as a man speaks to his friend." Doesn't this mean that God has a body like Moses had a body?

Remember, when Scripture describes God it always does so in some nonliteral way. Sometimes this is easy to spot, such as in Psalm 91:4 (NIV), which says God "will cover you with his feathers, and under his wings you will find refuge." We know this passage teaches us about God's love, not his wingspan. This and other passages that describe God as having a material form are nonliteral, because Scripture and reason teach us that God is immaterial.

Through reason we know that God is not physical because he created not only all physical objects, but even the space and time in which those objects reside. If God were material, then space and time would have to have preceded him, and God would thus be downgraded from "omnipotent Creator" to mere "cosmic craftsman." He would be a being that inexplicably resides in a preexisting space-time universe and cobbled together out of eternal matter the world in which we live.[373] But since the universe requires an explanation for its existence, it follows that God created it and so he transcends it by being immaterial (or beyond space) and eternal (beyond time). If God were not so, then he would hardly be different from the creatures he made, who are confined to the space and time he created.

Scripture, too, reveals that God is the Creator of all things. For example, the mother in 2 Maccabees 7:28 told her sons, "Look at the heaven and the earth and see everything that is in them, and recognize that God did not make them out of things that existed." John 1:3 reveals that not a single thing was made apart from God, and Colossians 1:16 says, "in him all things were created, in heaven and on earth, visible and invisible." The *Catechism* affirms that "God needs no pre-existent thing or any help in order to create, nor is creation any sort of necessary emanation from the divine substance. God creates freely 'out of nothing'" (CCC 296).

As the Creator of all, God is not a physical being, but immaterial being itself. In Jeremiah 23:24 God rhetorically asks, "Can a man hide himself in secret places so that I cannot see him? Do I not fill heaven and earth?" In John 4:24 Jesus says, "God is spirit" and he also makes it clear in Luke 24:39 that "a spirit has not flesh and bones." The second-century Church Father St. Irenaeus likewise taught that God "is simple, not composed of parts, without structure, altogether like and equal to himself alone. He is all mind, all spirit . . ."[374]

It's important to remember that although God is a spirit he is also all-powerful. God can do anything that is logically possible, including become the man Jesus Christ. So, although God can and did acquire a human body, he doesn't *need* a body, and the Father and Holy Spirit exist without one.

God Is Not a Man

Some people, whether it's atheists who think the Bible contradicts itself or Mormons who think that God is an exalted man, believe the Bible teaches that God has a physical body.[375] Gerike insists that "the obvious meaning" of man being made "in the image of God" is that God has a physical body that resembles human bodies.[376]

However, the pairing of the Hebrew words used in these passages for image (*tselem*) and likeness (*demuth*) more likely refer to royal authority and filial adoption by God and not mere human appearance.[377] In the ancient Near East it was commonly believed that only rulers were "of God," which is reflected in an ancient Sumerian proverb that said, "Man is the shadow of god, but the king is god's reflection."[378] Genesis, however, turns this idea on its head and says that all human beings bear the image and likeness of God, not just the ruling class (Gen. 1:26; 5:1).

The interpretation that "image and likeness" refer to immaterial qualities in man (and not physical likeness) is also bolstered by Genesis 9:6, which states, "Whoever sheds the blood of man, by man shall his blood be shed; for God made man in his own image." God doesn't condemn killing humans because they physically look like him, but because they possess immaterial qualities like intrinsic value and God-given authority over Creation. The Pentateuch's declaration that "God is not man" (Num. 23:19) and its prohibition on creating images of God (Exod. 20:4) are also evidence that its ancient authors conceived of God as being vastly different from everything in Creation.[379]

But if God doesn't have a body, and isn't a man in his divine nature (though God the Son does have a human nature), then in what sense can God be a "he"? The *Catechism* explains,

> [B]y calling God "Father," the language of faith indicates two main things: that God is the first origin of everything and transcendent authority; and that he is at the same time goodness and loving care for all his children. God's parental tenderness can also be expressed by the image of motherhood, which emphasizes God's immanence, the intimacy between Creator and creature . . . [but] God transcends the human distinction between the sexes. He is neither man nor woman: he is God. He also transcends human fatherhood and motherhood, although he is their origin and standard: no one is father as God is Father (CCC 239).[380]

Peter Kreeft and Ronald Tacelli give us another reason to understand why God, though he is not a literal male, chose to reveal himself as "he" instead of "she." They root this in Judaism's unique theology of transcendence:

> As a man comes into a woman from without to make her pregnant, so God creates the universe from without rather than birthing it from within and impregnates our souls with

grace or supernatural life without. As a woman cannot impregnate herself, so the universe cannot create itself, nor can the soul redeem itself.[381]

HAS ANYONE SEEN GOD?

Another reason to believe God is not an embodied being is because Scripture teaches that God cannot be seen. Job 9:11 says of God, "He passes by me, and I see him not; he moves on, but I do not perceive him." In the New Testament, 1 Timothy 1:17 and Colossians 1:15 describe God as being invisible, and 1 Timothy 6:16 tells us that God "dwells in unapproachable light, whom no man has ever seen or can see." Of course, a skeptic might object that many Scripture passages describe people seeing God (such as Gen. 32:30, Isa. 6:1, and Amos 9:1).[382] How can these passages be reconciled with those that say God is invisible and immaterial?

Even though God is invisible and immaterial, he can still appear to human beings under a visible form, in what theologians call a "theophany." These are experiences in which human beings interacted with a God who accommodated himself to their finite nature. These were not cases of human beings seeing God's true glory and essence.

One example of a theophany would be God's "walking" through the Garden of Eden (Gen. 3:8), as would God's appearances to Isaiah (6:1), Amos (7:7), and patriarchs like Jacob, for whom God took the form of an angel who wrestled with him (Gen. 32:24–32). When Moses spoke to God "face-to-face (Exod. 33:11)," this was an expression of the intimacy Moses had with God (even a blind man can speak to someone "face-to-face").

In fact, the reason people in the Gospels could see a fully divine Jesus is because Christ voluntarily set aside his divine glory in order to become human (Phil. 2:7). Jesus even said, referring to himself, "Not that any one has seen the Father except him who is from God; he has seen the Father" (John 6:46). In other words, no one has ever seen God except for his Son because the

Son is as fully divine as the Father. Fortunately, through the greatest act of divine condescension, the invisible God is made visible through his Son Jesus Christ (Col. 1:15). In the words of St. Irenaeus,

> Christ Jesus, the Son of God, because of his surpassing love for his creation, *condescended to be born of the virgin* [emphasis added]. He himself uniting man through himself to God, and having suffered under Pontius Pilate, and rising again, and having been received up in splendor, shall come in glory, the Savior of those who are saved.[383]

14

An Imperfect God?

The Claim: Some Bible passages say there is only one God who is all-knowing, all-powerful, and all-good. But other passages depict God existing alongside other gods, not knowing some things, not being able to do some things, and actually being the source of evil.

Since reason shows us that God is infinite and lacks nothing, it follows that God must know all real and possibly real things. In other words, God knows everything that was, is, and will be—that is, God is *omniscient*, or all-knowing.[384] To say that God is ignorant of some truth would impose a limit on unlimited being, which is contradictory. Indeed, Hebrews 4:13 says of God, "Before him no creature is hidden, but all are open and laid bare to the eyes of him with whom we have to do," and Psalm 147:5 says, "his understanding has no limit" (NIV).

When Scripture speaks as if God does not know something, it is speaking metaphorically. For example, in Hosea 8:4 God says of Israel, "They made kings, but not through me. They set up princes, but without my knowledge."[385] Was God unaware of Israel's coronation ceremonies? No, this verse means that Israel broke God's covenant by trusting solely in rulers to address their worldly concerns instead of trusting God to be their king (Hos. 8:1; see also Ps. 146: 3–5).

Another example would be Genesis 3:9, where God called out in the Garden of Eden to Adam, "Where are you?"[386] The reason God did this, or the reason the sacred writer describes God doing this (since we know Genesis 3 uses figurative language), is not to portray God as having lost Adam, but precisely the opposite. The text underscores the fact that Adam has cut himself off from God through his own disobedience. In response to the objection that God asking a question proves he is not omniscient, I would answer, "Is it possible to ask a question in order to make a point instead of to gather information?"

God Does Not Change

As creatures we change in order to gain a good or avoid an evil. But since God is all-knowing goodness, he has no need or desire to change. As James 1:17 says, "Every good endowment and every perfect gift is from above, coming down from the Father of lights with whom there is no variation or shadow due to change." God himself bluntly says in Malachi 3:6, "I the Lord do not change." Or does he?

The book of Jonah describes how God called the titular prophet to preach the need for repentance to the people of Nineveh. Jonah, however, decided to flee from God's call and, one fish story of a detour later, ended up right at Nineveh to preach God's judgment. As a result of his preaching, the people of the city repented and Jonah 3:10 says, "When God saw what they did, how they turned from their evil way, God repented of the evil which he had said he would do to them; and he did not do it."

But how could an immutable God change his mind about destroying Nineveh? Wouldn't an omniscient God have known he would change his mind before it ever happened?[387]

Notice that in Jonah 1:2 God told Jonah, "Arise, go to Nineveh, that great city, and cry against it; for their wickedness has come up before me." In Jonah 3:4 our hero preaches the specific message God gave him: "Forty days, and Nineveh shall be overthrown." Since God was known to be merciful the people trusted that this message implicitly ended with the caveat "unless you repent" (Jon. 3:8–9). Indeed, God always knew that the people of Nineveh would repent; it was *the people of Nineveh* who did not know they were capable of repentance. Therefore, when the text says God changed or repented from evil, this is a metaphorical way of saying that human beings changed, or *they* repented, not that God changed in any way.

But what about passages that seem to describe God regretting that he did something? Wouldn't an omniscient being have foreknown his course of action was a bad idea before he could ever regret it? Consider Genesis 6:7, where God decides that mankind's wickedness has reached epidemic proportions. With the flood in mind, God says, "I will blot out man whom I have created from the face of the ground, man and beast and creeping things and birds of the air, for I am sorry that I have made them." St. Thomas Aquinas says of this passage,

> These words of the Lord are to be understood metaphorically, and according to the likeness of our nature. For when we repent, we destroy what we have made . . . God is said to have repented, by way of comparison with our mode of acting, in so far as by the deluge he destroyed from the face of the earth man whom he had made.[388]

What Aquinas means is that this passage, and others like it, describe God literally punishing mankind through the nonliteral language of repentance.[389] Just as when humans repent of something, they do their best to get rid of the evil they've created (for example, a man repents of buying pornography, so he throws it away), when God "repents" of the evil that came from his creatures he does so by ending those creatures' existence. The Protestant Reformer Johannes Brenz put it this way: "In [God']s own nature, he has neither hands nor feet, but his *power* is called his 'hands' . . . And he is said to repent when he destroys something he previously had made."[390]

GOD IS ALL-POWERFUL

Since God is not limited in his being and sustains everything in existence, it follows that he is not limited in power. Luke 1:37 says, "For with God nothing will be impossible," and the angels in heaven cheer, "Hallelujah! For the Lord our God the Almighty reigns" (Rev. 19:6). In ancient cultures, "almighty" was a synonym for all-powerful or omnipotent.[391] According to the *Catechism*, "Of all the divine attributes, only God's omnipotence is named in the Creed: to confess this power has great bearing on our lives. We believe that his might is *universal*, for God who created everything also rules everything and can do everything" (CCC 268).

However, some critics say that the Bible describes God as being unable to do certain things, which would seem to negate his omnipotence. One example is Hebrews 6:18, which says, "It is impossible for God to lie" (NIV). But this verse does not negate God's omnipotence because omnipotence only involves the ability to do the logically possible.[392] God can do anything that can be done, but the concept of a perfect being acting in an imperfect way (by destroying himself, or committing a sin, for example) is as logically impossible as a square being a circle. As St. Augustine says, "God cannot do some things for the very reason that he is omnipotent."[393] If God were to be imperfect, this would contradict his perfection, not reinforce his omnipotence.

Another objection to God's omnipotence, one that inspired the creation of an atheist website, is Judges 1:19. This passage describes the Israelites attempting to drive the remaining Canaanites out of the Promised Land and says, "the Lord was with Judah, and he took possession of the hill country, but he could not drive out the inhabitants of the plain, because they had chariots of iron."[394]

Is God all-powerful? Or are iron chariots too much of a challenge for him?

It doesn't make sense to say that God was incapable of driving out the Canaanites, because Judges 4:15 describes how God "routed" the Canaanite commander, Sisera, and his 900 iron chariots (not to mention that in Genesis God was powerful enough to create the entire universe). This is an example of misreading the biblical text. The pronoun "he" in this verse refers to the nearest proper noun, the tribe of Judah.

It was *Judah* who took possession of the hill country but failed to secure the plains, not God. This is similar to Genesis 39:2, which says, "The Lord was with Joseph, and he [or Joseph] became a successful man; and he was in the house of his master the Egyptian." It's true the Lord was "with Judah," but this only means that God did not abandon Judah during his failure to capture the valley. According to James Jordan's commentary on Judges,

> Chariots could not function in the hills, so Judah did not have to fight them there. Where the iron chariots could function, however, Judah did not succeed . . . as Judges 4 and 5 will show, God is fully capable of dealing with iron chariots. Thus, the problem was not the iron chariots. The problem was faith, or rather the lack of it.[395]

God Is All-Good

Psalm 145:17 says, "God is just in all his ways and kind in all his doings." St. Paul echoes this in Romans 8:28: "We know that in everything God works for good with those who love him, who are called according to his purpose." Critics respond to this, however, with verses they say not only deny God's goodness, but prove he is the author and creator of evil. Here are three of the most commonly cited passages:

- "I form the light, and create darkness: I make peace, and create evil: I the Lord do all these things" (Isa. 45:7, KJV).
- "Does evil befall a city, unless the Lord has done it?" (Amos 3:6).
- "Is it not from the mouth of the Most High that good and evil come?" (Lam. 3:38).

Before we examine these verses we need a precise definition of "evil." Evil is not a thing God created, because everything God made is good (Gen. 1:31). Evil is instead a privation or absence of good.[396] This doesn't mean that evil is "nothing" or that it is illusory in nature. Evil is real, but it only exists as an absence or corruption of a good—the way rust only exists as a corruption of metal and has no real existence on its own. There also different kinds of evil: moral and natural.

Moral evil refers to a rational being acting against the good, and natural evil (also called physical evil) refers to suffering or pain that have nothing to do with making evil choices. This kind of evil doesn't come from someone acting against the good, but an absence of a good that is natural and due to a thing.[397] One example of this would be the absence of sight a blind person should possess. God cannot engage in moral evil because it is impossible for God to act against what he is—goodness itself. The Catechism teaches, "God is in no way, directly or indirectly, the cause of moral evil. He permits it, however, because he respects the freedom of his creatures and, mysteriously, knows how to derive good from it" (CCC 311). However, God can directly or indirectly cause physical evils like pain or suffering. That's because these bad things can serve God's ultimately good ends (CCC 310).[398] As C.S. Lewis once said, "God whispers to us in our pleasures, speaks in our conscience, and shouts in our pain, it is his megaphone to rouse a deaf world."[399]

Do the three passages listed above describe God creating physical evils like pain, or do they describe God creating moral evils that contradict his perfectly good nature? Let's begin with Isaiah 45:7, which reads in some English translations, "I make peace and create evil," or, with the Hebrew words substituted, "I make shalom and create ra."

The word shalom is a greeting that means "peace" and is an informal way of wishing someone well (similar to "Peace be with you"). The Hebrew word that the King James Version translates as "evil" in this passage, ra, can mean moral evil. For example, in Genesis 2:9 it refers to "the tree of the knowledge of good [tov] and evil [wa-ra]." But this does not mean, as Dan Barker suggests, "The Hebrew word ra clearly [or only] means 'moral evil.'"[400]

Ra can also refer to natural evil, as in Psalm 34:19, which says, "Many are the afflictions [ra-ot] of the righteous; but the Lord delivers him out of them all." Obviously Psalm 34:19 does not mean "many are the moral evils of the righteous." It means instead, "many are the trials or difficulties of the righteous." These trials can come from the moral evils of bad people who oppose the righteous or even natural evils like sickness or accidents.

Prior to this verse, Isaiah describes how God is in complete control of the universe. The Israelites' suffering is not the result of God being unable to fend off other gods, but is instead part of God's providential plan for Creation. The Catholic edition of the Revised Standard Version of the Bible accurately communicates this message by rendering Isaiah 45:6–7: "[T]here is none besides me; I am the Lord, and there is no other. I form light and create darkness, I make weal [*shalom*] and create woe [*ra*], I am the Lord, who do all these things."

Just as the opposite of light is darkness, the opposite of peace is unrest or calamity, not necessarily moral evil (though moral evil could cause calamities). Isaiah 45:7 simply describes how God is the ultimate cause of both what we enjoy and what we suffer. According to the *Catholic Commentary on Holy Scripture*, "No distinction was made between direct causality and mere permission. The Israelites were satisfied that Yahweh was the ultimate cause of every event and did not ask how precisely he was the cause both of good and evil."[401]

This also explains Amos 3:6, which the Catholic Revised Standard Version (RSV:CE) renders, **"Does evil befall a city, unless the Lord has done it?"**

The second chapter of Amos indicts Israel for oppressing the poor ("they trample the head of the poor into the dust of the earth, and turn aside the way of the afflicted") and sexual immorality ("a man and his father go in to the same maiden, so that my holy name is profaned") (Amos 2:7). The third chapter of Amos describes God delivering his judgment against Israel in the form of the invading Assyrian army. God is certainly causing a disaster, and using the moral evil of others to bring it upon the Israelites, but he is not engaging in an act of moral evil by allowing these events to take place.

What about Lamentations 3:38? Do "evil and good" proceed from the mouth of God? The book of Lamentations describes the aftermath of the destruction of Jerusalem in 587 B.C. The author uses poetic language to help the reader understand why a good God would allow something so terrible to happen. The author says, "The Lord is good to those who wait for him" (Lam. 3:25), but he also candidly admits, "though [the Lord] causes grief, he will have compassion according to the abundance of his steadfast love; for he does not willingly afflict or grieve the sons of men" (Lam. 3:32–33).

The author of Lamentations, traditionally thought to be Jeremiah, is walking a fine line between two unorthodox views of God. The first is to say there are events that happen outside of God's control, such as the suffering of morally upright people. However, this contradicts the biblical notion of God's sovereignty, or his complete control of the universe. According to biblical scholar John Walton, "The Israelites, along with everyone else in the ancient world, believed that every event was the act of deity – that every plant that grew, every baby born, every drop of rain and every climactic disaster was an act of God. No 'natural' laws governed the cosmos; deity ran the cosmos or was inherent in it."[402]

Jeremiah avoids detracting from God's sovereignty by admitting that the Lord causes grief. But God doesn't just stand by and helplessly watch it happen or delight in our suffering for its own sake. Jeremiah makes that clear by saying God "does not willingly afflict or grieve" us (Lam. 3:33). Instead, God uses suffering to call us to repentance. This is the context in which Lamentations 3:38 is best understood. The text says, "Who has commanded and it came to pass, unless the Lord has ordained it? Is it not from the mouth of the Most High that good and evil come? Why should a living man complain, a man, about the punishment of his sins? Let us test and examine our ways, and return to the Lord!"

Jeremiah is essentially telling his fellow Jews, "Who are we to say God is evil when our own evil deeds brought this punishment upon us? Both good and evil exist by God's will, and it is not our right to question him. We must obey God and turn away from the evil we have embraced."

God Is One

Since God is *ipsum esse*, pure being that exists without limit or deficiency, he must be one. In other words, there is only one God. If there were another God then the God we worship would be limited by this other divine being. Plus, if there were two "Gods" then there would be a difference between these two beings due to one of them having a perfection the other lacked. But the true God is not *a* being who competes with others. He is infinite being that lacks nothing and possesses all perfections. Two incomplete but powerful beings would just be an example of gods with a lowercase "g," not God with a capital "G" since *ipsum esse,* or the true God, is not divided or challenged in any way.[403]

Scripture also reveals this truth in passages like Isaiah 45:5, where God says, "I am the Lord, and there is no other, besides me there is no God." God also makes it clear in Isaiah 43:10 that "Before me no god was formed, nor shall there be any after me." This can't refer to false gods or idols, because many of those are still "formed" to this day. Instead, Isaiah says that no other God besides the true God ever has existed and no other God ever will exist.

Jesus described God as "the only God" (John 5:44) and "the only true God" (John 17:3). St. Paul describes God as "the only wise God" (Rom. 16:27) and the only being who possesses immortality (1 Tim. 6:16). St. Ignatius wrote in the early second century that Christians were persecuted because they "convince[d] the disobedient that there is *one God* [emphasis added], who manifested himself through his Son, Jesus Christ (*Letter to the Magnesians* 8:1)."

However, some critics say that the Bible contradicts itself on this point because it mentions "other gods" (Exod. 23:13, Deut. 5:7, Jer. 25:6) and forbids believers from worshipping them. The First Commandment even says, "You shall have no other gods before me" (not "I am the only God"), and St. Paul says, "There are many 'gods' and many 'lords'" (1 Cor. 8:5).

It's true these texts acknowledge that other, false gods do exist—but they exist in name only. Paul makes it clear that they are only "so-called gods" because "an idol has no real existence" (1 Cor. 8:4). But what are we to make of passages in Scripture that seem to endorse the actual existence of deities besides the God of Israel? In Genesis 1:26 God says, "Let *us* make man in our image," and the psalmist declares, "God presides in the great assembly; he renders judgment among the 'gods'" (Ps. 82:1, NIV).

There are actually several ways we can approach these texts.

First, the *Catechism* says that God created the angels and heavenly realm before he created the earth (CCC 331–333). Therefore, the use of the plural in Genesis 1:26 could be a "plural of majesty," or God speaking as a magnificent king whose actions reflect what the entire heavenly realm is ordered toward. This use occurs throughout the Old Testament, such as in Isaiah 6:8, where after the prophet Isaiah sees God and his angels (one of whom cleanses Isaiah's lips of impurities), God says, "Whom shall I send? Who will go for *us?*"

In addition, the word for God that is used in this passage, *elohim*, may refer to the multiplicity of powers found in God (God the all-powerful, God the all-knowing, God the all-good, and so on). *Elohim* does not require the existence of multiple deities, because even though it is a plural noun it is often joined with a singular verb, such as in Genesis 1:26, which says, "Then God said [singular form], 'Let us make man in our image.'" The sacred writer understood that the God of Israel was one being, even though he could be described as having a magnificence that is best represented in human language through a plurality.

Human rulers and judges are sometimes called "gods" (for example, Exod. 22:8–9) or *elohim* in the Bible. Psalm 82:7 says these *elohim* will "die like men," so these beings were not actual gods. Jesus even quoted Psalm 82 because it criticized human judges like the Pharisees, who were unfair or wicked and fell short of God's moral law. When the Pharisees accused Jesus of blasphemy for making himself equal with God (John 5:18), Jesus said to them in response, "Is it not written in your law 'I said, you are gods'?" (John 10:34). Jesus' point was that if the corrupt human leaders in Psalm 82 could be called "gods" then why couldn't he, who "the Father has sanctified and sent into the world" (John 10:36), be called God. After all, he actually is God!

GRADUAL REVELATION

It could also be the case that these verses carry with them remnants of Israel's henotheistic past. *Polytheism* is the worship of many gods; henotheism is the worship of one god among many others. This god may even be worshipped because he created all the other divine beings. Consider Deuteronomy 32:8–9, which says, "When the Most High gave to the nations their inheritance, when he separated the sons of men, he fixed the bounds of the peoples according to the number of the sons of God. For the Lord's portion is his people, Jacob his allotted heritage."

Traditional commentaries say this text describes God giving the nations to angels ("sons of God") who keep charge over them while God keeps charge over Israel because of his love for and fidelity to his people. Critics, on the other hand, say that the "Most High" in this text is not Yahweh, but the Canaanite god El. They say that the ancient Israelites believed their god was just a junior deity amidst a pantheon of other gods.[404]

How should Catholics answer these claims?

First, there's no doubt that at least some ancient Israelites believed in the existence of other gods. This explains Israel's frequent bouts of idolatrous worship and the need to condemn this practice, such as when Joshua told the Israelites at Shechem, "Put away the foreign gods which are among you, and incline your heart to the Lord, the God of Israel" (Josh. 24:23).

Even Pope Benedict XVI said that ancient Israel "no more denied the existence of Sheol than, at first, it denied the existence of other gods than Yahweh."[405] This means that just as the ancient Israelites believed in a gloomy underworld, at least some of them believed in the existence of other deities. But just as God progressively revealed the nature of the afterlife as well as the nature of the Trinity to his people, God progressively revealed to them that he was the only God that existed.

However, this doesn't mean that polytheism or henotheism were the only strains of divine belief in ancient Israel; belief in multiple gods wasn't the only religious framework in the ancient Near East. In the fourteenth century before Christ, Pharaoh

Akhenaten of Egypt promoted the worship of one God named
Aten and denied the existence of other popular gods (although
his reform collapsed shortly after his death and Egypt reverted
to polytheism).[406]

When it comes to the Israelites, the earliest books of the Old
Testament, like Job and Genesis (especially Gen. 14–15), describe monotheistic beliefs in one "almighty God." Although
the Bible contains progressive revelation about God's unique
existence, it's important to remember, in the words of Jewish
scholar Benjamin Sommer, "Never do other nation's deities in-
teract with YHWH or contact human beings on their own in
the biblical narrative . . . the fact that the Hebrew Bible as a
whole fails to attest any [texts] that must be read in a polytheistic
fashion justifies the conclusion that this anthology is indeed a
monotheistic one."[407]

There is also evidence that the God of the Israelites, Yahweh,
was worshipped in Canaan under the name El, who was the
supreme god of the Canaanite pantheon of deities. According to
Old Testament scholar Mark Smith, although the Bible fiercely
criticizes other pagan deities like Baal, "there are no biblical polemics against El. At an early point, Israelite tradition identified
El with Yahweh or presupposed this equation."[408] In fact, the
name Israel means "El will rule."[409]

Smith also says, "Psalm 82, like Deuteronomy 32:8–9, pre-
serves the outlines of the older theology it is rejecting."[410] Theologian Matthew Ramage makes a similar point. "Israel's fundamental belief in Yahweh's superiority over 'sons of the gods' led
to recognition that these beings were not gods at all."[411] Once
again, we see an example of God progressively revealing himself to a people steeped in polytheism and henotheism. As Pope
Benedict XVI said, "from the denial of the gods of myth, and
from faith in the unicity of Yahweh, there gradually came about
distinct changes in the Israelite picture of reality."[412]

In other words, over time God's people came to learn that
their God was unique not just in power or goodness, but also in
existence. He was and is "the only true God" (John 17:3).

For This Is God

Although some passages in Scripture can be isolated and interpreted to mean God is limited or imperfect, we must remember the analogy of faith. These passages must be interpreted against the backdrop of both the whole of Scripture and also what we know about God from philosophical reflection. In fact, even ancient people were able to see that, in spite of ubiquitous, incorrect mythological descriptions of God, one could still come to know the real, perfect, and infinite God.

Xenophanes, whom we discussed in the previous chapter, rejected anthropomorphic conceptions of God while simultaneously believing in "one god, greatest among gods and humans, like mortals neither in form nor in thought."[413] Likewise, Aristotle said that even though gods like Zeus existed "in the manner of myth," there was one true God who "is a living being, eternal, most good, so that life and duration continuous and eternal belong to God; for this is God."[414]

What applies to our modern descriptions of God also applies to descriptions found in Scripture. The *Catechism* says, "We really can name God, starting from the manifold perfections of his creatures, which are likenesses of the infinitely perfect God, even if our limited language cannot exhaust the mystery" (CCC 48).

A Dysfunctional God?

The Claim: The Bible praises God for being kind and merciful,
but it also depicts God as being jealous, capricious, and even causing
people to do evil. Either the Bible contradicts its own descriptions
of God, or God has a serious personality disorder.

Many years ago a friend of mine was struggling to find healing
after moving out of her dysfunctional home. After I gave her a
book on overcoming troubled childhoods, I remember her reading one passage that brought her to tears. "Oh my gosh," she
said, "this is my father!"

The passage described an attitude the author called "king-baby syndrome." According to the book, in a dysfunctional family
the "king-baby" rules like a king whose orders must be unques-
tioningly obeyed. But this person also acts like a baby whose
needs everyone else must meet. The alcoholic father who demands money for beer and then wants someone to console him
during his hangovers is a classic example of the "king-baby."

Some critics of the Bible argue that God is a kind of "king-
baby." They say that God is an irrational king who demands
blind obedience and is also a baby who needs people to appease
him. But it is not God's temperament that needs adjustment. Instead, it is the critic's understanding of certain passages in Scripture that describe God that needs to be adjusted.

A JEALOUS GOD?

In Exodus 34:14 God tells his people, "You shall worship no other
god, for the Lord, whose name is Jealous, is a jealous God." As
we've seen, God has no deficiencies, so he does not become upset when his creatures fail to worship him. Language like this is

another example of an anthropomorphic description of God. It is designed to help the reader understand the importance of worshipping only the one true God, but it should not be taken literally.

In fact, the words translated as "jealously" in this text, the Hebrew *qanah* and the Greek *zelotes*, can also mean "zeal" or "passion." For example, 2 Samuel 21:2 uses this word to describe Saul's "zeal" for Judah and Israel. Paul told the Corinthians that he boasts of their zeal (*zelos*) and that it "has stirred up" other churches to be just as zealous for the faith (2 Cor. 9:2). When Jesus drove the money-changers out of the temple, this act reminded the apostles of Psalm 69:9: "Zeal [*zelotes*] for your house will consume me" (John 2:17). God is indeed zealous for his children and does not tolerate worship of false gods that can cause his children harm. He even warned his people in Deuteronomy 12:30–31 that, when it comes to pagan religions, "Do not inquire about their gods, saying, 'How did these nations serve their gods?—that I also may do likewise.' You shall not do so to the Lord your God; for every abominable thing which the Lord hates they have done for their gods; *for they even burn their sons and their daughters in the fire to their gods* [emphasis added]."

By saying that God is "jealous," the biblical writer is not asserting a literal truth about God's emotions. He is instead asserting a truth about God's zealous desire for our good.

Tempted to Do Evil

James 1:13 says, "God cannot be tempted with evil and he himself tempts no one." But what about the case of God causing the Egyptian pharaoh not to let the Hebrew slaves go free? Wouldn't that be a case of God causing someone to sin? Mark Roncace writes of these passages in Exodus: [W]hy didn't Pharaoh let the people go? This is not a joke. Answer: God himself hardens Pharaoh's heart. God manipulates Pharaoh, so that he will not cooperate. The text does not say this one time in passing; on the contrary, it states this repeatedly so it's difficult to miss (7:3; 9:15–16; 10:1–2, 27; 11:10; 14:1–4; 14:17–18)."[415]

Exodus 4:21 is the first time we learn that God would harden Pharaoh's heart. In the next chapter, Moses and Aaron demand that Pharaoh let the Israelites go worship in the desert. Pharaoh not only curtly dismisses them, he demands that the Israelites make bricks without straw as a punishment for their request. All of this takes place without any hint of God prompting Pharaoh's overreaction.

God then reminds Moses in Exodus 7:3 that he will harden Pharaoh's heart. Then, in Exodus 7:14 and 7:22, we read that Pharaoh's heart was hardened, but the text does not say by whom. But in Exodus 8:15, 8:32, and 9:34 we learn that it was *Pharaoh* who hardened his own heart by "sinning yet again"— verses that Roncace leaves out of his argument. According to Old Testament scholar Christopher Wright,

> Pharaoh hardened his heart eight times before we read of God's involvement again. In other words, the sequence is clearly Pharaoh's own stiffening resolve to reject the requests of Moses and the advice of his own counselors. Altogether we read that Pharaoh hardened his heart twelve times, whereas God is the subject six times, and five of these are towards the end of the story when Pharaoh's resistance has become irrevocable.[416]

When we read that God hardened Pharaoh's heart it's easy to assume that God did something *to* Pharaoh in order to cause his heart to become stubborn and "hard." But you can cause something to become hard just by leaving it alone, like when bread is left out on the counter overnight. It seems that God hardened Pharaoh's heart by removing what little presence of his grace was left in it. As St. Augustine says, "It was that both God hardened him by his just judgment, and Pharaoh by his own free will."[417]

Pharaoh had the chance to peacefully release the Hebrews, but instead he ignored God's warnings and "hardened his heart." As a result, God allowed Pharaoh's heart to reach its maximum level of stubbornness, and Israel's freedom was purchased at a heavy price for the Egyptians. Indeed, this mirrors other times in salvation history when God punished sinners not with an external punishment like a plague, but by allowing them to suffer the awful consequences of their own decisions. God even did this with Israel after the Exodus, or, as Psalm 81:11–14 says, "But my people did not listen to my voice; Israel would have none of me. So I gave them over to their stubborn hearts, to follow their own counsels. O that my people would listen to me, that Israel would walk in my ways! I would soon subdue their enemies, and turn my hand against their foes."

God does not cause us to commit evil, but he can punish us by withholding his grace from our souls. If he does this, then *we* may punish ourselves by freely choosing evil and reaping the consequences of our sinful actions.

GOD IS IN CONTROL

Other commenters have noted that the author of Exodus was probably writing during a time in Jewish history when sacred writers stressed the sovereignty of God.[418] Devotees of other religions might have heard the Exodus account and wondered how a mere man like Pharaoh could have foiled God's plan to release the Israelites. To keep this speculation from occurring, the writer of Exodus said God "hardened Pharaoh's heart" in order to show that God was using Pharaoh's stubbornness as part of his plan to free Israel. This plan included not just the liberation of Israel, but also the departure of a "mixed multitude" of Egyptians who joined the Israelites to presumably worship their God (Exod. 12:38).

This theme of God's sovereignty can also be seen in the case of David's census. 2 Samuel 24:1 says that God was "angered at Israel," and so he moved David to take a census. But 1 Chronicles 21:1 says that it was Satan who moved David to take the illicit census, not God. So who was it? God or the devil? The answer is: both.

In the ancient world, a person could only conduct a census of what he owned. Since the people of Israel belonged to God, and not to a mortal ruler, only God could call a census. David knew that it was wrong of him to take a census and trust in his military more than God, but he did it anyway. David's pride in his army may also have reflected a national pride that rejected God and embraced worldly principles. As punishment for this attitude, God allowed the disastrous census and subsequent inflaming of national pride that followed. Since God is all-powerful and all-knowing, he was able to use Satan's temptation of David, as well as David's prideful yielding to that temptation, as part of his divine plan.

The incidents involving David and Pharaoh teach us that God sometimes punishes us with the consequences of our own sins. But as soon as we repent, God will deliver us from the eternal consequences our sins (though we might still suffer the temporal consequences for what we've done). God was not the primary cause of either Pharaoh or David sinning, and he would have allowed either of these men to repent if they had chosen to do so. The fact that Pharaoh ultimately did not repent and perpetually hardened his heart speaks volumes about his own moral failings, not God's.

Sins of the Fathers

In North Korea, someone who opposes the government can be inflicted with "three generations of punishment." This means that their grandparents, their parents, and their children are sent to languish and probably die with them in work camps.[419] Most people recoil at this kind of punishment because deep down we know it is true that the punishment ought to fit the crime and the innocent should not be punished in place of the guilty.

The Bible also teaches that punishment must be meted out justly and that the innocent should not be punished on behalf of the guilty. For example, in the world of the ancient Israelites, if a man was killed, his family would often target the killer's family and try to wipe them out in retaliation. That's why Exodus's teaching of "an eye for an eye, a tooth for a tooth" was so countercultural (Exod. 21:24). It tried to limit the punishment a mob might impose on an innocent person as well as limit excessive punishments imposed on the guilty party (such as the death penalty for a nonlethal assault).

The principle of not punishing the innocent is also clearly spelled out in Deuteronomy 24:16, which says, "The fathers shall not be put to death for the children, nor shall the children be put to death for the fathers; every man shall be put to death for his own sin."[420] But what about passages in the Bible that speak of God punishing children for what their parents have done? In Exodus 34:7 God speaks of "visiting the iniquity of the fathers upon the children and the children's children, to the third and the fourth generation."

Sometimes when the Bible speaks of punishing a sinner's future descendants it means that those descendants will engage in the same sins as their ancestors. As a result, they will lawfully earn the same punishment as their ancestors. Consider Jeremiah 16, where God tells his prophet how to answer the people when they ask, "Why has the Lord pronounced all this great evil against us?" God says Jeremiah should tell them, "Because your fathers have forsaken me, says the Lord, and have gone after other gods and have served and worshiped them, and have forsaken me and have not kept my law" (Jer. 16:11). This may seem unfair until we read the next verse, which says, "and because *you have done worse* [emphasis added] than your fathers, for behold, every one of you follows his stubborn evil will, refusing to listen to me."

In other cases that seem to describe God punishing future generations, we must distinguish between direct punishment for sin and allowing the consequences of sin to harm those who never sinned in the first place. Consider the following analogy: Imagine that a man wins the lottery. If he chooses to, he can invest his earnings into a savings account that will allow all his descendants to be prosperous. But let's say the man breaks the law and tries to cheat at the lottery so he can have even more money. Unfortunately for him, he is caught and forced to return all his original winnings. Now, instead of living in comfort and prosperity, his descendants will have to work much harder than they would have if he had not committed his crime.

When the Bible speaks of "visiting the iniquity of the fathers upon the children and the children's children, to the third and the fourth generation (Deut. 5:9)" it is talking about the lasting negative effects sin has on one's descendants, the consequences they inherit or the behavior they imitate—not to punishments they received solely because of their ancestor's crimes. God even forbade the Israelites from quoting a famous proverb that shifted blame for sinning upon one's ancestors ("The fathers have eaten sour grapes, and the children's teeth are set on edge"). Instead, God instructed Jeremiah to say, "Every one shall die *for his own sin*; each man who eats sour grapes, *his teeth* shall be set on edge [emphasis added]" (Jer. 31:29–30).

Perhaps the clearest example of this kind of punishment is the curse of original sin that all humans inherit because of Adam and Eve's disobedience in the Garden of Eden. The *Catechism* teaches that original sin does not involve God *punishing* us for Adam's sin (CCC 405). Instead, original sin is a *consequence* of Adam and Eve losing the graces God initially gave them. Since our first parents lost the divine protections from death and suffering, they could not pass them on to their descendants, who in turn could not pass them on to us. The *Catechism* even says, "By yielding to the tempter, Adam and Eve committed a personal sin, but this sin affected the human nature that they would then transmit in a fallen state" (CCC 404).

If it seems unfair to allow a person's bad decision to hurt his descendants, then wouldn't it also be unfair to allow a person's good decisions to *benefit* his descendants? After all, in both cases a group of people receives something they didn't "earn" (hardships in the former case and blessings in the latter). For example, I know one family whose children have a perpetual college fund because their grandparents set up a trust decades earlier that continues to bless them to this day. On the other hand, I also know a family whose mother has infertility issues because one of her great-grandparents contracted syphilis through extramarital intercourse. If human freedom is to be meaningful, then all the consequences of our free choices must be allowed to exist, both for good and for ill.

Of course, God could have eliminated inherited evil by never creating human beings in the first place, or by never letting humans procreate, or by causing all of our actions and thoughts to be only good. But as St. Augustine said, "God judged it better to bring good out of evil than not to permit any evil to exist."[421] Along with the goods of freedom, love, compassion, and sacrifice that have come with allowing mankind to sin, another good was brought from it—God's act of love on the cross that redeemed us from our freely chosen sins. This sentiment is enshrined in the Exultet sung at the Easter Vigil Mass, which joyously proclaims, "O happy fault! O necessary sin of Adam, which gained for us so great a Redeemer!"

Two Different Gods?

Old Testament professor David Lamb tells us in his book *God Behaving Badly* that he asks his students this question: "Why does the wrathful God of the New Testament seem so different from the loving God of the Old Testament?"[422] Lamb's question seems backwards, doesn't it? Don't you hear most people say that they like the God of the New Testament, who preaches love, but they hate the "fire and brimstone" God of the Old Testament? This attitude isn't new and can be traced all the way back to the second-century heretic Marcion of Sinope.

Marcion was at one time a faithful Christian who lavishly supported the Church at Rome with profits from his shipbuilding business.[423] But his donations were returned to him after he was excommunicated for advocating heresy. Marcion believed that there were actually two gods: the inferior god of the Old Testament, who directly created the material world, and the superior god of the New Testament, who created everything, including the god of the Old Testament.[424] Marcion also said the only books of the Bible that were inspired were those that advocated the worship of the superior God, which ended up including only Luke's Gospel and some of Paul's writings. The rest of the New Testament, as well as the entirety of the Old Testament, was declared to be uninspired rubbish.

Fortunately, Marcion's efforts to rewrite Scripture failed and the Councils of Hippo and Carthage reaffirmed the canonical status of all the books we recognize today as being part of the Bible. But Marcion's challenge still exists for many. Why does the God of the Old Testament seem so different from the God of the New Testament? It turns out this question usually betrays a selective remembering of the Bible. Consider the following two passages:

- "By your hard and impenitent heart you are storing up wrath for yourself on the day of wrath when God's righteous judgment will be revealed."
- "The Lord has called you like a wife forsaken and grieved in spirit, like a wife of youth when she is cast off, says your God. For a brief moment I forsook you, but with great compassion I will gather you."

The first passage is not one of God's decrees in the Old Testament, but a judgment given by the apostle Paul in Romans 2:5. As you might expect, the second passage comes not from a pastoral letter in the New Testament, but from Isaiah 54:6–7. And consider this: the idea of eternal damnation is only hinted at in the Old Testament (Dan. 12:2) but is made explicit in the New Testament's teachings about hell. Jesus even said, "If your eye causes you to sin, pluck it out; it is better for you to enter the kingdom of God with one eye than with two eyes to be thrown into hell, where their worm does not die, and the fire is not quenched" (Mark 9:47–48).

It is incorrect to say that the Old Testament portrait of God radically differs from the New Testament portrait. That would be like comparing a couple's parenting of a newborn with their parenting of that same child twenty years later, then saying the difference proves the child had two different sets of parents! Instead, just as a parent treats a young child differently than an older one, God gave a different revelation to the Israelites, who were struggling in a fierce, polytheistic culture, than the one he gave to second-temple Jews living under Roman occupation.

Pope St. John Paul II said of a contemporary resurgence of Marcionism,

"[T]he Church firmly rejected [the Marcionite] error, reminding all that God's tenderness was already revealed in the
Old Testament. Unfortunately the Marcionite temptation is
making its appearance again in our time. However what occurs most frequently is an ignorance of the deep ties linking
the New Testament to the Old . . . To deprive Christ of his
relationship with the Old Testament is therefore to detach
him from his roots and to empty his mystery of all meaning.
Indeed, to be meaningful, the Incarnation had to be rooted in
centuries of preparation. Christ would otherwise have been
like a meteor that falls by chance to the earth and is devoid of
any connection with human history."[425]

As I said before, critics of the Bible have claimed there are
hundreds, if not thousands, of alleged contradictions within its
pages. This claim is nothing new, and even the early Church Fathers were concerned about harmonizing alleged contradictions
presented by their pagan opponents. So how should believers
respond to these allegations?

You can consult one of the large encyclopedias of Bible difficulties published by Christians who have addressed these issues in detail. Unfortunately, the majority of the authors of
such works are non-Catholics, so some of their explanations
may conflict with Catholic teaching. They can be helpful, but
their proposals should be approached with caution and evaluated
against the teaching authority of the Church.

Karl Keating presents a good attitude to have in the face of
alleged contradictions:

The Bible appears to be full of contradictions only if you approach it in the wrong way. If you think it is supposed to be
a listing of theological propositions, you won't make heads
or tails of it. If you think it is written in literary forms you're
most familiar with, you'll go astray in interpreting it. Your
only safe bet is to read it with the mind of the Church, which

affirms the Bible's inerrancy. If you do that, you'll see that it contains no fundamental contradictions because, being God's word inspired, it's wholly true and can't be anything else.[426]

Part III

Moral Difficulties

16

An Evil Bible?

The Claim: The Bible is a disgusting collection of stories promoting violence and even pornography. No child should be allowed to read it!

One of the most interesting "translations" of the Bible I've ever read is Brendan Powell Smith's *The Brick Bible*. It features hundreds of photographs of small Lego toys intricately arranged to depict various Bible stories. The cover, with its image of God the Father as a little yellow man with a white plastic beard, seems harmless enough. But this Bible was not created as a loving tribute to Scripture.

According to an interview in *Rolling Stone*, Smith is an atheist and he purposely dramatized the most "intense" scenes in the Bible. The interview went on to say that Smith "publishes his work in glossy, coffee-table-friendly books—if incest, gang rapes, beheadings, bestiality, and wholesale genocide are your idea of parlor chit chat."[427] The retail outlet Sam's Club refused to sell *The Brick Bible* because some customers complained that it was "vulgar and violent."

For Christians who only recall Sunday school stories about Noah's Flood or David and Goliath, Smith's Lego depictions of biblical murder and rape can come as quite a shock. But they aren't that out of place if you remember that the Bible shows how God saves human beings from their sins—including wicked and downright sickening sins.

EVIL BIBLE OR JUST EVIL PEOPLE?

The writings of the influential Revolutionary War pamphleteer Thomas Paine are typical of many unbelievers' attitudes toward the Bible: "Whenever we read the obscene stories, the

205

voluptuous debaucheries, the cruel and torturous executions, the unrelenting vindictiveness, with which more than half the Bible is filled, it would be more consistent that we called it the word of a demon, than the word of God."[428]

Paine is exaggerating when he says this content makes up "more than half the Bible," but the Bible does describe some disturbing episodes. However, these descriptions simply exemplify Bible-reading rule number fourteen: *Just because the Bible records it doesn't mean God recommends it.* The Bible is not evil because of the evil deeds it describes any more than high school history textbooks are anti-Semitic because they document the Holocaust.

The Bible records depravities like rape (Gen. 34:2, 2 Sam. 13:14), adultery (2 Sam. 11:4), and murder (Gen. 4:8, Mark 6:27), but it does not condone these acts.[429] This should be a commonsense principle, but you'd be surprised at how many critics simply list Bible passages that sound evil and then make the incorrect inference that the Bible itself is evil. Here are just a few examples:

- "Are they not finding and dividing the spoil? A maiden or two for every man" (Judg. 5:30).[430]
- "Plunder the silver, plunder the gold! There is no end of treasure, or wealth of every precious thing" (Nah. 2:9).[431]
- "As for these enemies of mine, who did not want me to reign over them, bring them here and slay them before me" (Luke 19:27).[432]

First, Judges 5:30 was not a divine command for the Israelites. It was instead a war song the Israelite judge Deborah sang after the death of the Canaanite commander, Sisera. The song imagines Sisera's mother hoping that the reason her son is delayed is because he is taking spoil from the Israelites. In reality, Sisera was delayed because Deborah's fellow Israelite Jael killed him by driving a stake through his head while he slept. Likewise, Nahum 2:9 isn't a record of God commanding the Israelites to plunder. Instead, it is a poem describing what the

Babylonians thought to themselves when they conquered the Assyrian capital of Nineveh.

Finally, Luke 19:27 does record something Jesus said, but it was a parable, not instructions. It compared those who serve God with those who serve nobility. The people who are slain at the end of the parable, like those enemies killed by ancient kings for plotting rebellion, represent those who will lose their eternal salvation because they rebel against God's authority. Matthew's version of the parable explicitly reveals this meaning since it ends with the Master saying, "Cast the worthless servant into the outer darkness, where there will be weeping and gnashing of teeth" (Matt. 25:30).

If someone presents you with a disturbing verse in the Bible in order to prove that the Bible is bad, you should first read it in context (rule six), then note that just because the Bible records someone doing evil, it does not mean that the Bible is evil (rule fourteen). With that in mind, let's look at what might be the paradigmatic example of a biblical story about evil actions that is fallaciously used to condemn the Bible as an evil book in general.

THE ATROCITY OF GIBEAH

After the death of Samson there was no one to lead Israel, and Judges 19:1 grimly reminds the reader, "there was no king in Israel." In other words, there was no central authority to maintain order, so lawlessness was rampant. We are then introduced to an unnamed Levite and his concubine, who are about to spend the night in the city square of Gibeah. An old man sees them and takes them into his home, apparently because he is afraid for what might happen should they spend the night in the square.

His fears are soon realized as the men of Gibeah come to his home and demand to rape the Levite staying there. The old man tries to protect his male guest and so he begs the mob to rape either his daughter or the Levite's concubine instead.[433] The men choose the concubine, and verse 25 says they "abused her all night." The next morning, the woman was found on the doorstep of the house and the Levite proceeded to cut her body into twelve pieces and send the pieces throughout Israel. One atheist website places this account in its list of "Top 20 Evil Bible Stories."[434]

But does this story prove that the Bible is evil? No. It only proves that the inhabitants of Gibeah were evil. God never commanded this behavior and the text does not approve of what happened. In fact, the entire passage serves as proof that Israel had descended into moral madness during the time of the Judges.[435] Even the Levite's actions demonstrate how far Israel had fallen.

First, upon finding his violated concubine on the doorstep of the house, he only said, "Get up, let us be going" (Judg. 19:28), as if her being gang-raped was only an inconvenience for *him*! Second, the fact that he was able to dismember the woman's corpse communicates how bad the situation was in Gibeah.[436] In fact, the other tribes said that such an evil "has never happened or been seen from the day that the sons of Israel came up out of the land of Egypt" (Judg. 19:30).

As bad as this was, the situation continued to spiral out of control when the leaders of the tribe of Benjamin (where Gibeah was located) refused to hand over those responsible for this crime. This prompted a war among the tribes that resulted in the death of all but 600 members of the tribe of Benjamin (Judg. 20:46–48). In order to keep the tribe from going out of existence, the Israelites resorted to kidnapping dancing girls from Shiloh for the men of the tribe of Benjamin to marry (Judg. 21:21–23).

One atheist website says of this disturbing episode, "These sick [people] killed and raped an entire town and then wanted more virgins, so they hid beside the road to kidnap and rape some more. How can anyone see this as anything but evil?"[437] John Loftus wrote, "Why should we trust the writings of people who saw nothing wrong with this?"[438]

But how do Loftus and other critics like him know that the author of Judges saw nothing wrong with this? No morally sane person (including the author of the book of Judges) would disagree with Loftus's assessment that the events described in

Judges 19–21 are evil.[439] But the mere fact that these acts were
evil does not prove that *the Bible* that recorded them is evil.

The author of Judges didn't think his audience was so inept
that he needed to write in block letters, "WHAT THESE PEO-
PLE DID WAS BAD." Instead, the final verse in Judges haunt-
ingly indicts Israel's decrepit condition: "In those days there was
no king in Israel; every man did what was right in his own
eyes" (Judg. 21:25). Judges is not an instruction book on how we
should live our lives. It is instead a warning about what happens
when God's authority is rejected. Pope Pius XI said, "As should
be expected in historical and didactic books, [the Old Testament
books] reflect in many particulars the imperfection, the weakness and sinfulness of man."[440]

THE ATHEIST'S DILEMMA

Ironically, atheists like Loftus who loudly protest the evil deeds
in these stories don't have a metaphysical leg to stand on. They
act as if it is a *fact* that what the people of Gibeah and the rest of
Israel did was wrong. But how would an atheist prove this "fact"
is true?

Other facts, like the size of the earth or its distance from the
sun, can be proven empirically, or they can be proven with tools
that measure and quantify reality. "Right" and "wrong," however, are immaterial, universal concepts that can't be proven in
an empirical way. There's no experiment a scientist can perform
and no measuring device that can tell us if a certain action is
morally right or morally wrong.[441]

In the atheistic worldview, the concept of a moral wrong only
means "something I don't like," because if it meant "something
that ought not to be," that would imply there is a way that our
actions "ought to be." But if our actions, or even the universe
itself, "ought to be" a certain way, that further implies that there
is a cosmic plan for human beings, their moral behavior, and
even the universe itself. And if there is a cosmic plan, then that
implies the existence of a cosmic planner, or what we call God.

On the other hand, if there is no way the world *ought* to be, then, to quote Judges 21:25, each man could simply do "what was right in his own eyes." There would be no objective truth about how he ought to live. There would instead only be other people's opinions about how we should live, and who's to say one person's opinion is better than anyone else's?

The existence of such objective moral truths, like the fact that what happened in Gibeah was wrong no matter what anyone says, actually provides evidence *against* the atheistic worldview. As the famous atheist philosopher J.L. Mackie put it, "Moral properties constitute so odd a cluster of properties and relations that they are most unlikely to have arisen in the ordinary course of events without an all-powerful god to create them."[442] Mackie opted to reject objective morality in favor of his atheism, but for the rest of us who believe that moral truths are objective facts and not matters of opinion, a better approach would be to reject atheism.

Bearing False Witness

Other critics say that the Bible is evil because it rewards people for performing evil acts, even when those acts contradict God's other commands to refrain from doing evil. For example, the eighth commandment says, "You shall not bear false witness against your neighbor" (Exod. 20:16), but what about cases where God seems to reward lying? Two examples that critics commonly bring up are the Egyptian midwives in the book of Exodus and Rahab's actions in the book of Joshua.[443]

In the first, the Egyptian pharaoh feared that the Hebrew slave population was growing too quickly, and so he ordered two Egyptian midwives, Shiphrah and Puah, to kill any newborn Hebrew males. But according to Exodus 1:17, "the midwives feared God, and did not do as the king of Egypt commanded them, but let the male children live." When they were brought before Pharaoh and asked why they let the children live, the midwives responded, "Because the Hebrew women are not like the Egyptian women; for they are vigorous and are delivered before the midwife comes to them" (Exod. 1:19). The next verse then says that, "God dealt well with the midwives."

Did God "deal well" with the midwives because they lied to Pharaoh? That's doubtful, because the midwives' lie gained nothing for the Hebrews. Instead, God "dealt well" with the midwives because they feared him more than Pharaoh and chose not to kill the Hebrew children. The fact that they later lied in order to save their own lives is something that God tolerated but did not necessarily reward or praise.

In the second case, we read that Joshua sent two spies into the Canaanite fortress city of Jericho. The spies lodged with a prostitute named Rahab, but when the king of Jericho became aware of the spies' presence he demanded that Rahab hand them over. The story takes an interesting turn when she decides not to, but instead to hide them under the flax on her roof. She told the king, "True, men came to me, but I did not know where they came from; and when the gate was to be closed, at dark, the men went out; where the men went I do not know; pursue them quickly, for you will overtake them" (Josh. 2:4–5).

Unlike the midwives, whose lie was not instrumental in their plan to save the Hebrew children, Rahab's lie was necessary in order to keep the spies from being discovered. Not only did Joshua praise Rahab for her actions, so did the author of the letter to the Hebrews. He lists Rahab alongside Jewish heroes like Moses and David (Heb. 11:23–40). James 2:25 also says that Rahab was "justified" for receiving the Israelite messengers and sending them out undetected. Isn't this, then, a case of the Bible praising someone because she lied? Not necessarily. Just as the midwives were rewarded because they feared God and did not kill the male infants, Rahab was rewarded, not for her lie per se, but because she feared God and did not turn in the spies.

After Jericho's destruction, Joshua spared Rahab and her family because, in his words, "she hid the messengers that we sent" (Josh. 6:17). Her decision proved that she had remarkable faith, and it was that faith in God, not the deception she used to protect the spies, that is praised in Hebrews 11:31. It says, "By faith

Rahab the harlot did not perish with those who were disobedient, because she had given friendly welcome to the spies." Likewise, James 2:25 does not say that Rahab's lie was the reason she found favor in God's sight. The verse only mentions the fact that Rahab took in the spies and sent them out another way as the reason she was justified, or made righteous before God.

In both cases, God rewarded those who believed in him not because of their sins, but in spite of them.[444] Rahab was a prostitute and, like the Egyptian midwives, she had probably spent her whole life worshipping false gods. But God was pleased that these women chose to protect his people and acknowledge his authority even though it could have cost them their lives. Just because they may have committed sins in the process of serving God does not nullify God's gratitude for revering him and helping his chosen people.

THOU SHALL NOT STEAL

Dan Barker says the seventh commandment, "Thou shall not steal" (Exod. 20:15), contradicts Exodus 12:35–36, which describes how the Israelites were ordered to "spoil" or "plunder" the Egyptians. He says, "I was taught as a child that when you take something without asking for it, that is stealing."[445] But look at the context of Exodus 12 (remember rule six!).

After God sent the series of destructive plagues, the Egyptians came to believe that the Hebrews had legitimate divine protection and as a result, the Egyptians were more than happy to let them leave. Exodus 12:33 tells us, "The Egyptians were urgent with the people, to send them out of the land in haste; for they said, 'We are all dead men.'" Verses 35–36 then say that the people of Israel "asked of the Egyptians jewelry of silver and of gold, and clothing; and the Lord had given the people favor in the sight of the Egyptians, so that they let them have what they asked. Thus they despoiled the Egyptians."

According to the *Catechism*, "The seventh commandment forbids *unjustly* [emphasis added] taking or keeping the goods of one's neighbor and wronging him in any way with respect to his goods" (CCC 2401). This wasn't stealing. It was a case of the Hebrews asking for and receiving just compensation for slavery, or what we would now call reparations.

DASHING BABIES AGAINST THE ROCK

Some people think that Psalm 137:8–9 is indisputable proof that the Bible not only records evil, but that it commands and even applauds it. *The Oxford Handbook of the Psalms* even calls this passage "the most horrifying psalm of all."[446] It reads, "O daughter of Babylon, you devastator! Happy shall he be who repays you with what you have done to us! Happy shall he be who takes your little ones and dashes them against the rock!"

This certainly stands in stark contrast to Jesus' command to "love your enemies," but is it an irresolvable moral difficulty? Remember that we must evaluate Scripture passages in light of their genre. One reason we know this passage is in the poetic genre is because it is found in the Psalms, but it also falls under a special category of psalmic literature known as *imprecatory psalms*. These are psalms that involve the author asking God to curse or harm his enemies. According to the *Catholic Bible Dictionary*,

> [The Psalm's] theological message is expressed through a range of human emotions and sentiments, from joy and contentment to sadness and despair, and even to anger and indignation. Even curses have their place in the psalms . . . The imprecatory psalms represent anguish of a nation beset by its enemies who do not acknowledge the One God. Even these "curse" Psalms are an acknowledgment of God's suzerainty [i.e., Lordship] over the whole world.[447]

The prayers in the Psalms help us resist the temptation to treat God as our "employer," or someone we hide our true feelings from because we are afraid of being disciplined. True, we must obey and respect God as we do an employer, but unlike most employers God is our Father (Matt. 6:9, Rom. 8:15) and he wants us to cast all our anxiety on him because he cares for us (1 Pet. 5:7). The Psalmist understands this, so when he feels forsaken by God, he says so (Ps. 22:1), but when he feels like an unworthy worm, he says that, too (Ps. 22:6). And in some cases, the Psalmist expresses heartfelt anger at what seems to be a lack of punishment against evildoers. Psalm 137 is one of these cases where a believer pours out his heart to God in prayer.

In this psalm, the author laments how he and his fellow Jews have been taken into captivity in Babylon. Keep in mind that when cities in the ancient world were conquered, the inhabitants were rarely shown mercy, regardless of how young they were. When the Psalmist talks about babies being dashed against a rock he no doubt thought of his fellow Jews, and possibly his own family, who had been brutally murdered. This theme is also found in passages like Hosea 13:16 and 2 Kings 8:12, which describe pregnant women being cut open and having their unborn children ripped out of them.

Psalm 137 is a cry to God to justly punish the Babylonians; it is not, as atheist Ophelia Benson interpreted it, "God tell[ing] you to dash the Babylonian babies against the rocks."[448] The psalm takes the form of a warning, telling the Babylonians that, even though they gleefully devastated Jerusalem, there will come a day when another empire (in this case, the Persians) will gleefully carry out the same atrocities against them.

Do the imprecatory psalms prove the Bible is evil? No. They only prove that the word of God is fully divine in its inspiration and fully human in its composition. In other words, human beings were the real authors of Scripture, so human worldviews and human emotions can be found within the Bible's pages. Also keep in mind that the psalmist's worldview was limited. He did not know of Christ's future victory over evil and Christ's future command to love our enemies. As a result, the best response he hoped for in the face of the tremendous evils he and his family suffered was some kind of retributive justice in this life.

But God was able to use this author's words to convey a literal truth about war as well as a deeper spiritual truth for believers who read the Psalms today. One example is found in St. Augustine, who said of this passage, "What are the little ones of Babylon? Evil desires at their birth . . . by no means let it gain the strength of evil habit; when it is little, dash it. But you fear, lest though dashed it die not; 'Dash it against the Rock; and that Rock is Christ'" (1 Cor. 10:4).[449]

OBSCENE PORNOGRAPHY?

In Hong Kong, the Obscene Articles Tribunal censors books and materials that are deemed "indecent" or "obscene." In 2007, the tribunal ruled that a student magazine that asked readers if they ever fantasized about incest or bestiality was indecent and should be banned. In response to the government's decision, over two thousand Hong Kong residents petitioned the government to rule that the Bible was also indecent because it referred to things like cannibalism and rape.[450] Critics in the United States have also likened the Bible to pornography because it contains "sex, obscenity, and filth."[451]

Is it accurate to say that the Bible contains obscenity or pornography?

Pornography comes from the Greek words *pornea*, which means "prostitute," and *graphas*, which means "writings." Pornography is literally, "the writings of prostitutes." It accomplishes through paper or pixel what a prostitute does with her body: the sexual arousal of a client. The difference between tasteful art or educational materials that feature nudity and pornography is that the latter uses the naked body as a means to arouse the viewer while the former wills a completely different end. For example, if you told Michelangelo that the nude images on the Sistine Chapel ceiling were arousing he would be perplexed or disgusted, but if you said the same thing to a pornographer he wouldn't be surprised at all, because arousal is the goal of his "craft."

Of course, it's not always easy to define what is and isn't pornography, but when it comes to recognizing that something is pornographic we can agree with the sentiment of Supreme Court Justice Potter Stewart: "I know it when I see it."[452] In that respect, the Bible is not pornographic, because it does not describe sexual acts with the intention of arousing the reader.

When the topic of sex comes up, the biblical authors use euphemism or generic language in their descriptions. People in the Bible may "lie together" or "come into" someone, but there are no pornographic descriptions designed to titillate and arouse the reader. After all, do you know anyone who hid the Bible under their bed so that their parent's wouldn't find their naughty collection of ancient texts?

But that doesn't mean that the theme of healthy sexuality isn't celebrated in Scripture. For example, in the Song of Solomon, a lover says to his beloved, "Your two breasts are like two fawns, twins of a gazelle . . . A garden locked is my sister, my bride. A garden locked, a fountain sealed . . . Awake, O north wind, and come, O south wind! Blow upon my garden, let its fragrance be wafted abroad. Let my beloved come to his garden, and eat its choicest fruits" (Song of Sol. 4:5, 12, 16).

But not all the metaphors in the Bible are as veiled as this one. Consider Ezekiel's metaphorical description of Israel's idolatry. He writes, "She lusted after her lovers, whose genitals were like those of donkeys and whose emission was like that of horses" (Ezek. 23:20, NIV). Dan Barker says of verses as graphic as this one, "God uses language that would never be allowed in Church . . . Is this proper language for a moral example?"[453]

Certainly, these verses contain graphic descriptions that may not be appropriate for some audiences, but how does that prove that the Bible itself is immoral or uninspired? History and medical textbooks include images and descriptions that might upset the young or the squeamish, but they are good for educating those who can properly receive their contents. The same is true for the small number of graphic texts in the Bible that powerfully communicate important truths to God's people. Indeed, some people need to be shocked or unsettled (at least at first) in order to receive a message they may not have wanted to hear in the first place. Just because a biblical writer employed a graphic way of revealing God's truth does not prove his account is in error or uninspired.

Bad Role Models?

The Claim: The Bible has a terrible moral compass when it comes to its own heroes. These men murder innocent people and even allow their daughters to be raped or burned alive. Even supposedly perfect Jesus teaches people to do things like hate their families and cut off their limbs!

Pope Benedict XVI said in *Verbum Domini,* "Revelation is suited to the cultural and moral level of distant times and thus describes facts and customs, such as cheating and trickery, and acts of violence and massacre, without explicitly denouncing the immorality of such things."[454] He goes on to say that modern readers can often be taken aback by these incidents and miss the context that explains them. So let's take a look at a few of these cases and fill in the context a modern reader might miss.

Righteous Lot

Genesis 19 tells the story of how Abraham's nephew Lot, along with his family, escaped the city of Sodom just before God destroyed it. 2 Peter 2:7 references this event and says that God "rescued righteous Lot, greatly distressed by the licentiousness of the wicked."

However, it seems odd that the Bible calls Lot "righteous" given what Lot did when an angry mob of Sodomites tried to rape the angels who were lodging with him. Instead of standing up to the mob, Lot offered his two daughters for the mob to rape! In Genesis 19:7–8, Lot says, "I beg you, my brothers, do not act so wickedly. Behold, I have two daughters who have not known man; let me bring them out to you, and do to them as you please; only do nothing to these men, for they have come under the shelter of my roof."

How can the Bible say Lot was righteous when he was willing to do something so terrible to his own daughters? Jason Long says, "A man with the moral qualities of Lot cannot be regarded as righteous unless you discount the inherent rights of all people, more specifically, the inherent rights of women."[455]

In order to understand why 2 Peter 2:7 calls Lot righteous, we need to look at the whole chapter's context. In 2 Peter 2, the author is warning Christians about false teachers who were spreading heresy. The author reassures listeners who may have faced these heretics, telling them, "the Lord knows how to rescue the godly from trial, and to keep the unrighteous under punishment until the day of judgment" (2 Pet. 2:9). Peter's evidence for this included references to God rescuing Noah and Lot's families because those men were beacons of righteousness in their respective fallen communities.

When it comes to Lot, 2 Peter 2:7 says he struggled against Sodom's sexual sins and Genesis 19:1 says Lot sat at "the city gate." In the ancient world the city gate was a place for commercial activity as well as a place where disputes were settled. For example, Deuteronomy 21:18–21 says that an unruly son would be brought to judges at the city gate, and Ruth 4:1–11 describes how Boaz met with elders at the city gate in order to settle a legal dispute.

Therefore, Lot probably held a position of influence in Sodom and may have mediated disputes among its residents.[456] Since even evildoers want justice when they've been wronged, Lot's position as a judge is evidence of his impartiality and righteousness.

However, this may also have caused Sodom's residents to resent him. Indeed, the mob at Lot's door berates him for refusing to hand over his guests, saying, "This fellow came to sojourn, and he would play the judge! Now we will deal worse with you than with them" (Gen. 19:9).

Lot's righteousness is also seen in his hospitality toward strangers, which was a sacred duty in ancient Mesopotamia. In a time when you couldn't go to a department store for clothes or check in at a motel when you needed shelter, the kindness of strangers could mean the difference between life and death. Lot understood that anyone who slept outside in Sodom was in grave danger of being attacked. Therefore, he offered the city's visitors shelter and wouldn't take no for an answer (Gen. 19:1–3).

Even Lot's misguided decision to offer his daughters to the mob can be seen as an act of hospitality meant to protect the guests dwelling under his roof. The *Catholic Encyclopedia* says, "Lot interceded in behalf of his guests in accordance with his duties as host, which are most sacred in the East, but made the mistake of placing them above his duties as a father by offering his two daughters to the wicked designs of the Sodomites."[457]

It's important to remember that righteousness is not a synonym for perfection.[458] John the Baptist's father, Zechariah, was called righteous even though God punished him for not believing the angel's message about the future birth of his son (Luke 1:6–20). Saying Lot was righteous does not mean the author of 2 Peter condoned Lot's decision to offer his daughters to the mob. Of course, a critic could object that if God was willing to punish the Sodomites for their wicked behavior, then why didn't God punish Lot for his wicked cowardice? But the Genesis narrative actually implies that Lot was punished, since he later gets what can only be described as a humiliating form of "just deserts."

After fleeing into the hill country, Lot's daughters realize there are no men living in the vicinity. Perhaps due to the depraved lifestyle they observed in Sodom, the girls made up for this dearth of men by getting their father drunk and having sex with him (Gen. 19:30–36). In an ironic turn of events, Lot, who had previously offered his daughters up to be raped, has now been raped by his own daughters. Even worse, Lot's progeny go on to become the ancestors of Israel's enemies, the Moabites and the Ammonites (Gen. 19:37–38).

Critics like Brian Baker, who read this story and conclude in capital letters that "BIBLICAL FAMILY VALUES—INCLUDES INCEST!" completely miss the point of the story.[459] To their complaints we can say, "The Bible is not a sterile collection of perfect people who always follow God's will. It is instead a drama about how God redeemed imperfect people and used them, in spite of their flaws, to accomplish his sovereign and holy will for mankind."

SCHEMING JACOB

In Genesis 27, Jacob steals the familial blessing by pretending to be his brother, Esau, in front of his nearly blind father, Isaac. Even though Jacob is one of the three revered patriarchs, or founding fathers of the nation of Israel, his deception seems to make him a bad role model for believers. Steve McRoberts says of the Bible, "This is supposed to be our 'moral instruction book.' I wonder what kind of an example Jacob is setting for us here."[46]

But as we've seen, the Bible was not written as an "instruction book." The biblical authors do not always recommend what they record and sometimes what they record is an abject lesson in what *not to do*. Notice, for example, that God does not command or praise Jacob's deception. We can even see how God tolerated it in order to allow Israel to become a mighty nation. But that doesn't mean God let Jacob off the hook. Through divine Providence, God allowed Jacob to be punished in the future with evils similar to the ones he committed against Isaac and Esau.

In Genesis 29, Jacob's uncle Laban had his less attractive daughter, Leah, impersonate his more attractive daughter, Rachel, in order to trick Jacob into marrying her. Just as Jacob impersonated Esau to steal the blessing, Leah impersonates Rachel so that Laban could essentially steal Jacob. Or consider Genesis 37, which describes how Jacob's sons lie to him and say wild animals have killed their brother Joseph, when in reality the brothers sold Joseph into slavery. As proof of their story, the brothers show their father the tattered, blood-soaked remains of the coat Jacob gave Joseph. Just as Jacob duped Isaac by donning animal skin that concealed his true identity, the brothers dupe Jacob with animal skin that also conceals the truth.[461]

However, after Joseph is sold to the Egyptians he becomes a high-ranking official and ends up saving his family, along with the rest of Egypt, from a famine. When Joseph revealed to his brothers who he was, he said of their original crime, "you meant evil against me; but God meant it for good, to bring it about that many people should be kept alive, as they are today" (Gen. 50:20). In other words, the stories about Jacob's deceptions don't teach the value of lying. They show instead that our sins always have a way of catching up with us. Fortunately, God can use our moral failings to bring about even greater goods.

Rash Jephthah

The book of Judges recounts how Israel constantly fell into idolatry and, as a result, was punished through foreign domination. But God had mercy on Israel and sent a series of judges to deliver his people from their oppressors. While some of these judges were good people, others were of a quality that apostate Israel deserved. One of those less-than-desirable judges was Jephthah, a man whose half brothers had previously driven him out of his own home and stolen his inheritance. This act of betrayal drove Jephthah to a life of crime in order to support himself.

However, Jephthah's life took a dramatic turn when the leaders of a region of Israel called Gilead asked him to drive out the Ammonites who were oppressing them. Jephthah accepted their offer and, after a peaceful approach failed, he prepared to go to war. He didn't know if he could defeat the Ammonites, so he made the following vow to God: "If you will give the Ammonites into my hand, then whoever comes forth from the doors of my house to meet me, when I return victorious from the Ammonites, shall be the Lord's, and I will offer him up for a burnt offering" (Judg. 11:30–31).

Sure enough, in the next verse God delivered the Ammonites into Jephthah's hands and Jephthah returned home, to be shocked by the unintended consequence of his vow. Judges 11:34–35 says,

> Then Jephthah came to his home at Mizpah; and behold, his daughter came out to meet him with timbrels and with dances;

she was his only child; beside her he had neither son nor daughter. And when he saw her, he tore his clothes, and said, "Alas, my daughter! you have brought me very low, and you have become the cause of great trouble to me; for I have opened my mouth to the Lord, and I cannot take back my vow."

Some exegetes say that Jephthah did not actually burn his daughter alive but offered her up as a consecrated virgin.[462] But this seems to contradict verse 39, which says Jephthah "did with her according to his vow which he had made." The vow only mentions "burnt offerings," not consecrated virginity.

Therefore, let's suppose that the worst-case scenario is true, that Jephthah kept his vow to God and offered his daughter as a burnt sacrifice. What would this prove? It's certainly a sad story, but the biblical text does not praise Jephthah for what he did, and even Jephthah realized that the vow he made was foolish. Remember, the book of Judges is more a description of what not to do then it is a model for how believers should behave.

Endorsing Human Sacrifice?

Some critics say that this story is evidence that the Bible possesses moral failings, including a heinous acceptance of human sacrifice. Scripture scholar and inerrancy critic Thom Stark says that Jephthah's actions only make sense if the Israelites thought that God would accept a human sacrifice. According to him, "No repudiation of the sacrifice is found here. Nor does Yahweh intervene to spare the life of Jephthah's daughter."[463] Mark Roncace agrees, "The lack of divine intervention stands in striking contrast to the Abraham and Isaac story."[464]

But God had already told the Israelites that sacrificing sons and daughters as burnt offerings was "abominable" (Deut. 12:31). This lesson was taught as far back as the story of Abraham and eventually became part of Israel's national identity. This text in Judges doesn't have to explicitly condemn Jephthah any more than other texts that describe wicked behavior have to condemn what they record.

As for God's lack of intervention, unlike in the case of Isaac, God never commanded Jephthah to offer his daughter as a sacrifice. Instead, as God often does in Scripture (and life in general), he allowed the consequences of Jephthah's bad decisions to be his own punishment—even if that involved Jephthah harming someone he cared about. Jephthah wasn't planning to sacrifice his child to God, since he only had one daughter, and he was devastated at the thought of sacrificing her (Judg. 11:34–35). This would be a strange reaction if Jephthah had planned to sacrifice her all along. But that raises another question: who or what did Jephthah intend to sacrifice if not his own daughter?

Perhaps he thought he could sacrifice a pet that greeted him when he returned. The Hebrew word *asher* in Judges 11:31 can be translated as "whatever" instead of "whoever." Therefore, Jephthah could have said, "*whatever* comes forth from the doors of my house to meet me . . ."[465] Indeed, when many modern people return home their dogs are the first to greet them.

Stark says this is a tenuous conclusion because most animals were kept outside. But smaller farm animals and domestic animals could wander in and out of ancient Israelite houses. Some houses were even built to house animals on the first floor and people on the second.[466] Archaeologists in Israel have also discovered the bones of an elderly woman who was buried with a puppy in the year 10,000 B.C., and the book of Tobit describes a young Jew who had a dog as a companion (Tob. 11:4).[467]

But it is also plausible that Jephthah planned to sacrifice one of his slaves to Yahweh in exchange for a military victory. Even if this were the case it doesn't demonstrate an endorsement of that behavior on the part of the narrator. Most of the protagonists in the book of Judges engaged in wicked behavior, so we shouldn't expect all their actions to be commendable. Jephthah may have believed that Yahweh would accept a human sacrifice, not because Yahweh revealed this to the Israelites, but because other nations sacrificed humans to their deities and military victories sometimes followed these barbaric rituals.[468]

According to *The Bible Knowledge Commentary*, "Though Jephthah made his rash vow, he probably knew something about
the prohibitions of the Mosaic Law against human sacrifice. Yet
his half-pagan background, combined with the general law-
less spirit dominating the period of the Judges (e.g. 17:6; 21:25),
could readily account for his fulfilling this vow."[469]

Another argument critics make is that Judges 11:29 says that
"the spirit of the Lord came upon Jephthah." Doesn't that mean
God wanted Jephthah to sacrifice his daughter? The spirit of the
Lord did come upon Jephthah, but that doesn't mean that God
endorsed everything Jephthah did after that point. For example,
the spirit of the Lord came upon Samson in Judges 15:14, but
not long after that Samson visited a prostitute. According to
Old Testament scholar Christopher Wright, "One thing that is
said quite often about these 'judges' is that the Spirit of the Lord
(Yahweh) would come upon them. When this happened it was
a signal for action. Empowered by the Spirit of the Lord, they
could exercise charismatic leadership and do valiant exploits
that were recited around the campfires of Israel for generations
to come."[470]

Wright then lists seven instances where this phrase is used, and
each describes a person being strengthened for war (including Jephthah). The passages do not describe the person being protected
from sin in general. For example, Wright says the superhuman
power given to Samson clearly exposed his all-too-human weaknesses. A similar analysis can be applied to Jephthah, whose skill
in combat did not aid him in fighting spiritual temptations.[471]

Finally, the critic could object that Jephthah was praised in
Hebrews 11 alongside other heroes of the Jewish faith, and so
God did condone his sacrifice.[472] Hebrews 11:32–33 says, "For
time would fail me to tell of Gideon, Barak, Samson, Jephthah,
of David and Samuel and the prophets—who through faith conquered kingdoms, enforced justice, received promises, stopped
the mouths of lions."

But the list of "heroes" in this chapter only describes people
who were able to do mighty deeds because of their faith in God.

Hebrews 11 does not say that these people were without serious character flaws. After all, Rahab was a prostitute, Gideon practiced idolatry, Samson had a weakness for women, and David committed adultery and murder. Jephthah's rash vow only shows that he was a sinful human being who God used for the benefit of Israel—not that God willed or desired that Jephthah engage in human sacrifice.

FOOLISH SAMSON

Samson was the last recorded judge to rule over Israel, and critics often use his exploits as ammunition against the Bible's morality. Best-selling author and cognitive psychologist Steven Pinker described Samson this way:

> Samson establishes his reputation by killing thirty men during his wedding feast because he needs their clothing to pay off a bet. Then to avenge the killing of his wife and her father, he slaughters a thousand Philistines and sets fire to their crops; after escaping capture, he kills another thousand with the jawbone of an ass. When he is finally captured and his eyes are burned out, God gives him the strength for a 9/11-like suicide attack in which he implodes a large building, crushing the three thousand men and women who are worshipping inside it.[473]

Although it's possible that these stories are not literal, most critics would probably still object to them because they promote immorality. But as is often the case with critiques of the Bible, this summary grossly oversimplifies the events in question and ignores their historical context.

During this time in history, God allowed the Philistines to oppress the Israelites because of Israel's constant unfaithfulness to God. Samson was born in the midst of this struggle and was consecrated from birth to be a Nazarite (Judg. 13:7). According to the Nazarite vow, Samson was expected to abstain from alcohol, not touch corpses, and never cut his hair (Num. 6:1–21). The angel of the Lord even told Samson's mother that he "shall begin to deliver Israel from the hand of the Philistines" (Judg. 13:5).

But when it came to being a hero for his people, Samson was not a flawless "Captain Israel" as much as he was an antihero—a generally good person with deep character flaws. For example, the Philistines were oppressing the Israelites, but Samson wanted to marry a Philistine woman. Even though his parents disapproved of the marriage, God anticipated Samson's foolish decision and was "seeking an occasion against the Philistines" (Judg. 14:4).

More evidence of Samson's flaws is seen in the fact that, while on the way to his wedding, Samson broke his Nazarite vow by handling a lion's corpse and eating honey that had formed in it (Judg. 14:8–9). In fact, the honey incident inspired Samson to make a bet with the thirty Philistine groomsmen at his wedding. If they could answer Samson's riddle then he would give them each a set of fine linens. The riddle was, "Out of the eater came something to eat. Out of the strong came something sweet" (Judg. 14:14). The Philistines couldn't solve the riddle and threatened to burn Samson's wife and her father to death unless she found out for them.

Samson's wife begged him for the answer, and when she got it, she told the Philistine groomsmen. Samson knew they only discovered the answer by threatening his wife, so "the Spirit of the Lord came mightily upon him, and he went down to Ashkelon and killed thirty men of the town, and took their spoil and gave the festal garments to those who had told the riddle" (Judg. 14:19). Samson didn't kill thirty innocent people because he was mad that he lost an honest bet. The actions of the Philistines finally made it clear to him what kind of people they were. Samson was now motivated to strike at Israel's enemy just as God intended—and he did just that in Ashkelon, which Joshua 13:3 tells us was a prominent Philistine city.

After the wedding incident, Samson's father-in-law gave his fiancée to his best man, which prompted Samson to retaliate by setting the Philistine's crops on fire (Judg. 15:4–5). The Philistine then retaliated by burning Samson's ex-fiancée and her father to death. In order to keep the situation from escalating further, the Israelites handed Samson over to the Philistines, but to the Philistines' surprise he broke free from his bonds and killed a thousand of their soldiers with the jawbone of an ass. Once again, Samson did not go on a senseless killing spree. He was more like Rambo fighting a much larger military force that was unjustly occupying and oppressing the Israelites.

After he escaped, Samson fell in love with a woman from the valley of Sorek named Delilah, who later betrayed him to the Philistines. His story ends with him chained to two pillars in the temple of Dagon, where he was mocked during a sacrifice to the Philistine deity. Samson prayed to the Lord to have his strength return to him, and when God granted his prayer Samson tore down the temple's main pillars. It collapsed, and three thousand of the people gathered there, including the lords of the Philistines, perished.

In his book *Laying Down the Sword: Why We Can't Ignore the Bible's Violent Verses,* Philip Jenkins asks, "Could a text offer better support for a modern-day suicide attack, in Gaza or elsewhere?"[474] But was this a suicide attack, as Pinker and Jenkins allege? Hardly. Imagine an imprisoned soldier chained up in a stadium full of enemy troops. They mock him, and revel in their victory over "the enemy" as they wait to execute him. If such a soldier was able to kill his captors before his own execution, we would probably consider it a fair retaliation and not a cold and heartless "terror attack" designed to strike at innocent civilians.

Samson's exploits were certainly violent, but when read in their proper context we see they were the actions of an imperfect man God used to strike at the enemy of his people. St. Augustine made the same point when he said the following about the stories found in Judges: "The Spirit of the Lord is at work in those who do good and those who do evil, in those who are aware and those who are unaware of what he [the Spirit] knows and does."[475]

Finally, Matthew Ramage offers us a helpful insight into why Sacred Scripture would include the moral failings of God's people. The sacred author, he said, "probably has the practical goal of getting his audience to learn from the failures of his ancestors and to appreciate the work of divine pedagogy that had led the nation despite the successes and failures of its great men."[476]

Sinful Jesus?

Because Jesus lived in a foreign culture thousands of years ago, it can be easy to misunderstand things he said. Take Mark 4:11–12, in which Jesus says, "To you has been given the secret of the kingdom of God, but for those outside everything is in parables; that they may indeed see but not perceive, and may indeed hear but not understand; lest they should turn again, and be forgiven." Does this mean that Jesus confuses people so they will be damned?

To understand this passage, we must recognize that Jesus is quoting part of Isaiah's call to be a prophet (Isa. 6:9). In that context, God is basically saying to Isaiah, "Go ahead and preach my judgment, but don't expect anyone to listen to you." The parable of the sower illustrates that God's message will sometimes be received by hard-hearted people who will not "turn and be forgiven." The message is preached, however, for the benefit of the openhearted, who are like "good soil"—people who *will* turn and be forgiven. Just because some won't accept the message doesn't mean it should not be preached for the benefit of those who will.

Consider also Jesus' assertion, "If any one comes to me and does not hate his own father and mother and wife and children and brothers and sisters, yes, and even his own life, he cannot be my disciple" (Luke 14:26). Does Jesus really want us to hate our families and even ourselves?

First, we should remember that as a good Jew, Jesus obeyed the Ten Commandments, including the fourth: Honor your father and mother. He even criticized the Pharisees for shirking this responsibility (Mark 7:9–13). In Hebrew, the phrase "to hate someone" does not necessarily mean unconditionally despising; it can also mean "to love less than others."[477] Jesus knew that everything on earth, even love of family, must be second to our love of

God. Matthew 10:37–38 describes the same saying, but rephrases it slightly so that the meaning is easier to discern: "He who loves father or mother more than me is not worthy of me; and he who loves son or daughter more than me is not worthy of me; and he who does not take his cross and follow me is not worthy of me."

This also explains Jesus' seemingly harsh words in Matthew 10:34: "I have not come to bring peace, but a sword." What Jesus meant is that his gospel is not going to unite people under comfortable truths. It's going instead to divide them because of its uncomfortable truths. According to Craig Evans, "This was very true in the first several decades of the young Church, for in its infancy the church was made up entirely of Jewish people . . . The result was division in Jewish families and in synagogues."[478] This confirms Christ's prediction that his Church would be persecuted (i.e., "the sword") and that all Christians, then and now, must be ready for hatred and rejection—even from their own family members.

What about the seeming contradiction involving Jesus telling people that if they call people fools they are liable to go to hell (Matt. 5:22), while he himself called the Pharisees fools (Matt. 23:17)?[479] Once again, we must ask what the context is behind these verses. In Matthew 5, Jesus is saying that not only should we obey the Commandments, we should purge from our hearts the attitudes and emotions that lie at the root of the offenses against the Commandments. For example, lust is always the root cause of adultery, so just as we shouldn't commit adultery, we shouldn't lust either (Matt. 5:27–28). Likewise, anger is the root cause of murder, so we should not be unjustly angry with our brothers (Matt. 5:21–22). In Matthew 5:22, Jesus is condemning unjustified anger and envy that motivated murderers like Cain. He was not condemning *righteous* anger or even strong admonishments against those who commit legitimate evils, such as the Pharisees.

Another example is the incident in which Jesus curses a fig tree for its unfruitfulness (Matt. 21:18–22, Mark 11:12–25). What sane person would curse a tree for not bearing fruit, especially when it wasn't even the season for fruit? Here Jesus is using the example of the fig tree to make a larger point about Jerusalem. Just as the fig tree will be destroyed because its fruit was not ready for an unexpected encounter, so too will Jerusalem be destroyed by the Romans—it happens in A.D. 70—because the spiritual fruitlessness of the people, caused by their hardness of heart, will bring God's judgment upon them.[480]

JESUS' BAD ADVICE?

The Jewish comedian Jackie Mason once said, "A rabbi would never exaggerate. A rabbi composes. He creates thoughts. He tells stories that may never have happened. But he does not exaggerate!"[481]

Of course, hyperbole or exaggerated rhetoric has been a common tool among rabbis since before the time of Christ. The Talmud (a collection of ancient rabbinical writings) records the second-century Rabbi Bar Yochai saying, "Better had a man throw himself into a fiery furnace than publicly put his neighbor to shame."[482] This is very similar to Jesus' words in Matthew 5:29: "If your right eye causes you to sin, pluck it out and throw it away; it is better that you lose one of your members than that your whole body be thrown into hell."

Should we actually pluck our eyes out or jump into furnaces? No. Jesus is just showing us that sin is serious and we should do whatever it takes to avoid it. Jesus' other commands to exceed the righteousness of the scribes and Pharisees (Matt. 5:20), sell all you have and distribute it to the poor (Luke 18:22), and his warning that "it is easier for a camel to go through the eye of a needle than for a rich man to enter the kingdom of God" (Luke 18:25) must be interpreted according to this hyperbolic framework.

They also must be interpreted within the context of wealth in the ancient world where, unlike today, it was almost always acquired by oppressing the poor. According to biblical scholar Bruce Malina,

By and large, only the dishonorable rich, the dishonorable nonelites, and those beyond the pale of public opinion (such as city elites, governors, regional kings) could accumulate wealth with impunity. This they did in a number of ways, notably by trading, tax collecting, and money lending . . . In the first century [these methods] would all be considered dishonorable and immoral forms of usury."[483]

The ethical demands in passages like Luke 18:22–25 and Matthew 5:20 should not be ignored (e.g., strive for virtue, don't love possessions more than God), but the passages themselves should not be taken literally, lest one thinks he must become a homeless student of the Talmud in order to get to heaven.

Rabbinic hyperbole also explains this promise Jesus made to his disciples: "Truly, I say to you, whoever says to this mountain, 'Be taken up and cast into the sea,' and does not doubt in his heart, but believes that what he says will come to pass, it will be done for him. Therefore I tell you, whatever you ask in prayer, believe that you receive it, and you will" (Mark 11:22–24; see also Matt. 21:22, John 14:14). The phrase "move mountains" is probably a metaphor referring to the ability to do amazing or impossible feats in general (the Talmud calls some exceptional rabbis "uprooters of mountains").[484] However, a question still remains: why don't we always receive what we ask for in prayer?

James 4:3 says it is because "we ask wrongly" or because something we ask for contradicts God's will. This can mean requests that knowingly contradict God's will (e.g., selfish or sinful prayers) or that unknowingly contradict God's will. This happens because our limited human knowledge doesn't allow us to see the good plan God has for us in spite of present suffering or hardship.

The point of prayer isn't to get what we want. It's to come before God in childlike humility, recognizing that we depend on him for everything. By offering up our prayers in this way, over time our wills become more aligned to God's will. Then, when we ask for something that corresponds to God's will, our prayers have the dignity of being real causes in the world. They really cause the effect for which we petition.[485] The *Catechism* says,

What is the image of God that motivates our prayer: an instrument to be used? or the Father of our Lord Jesus Christ? . . . All our petitions were gathered up, once for all, in his cry on the Cross and, in his Resurrection, heard by the Father. This is why he never ceases to intercede for us with the Father. If our prayer is resolutely united with that of Jesus, in trust and boldness as children, we obtain all that we ask in his name, even more than any particular thing: the Holy Spirit himself, who contains all gifts" (CCC 2735, 2741).

Of course, much more can be said on the topic of prayer, but the main point is this: passages like Mark 11:22–24 are not proof that "nothing fails like prayer," because the passages are metaphorical. They teach us that we must completely trust in God's will when we pray, not that God is a kind of genie who will grant us unlimited wishes.

There are many other examples of Jesus saying things that, to our modern ears, may seem absurd or even impossible. But it's important to remember that theologians and biblical scholars have examined these sayings for centuries and have provided explanations that help us more clearly understand what Jesus meant. If Jesus is the resurrected Son of God, then we must give him the benefit of the doubt. Since the Son of God cannot sin or give us bad advice, it follows that Jesus' hard sayings must only be "hard" because we don't understand what he meant—not because he made a mistake.

18

Anti-Woman?

The Claim: The Bible consistently portrays women as being less valuable than men, and it encourages men to mistreat women. This ranges from the demeaning command to be "silent in church" to the barbaric command to rape female prisoners of war.

During one of my appearances on the radio show *Catholic Answers Live,* we invited callers to answer the question "Why are you an atheist?" One woman gave this rationale: "The reason I am an atheist is because when you read the Bible you see that it is very anti-woman. I mean Paul says women shouldn't be allowed to speak in Church."

What's baffling about this response is that, at most, all this would prove is that some parts of the Bible are not divinely inspired. Although I wouldn't recommend it, one could still believe in God and Christ's divinity without affirming the truth of everything in Sacred Scripture. So why do atheists like this woman not consider this option?

I think that when some people read Scripture passages that seem to denigrate women or endorse a moral evil, their negative emotional reaction clouds their ability to assess the issue. They instead hastily leap to the conclusion that the Bible's "anti-woman" rhetoric is proof the Bible is only the product of fallible human authorship.

Of course, it's true that in the contexts of ancient Judaism and Christianity women were subject to male rule and had fewer rights than men. They lived in a patriarchal culture that had always existed and would continue to exist for many centuries. Women around the world still struggle for equality with men. But this does not mean that the biblical writers endorsed the view that women were merely property or that men could mistreat them. In fact, Scripture teaches God's ideal of male and female equality along with the positive steps God's people took to promote that equality.

MAN AND WOMAN HE CREATED THEM

Genesis 1:27 says, "God created man in his own image, in the image of God he created him; male and female he created them." It is not simply biological males who share in the image and likeness of God; women, too, share this honor. In fact, God's eternal wisdom is personified as a woman (Prov. 8). But doesn't Genesis 2:18 contradict this notion of equality when it says that Eve will be Adam's "helper"? That doesn't sound very honorable, at least in modern translations that make Eve sound like Adam's secretary and cook.

The Hebrew word often translated "helper," *ezer,* more closely represents a combination of the concepts "rescue" and "strength" than it does "domestic servant."[486] In the Old Testament, the only human ever described as an *ezer* is Eve.[487] In every other case this word refers to things like armies helping kingdoms or God helping his people. If Genesis 2:18 is offensive because it says Eve is Adam's helper, then Psalm 115:11 is offensive because it says God is our helper. The Psalmist says, "You who fear the Lord, trust in the Lord! He is their help (*ez-ram*) and their shield."

God's ideal for men and women was equality and mutual servitude, but the Bible is also a story of man's fall from grace. Paul says man is a slave to sin (Rom. 7:14) and his appetite for evil manifests itself in disordered desires and perversions of the good. For example, sexual union is a good thing, but when it occurs between the unmarried it perverts the good of sex and often results in evils like sexually transmitted diseases, children born out of wedlock, and abortion. Or consider money, which is not evil itself, but becomes evil when its use is perverted out of greed or "the love of money" (1 Tim. 6:10).

Just as sin corrupts sex and money, it also corrupts the naturally good relationship that exists between men and women. For example, after Adam and Eve disobeyed God, they were told of the consequences of their disobedience, both for themselves and their descendants. Adam was cursed with painful labor in the field while Eve was cursed with painful labor at birth (Gen. 3:16–19). Eve was also told, "your desire shall be for your husband, and he shall rule over you" (Gen. 3:16). Since this verse is included with the curses associated with the fall, and not with God's original plan for life in Eden, we can assume it was not something God intended for human beings. Instead, as Pope St. John Paul II noted in his encyclical *Mulieris Dignitatem*,

> [T]he words of the biblical text [Gen. 3:16] directly concern original sin and its lasting consequences in man and woman. Burdened by hereditary sinfulness, they bear within themselves the constant "inclination to sin," the tendency to go against the moral order which corresponds to the rational nature and dignity of man and woman as persons.[488]

THE FALL

Critics often describe the Bible's depiction of the fall of man as an account that places the blame for humanity's suffering squarely on Eve's shoulders. But this is not an accurate summary of Genesis 3. For example, when the serpent assures Eve, "You will not die" (Gen. 3:4), the Hebrew word for "you" is in the plural form, as when we say "you all" or "y'all." When Eve partakes of the fruit, the narrator says, "she also gave some to her husband, and he ate" (Gen. 3:6), evidence that Adam was standing right next to Eve when the temptation occurred, so he is to blame as well. Even if that were not the case, God had already told Adam not to eat the fruit (Gen. 2:17), so he would be culpable both for disobeying God and for failing to protect Eve.

The New Testament also primarily places the blame for mankind's original sin on Adam, not Eve. In Romans 5:12, we learn that "sin came into the world through *one man* [emphasis added] and death through sin, and so death spread to all men because all men sinned." In 1 Corinthians 15:22 Paul declares, "or as in *Adam* [emphasis added] all die, so also in Christ shall all be made alive."

That is not to say that Paul did not assign some blame to Eve, which is evident in 1 Timothy 2:14: "Adam was not deceived, but the woman was deceived and became a transgressor."[489] It's easy to assume that in this verse Adam is being praised for "not being deceived," but actually the opposite is true. As George Montague put it in his commentary on 1 Timothy,

> Paul's argument is not that Adam did not sin whereas Eve did, but that Eve failed by *being deceived* . . . Adam was not deceived; he just *did* it. That, morally speaking, was worse not only because he disobeyed God's explicit command but because he failed to exercise his responsibility to intervene with Eve at the moment of her weakness.[490]

INHERENT IMPURITY?

The book of Genesis isn't the only place in the Pentateuch where critics say women are demeaned. Leviticus 12:1–5 says that if a woman gives birth to a male child she will be unclean for one week and must be purified for thirty-three days. But if she gives birth to a female child she will be unclean for two weeks and must be purified for sixty-six days. Does this text mean that women are more unclean and so giving birth to them requires more purification than birthing men?[491]

Keep in mind that the uncleanness referred to in this passage is not moral in nature. It instead refers to ritual uncleanness that comes from touching bodily fluids. It's similar to other parts of Leviticus that tell women how to be purified from menstrual flows (Lev. 15:19) and men how to purify themselves after the involuntary emission of semen (Lev. 15:16). These biological functions aren't sinful; they just require ritual cleansing because they involve contact with powerful bodily fluids that were necessary for the creation of human life.

Still, why is the birth of a female child treated differently than the birth of a male child? Scholars have not reached a definitive answer and so several options have been proposed.[492] The Israelites may have accepted the popular ancient belief that women took longer to heal after giving birth to a girl than to a boy.[493] Another reason could be that newborn female infants often bleed from their vaginas and so their births would require more cleansing than a male's because more blood would be present.[494]

Of course, many critics say that the reason was that women were seen as being inferior to men and thus in need of more cleansing, but as Mark Rooker notes in his commentary on Leviticus, "[T]he sacrifices for male and female infant are identical [Lev. 12:6]. This observation supports the view that the male and female infants as well as male and female adults were considered equal in value before God."[495]

POLYGAMY

While attending a debate about whether marriage should be redefined to include same-sex couples, I noticed a person in the audience wearing a T-shirt adorned with the phrase "The Biblical View of Marriage." Underneath it were many different types of marriages that were allegedly recorded in the Bible, including polygamous marriages, in which one man had several wives. A critic might say, "Why should we care what the Bible says about marriage when it endorsed an evil like polygamy?"

But the Bible does not contain a general instruction for believers to be married to more than one person at the same time. In fact, Leviticus 18:18 prohibits a man from marrying his sister-in-law while his wife is still alive, and Deuteronomy 17:17 says that a ruler should not "multiply wives for himself" lest his heart turn away from God.

Some critics, however, erroneously conclude that 1 Timothy 3:2 ("a bishop must be above reproach, the husband of one wife") is evidence that early Christians practiced polygamy because bishops were warned not to have more than one wife. But

Paul uses a similar construction in 1 Timothy 5:9–12, where he says that a woman who has been previously consecrated to religious life may not marry, even though Paul allows remarriage upon the death of a spouse for laity (Rom. 7:2–3).

Paul's admonition in 1 Timothy 3 was probably against ordaining men to the office of bishop who had remarried. That's because the ideal candidate for that position was a celibate man. Although married men could assume this office (they may have been married when they first heard the gospel), it was not given to men who chose marriage over celibacy when given the opportunity to do so after the death of a spouse.[496]

The only verses that seem to explicitly contradict the Bible's negative stance on polygamy are the descriptions of David and Solomon's many wives. But remember rule number fourteen: "Just because it's recorded doesn't mean it's recommended." The book of 1 Kings 11:3 says that Solomon had 700 wives and 300 concubines, but it also says these women caused Solomon to "turn away his heart after other gods," just as Deuteronomy 17:17 said would happen.

The Bible's other depictions of polygamy fare no better. Its first description of polygamy, in Genesis 4:19, involves Lamech, who was a violent murderer. Jacob's polygamous relationship with Rachel and Leah led to marital discord and competition between his wives. Finally, many of the "bad kings" who reined during the divided kingdom, like Rehoboam, Abijah, Jehoiachin, and one of the worst kings of all, Ahab, practiced polygamy.[497]

So why didn't God condemn polygamy in the Old Testament if it was so harmful? Think back to when the Pharisees questioned Jesus about divorce. They asked Jesus, "Why then did Moses command one to give a certificate of divorce, and to put her away?" Jesus answered them, "For your hardness of heart Moses allowed you to divorce your wives, but from the beginning it was not so" (Matt. 19:8). Jesus then appealed to Genesis 2 as evidence that God's primary plan for marriage was permanence. The fact is, God did not intend marriage to include

ANTI-WOMAN? 241

divorce, and God even said he hates divorce (Mal. 2:16). Divorce was only allowed as an example of the divine accommodation of human weaknesses. St. Thomas Aquinas even argued that the evil of divorce was tolerated so that the greater evil of wife-murder would be prevented![498]

This brings us to rule fifteen: *Just because the Bible regulates it doesn't mean God recommends it.* For example, Exodus 21:18 describes what should happen "if men quarrel and one strikes the other with a stone or with his fist and the man does not die but keeps his bed." Clearly the sacred author is not commanding people to hit each other in the head with rocks. He is just giving sound advice about what should be done if something like this happens. Likewise, Exodus 21:10 and Deuteronomy 21:15 both describe a man with two wives and how he should treat his wives and children, but the texts don't recommend marrying two women in the first place.

Just as God tolerated the widespread practice of divorce even though it contradicted marriage's essential permanence, God allowed the ubiquitous practice of polygamy even though it contradicted marriage's essential exclusivity. This is another example of God patiently leading people to holiness instead of just giving them blunt commands that would have been ignored. Even today the Church has to regulate polygamy in spite of its strict prohibition of the practice. The *Catechism* says polygamy is a violation of the moral law but also says, "The Christian who has previously lived in polygamy has a grave duty in justice to honor the obligations contracted in regard to his former wives and his children" (CCC 2387).

This is not uncommon in places like Africa, where some men who come into the Church have more than one wife. In these cases the virtue of chastity compels these men to have sexual relations only with their actual spouse (which is usually the first woman they married), while the virtue of justice compels them to not abandon the women and children who have become dependent on them through legally contracted, civil marriages.

WOMEN AS WAR BOOTY?

The only thing more misogynistic than polygamous marriages, say many critics, are the Bible's "POW marriages." They usually cite Deuteronomy 21:10–14:

> When you go forth to war against your enemies, and the Lord your God gives them into your hands, and you take them captive, and see among the captives a beautiful woman, and you have desire for her and would take her for yourself as wife, then you shall bring her home to your house, and she shall shave her head and pare her nails. And she shall put off her captive's garb, and shall remain in your house and bewail her father and her mother a full month; after that you may go in to her, and be her husband, and she shall be your wife. Then, if you have no delight in her, you shall let her go where she will; but you shall not sell her for money, you shall not treat her as a slave, since you have humiliated her.

Many people become distressed when reading this passage because they assume that God is commanding the Israelites to kidnap women in order to marry them. But like most of the things we find abhorrent in the Bible (like polygamy), this is a case of regulating a common practice and teaching God's people to eventually reject it. Why should we believe that is the case?

First, notice that God is only involved in the defeat of the enemy army ("The Lord gives them into your hands"). After the victory, it is the Israelites who decide what should be done and, like many armies in the ancient world, they often took brides from among their captives. In most ancient societies, marriage rites would have been skipped and the women would just have been raped and abandoned. But in ancient Israel rape and defilement of women was never tolerated. Shechem learned this lesson the hard way in Genesis 34, when the relatives of the woman he raped slaughtered him and his entire village.

The text in Deuteronomy also gives us several clues that the biblical writer is exhorting those who practiced forced marriage to reconsider their actions.[499] First, the captive woman the man wants to marry is told to shave her head, and the man must provide her with new clothes. Since long hair was a sign of beauty and clothes were very expensive, this may have been a way to dissuade the Israelites from engaging in forced marriage. Second, the woman is allowed to mourn her loss for an entire month, and only then could a marriage take place. Once again, it is hoped this prescription would instill a sense of compassion in the Israelites and motivate them not to marry such a woman against her will.

But if the man does marry a woman he's captured and is later displeased with her, he can't sell her as a slave. He must see her as his legitimate wife. If he wants to end the marriage, then he has to let her go because, and here is the important part, the text says the man has "humiliated her" (Deut. 21:14). Deuteronomy makes it clear that the taking of a bride in wartime was wrong because it dehumanized the victim and treated her like an object.

In fact, in her study of the position of women in Deuteronomy's laws, Carolyn Pressler agrees that this law does not *encourage* marrying female POWs but "provides a means for the man to marry a woman in a case where the normal procedures for marriage are not possible [due to her foreign status]."[500] If a man chooses to marry a woman under these conditions, then the law gives him instructions that minimize the woman's dehumanization; the laws do not treat her as property he has acquired. According to Pressler, "The man's humiliation of or imposition on the woman is recognized by the motive clause [in the passage]. Acknowledging that she can be imposed upon acknowledges her personhood; chattel cannot be debased."[501]

This also helps us understand how women were treated after the Israelites defeated Midian in Numbers 31. Upon returning from the battle, the army officers discovered that Moses was angry because they let the women live. According to Moses, these women "caused the sons of Israel, by the counsel of Balaam, to act treacherously against the Lord" (Num. 31:16). Specifically, they enticed the men to commit idolatry. Moses then ordered the men to "kill every male among the little ones, and kill every woman who has known man by lying with him. But all the young girls who have not known man by lying with him, keep alive for yourselves" (Num. 31:17–18).

We will discuss the ethics of the Israelites killing noncombatants as well as the possibility that these texts may not be strict historical accounts in chapters 23 and 24. For now, let's address the accusation that the distinction made between virgins and nonvirgins was made because the Israelite soldiers were just "virgin-obsessed" barbarians.

As we've already seen, other ancient armies would have raped and abandoned their victims, but the Israelites were prohibited from doing that. An Israelite soldier could marry one of these prisoners, but only if doing so did not threaten Israel's religious-social order. The fact that the Midianites had previously led Israel into idolatry motivated the command to destroy the paganizing influences within that culture. According to Old Testament scholar Sarah Shechtman,

> There is no concept of a process of conversion to Israelite religion in the Hebrew Bible, marriage constituting the closest thing to it; a woman would have taken on the religious identity of the man she married (or at least this is the assumption). A woman who has married a Midianite man, therefore, is more fully a Midianite, religiously speaking. An unmarried virgin, however, has not yet cemented her loyalties in such a fashion.[502]

So we see that the distinction that was made between virgins and non-virgins was not made out of sexual preference, but out of a need to protect Israel's religious identity. Is this an ideal solution to tribal conflict and religious opposition to Israel's worship of God? No, but it was a workable solution that God tolerated (remember Moses gave these commands, not God) in order to protect Israel's distinct identity and allow his people to prosper in a hostile environment.

ars almost never grant that title to St. Paul. The following excerpts from his letters may explain why:

from woman, but woman from man. Neither was man

cerpts from his letters may explain why:

Paul the Misogynist?

While Jesus' openness to women within his ministry has earned him the moniker of "feminist" by some academics, these scholars almost never grant that title to St. Paul. The following excerpts from his letters may explain why:

- "The head of every man is Christ, the head of a woman is her husband, and the head of Christ is God . . . man was not made from woman, but woman from man. Neither was man created for woman, but woman for man" (1 Cor. 11:3, 8–9).
- "As in all the churches of the saints, the women should keep silence in the churches. For they are not permitted to speak, but should be subordinate, as even the law says. If there is anything they desire to know, let them ask their husbands at home. For it is shameful for a woman to speak in church" (1 Cor. 14:34–35).
- "Let a woman learn in silence with all submissiveness. I permit no woman to teach or to have authority over men; she is to keep silent" (1 Tim. 2:11).[503]

How should we understand Scripture passages that seem to conflict with our belief that men and women should be treated equally? Let's address the first passage, which New Testament professor Robert Gagnon explained in this way:

> Paul is careful to qualify his argument for male headship with the point that neither male nor female exists without the other and that men are born from women (1 Cor. 11:11–12) . . . Elsewhere in his letters Paul undermines conventional, subordinate roles for women. In Romans 16, for instance, he mentions numerous female co-workers. In 1 Corinthians 7:3–4 he insists on the mutuality of conjugal rights. Finally, he pronounces that in the community of the baptized there is "neither male and female" (Gal. 3:28).[504]

Paul acknowledges the equal value of all the members of the Body of Christ, but he does not consider each member to be the same as every other member. He recognized that the different parts of the body each possessed different gifts, and so each part served the whole body in a unique way (1 Cor. 12:14–31). Paul also recognized the commonsense truth that men and women are different. As a result, he taught that each sex has a particular role to play in the Church, but this did not mean that one sex was inherently better than the other.

A critic might appeal to 1 Peter 3:7 as proof that the Bible does say that men are better than women. That passage says, "Husbands, live considerately with your wives, bestowing honor on the woman as the weaker sex." But according to New Testament scholar Daniel Keating,

> Given the overall context of the letter, by weaker he probably means weaker in physical strength, and therefore subject to intimidation and abuse by husbands, and also weaker in social standing and influence in society, and so in need of being established and honored by husbands. In these ways wives were vulnerable, and so Peter counsels husbands to show special honor to them."[505]

AN ARGUMENT FROM SILENCE

But what about 1 Corinthians 14:34–35, where Paul says that a woman should keep silent in church? Doesn't that imply that he thought less of women? The problem with this conclusion is that Paul never absolutely forbids women from speaking in church. In fact, he describes quite the opposite. In 1 Corinthians 11:4–5, he says, "Any man who prays or prophesies with his head covered dishonors his head, but *any woman who prays or prophesies* [emphasis added] with her head unveiled dishonors her head—it is the same as if her head were shaven."

One of the differences between praying and prophesying is that the latter involves speaking out loud what God has internally revealed to the person. Pope Benedict XVI said of this passage, "The apostle accepts as normal the fact that a woman can 'prophesy' in the Christian community (1 Cor. 11:5), that is, speak openly under the influence of the Spirit, as long as it is for the edification of the community and done in a dignified manner."[506]

It turns out women were allowed to speak in church just as men were allowed to speak. But just as the average man in the pew cannot give the homily at Mass, women may not give similar instruction because they do not have clerical authority.[507] It is only the priest or the bishop who can give such instruction, or have "authority over man."[508]

Paul may have also been addressing a pastoral issue in Corinth that involved certain women openly questioning teachings they were receiving in church. Paul advised these women to save their questions for their own homes. Since the first Christian services were held in a believer's home, it was tempting for those gathered there to treat the occasion with an inappropriate sense of informality. New Testament scholar Ben Witherington wrote,

> The argument is not gender specific. Paul requires respect, submission, and silence of any listener when any prophet is speaking (1 Cor. 14:28–32), and his dealing with some women who are asking questions (1 Cor. 14:34f.) is a specific implementation of principles already applied to everyone. One must assume that he singles these women out for comment because he has heard that some of them were notable violators of these principles. Throughout the chapter Paul is correcting abuses, and his words must be read in that context."[509]

What is important to understand from this analysis is that Paul's condemnation is not a strict division between men and women, but is instead a division between laity and clergy. According to the Congregation for the Doctrine of the Faith's 1976 document *Inter Insigniores*,

> Paul in no way opposes the right, which he elsewhere recognizes as possessed by women, to prophesy in the assembly (1 Cor. 11:5); the prohibition solely concerns the official function of teaching in the Christian assembly. For St. Paul this

prescription is bound up with the divine plan of creation (1 Cor. 11:7, Gen 2:18–24): it would be difficult to see in it the expression of a cultural fact.

But even if we can provide a sensible explanation for why Paul seems to condemn women speaking in church, most of us still wonder about Paul's view on the relationship between husbands and wives. In Ephesians 5:22–24 he writes, "Wives, be subject to your husbands, as to the Lord. For the husband is the head of the wife as Christ is the head of the church, his body, and is himself its Savior." What does Paul mean when he says that wives should be "subject to" their husbands or that a husband is the "head" of a woman? Pope St. John Paul II explained it this way:

> The author knows that this way of speaking, so profoundly rooted in the customs and religious tradition of the time, is to be understood and carried out in a new way: as a "mutual subjection out of reverence for Christ" (cf. Eph. 5:21). This is especially true because the husband is called the "head" of the wife as Christ is the head of the Church; he is so in order to give "himself up for her" (Eph. 5:25), and giving himself up for her means giving up even his own life. However, whereas in the relationship between Christ and the Church the subjection is only on the part of the Church, in the relationship between husband and wife the "subjection" is not one-sided but mutual.[510]

Equals to the End

We've examined several passages that critics use to indict the Bible as being a sexist relic of the past, but we should not forget passages that teach about the equality that exists between the sexes. For example, Scripture verses that command children to honor their parents always say to honor both father *and* mother. Likewise, a child could be punished for cursing either his father or his mother (Exod. 21:17). When the book of Proverbs encourages listening to a father and not mocking him, it also says children should not despise or scorn their mothers (Prov. 23:22). In fact, fathers are sometimes singled out if they are failing at their vocation. Ephesians 6:1, 4 states, "Children, obey your parents in the Lord, for this is right . . . Fathers, do not provoke your children to anger but bring them up in the discipline and instruction of the Lord."

Also, women often served God's purposes by being the heroes in salvation history who paved the way for the coming of the Messiah. Jesus' genealogy includes Tamar, who outwitted her uncle Judah and exposed his moral hypocrisy; Rahab, who protected the Israelite spies and allowed them to conquer Jericho; Ruth, who courageously left her Moabite heritage and became an Israelite; and Bathsheba, who secured Solomon's succession to David's throne.

Let's not forget the other women in Israel's history, like Deborah, who led Israel to victory against the Canaanites; Judith and Esther, who saved the Jews from extermination; and of course, Mary, the Mother of God, who the Bible says all generations will call "blessed" (Luke 1:48). No other man in the Bible, save for her son Jesus Christ, is given such an honorific title.

19

Bizarre Laws and Cruel Punishments?

*The Claim: Christians pick and choose which Bible rules to
follow since deep down they know some of these rules, along with
the cruel punishments that accompany them, are absurd and
have no place in a modern, civilized society.*

In the late 1990s, advocates of homosexual behavior criticized
popular talk-radio host Laura Schlessinger for saying this behavior was a "biological error" and for using the Bible to justify her
condemnation. One of these critics was Canadian writer J. Kent
Ashcraft, who sent Schlessinger a tongue-in-cheek letter that is
still being circulated on the Internet. It was even adapted for a
scene in the television show *The West Wing*. His letter begins,

> Thank you for doing so much to educate people regarding
> God's Law. I have learned a great deal from your show, and
> try to share that knowledge with as many people as I can.
> When someone tries to defend the homosexual lifestyle, for
> example, I simply remind them that Leviticus 18:22 clearly
> states it to be an abomination . . . end of debate. I do need
> some advice from you, however, regarding some other ele-
> ments of God's Laws and how to follow them. [Ashcraft then
> asks a series of questions that include the following:]

- I know that I am allowed no contact with a woman while she
  is in her period of menstrual unseemliness—(Lev. 15:19–24).
  The problem is how do I tell? I have tried asking, but most
  women take offence.
- I have a neighbor who insists on working on the Sabbath. Exodus 35:2 clearly states he should be put to death. Am I morally
  obligated to kill him myself, or should I ask the police to do it?

- Most of my male friends get their hair trimmed, including the hair around their temples, even though this is expressly forbidden by Leviticus 19:27. How should they die?
- A friend of mine feels that even though eating shellfish is an abomination (Lev. 11:10), it is a lesser abomination than homosexuality. I don't agree. Can you settle this? Are there "degrees" of abomination?

Ashcraft ends his letter with sarcastic gratitude. "Thank you again for reminding us that God's word is eternal and unchanging."[511]

Of course, Ashcraft thinks God's law has changed since nearly all Jews and Christians neglect the Old Testament's impractical or seemingly bizarre prohibitions.[512] Critics like Ashcraft wonder, "Why should we take the Bible seriously when it contains nonsensical rules like these? Why don't we just ignore these rules and reject the Bible's moral authority?"

KEEPING IT KOSHER

There are two aspects of the Old Testament's laws critics usually object to: what they require, and the punishments for violating them. Before we examine those points, however, it's important to know that many of these laws served practical purposes that still make sense today. These included placing fences on roofs to prevent accidental falls (Deut. 22:8), leaving some crops behind for the poor to eat (Lev. 23:22), and requiring weights and scales to be accurate (Lev. 19:36). When circumstances change, laws like these also change because they are no longer required. For example, today fences aren't needed on roofs because, unlike in the ancient world, they aren't a popular place for people to congregate.

Of course, critics still say that many of the Old Testament's laws are impractical or even absurd. Along with the previously referenced laws, a critic might ask, "Why would God care if I mix meat and dairy (Exod. 23:19), or eat shellfish (Lev. 11:12), or wear fabrics made of two different materials (Lev. 19:19)? Aren't these strange laws evidence that the Bible is not divinely inspired?"

In Galatians 3:24–26, Paul says, "the [Mosaic] law was our custodian until Christ came, that we might be justified by faith. But now that faith has come, we are no longer under a custodian; for in Christ Jesus you are all sons of God, through faith." The word rendered "custodian" is *paidagogos,* from which we get the English word "pedagogy." In the ancient world, a *paidagogos* was a kind of babysitter who taught children in his care valuable lessons, similar to the fictional nanny Mary Poppins (but without a magical bag and flying umbrella).[513]

As a *paidagogos,* the Mosaic Law taught the Israelites how to be distinct from their pagan neighbors as well as how to understand the unique and absolute holiness of their God. Old Testament scholar John Goldingay put it this way:

> Food is an expression of identity. God takes that fact and makes it contribute to the forming and articulating of Israel's identity. Jews don't eat pork; it's one of the things that makes them stand out and keeps them separate . . . God is holy, which means being different, being set apart. Israel is holy, which means being different, being set apart, as the Jewish people have always been . . . their distinctive customs meant they were always distinguishable from other peoples.[514]

Laws that required the sacrifice of animals taught the Israelites that even if other cultures worshipped animals or animal-shaped idols, these creatures were not gods, because the Israelites had the authority to kill these animals. These laws also taught the Israelites that God deserves our highest form of worship. Animals like bulls or goats were very valuable in the ancient world, so sacrificing them showed that the believer valued God more than worldly goods.

These sacrifices also prepared God's people for Christ's sacrifice, which took away the sins of the entire world.[515] The *Catechism* says that God's revelation "involves a specific divine pedagogy: God communicates himself to man gradually. He prepares him to welcome by stages the supernatural Revelation that is to culminate in the person and mission of the incarnate Word, Jesus Christ" (CCC 53).

But why were some animals acceptable to eat and sacrifice but others were not? One proposal says that these laws were issued for health reasons, to protect the Israelites from animals that carried disease (such as bats or scavengers, like vultures). However, this doesn't explain why Christians in the first century, who also needed to be protected from disease, were not required to follow the same guidelines. In fact, the New Testament *forbids* following these laws, so it seems incredibly unlikely that they had a medicinal purpose. Instead, the law's purpose seems to have been pedagogical, or as Old Testament scholar Paul Copan has written,

> A number of scholars reasonably claim that God was reminding Israel of her own distinctive, holy calling even in the very foods Israel was to eat. Animals that "crossed" or in a sense "transgressed" the individual and distinctive spheres of air, water, or land were considered unclean.[516]

The Old Testament's dietary restrictions came from the idea of food being "fit" for consumption, or in Hebrew, *kashrut* (from which we get the English word "kosher"). Animals that were fit to eat were ones that were true to the typical animal of their kind. What makes the typical fish a fish is that it has scales and fins. Aquatic animals that don't have these characteristics, like shellfish, were considered a deviant offshoot of what a fish should be and were thus unfit for consumption (Lev. 11:9–12). The same is true of land animals, among whom the common edible examples were beasts that had cloven hooves and "chewed the cud" (Lev. 11:3–7). Animals that lacked the former trait (such as rabbits), the latter trait (pigs), or both traits (reptiles) were deemed unfit for consumption.

The dietary restrictions also provided a practical way to keep Israel distinct from her pagan neighbors. This is similar to how a vegan's dietary restrictions keep him distinct from his animal-eating friends. Such dietary laws could even serve as an opportunity for the Jews to share with their neighbors what makes them Jewish and why Jews worship and live the way they do.

PREVENTING "MIX-UPS"

The goal of being distinct from surrounding pagan culture is also seen in laws that condemned activities like cross dressing (Deut. 22:5), planting more than one seed in a field, or wearing fabrics composed of different materials (Lev. 19:19). Notice that all these offenses involve the idea of illicit mixing. The matters treated in these laws may have been minor, but the idea they taught was of major importance to Israel—what naturally belongs apart should not be illicitly joined together. The Israelites had to learn that they could not worship the true God and also indulge in the sinful practices of, or intermarry with, people who rejected God.

Part of this pedagogy included bans on grossly immoral practices, such as child sacrifice and cultic prostitution, as well as bans on seemingly innocuous things that modern readers often misunderstand. For example, there was a case involving a Christian baker who refused to bake a cake for the wedding of two men. One critic said the baker was hypocritical because even though he believed in the Bible, he also sported tattoos, which seems to contradict Leviticus 19:28: "You shall not make any cuttings in your flesh on account of the dead or tattoo any marks upon you." If Christians ignore this strange prohibition on tattoos, then why not ignore Leviticus's prohibition on homosexual behavior?

Although tattoos may seem relatively harmless to us, in the ancient world they often signified that you belonged to a pagan religion. For example, tattoos discovered on mummified Egyptian women suggest that they were used to seek help from the gods during pregnancy.[517] *A Catholic Commentary on Holy Scripture* also notes that the verse preceding this one, which prohibits trimming hair around the temples (Lev. 19:27, the verse Ashcraft cites in his letter), relates to a common, ancient superstition

associated with priests from idolatrous desert tribes.[518] These
laws are on par with modern rules that prohibit children from
shaving their heads in order to keep them from resembling racist
"skinheads," or dress codes that prohibit students from wearing
clothes that are affiliated with local gangs. The rationale behind
rules like these is that even though hairstyles and clothing are
not bad in and of themselves, they can come to be identified
with bad people and thus need to be avoided.

Ritual versus Moral Laws

St. Paul taught that the Mosaic Law was useful in teaching the
Jews how to be holy, but it was incapable of saving them from
sin (Gal. 3:10). That's because no one could perfectly follow the
Law and the Law didn't fix the root of why we sin—our fallen,
sinful nature. The Law was holy, good and just (Rom. 7:12),
but it made nothing perfect (Heb. 7:19).[519] It contained what
the Second Vatican Council calls "imperfect and provisional"
things like animal sacrifices or ritual cleansing that would not be
a part of God's final, universal plan to redeem all of humanity.[520]

Simply put, we are not saved by obeying the Law of Moses,
but by obeying the Law of Christ (Gal. 6:2). We rely on his
grace (Eph. 2:8–10) to purify us from sin (1 John 1:7) and make
us God's adopted children (Rom. 8:15). It is only through grace
that we are able to follow Jesus' command to be perfect "as your
heavenly father is perfect" (Matt. 5:48). But, even though some
of the Old Testament's laws were abrogated, not all of them
were. According to Scripture professor Mark Giszczak,

> Moral law has to do with universal principles of right and
> wrong. Ritual or ceremonial law has to do with symbolic, re-
> ligious cleanness and uncleanness in Old Testament religion.
> Judicial or civil law involves structures for the administration of
> the law in the Old Testament . . . Aquinas teaches that the ritual
> and judicial laws have been abrogated, but that the moral law
> still holds. So we *can* eat bacon, but we can't eat our neighbor.[521]

Here's an analogy to help understand this distinction: When I was a child my mom gave me two rules: hold her hand when I cross the street, and don't drink what's under the sink. Today, I only have to follow the latter rule. The former rule is no longer needed to protect me and, in fact, following it would now do me more harm than good.

The ritual/judicial laws were like mom's hand-holding rule. They helped the Israelites understand the internal purity God's law requires, just as hand-holding helped me understand the vigilance that crossing the street required. These laws also protected the Israelites from pagan influences, just as the hand-holding rule protected me from careless motorists. But by the time of the New Covenant, these laws were no longer needed. In fact, the burden of following them hindered the goal of bringing non-Jews into communion with God (such as the requirement to be circumcised).

As a result, Christ's Church, endowed with his authority (Matt. 16:18, Luke 10:16), removed the necessity of following these laws (Acts 15:6–21).[522] Through the coming of Christ, we have been discharged from following the entire Mosaic Law (Rom. 7:6), and Jesus himself "declared all foods clean" (Mark 7:19). The *Catechism* says, "Jesus perfects the dietary law, so important in Jewish daily life, by revealing its pedagogical meaning through a divine interpretation . . . 'What comes out of a man is what defiles a man. For from within, out of the heart of man, come evil thoughts'" (CCC 582).

However, unlike its ritual or temporary judicial laws, the Old Covenant's moral laws forbade evils like murder or adultery and were not pedagogical in nature. They were meant to permanently protect God's people from sin. That's why, even though Jesus declared all foods clean, he did not declare all sexual relationships to be clean, and so he affirmed the Mosaic Law's prohibition on adultery (Matt. 5:27–28). Or, to cite another example, even though Paul said circumcision was not necessary for and could even hinder one's salvation, he also said that the man in 1 Corinthians 5 who was having sex with his stepmother (a violation of Leviticus 18:8 and Deuteronomy 22:30) should be cast out of the community.

These unchanging moral laws related to sinful sexual behavior (along with laws related to other evils like idolatry or murder) are as permanent as my mother's ban on Drano martinis. I might have grown up enough to cross a busy street without help, but there's no age that would protect me from drinking poison. Likewise, God's people no longer needed the ceremonial laws to be holy, but there is no circumstance in which sins like murder or fornication could ever be appropriate. Even most die-hard critics of the Bible admit that the Old Testament's prohibitions on child sacrifice, bestiality, and incest are still worth following.

But are Leviticus's prohibitions on same-sex intercourse part of the Old Testament's abrogated ceremonial law, or are they part of the permanent moral law that is still binding?

First, notice that Leviticus 18:22 is sandwiched between moral laws—not ceremonial ones. Verse 20 condemns adultery, verse 21 condemns child sacrifice, and verse 23 condemns bestiality.[523] Second, Leviticus makes it clear that actions like adultery, bestiality, and same-sex relations were part of the moral law that also applied to non-Jews (only Jews were expected to follow things like the dietary laws). God had even judged the other pagan nations for engaging in these "defilements" and expelled them from the land for doing so (Lev. 18:24–25).

Finally, unlike the punishments associated with idolatry, murder, or adultery, the Bible never prescribes the death penalty for violating ceremonial laws.[524] The fact that both partners in same-sex intercourse stand in danger of being executed for their behavior shows that this was not a violation of a ritual purity law. Instead, homosexual behavior was a violation of a deeper moral truth that all people, even those who had never been taught the Old Testament's laws, should know and obey (a point Paul makes in Romans 1:18–32 about this same subject).

CRUEL AND UNUSUAL PUNISHMENTS?

What about the punishments associated with the still-binding moral laws? Are they still valid? John Shelby Spong gives some examples of capital offenses in Scripture that seem extreme from his perspective:

> The execution squads would have to work overtime to keep up with the number of texts from the Bible that call for the death penalty. Violating the Sabbath (Exod. 35:2), cursing (Lev. 24:13–14) and blaspheming (Lev. 24:16) are among them. Such judgments would fall most heavily on athletic locker rooms used in preparation for Saturday or Sunday football games![525]

Given that we live in a country where the death penalty isn't even allowed for the crime of child rape, it's no surprise that many people consider the Old Testament's use of capital punishment to be excessively harsh.[526] However, there's no evidence that anyone in ancient Israel was executed for having a shrimp cocktail or a slice of bacon. Instead, capital punishment was reserved for serious crimes that involved breaking one of the Ten Commandments.

This included the first commandment (against idolatry, defiling holy objects, necromancy), the second commandment (cursing God), the third commandment (breaking the Sabbath), the fourth commandment (cursing one's parents, rebelling against them), the fifth commandment (murder, child sacrifice, negligent homicide), the sixth commandment (adultery, rape, incest), the seventh commandment (kidnapping), and the eighth commandment (perjury related to a capital offense). The last two commandments deal with hidden, sinful desires (coveting a neighbor's wife or goods), and so they cannot be punished. It was only when these desires manifested themselves in actions (such as adultery or stealing) that a punishment would be administered.

When we discuss whether these punishments were too severe, we must be careful about being anachronistic. Yes, some of them may seem too severe for *our* time and *our* culture, but they weren't necessarily so for the ancient Israelites. They lived in a time when prisons did not exist and a group's resources went to the community's survival (preventing food shortages, fighting invading tribes). As a result, there were few ways to punish and deter serious criminals besides the threat of death or exile. Take, for example, the execution of perjurers found in Deuteronomy: "If the witness is a false witness and has accused his brother falsely, then you shall do to him as he had meant to do to his brother; so you shall purge the evil from the midst of you. And the rest shall hear, and fear, and shall never again commit any such evil among you" (Deut. 19:16–20).

According to Deuteronomy, the people will learn that they should not falsely accuse their fellow Israelite because if their perjury is discovered, they will receive the penalty that would have been given to the accused. In the case of accusations involving capital crimes, the punishment would be death. We have the luxury of choosing other ways to deter the evil of perjury, but for ancient people this was a very fair and simple way to uphold the justice system and prevent deaths caused by false testimony.

Killed for Gathering Firewood?

Most critics understand why crimes like murder or false witness in capital cases require harsh deterrents, but they still complain that crimes like idolatry (Deut. 17:2–7), blasphemy (Lev. 24:16), rebelling against one's parents (Deut. 21:18–21), and adultery (Deut. 22:22) do not deserve to be punished with death. However, these crimes were (and still are) very serious offenses. Those who committed them challenged the authority of the people who led the community—namely, God, parents, and husbands. Because of this insolence, strict laws were passed in order to preserve tribal unity and prevent the foundation of Israel's holiness from being undermined.

Consider, for example, the man who is executed in Numbers 15:32–36 for picking up sticks on the Sabbath (an example atheists often cite). According to Church Fathers like St. John Chrysostom and St. John Cassian, laws that punished seemingly minor infractions were necessary for making an example of those who would defy civil and religious authority figures. According to St. John Chrysostom, though this man's sin was not as grave as others, he had to be punished, because "if the laws were obstinately despised even at the beginning, of course they would scarcely be observed afterwards."[527]

Other scholars argue that the man was treated so harshly because he was using fire, a sacred element, in order to incite idolatrous worship of another god.[528] This would explain why this story is included in a section of Numbers that deals with grave, premeditated sin.

Unfortunately, many people today do not think crimes like blasphemy or adultery are grave sins, but in the ancient world they threatened to unravel the social fabric. This could happen by creating children out of wedlock that may have been abandoned or by rejecting the sovereign Lord who sustained Israel amidst hostile peoples and elements. As Giszczak says, "Life was harsher, shorter, and involved a lot of messy things. War was frequent and involved personal combat with bronze swords, spears, and bare hands. Infant mortality was normal. Plagues and famines were common. Laws were simple because life was brutal."[529]

THE THREAT OF PUNISHMENT

There is a question of whether these punishments were actually carried out or if they belong to a nonliteral genre and were composed to teach the Israelites a valuable lesson.[530] Old Testament scholar Raymond Westbrook wrote,

> Since the law codes were theoretical documents, it is difficult to know how far they represent the law in practice . . . some of the punishments reflect the scribal compilers' concern for perfect symmetry and delicious irony rather than the pragmatic experience of the law courts."[531]

In fact, laws that punished serious crimes may have been written with very high maximum penalties, when in practice lighter punishments were more routinely administered. For example, Exodus 21:29–32 says that if the ox of a negligent owner gores someone to death, the owner can pay a ransom to the victim's family in place of being executed for his crime. But Numbers 35:31 says that when it comes to someone guilty of premeditated murder (the most serious crime one could commit against a fellow Israelite), "you shall accept no ransom for the life of a murderer, who is guilty of death; but he shall be put to death."[532]

It's plausible to assume that for most crimes a less severe penalty could be issued than what was recorded in the law codes. This is similar to the practice of placing a warning on films that threaten those who might copy them with a $250,000 fine and a five-year prison sentence. That's a fairly severe punishment for making a friend a copy of a movie you just purchased. In a case like that, the maximum punishment would probably not be administered to you, but instead be saved for a more serious offender, like someone who makes a lot of money selling illegally copied movies. The goal of such a severe sanction and stern warning, then, would be to deter crime rather than to punish it harshly in every case.

Likewise, even though the punishments in ancient Israel may have been very severe on paper, we have little evidence they were actually carried out in all their severity.[533] For example, Exodus 22:18 says, "You shall not permit a sorceress [or in some translations, "a witch"] to live," but 1 Samuel 28:3–25 shows that by the time of King Saul mediums were still present in Israel. Even though Saul had previously deported them, he was still able to ask his servants to find him a medium so he could communicate with the deceased prophet Samuel. According to Richard Hiers in his book *Justice and Compassion in Biblical Law,* "the story instances an occasion when the severity of the [biblical] provision was mitigated in practice."[534]

Condoning Rape?

Some critics object that the Old Testament's laws were unfair because the victim is punished more than the perpetrator. A commonly cited example is Deuteronomy 22:28–29, which critics say forces rape victims to marry their rapists. The passage says,

If a man meets a virgin who is not betrothed, and seizes her
and lies with her, and they are found, then the man who lay
with her shall give to the father of the young woman fifty
shekels of silver, and she shall be his wife, because he has violated her; he may not put her away all his days.

In order to understand this passage we must review the verses
that come before it. Verses 22–24 say that if a man has sex in the
city with a married woman and the two are found out, both the
man and woman will be put to death for the crime of adultery.[535]
But verses 25–27 describe a very different scenario. They say,

But if in the open country a man meets a young woman who
is betrothed, and the man seizes her and lies with her, then
only the man who lay with her shall die. But to the young
woman you shall do nothing; in the young woman there is no
offense punishable by death, for this case is like that of a man
attacking and murdering his neighbor; because he came upon
her in the open country, and though the betrothed young
woman cried for help there was no one to rescue her.

These last verses are remarkable in that the writer is patiently
explaining to his readers why they should reject the prevailing
cultural norms of the ancient Near East that say a woman who is
a victim of rape deserves to be punished with death. Even today
in some parts of the Middle East a woman can be executed for
being the victim of rape.[536]

The law in Deuteronomy even gives the woman the benefit
of the doubt by asserting that she probably summoned help (and
thus did not consent), even though there were no witnesses to
hear her cry out. The fact that such a presumption would have
allowed some adulterers to go free was tolerated because punishing a victim of rape was considered worse than failing to punish
someone guilty of adultery.

Women accused of adultery were also given the benefit of the
doubt because the trial they underwent, drinking water mixed

with dust from the floor of the tabernacle, could not hurt them if they were innocent. A guilty woman, on the other hand, would only be rendered infertile through divine intervention (Num. 5:11–22). This differs from other ancient adultery trials, such as those found in the Code of Hammurabi, which involved throwing women into rivers with the erroneous assumption that only the guilty (and not innocent non-swimmers) would sink.[537]

Righting a Wrong

We've seen that Deuteronomy describes the penalties for consensual adultery as well as the rape of a married woman, but what about sex with an unmarried woman? Verses 28–29 seem to be describing the rape of an unmarried woman, but they also contain language that could apply to consensual encounters. For example, the passage includes the conditional clause, "and they are found," which is absent from the previous nonconsensual cases and may refer to a consensual yet illicit sexual encounter.

The language in this passage might even refer to other kinds of nonconsensual sex like statutory rape.[538] The law would then be similar to the provision found in Exodus 22:16, which says, "If a man seduces a virgin who is not betrothed, and lies with her, he shall give the marriage present for her, and make her his wife." The Hebrew word translated "seduced," *patah,* means "deceive" rather than the more violent "take."[539] The flexibility of the language in these verses may be because the punishment for either consensual or nonconsensual sex with an unmarried woman was the same: the man who violated this woman must marry her and can never divorce her.

Although the rape of a married woman is framed as a violation of "your neighbor's wife," the rape of an unmarried woman is not framed as a violation of "your neighbor's daughter." Instead, the text simply says the rapist "violated her." Indeed, in addition to inflicting the trauma of rape, the rapist would also have made this woman "damaged goods," unmarriable in the eyes of nearly all the other men in the community.[540] This is certainly unfair, but that was the social climate present in the ancient world. The laws of Deuteronomy had to regulate life in this environment (remember rule fifteen).

A woman's inability to marry was devastating, because marriage was the primary way she could attain a stable economic existence. Because of a lack of employment for women, the unmarried could either rely on their fathers to provide for them (which couldn't last forever), be as economically afflicted as widows (including the risk of dying of starvation), or resort to prostitution to provide for themselves.

Sure, the man who raped an unmarried woman might be executed in the same way that a man who raped a married woman might be, but the married woman at least had a husband and family who could provide for her. For the unmarried victim, mandated marriage would serve as a form of restitution, requiring the rapist to provide his victim with the economic security he had stolen from her. The perilous social status of widows also explains Israel's Levirate law, which required a man to marry the wife of his deceased brother. Far from being misogynistic, this law protected women from extreme poverty and even empowered them to shame an uncooperative brother-in-law by publicly taking off his sandal and spitting in his face (Deut. 25:9).

Keep in mind that while this solution to the problem of rape may seem shocking to us, for a woman living in ancient Israel it would have provided at least some relief of her plight. Consider, for example, the episode that took place between King David's children Amnon and Tamar. Amnon fell in love with his half sister Tamar, and when she refused to have sex with him he raped her. Surprisingly, Tamar begs her half brother before the rape to stop and to marry her (2 Sam. 13:13). Even after the rape she pleads for Amnon to not send her away and says, "No, my brother; for this wrong in sending me away *is greater than the other which you did to m*e [emphasis added]" (2 Sam. 13:16).

Tamar's plea reflected the ancient attitude that marriage was an institution that promoted survival and family stability more than it promoted romantic relationships. Of course, this should not be taken to mean that people in the ancient world didn't marry out of love for one another (the book of Ruth is evidence against that thesis). It simply shows that marriage was a more robust social institution than it is in today's world. But this doesn't mean the forced-marriage solution was always utilized for the crime of rape. Exodus 22:17 says that a father could refuse to give his daughter to the man who violated her. He could compel the rapist to provide monetary restitution instead.

Rather than being "pro-rape," the Bible makes it clear that rape is a crime committed by men, not women, and so women are not punished when they are the victims of rape. It further makes it clear that rape was a crime that reflected not just on the individual, but on the community as a whole. According to one commentary, "In all three texts, the rape of a woman—Dinah in Genesis 34, the Levite's concubine in Judges 19, and Tamar in 2 Samuel 13—points to the unraveling of the larger social fabric."[541]

This law's primary purpose was to deter men from thinking that they could rape or seduce a woman without any negative consequences for themselves. Even critics of the Bible's inerrancy see the positive elements in laws like those found in Deuteronomy 22:28–29. For example, Kenton Sparks wrote of this passage, "Though I freely admit that I am troubled by the law as it stands, the law is 'good' in ways I would not have expected because my world is so profoundly different from the world of ancient Israel."[542] Indeed, this profound difference must be taken into account when we examine all of ancient Israel's laws. This includes the laws related to slavery that we will examine next.

20

Endorsement of Slavery? Part I

*The Claim: The easiest way to disprove the Bible as our standard
of morality is to ask what the Bible's position on slavery is.
Why should we heed the words of a book that tells "slaves to obey your
masters," yet fails to tell the masters to free their slaves?*

On April 13, 2012, self-identified gay columnist Dan Savage delivered an address at a high school journalism conference. Although he was billed as an anti-bullying advocate, he chose to deliver a profanity-laced tirade against Christians who believe homosexual behavior is wrong.[543] In an article he wrote two weeks after the incident, Savage apologized for his name-calling, but not for his attack on the Bible. He referenced another one of his writings, in which he had made the same point in a less angry way:

> We ignore what the Bible says about slavery in both the Old and New Testaments. And the authors of the Bible didn't just fail to condemn slavery. They *endorsed* slavery: "Slaves obey your masters" [Col. 3:22]. In his book *Letter to a Christian Nation*, Sam Harris writes that the Bible got the easiest moral question humanity has ever faced wrong. The Bible got slavery wrong. What are the odds that the Bible got something as complicated as human sexuality wrong? I'd put those odds at about 100%.[544]

The word "slavery" arouses deep emotions within nearly everyone. When this word is uttered we imagine people being kidnapped, shackled, whipped, and forced into hard labor. If God is the author of the Bible, then why doesn't the Bible explicitly denounce slavery? In order to answer this question we need to examine what slavery actually is.

What Is Slavery?

When most people think of slavery they think of the kidnapping, imprisonment, and forced labor of Africans that took place in the New World between the sixteenth and nineteenth centuries. However, these events aren't a good *definition* of slavery because slavery existed before and after this time period (including in the present day), and not all slavery is like what happened in the antebellum or pre-Civil War South. Hector Avalos, an atheist scholar who is extremely critical of the Bible and its view of slavery, defines slavery as "a socioeconomic system centering on the use of forced laborers, who are viewed as property or as under the control of their superiors for whatever term was determined by their masters or by their society."[545]

Avalos's definition includes forced laborers who are considered property ("chattel slavery"). It also includes people whose labor—rather than their person—is owned by another for the purpose of remunerating a debt ("debt slavery"). Avalos's definition even includes criminals who are forced to work in prison. After all, criminals are "under the control of a superior" for a period of time that is determined by society. The United States Government Accounting Office even said, "The courts have held that inmates may be required to work and are not protected by the constitutional prohibition against involuntary servitude. They have also consistently held that inmates have no constitutional right to compensation and that inmates are paid by the "grace of the state."[546]

Granted, prisoners in the United States aren't *chattel* slaves because they retain certain basic rights. These include the right not to be tortured, the right to legal counsel, and the right to be provided with food, clothing, and medical care (among other things). But imprisoned criminals have been deprived of their freedom, and so their condition can be considered a kind of de facto slavery. This means that, at least in some circumstances, it is not wrong to deprive someone of his freedom or reduce him to the status of being a slave. Thus, slavery is not *intrinsically* evil.

St. Thomas Aquinas said, "The fact that this particular man should be a slave rather than another man, is based, not on natural reason, but on some resultant utility."[547] What St. Thomas means is that no one is naturally ordered toward being a slave in the same way that he or she may be naturally ordered toward being a father or a mother. He therefore would have opposed antebellum slavery, which enslaved people based on their skin color or some other aspect of their nature. Instead, Thomas argued that slavery is a human construct that exists because in some circumstances slavery can be just and beneficial. For example, it might be necessary to the common good to force criminals or prisoners of war to work against their will. If that's true, then it's not surprising the Bible does not universally denounce slavery, because not all kinds of slavery are wrong.

Of course, most people will say that although criminals *deserve* to be enslaved, innocent people do not, and the Bible teaches that this latter form of slavery is acceptable. But this is not an accurate assessment of what the Bible teaches.

SLAVERY IN THE OLD TESTAMENT

Almost everything we know about economics in the ancient Near East comes from the records of temples, palaces, and private merchants. Of these three entities, religious and civil authorities controlled the majority of what could be called "the means of production." They had dominant access to craftsmen, metalworks, land, and natural resources like water or animals. *The Dictionary of the Ancient Near East* says,

> The temple estates in third millennium B.C. Mesopotamia were huge. Temples owned land and animals, employed workers and artisans and commissioned merchants. Dependent workers were tied to the land and paid in rations. Temples functioned as redistributors of food and other goods. Palace estates and private holdings also existed, however, and the overall administrative role of the palaces gradually increased with time.[548]

As civil authorities grew in power they gained the ability to force their subjects to produce food surpluses for them as well as construct massive building projects. Slave labor used to harvest farms and build monuments in ancient Egypt would be an example of this kind of conscription. Another would be the feudal states found in the land of Canaan that came about, according to Daniel Snell, historian of the ancient Near East, because "rich people bought up the land held by the poor and destroyed the old agrarian order, replacing it with their own farms."[549]

For the average person, survival meant being able to produce not only enough food to feed one's own family, but enough food or resources (including hides, wool, and so on) to pay for the resources that were needed to farm and shepherd in the first place. Since these resources were not cheap, farmers inevitably had to borrow from wealthier landowners in order to obtain them. Unfortunately, this created a cycle of debt that Gregory Chirichigno ably summarizes in his monograph on ancient Near Eastern slavery,

> Once this dependency [on large landowners] was established the small landowners were often forced into procuring loans which often included high interest rates. If their crop(s) failed or was below expectation, then the debtors would be hard pressed to pay back the loan. Therefore, many of these small landowners were likely to become insolvent, since they were able to engage only in subsistence farming. As a result of their insolvency farmers were forced to sell or surrender dependents into debt-slavery.[550]

This is the kind of slavery that is usually described in the Old Testament: an institution that provided people with a reliable source of income in order to pay off their debts.[551] This situation is also called "indentured servitude," and was common even up to the eighteenth and nineteenth centuries. Some studies estimate that during these centuries one third to one half of all immigrants to the United States were forced to work off debts they incurred to travel to their new homeland.[552]

In contrast to antebellum slavery, it was the worker who initiated the arrangement of being a debt slave. Genesis 47:19 provides an example of this when the people of Egypt, distraught at the effects of a recent famine, plead to Joseph, "Buy us and our land for food, and we with our land will be slaves to Pharaoh; and give us seed, that we may live, and not die, and that the land may not be desolate." In addition, unlike what occurred in the African slave trade, Exodus 21:16 forbade the kidnapping and selling of anyone into slavery. It specifically prescribes the death penalty for anyone who "steals a man, whether he sells him or is found in possession of him."[553]

Even though slavery was common, the Bible's authors did not endorse or celebrate it. As with polygamy or divorce, the sacred authors of Scripture attempted to limit the harm caused by this ubiquitous yet degrading human institution. To repeat what Pope Benedict XVI said, "God's plan is manifested progressively and it is accomplished slowly, in successive stages and despite human resistance."[554]

Instead of issuing shrill, universal condemnations of slavery that would have been ignored by most people (just as condemnations of abortion fall on deaf ears for many today) the laws set down in Scripture progressively guided God's people toward the eventual rejection of slavery. The laws did this while tolerating the existence of slavery because of the "hard hearts" of people who believed it was an indispensable source of labor. As Scripture scholar Richard Bauckham wrote, the Bible "accepts the fact of slavery but treats it as an abnormality to be minimized as far as possible."[555]

For example, the Old Testament does not instruct the Israelites to treat slaves in the same way one would treat an animal or a chair. If a master seriously injured a slave by knocking out a tooth or an eye, he had to set the slave free (Exod. 21:26–27).[556] Slaves could not work on the Sabbath (Exod. 20:10), and were allowed to participate in religious festivals (Exod. 12:44), a freedom that was unheard of in the ancient world. Slaves could marry free persons (1 Chron. 2:34–35), own property, and even own other slaves (2 Sam. 19:17). If an ox killed a slave then the ox would be stoned, which was the same punishment that was administered for the killing of a free person (Exod. 21:28–36). Fugitive slaves from other nations could not be returned to their masters and were allowed to live without oppression in the land of Israel (Deut. 23:15–16).

In many respects, Israel's slave laws were superior to those in the surrounding cultures. The Code of Hammurabi, for example, prescribed the death penalty for sheltering fugitive slaves and only required a modest fine for the crime of injuring someone else's slave.[557] The code did not prescribe a punishment for mistreating one's own slave. According to C.J. Wright, "No other ancient Near Eastern law has been found that holds a master to account for the treatment of his own slaves (as distinct from injury done to the slave of another master), and the otherwise universal law regarding runaway slaves was that they must be sent back, with severe penalties for those who failed to comply."[558]

The authors of the Old Testament also understood the crushing cycle of debt that afflicted their kinsmen. That's why Exodus 21:26 says that Hebrew slaves had to be set free and released from their debts every six years (this is not unlike our modern legal practice of allowing someone to file for bankruptcy once every seven years). Deuteronomy states this requirement explicitly:

> Take heed lest there be a base thought in your heart, and you say, "The seventh year, the year of release is near," and your eye be hostile to your poor brother, and you give him nothing, and he cry to the Lord against you, and it be sin in you . . . You shall remember that you were a slave in the land of Egypt, and the Lord your God redeemed you; therefore I command you this today" (Deut. 15:9–15).

Crime and Punishment

Sometimes slavery in the Old Testament was used to punish criminals, a practice that even modern people can understand to some degree. For example, Exodus 22:1 lays out the instruction for punishing a thief: "If a man steals an ox or a sheep, and kills it or sells it, he shall pay five oxen for an ox, and four sheep for a sheep. He shall make restitution." Proverbs 6:31 likewise says, "If [a thief] is caught, he will pay sevenfold; he will give all the goods of his house." The criminal was expected to pay back more than what he stole for many possible reasons—to deter others from committing the same crime, to make up for the trouble he's caused the farmer beyond the theft itself (such as the time involved in punishing the thief), and to demand a justly deserved punishment in return for the serious crime he committed.

But what if the thief can't make restitution because he is poor and already sold or ate what he stole? Exodus 22:1 says, "If he has nothing, then he shall be sold for his theft." According to professor of biblical law Jonathan Burnside, "The sale appears to create a form of (temporary) debt slavery . . . the insolvent thief is sold only to secure repayment for the value of the stolen animal: he is not sold in order to make multiple restitution."[559] This punishment is similar to modern laws that punish thieves with fines that are much higher than the value of goods they stole, or jail time if the thief can't pay the fine and/or is guilty of a serious offense, like grand theft.

Some critics may still think this is a harsh punishment, but Israel's laws that required enslavement were more lenient than other ancient law codes. The Code of Hammurabi, for example, authorized the execution of thieves who could not repay what they stole.[560]

BEATING AND KILLING SLAVES

At this point some critics contend that the Bible does not merely regulate debt slavery. They say it also endorses "chattel slavery," or the treatment of slaves as property that can be abused for any reason. They might cite Exodus 21:20–21, which says, "When a man strikes his slave, male or female, with a rod and the slave dies under his hand, he shall be punished. But if the slave survives a day or two, he is not to be punished; for the slave is his money."

Striking someone with a rod was a common disciplinary procedure in the ancient Near East (it is still a common tool of discipline in many parts of the world). The rod was not supposed to be a lethal weapon, so if someone died immediately from being struck, it was proof that the person doing the striking had a murderous intent. But if a slave died of his injuries a few days or weeks later, then it would be an accidental killing.

This parallels the treatment of physical violence toward free men in Exodus 21:12–13: "Whoever strikes a man so that he dies shall be put to death. But if he did not lie in wait for him, but God let him fall into his hand, then I will appoint for you a place to which he may flee."[561] The man who accidentally kills a free man is not executed and is even given access to a sanctuary where he can be protected from the vengeance of the dead man's relatives. The same punishment is administered for the unintentional death of a slave, but no sanctuary is needed, since the slave's relatives (if he had any) probably lacked the social clout necessary to inspire "mob justice."

It's true that in the verse "for the slave is his money," the Hebrew word *kaspow* does mean "money," but that doesn't mean that a slave was only an object like a plough or an ox. The phrase "the slave is his money" probably means that the master lost the value of the slave's labor during his recuperation and was also required to pay for his healing.[562] This corresponds to verse 19, which says that if a free man injures another free man in a quarrel, "he shall pay for the loss of [the victim's] time, and shall have him thoroughly healed." Since slaves belonged to their masters, this responsibility would fall on them in lieu of any other punishment.

However, the slave is not considered to have the same value as money or tools. As we've seen, Exodus 21:20 explicitly says that a man who intentionally kills a slave would be punished. Indeed, the Hebrew word used for "punish," *naqam*, is ordinarily used to describe vengeance that comes through execution.[563]

Sex Slavery?

Some allegations of sex slavery in the Old Testament, such as the idea that women were sold into marriage after a man paid a "bride price" (Gen. 34:12), simply misunderstand ancient customs. The bride price, and its counterpart for grooms, called a dowry, is a sum of money or gifts families give to one another upon the occasion of a wedding. This is done to compensate the family for the loss of labor incurred by a child leaving to marry. The custom was ubiquitous in the ancient world and is still practiced in some areas. Paying the bride price was not and still is not a way to "purchase" a spouse.[564]

Other critics say Exodus 21:7–11 is evidence that the Israelites practiced a form of chattel slavery that some would call "sex slavery:"

> When a man sells his daughter as a slave, she shall not go out as the male slaves do. If she does not please her master, who has designated her for himself, then he shall let her be redeemed; he shall have no right to sell her to a foreign people, since he has dealt faithlessly with her. If he designates her for his son, he shall deal with her as with a daughter. If he takes another wife to himself, he shall not diminish her food, her clothing, or her marital rights. And if he does not do these three things for her, she shall go out for nothing, without payment of money.

First, most fathers in ancient Israel were not heartless monsters ready to make a few shekels off their little girls. In fact, Leviticus 19:29 condemns those who would practice this kind of exploitation: "Do not profane your daughter by making her a harlot, lest the land fall into harlotry and the land become full of wickedness." Second, a situation in which a father sold his daughter to another man probably came about because the father could not provide for her. He would not have been selling his child into sex slavery but into, as Gregory Chirichigno put it, "a type of marriage or adoption contract . . . which afforded to

a girl rights equal to that of a free-woman or wife, not a concubine or slave-wife."[565]

Is this an ideal solution to the problem of extreme poverty?
No. But it was a common one used at the time, and so the biblical
author tried to make the situation more tolerable for the woman
involved. This law provided destitute women with domestic and
economic security and protected them from exploitation. It did
not regulate their sale as if they were pieces of property.

Endorsement of Slavery? Part II

One argument against the previous interpretation of Israel's slave laws is that these beneficial laws applied only to Israelites. Critics say that Leviticus 25:44–46 shows that the Israelites were allowed to treat *foreign* slaves like chattel. The passage says,

> You may buy male and female slaves from among the nations that are round about you. You may also buy from among the strangers who sojourn with you and their families that are with you, who have been born in your land; and they may be your property. You may bequeath them to your sons after you, to inherit as a possession for ever; you may make slaves of them, but over your brethren the people of Israel you shall not rule, one over another, with harshness.

FOREIGN SLAVERY IN ANCIENT ISRAEL

Earlier I was careful to say that debt slavery was the *typical* form of slavery that existed in ancient Israel, not that it was the *only* one. It's not wise for Christians to say that slavery in Israel was only debt based and temporary. Leviticus makes it clear that foreign slaves could be bought and owned in perpetuity. But critics are wrong when they say these kinds of slaves could be treated like property.

Although other ancient law codes, such as the Code of Hammurabi, made explicit distinctions between the treatment of chattel slaves and former debt slaves, Leviticus 24:22 says, "You shall have one law for the sojourner and for the native."[566] The evidence strongly suggests that laws like those found in Exodus 21:26–27 and 21:20 protected all slaves regardless of their national or religious status. According to Chirichigno,

The biblical law in Exod. 21:20–21 not only prohibits mis-
treatment against chattel slaves, but this also stresses that own-
ership is a responsibility that requires owners to treat their
slaves like fellow members of the covenantal community . . .
these laws demonstrate the radical nature of the biblical slave
laws concerning assault, which place chattel slaves on a level
with freemen.[567]

In addition, laws that forbade returning or oppressing fugitive slaves from other countries contradict the idea these slaves
were treated like chattel in Israel. Indeed, Israel's fugitive slave
law provides indirect evidence that foreign slaves *desired* to live
under Israelite authority and were willing to risk severe punishment for that chance. According to Raymond Westbrook, "the
foreign fugitive was being granted the status of resident alien
without geographical limitation, which would protect him from
being enslaved by an Israelite."[568]

Finally, the Old Testament repeatedly exhorts the Israelites
to treat non-Israelites dwelling in their midst with kindness and
respect. Leviticus 19:34 says, "The stranger who sojourns with
you shall be to you as the native among you, and you shall love
him as yourself; for you were strangers in the land of Egypt:
I am the Lord your God." In Leviticus 25:23 God even says,
"The land shall not be sold in perpetuity, for the land is mine;
for you are strangers and sojourners with me." In other words,
God's people must be kind to foreigners and non-Hebrew slaves
because the Israelites are like foreigners in the eyes of the God,
who owns the land they have been given permission to inhabit.

PERMANENT SLAVERY IN ISRAEL

One point of contention still remains: why could Hebrew slaves
be set free after six years of service while non-Hebrew slaves
could be owned for life? The answer probably has to do with
land rights. We've already seen how farmers who were indebted
to land owners usually ended up being the ones who were

enslaved. Since God wanted to bless his chosen people with land to call their own, the Pentateuch divided the promised land among Israel's various clans and families (Josh. 13–19).

The goal of these regulations was to keep the land in possession of families and not allow it to be acquired by a few wealthy individuals. For example, the regulations prohibited the permanent selling of land to another person (Lev. 25:23), required that land be available for redemption if Israelite families could afford to reclaim it (Lev. 25:24–28), and prohibited foreigners from buying land in Israel.[569] Even today, the Israeli Land Authority does not sell land to foreign nationals. This is done to make sure the nation of Israel (which is constantly on guard against threats from its neighbors) is not "taken over" by Arab commercial interests.

The ancient version of this law protected Israel's unique identity, but it also made it difficult for non-Israelites to sustain themselves. Foreigners could either make a living as hired laborers (which, according to Deuteronomy 24:14–15, left them vulnerable to exploitation and poverty) or they could be permanently assimilated into a family they served. Even Hebrew slaves, who were required to be freed after six years and given provisions to survive on their own (Deut. 15:12–15), often chose to remain enslaved. Deuteronomy 15:16–17 says,

> But if [your slave] says to you, "I will not go out from you," because he loves you and your household, since he fares well with you, then you shall take an awl, and thrust it through his ear into the door, and he shall be your bondman for ever. And to your bondwoman you shall do likewise.

We see a similar example of this in Exodus 21:4–6:

> If his master gives [his slave] a wife and she bears him sons or daughters, the wife and her children shall be her master's and he shall go out alone. But if the slave plainly says, "I love my master, my wife, and my children; I will not go out free," then

his master shall bring him to God, and he shall bring him to the door or the doorpost; and his master shall bore his ear through with an awl; and he shall serve him for life.

It's possible that the "wife" is not a fellow slave, but a daughter of the master, who was given to the slave in hopes of securing him as a permanent worker in his household. This would be similar to the labor Jacob was required to provide in order to marry Laban's daughters in Genesis 31, or Sheshan, who gave his daughter in marriage to his slave Jarha (1 Chron. 2:35).[570] However, it's more likely the wife was a foreign slave or concubine who belonged in perpetuity to the master. In order to live with her and his children, the male slave would have to be formally assimilated into the master's house.

A Progressive Plan

Let's summarize where we are at so far: slavery was a universal institution in the ancient world that, like poverty and war, had no place in God's ultimate plan for humanity. God's desire was that there would be no poverty (Deut. 15:4), and that his people would transform their weapons of war into agricultural tools and never fight again (Isa. 2:4). However, in order to overcome the effects of sin and hardened hearts, God progressively revealed himself to his people and tolerated evils that their hard hearts embraced, like slavery and war. These evils were not meant to last forever, which is why God's word contained regulations designed to reduce and eventually eliminate them (see rule number fifteen).

This incremental approach could be compared to the current incremental approach many pro-life advocates take toward eliminating abortion in the United States. An absolute legislative prohibition could be issued, but since most people want at least some abortions to be legal, it would probably be ignored or voted down. Instead, a gradual, educational approach would better transform the country into one that protects unborn human life. In order to achieve this, a pro-life legislator might pass a law that restricts only the worst abortions (for example, a ban on partial-birth abortions), knowing that even if this does not end abortion outright it will start to turn public sentiment against the procedure.[571]

In the same way, the authors of the Old Testament passed laws that helped remove some of the worst abuses that were present in ancient Mesopotamian slavery and set the stage for God's people to eventually reject the institution of slavery in its entirety. Unfortunately, these preventive measures were not found in the laws of the Roman Empire, which forms the context for discussing slavery in the time of Christ and the apostles.

SLAVERY IN THE NEW TESTAMENT

Estimates of the slave population in the Roman Empire range from 15 to 90 percent of the population, but most scholars settle for a figure between to 25 and 40 percent.[572] Most of these slaves were either purchased from foreign merchants, acquired when Rome invaded other territories (for example, when Rome conquered Carthage during the First and Second Punic Wars), or were born into slavery. Although a few slaves were able to purchase their freedom, most endured a cruel existence. According to historian Sandra Joshel, slaves could not legally marry or own property because "The slave was res, a thing, property, an object . . . wounding or killing a slave was usually counted as damage to property; the owner, not the slave, sued for the recovery of a loss to property."[573]

The situation improved somewhat in the mid-second century A.D., when the Roman emperor Antoninus Pius passed legislation that forbade masters from killing their slaves without just cause.[574] The legislation also gave slaves the right to complain about harsh treatment from their masters, but even in cases of abuse, the law did not provide for the abused slave to be released. Instead, it prescribed the sale of the slave to a master who would treat him better. Of course, these reforms came long after the time of Christ's earthly ministry, when slaves, especially rural, farmland slaves, faced a miserable existence.

But if that's the case, then why didn't Jesus speak out against slavery?

First, the Bible tells us that Jesus said and did many things that are not recorded in it (John 20:30; 21:25), so we can't confidently assert that Jesus never said anything about slavery. Second, Jesus told a crowd in Nazareth that the prophet Isaiah's promise of an anointed one who would be "sent to proclaim release to the captives" was fulfilled in him (Luke 4:18). This implies that part of Jesus' mission was to free people from whatever held them captive—be it spiritual captivity, like sin or demonic possession; or material captivity, such as unjust taxation (Luke 19:1–10; 20:19–26); or oppressive, man-made religious traditions (Matt. 23:1–4, Mark 7:1–23). It's reasonable, then, to believe that Jesus thought of slavery as a similar kind of oppression that had no place in the kingdom of God.

However, some critics say Jesus' parables used images of slaves, which means he accepted slavery (Matt. 25:14–30). But Jesus did not condone everything found in his own parables. These stories used familiar circumstances in order to teach people less-familiar spiritual truths. For example, Jesus' description of the prodigal son being paid so poorly that he nearly starved to death does not mean that Jesus *condoned* such poor working conditions (Luke 15:14–17). It was just a fact of life to which his listeners could relate. In fact, Jesus' parables teach people to mercifully forgive debts (Matt. 18:23–35) and to pay laborers what they're worth (Luke 10:7), which are ideas that strike at the heart of slavery and other forms of economic exploitation. Scholar Jennifer Glancy says,

> Awareness of the dishonor associated with slavery should bring us a fresh appreciation of the newness of Jesus' mandate to his followers to embrace the role of "slave of all" [Mark 9:35]. Jesus died an excruciating and humiliating death, the death of a slave. This death is a model for the disciple's life.

Jesus does not condemn the institution of slavery. What he demands is something unexpected. He stipulates that his followers are to become a community of slaves serving one another [Matt. 20:26–27]."[575]

It's true that we have no record of Jesus explicitly rejecting the institution of slavery, but he did instill in his followers an implicit rejection of slavery that can be seen in the writings of his disciples and future apostles.

PAUL'S ADVICE FOR SLAVES

In his letters to Christian communities, St. Paul described himself as a slave who belonged to Christ (Rom. 1:1, Phil. 1:1), exhorted his listeners not to be slaves to sin (Rom. 6:15–23), and encouraged them to be slaves to one another (Gal. 5:13). Paul even said that Christ took on the nature of a slave and became poor for our sake (2 Cor. 8:9, Phil. 2:7). His audience knew what it meant to be a slave, which is not surprising since Christianity's compassion for the lowly earned it the reputation of being a "slave religion." The second-century pagan critic Celsus once sneeringly described converts to the Church as "foolish and low individuals" like "slaves, and women, and children."[576]

However, this language in Paul's letters does not mean that he endorsed slavery or that he thought it should be a part of God's kingdom. To understand why this is the case, let's look at the specific exhortations Paul gives to slaves, starting with one passage critics of the Bible often cite:

> Slaves, be obedient to those who are your earthly masters, with fear and trembling, in singleness of heart, as to Christ; not in the way of eye-service, as men-pleasers, but as servants of Christ, doing the will of God from the heart, rendering service with a good will as to the Lord and not to men, knowing that whatever good any one does, he will receive the same again from the Lord, whether he is a slave or free (Eph. 6:5–8).

Many critics of the Bible say these words are indefensible, but what advice should Paul have given Christian slaves in the Roman Empire? Should he have told them to rebel against their masters? One hundred years before Paul wrote this letter, a slave named Spartacus led a rebellion in southern France that scored a few victories but was ultimately defeated by the Roman general Marcus Crassus. Spartacus died in battle and six thousand of his comrades were crucified along the Appian Way.[577] A similar fate would have awaited any Christian uprising against slave owners.

Maybe instead of encouraging outright rebellion Paul could have said that slavery was wrong and encouraged slaves to simply revile their masters. But even that advice would have risked the persecution of the whole Church if the Roman authorities had become aware of it. In addition, Paul was more concerned about people being enslaved to sin than their being enslaved to other people (though, as we will see, Paul was also concerned about human slavery as well). This attitude parallels Jesus' warning that sinners become "slaves to sin" (John 8:34), as well as his exhortation to fear the one who can kill the body and the soul in hell, and not just the one who can kill the body (Matt. 10:28).

Paul's advice to Christian slaves was to endure their unjust condition by persevering in holiness. For example, Paul told Titus, "Bid slaves to be submissive to their masters and to give satisfaction in every respect; they are not to talk back, nor to pilfer, but to show entire and true fidelity, so that in everything they may adorn the doctrine of God our Savior" (Titus 2:9–10). A slave may not have had control over whether he would be enslaved in this life, but he could control whether he would be enslaved to Satan in the next life. St. Peter also taught this when he told slaves, "Be submissive to your masters with all respect, not only to the kind and gentle but also to the overbearing. For one is approved if, mindful of God, he endures pain while suffering unjustly" (1 Pet. 2:18–19).

Peter and the other apostles knew that slavery was wrong, but they also knew that it was better to conquer evil with good (Rom. 12:21) than to commit evil in order to achieve good. That's why

Peter rhetorically asks what good it does for a slave to commit evil against his master and then be beaten in return. At least, when a slave is beaten for no good reason and does not respond with evil (in imitation of Christ, who endured similar abuses without retaliation), he will stand blameless before God (1 Pet. 2:20). Loyalty to a master was also a common way for slaves in the Roman Empire to earn their freedom. After serving a master faithfully, a slave would be released as a *libertus*, who served his master in a new capacity as a freeman (we will see what that entailed shortly). Paul may even have exhorted slaves to acquire their freedom in this way:

> Every one should remain in the state in which he was called. Were you a slave when called? Never mind. But if you can gain your freedom, avail yourself of the opportunity. For he who was called in the Lord as a slave is a freedman of the Lord. Likewise he who was free when called is a slave of Christ. You were bought with a price; do not become slaves of men. So, brethren, in whatever state each was called, there let him remain with God (1 Cor. 7:20–24).[578]

This passage shows that Paul didn't think slavery was a good thing. In fact, he implicitly argued that men could not own other men because God owns all humans by virtue of having redeemed them on the cross (1 Cor. 6:19–20; 7:23). Being enslaved to men was an imperfect part of this life that had no place in the kingdom of God. In that kingdom, everyone, regardless of socioeconomic background, is a slave of Christ, our true Lord and Master. That's why in Galatians 3:28 Paul says, "There is neither Jew nor Greek, there is neither slave nor free, there is neither male nor female; for you are all one in Christ Jesus."

This was a revolutionary idea, given that Roman intellectuals, while lamenting some aspects of slavery, generally held slaves to be of lesser worth than free men.[579] However, slaves in the early Church were not stigmatized, and some, like Pius I (A.D. 140–155) and Callixtus I (218–223), even held the office of pope.

PAUL'S ADVICE FOR SLAVE OWNERS

Like Peter, Paul said that when it came to slaves and free people, God doesn't play favorites. Instead, every "wrongdoer will be paid back for the wrong he has done" (Col. 3:25). Just as Paul exhorted slaves not to sin against their masters, he exhorted masters not to sin against their slaves. His advice for slave owners is summarized in Colossians 4:1, where he says, "Masters, treat your slaves justly and fairly, knowing that you also have a Master in heaven," as well as in Ephesians 6:9, which adds the exhortation that masters should stop "threatening" their slaves.

The letter to Philemon also gives us a unique, pastoral anecdote concerning Paul's view of slavery. In this letter, Paul describes his desire to return a slave named Onesimus to his master, Philemon. Paul tells Philemon that he can command him to do the right thing, but for love's sake Paul makes an appeal instead (Philem. 8–9). He asks that Onesimus, who Paul is sending back to Philemon apparently on his own initiative (Philem. 12), be received "no longer as a slave but more than a slave, as a beloved brother, especially to me but how much more to you, both in the flesh and in the Lord" (Philem. 16).

Although interpretations of Philemon and Onesimus's relationship differ among scholars, I am partial to the view that these men were half brothers. If that's true, then both men had the same father, but Philemon was born to a free wife, thus giving him inheritance rights and authority, whereas Onesimus was born to a slave wife or a concubine, and was therefore treated with the same social status as his mother. This explains how the men could be brothers "in the flesh" as well as "in the Lord."

But even if this was not the men's relationship, a question still arises in the minds of critics. We know Onesimus was Philemon's slave, so why didn't Paul explicitly command Philemon to free him? In fact, why didn't Paul command all Christian slave owners to free their slaves?

First, slavery was tightly regulated in the Roman Empire, as is evidenced in the *Lex Fufia Caninia* and *Lex Aelia Sentia*, passed at the behest of Caesar Augustus. These laws required anyone seeking to free a slave, what is called manumission, to present good reasons to a Roman council. The Roman jurist Gaius, for example, said that one good reason for freeing a slave was if the slave were a family member.[580] This would explain why Paul wanted Philemon to have Onesimus return as "more than a slave," which could mean that he was asking Philemon to restore Onesimus to an equal, familial status through manumission.

These laws also forbade masters from freeing too many slaves at one time, which seemed to be necessary because manumission was extremely common. Augustus even banned this practice for any slave under the age of thirty, in order to keep the slave population in check.[581] Therefore, an exhortation to "free all the slaves" may have violated Roman law and been considered as seditious as demanding that the entire institution of slavery be abolished.

In addition, in ancient Rome freed slaves did not abandon their masters after settling into new employment. Instead, these slaves became "clients" (*liberti*) and their former masters became "patrons" (*patroni*), to whom they still owed loyalty, favors, and the fruit of their labor.[582] Freed slaves usually took the name of their former master's family, and the client/patron relationship helped the *liberti* overcome social stigmas and monetary hurdles that prevented them from climbing the Roman social ladder.

Since manumission was common, Paul may have taken for granted that slaves belonging to Christian masters would enjoy good living conditions until they were released at the right time to serve as *liberti*. This may even have motivated Paul to write about slaves who take advantage of a Christian master's kindness. He advised his disciple Timothy, "Those [slaves] who have believing masters must not be disrespectful on the ground that they are brethren; rather they must serve all the better since those who benefit by their service are believers and beloved" (1 Tim. 6:2).

This comports with Paul's other teachings that Christians are united in one Mystical Body (1 Cor. 12), and that all Christians, free or slave, are called to be slaves to one another (Gal. 5:13). In fact, when it comes to Onesimus, an ancient tradition tells us that he was freed and became a bishop in Ephesus.[583] But even if that was not the case, we can agree that Paul did not favor slavery. In fact, Paul's preaching of the gospel was aimed at undermining slavery through the imposition of religious and moral demands that made owning human beings antithetical to the Christian life. Renowned New Testament scholar James Dunn summarized the issue well:

> The economies of the ancient world could not have functioned without slavery. Consequently, a responsible challenge to the practice of slavery would have required a complete reworking of the economic system and complete rethinking of social structures, which was scarcely thinkable at the time . . . [Paul's] call for masters to treat their slaves "with justice and equity" assumes a higher degree of equality than was normal. And above all, the repeated reference to the primary relationship to the Lord (for both slave and free) highlights a fundamental criterion of human relationships which in the longer term was bound to undermine the institution itself.[584]

22

Drunk with Blood?

The Claim: The God of the Bible is the most prolific mass murderer in all of history. From drowning every living creature to sending bears to kill forty-two little children, the Bible is filled with tales of God killing human beings for any reason or for no reason at all.

In his unpublished short story "The Mysterious Stranger," Mark Twain describes the tale of three young boys who meet a handsome stranger named Satan, who assures them that he is a good angel and not like the "other Satan." But the boys soon notice that Satan despises other creatures and doesn't care about their well-being. For example, he impresses the boys by bringing clay sculptures to life, but then kills the creatures after they begin to annoy him. One of the boys describes Satan's destruction this way:

> "[T]he castle's wreck and ruin tumbled into the chasm, which swallowed it from sight, and closed upon it, with all that innocent life, not one of the five hundred poor creatures escaping. Our hearts were broken; we could not keep from crying."
>
> "Don't cry," Satan said; "they were of no value."
>
> "But they are gone to hell!"
>
> "Oh, it is no matter; we can make plenty more."[585]

Twain was no fan of religion and so it's no surprise that his "mysterious stranger" is supposed to resemble a God he believed had an equally callous disregard for human life. Twain would probably ask us, "If the boys were rightfully upset when the stranger killed little self-aware clay men, then shouldn't we be equally upset at the God of the Bible who has killed many more people?"

GOD THE SERIAL KILLER?

It's true that the Bible depicts God killing lots of human beings.
It describes him drowning all the inhabitants of the land except for the occupants of Noah's ark (Gen. 6:8). It says he killed
70,000 Israelites in punishment for David's census (2 Sam. 24:13),
and 185,000 Assyrian soldiers while they slept (2 Kings 19:35).
Steve Wells has even collected enough excerpts from his *The
Skeptic's Annotated Bible* to write a second book dedicated solely
to biblical accounts that describe God killing human beings.
The book is called *Drunk with Blood: God's Killings in the Bible.*

Wells claims that the Bible records God killing 2,821,364 humans, but he says the number could be as high as 25 million (the
unidentified deaths in Noah's flood account for the majority of
the estimated kills).[586] He admits that the New Testament has a
far lower "body count" than the Old, but even it records how
God killed Ananias and Sapphira because they lied about withholding their contributions to the apostles (Acts 5:1–11).

How should Christians respond to arguments like this?

First, in some cases Wells assumes that God has killed someone when the evidence does not conclusively show this. Take
the case of Ananias and Sapphira. The text only says that when
they heard Peter's indictment of their behavior, they "fell down
at his feet and died." The passage never says that God did anything to cause their deaths. Their fear at being caught could
have caused them to die. God might even have providentially
arranged the world so that Ananias and Sapphira would die of
natural causes after they lied to the apostles.

It's also possible that some of these fatal incidents were not
meant to be read as literal history. The stories of Noah's Flood,
the destruction of Sodom, and even the death of the firstborn
of Egypt during the Passover may have been designed to communicate a certain message about God rather than to chronicle
actual killings that took place in a historical context. But it's
also possible, and no doubt likely, that some of these stories are
historical, and they describe God directly ending people's lives.
Ananias and Sapphira's deaths can be plausibly interpreted this

way and so can many other accounts that describe God striking someone down (1 Sam. 6:19, 2 Sam. 6:7).

But even if some of these accounts do not describe literal events, they still affirm the moral permissibility of God directly killing innocent men, women, and children (as well as animals, in the case of Noah's flood). But what's wrong with that? Wells simply declares that these killings exhibit "unspeakable cruelty and obvious immorality," but he makes no argument for that assertion.[587] Indeed, underlying all the allegations that the God of the Bible is an evil "murderer" is a claim that is often assumed but rarely argued for—that God has no right to end our lives.

LICENSE TO KILL

I believe this is the most common reasoning behind the claim that God's killings in the Bible prove he is evil:

1. If a person like you or me were suddenly granted omnipotence and drowned every creature on earth or killed all the firstborn in a major city, we would be considered moral monsters.
2. God is a person with the same moral duties as people like us.
3. God killed innocent men, women, and children.
4. Therefore, God is a moral monster.

In fact, God forbade the killing of the innocent (Exod. 20:13, Prov. 6:16–17), and he must abide by his own rules. As Barker says, "Why is God special? Why should a deity get away with atrocities that would send you or me straight to prison?"[588] But there are several assumptions in this argument that need to be challenged.

We've already seen that the third premise might not be true (the killings might not have occurred in a historical context), but let's assume for the sake of the argument that these killings actually happened. The argument still doesn't succeed, because the second premise is false—God is not just a super-powered human being who must behave like all other human beings.

Even among humans there are cases in which a person with authority is permitted to do what someone under his authority may not do. For example, police officers may break the speed limit in order to apprehend a suspect, or a school principal may cancel classes for the day while a student may not.

Killing innocent humans might be wrong for *other humans*, but it may not be wrong for God, because God has ultimate authority over human life. Indeed, we often indict people who unethically create or destroy human life as "playing God." We recognize they don't have the authority to act toward human life in the same way God does. But certainly God has the authority to "play himself"!

Still, why think that God has the authority to kill innocent human beings and the rest of us do not? This is where a finer point in the second assumption needs to be challenged: the idea that God is just an all-powerful human or angelic person. An omnipotent human person would be terrifying because, as Lord Acton said, "Absolute power corrupts absolutely." But God isn't just an all-powerful cosmic genie.

As we already learned, God is *ipsum esse*, or the perfect act of being itself. God's power is not arbitrary, but is identical to his goodness and his will (CCC 271). He deserves our worship because he has perfect and supreme authority over our lives and is incapable of using his omnipotent power for evil. In fact, one reason to believe that God has authority over our lives is because he *gave us our lives in the first place*.

Life is a gift from God, which means that God is allowed to take it back whenever he wants to. This is reflected in the sentiments of the biblical protagonist Job, who, after learning that his children had been killed in a natural disaster, said, "Naked I came from my mother's womb, and naked shall I return; the Lord gave, and the Lord has taken away; blessed be the name of the Lord" (Job 1:21). None of us did anything to earn our lives, and so we have no basis for saying God wrongs us by taking away the lives he gave us. In other words, *Life is a gift from God, and he has complete authority over it.* That is Bible-reading rule number sixteen.

AN "INDIAN GIVER"?

Let's look at a few common objections to this defense of God's actions in the Bible. First, there's the "Indian-giver objection." "Indian giver" is a pejorative term that describes people who give gifts and then rudely ask for them to be returned. It originated with European settlers, who thought Native Americans were giving them gifts, when in reality the Natives Americans thought they were trading and expected a gift in return.[589] When they didn't get one, they took their gift back.

If God gives us life and is allowed to take that gift back whenever he chooses, then isn't he an "Indian giver"?

The problem with this objection is that not all gifts involve permanent exchanges. In some cases, a gift can take the form of a loan, such as when a father lets his grown child indefinitely use the family car with the caveat that the father can reclaim the car whenever he chooses. In fact, when there is a greater disparity in maturity or authority between the giver and the receiver of a gift, the giver generally possesses a greater right to retrieve the gift.

For example, if a mother gives a gift to her three-year-old son, she still has every right to take it back. She may do that because the child is misusing the gift, or because it is not good for others around the child, or because the mother has something better to give the child instead. The child may not always understand what his mother has done, and he may even think she is being unfair, but that's because he lacks the knowledge and maturity to understand her actions. Much the same, our finite and fallen human nature limits our understanding of why God only allows us to live for a certain amount of time or why he allows us to suffer in this life before we die.

I know some people will find this analogy distasteful or even horrible. Can we really compare depriving a child of something like a birthday gift with God depriving a child of seeing any future birthdays because of his premature death? But we have to step back from our emotional response to death and look at this fact of life from a rational and eternal perspective.

God never intended for us to die, and he endowed our first parents with special graces that would have allowed them to live indefinitely.[590] But after they sinned, those graces were lost and could no longer be passed on to their descendants. This is why the penalty for sin is death (Rom. 6:23). Although non-religious people believe that death is bad because it deprives a person of enjoyable experiences, loving relationships, and even existence itself, Christians know that death is not bad for at least the last reason. We have immortal souls that survive death and are destined for eternal life with God, which is why St. Paul triumphantly said, "O death, where is your sting!" (1 Cor. 15:55).

But Paul's confidence in the face of death doesn't mean that death is a good thing. Death is still bad, because through death humans are deprived of valuable earthly things like relationships with people we love or the opportunity to share Christ with others. That's why Paul said, "For to me to live is Christ, and to die is gain. If it is to be life in the flesh, that means fruitful labor for me" (Phil. 1:21–22). Death is also bad because the condition of being a soul without a body is not how we are supposed to exist (2 Cor. 5:2–4). This is why we rejoice at the Creed's affirmation of "the resurrection of the body" and the hope that God will provide us a glorified, embodied life in heaven that will outweigh any suffering that death or other evils cause us in this life.

A Cosmic Tyrant?

The next objection could be called the "murder objection." Since murder is wrong because it violates a person's right to life, it follows that God is a murderer because he violates that right whenever he kills innocent human beings. But this argument doesn't succeed. The right to life is the moral claim that a person deserves to live and may not be killed unjustly. But the reason humans have this right is because God made them in his image and commanded, in accordance with his perfect character and nature, that they not be killed unjustly.[591] God, however, is not bound by this command because he retains the right to end the earthly existence he gave us.

Now, a critic could say, "If the rules about killing don't apply to God, then what rules do apply to him? If we say people are evil when they kill innocent humans but God is good when he does the same thing, then the concepts of *good* and *evil* become meaningless. If everything God does is good by definition, then isn't saying that God is good is just the same as the tautology 'God is God?'"[592] But this objection only holds true with behaviors that are intrinsically evil, or evil by their very nature.

Acts like rape or sadistic torture, for example, are intrinsically evil and can never be good, even if God were to perform them. But other acts are not intrinsically evil, and become evil only in certain circumstance. For example, the killing of human beings is not intrinsically evil, because if it were, then it would always be wrong, even in self-defense. Therefore, killing human beings is evil only under certain conditions.

But wouldn't one of those conditions be the direct killing of the innocent? Pope St. John Paul II declared that abortion was intrinsically evil for that very reason, which seems to create a dilemma.[593] We must either reject God's goodness and moral perfection because he killed innocent human beings (including born and even unborn children), or we must reject the claim that it is intrinsically evil to kill innocent human beings.

We can't reject God's goodness or perfection, because those are as essential to the concept of God as three sides are essential to the concept of a triangle. If God exists, then he must be the perfect and complete act of being. As perfect goodness itself, God cannot be "bad" or "evil," because evil is a privation of good and God has no privation or absence of any kind. But this does not negate the intrinsic evil of killing innocent human beings. It just means that it is only intrinsically evil for *humans* to take innocent human life, because we lack the authority to do that.

To continue a previous analogy, if a father gives a gift to his son, the fact that the father can take the gift back does not mean the boy's older brother has the right to do the same thing.

Perhaps the brother could take the gift in rare cases, such as if his younger brother is going to harm himself with it, but the brother would not have the same "gift-retrieving" authority as his father.

Likewise, humans can rightfully deprive other humans of life in specific circumstances— for instance, in a just war, or killing in self-defense—but only God has the right to end our lives when he sees fit. That's because God is the perfect author and Creator of life. Even if a person might be better off if he died at a particular time—for example, if a sick person died in a state of grace after baptism or the sacrament of confession—it would still be wrong to kill that person, because humans lack the authority that God has to decide if someone should die at that moment.

There is also what we might call the "other creators" objection: "If parents give 'the gift of life' to their children, does that mean they can take that gift back? Is the threat 'I brought you into this world and I can take you out of it' not an empty one?" But these cases are not analogous to God's authority over human life. When humans beget offspring they do not create life in the same way that God creates life from nothing at all. In fact, they are examples of how God allows creatures to use the procreative gifts he gave them in order to cooperate with his creative will. Humans cooperate with God to create life, but God still retains ultimate authority over the life he creates through such cooperation.

The *Catechism* even says, "Every spiritual soul is created immediately by God—it is not 'produced' by the parents" (CCC 366). Therefore, humans can't take the life of their own offspring because those children are themselves gifts from God to whom we have moral responsibilities. However, God is able to end our lives whenever he sees fit since life is ultimately a gift from him.

Strange Fire

Now, let's take a look at three cases in the Bible that critics say are examples of God exercising his right to take life in a capricious or cruel way, thus negating his goodness. They involve the strange fire of Nadab and Abihu, Uzzah and the Ark of the Covenant, and Elisha and the she-bears. Concerning the first episode, Leviticus 10:1–2 says,

> Now Nadab and Abihu, the sons of Aaron, each took his censer, and put fire in it, and laid incense on it, and offered unholy fire before the Lord, such as he had not commanded them. And fire came forth from the presence of the Lord and devoured them, and they died before the Lord.

Jason Long says, "I'm always amazed how God kills people because they do something silly like build a displeasing campfire."[594] But is that all that's happening here? Various proposals have been offered to explain what offended the Lord in this scene, but two of those interpretations seem to be the most likely.

First, God spoke to Aaron right after this incident and said, "Drink no wine nor strong drink, you nor your sons with you, when you go into the tent of meeting, lest you die; it shall be a statute for ever throughout your generations" (Lev. 10:8–9). It's possible that Nadab and Abihu blasphemed the Lord by offering a sacrifice while they were in a drunken stupor. But this doesn't explain the quality of the *fire* they offered as being "strange." Another explanation is that Nadab and Abihu did something even worse than sacrifice to God in an unworthy manner—they sacrificed to another god in the presence of the Lord.

Scholars have zeroed in on the second verse's use of the Hebrew word *za'rah* to modify the word for fire. The Catholic edition of the RSV translates the word as "unholy," but older translations render it as "strange." Throughout the Old Testament, this Hebrew word refers to people who were strangers to the tribe of Israel and refers also to strange, foreign gods. Deuteronomy 32:16–17 says, "They stirred him to jealousy with strange (*be-zarim*) gods; with abominable practices they provoked him to anger. They sacrificed to demons which were no gods." According to Old Testament scholar Richard Hess,

The view that the sons of Aaron were performing a ritual associated with non-Yahwistic West Semitic cults is defensible. Like Aaron, who earlier in the narrative of the Golden Calf (Exodus 32) was condemned for worshiping other gods, his sons also engage in a rite that has its background in the worship of other deities and the appointment to their priesthood.[595]

Far from condemning Nadab and Abihu for unusual pyrotechnics, the brothers were punished for blaspheming the sovereign and holy God of Israel. They should have known better than to spurn the God of Israel, especially in the tent of meeting, which served as God's holy dwelling place among the Israelites after the Exodus. Nadab and Abihu were especially culpable for what they did because they were the sons of Aaron, Israel's first high priest.

"ARK" YOU OVERREACTING?

After the Philistines captured the Ark of the Covenant and took it to the city of Ashdod, God struck the people of that city with tumors and disease. In 1 Samuel 6 the Philistines realized the ark wasn't worth such trouble, so they returned it to Israel. As the Israelites were traveling with it to Jerusalem, they stopped in a city called Beth-she'mesh, where some people sacrificed to the God of Israel. Others, however, looked inside the ark, and as a result God killed them (v. 19).

Later, in 2 Samuel 6, the ark is almost back in Jerusalem when it begins to fall off the cart upon which it is being carried. 2 Samuel 6:6–7 says, "When they came to the threshing floor of Nacon, Uzzah put out his hand to the ark of God and took hold of it, for the oxen stumbled. And the anger of the Lord was kindled against Uzzah; and God struck him there because he put forth his hand to the ark; and he died there beside the ark of God."

Skeptics balk at the idea that this killing could be justified, and *Ken's Guide to the Bible* is even dedicated to "Uzzah the oxcart driver, who deserved better." But much like how Nadab and Abihu were killed because they blasphemed God in one of the most holy places in Israel, Uzzah and the men of Beth-she'mesh were killed because they showed a lack of respect for another incredibly holy object—the Ark of the Covenant.

One of the dominant themes of the Old Testament is that the people of Israel were different from their unbelieving neighbors because their God, the true God, was the king of Israel. The Israelites were called to be a kingdom of priests (Exod. 19:6) who faithfully served the only being who deserves unyielding loyalty—the almighty and perfect God who created the world.

Unfortunately, as time went on the Israelites desired to have a king just like the other nations; they acted like a teenager who demands a car because all his friends have one. The Israelites may also have felt that a human king would be easier to identify with, provide more protection, and be easier to persuade than a divine king. This brings us to the ark, which, because it contained God's words inscribed on the tablets given to Moses on Mount Sinai, was essentially a stand-in for God.[596] This is evident in the fact that ancient near-eastern kings would be transported on a litter, or a basket connected to poles carried by other people. The ark was carried in much the same way: indeed, the book of Exodus gives specific instructions to carry the ark on what is essentially a litter (Exod. 25:10–15).

However, when the Israelites rejected God as their king, they chose not to treat him or the object that represented him as having royal authority. Instead, it was put on a cart and not carried on anything resembling a litter. Putting the ark on a cart to be hauled by animals would be like asking the president of the United States to ride in the baggage compartment of Air Force One. The commander in chief would end up getting banged around like a piece of luggage.

In fact, the ark did shift and would have fallen off the cart if Uzzah had not steadied it. But when Uzzah casually touched the ark in order to keep it from falling, he violated the command that forbade anyone except the high priest from touching it (Num. 4:15). If the ark had been treated with respect and placed on a litter, then Uzzah would not have needed to steady it at all. In the same way, the men of Beth-she'mesh would not have been able to treat the ark like a roadside tourist attraction. Both cases showed the consequences of dishonoring the sovereign Lord who brought the Israelites out of slavery and into the promised land.

ELISHA AND THE SHE-BEARS

After Elijah was assumed into heaven, the prophet Elisha continued Elijah's ministry. 2 Kings 2:23–25 describes an event that took place soon after, and that disturbs many people:

> [Elisha] went up from there [Jericho] to Bethel; and while he was going up on the way, some small boys came out of the city and jeered at him, saying, "Go up, you baldhead! Go up, you baldhead!" And he turned around, and when he saw them, he cursed them in the name of the Lord. And two she-bears came out of the woods and tore forty-two of the boys. From there he went on to Mount Carmel, and thence he returned to Samaria.

One nineteenth-century commentary described this as "one of the stories which naturally repel us more than any other in the Old Testament."[597] But notice that, just like the incident involving Ananias and Sapphira, this text does not say that God killed the boys or even that Elisha summoned the bears to kill them. It only says that Elisha cursed the boys and then the bears attacked them. Just because one event happened after another does not mean the two events have a causal relationship. God may have known the bear attack was imminent and simply chose not to stop it. It may even be the case that this story comes from a past recollection of a tragedy that provided a basis for a narrative that is not in the historical genre.

Eric Ziolkowski wrote in his study of this episode, "Perhaps a mauling incident near Bethel really happened, not as the supernatural result of a curse, or as divine punishment, but as a natural calamity coinciding with Elisha's visit, of which this tale expresses a guilt-ridden recollection."[598] Julie Parker likewise wrote, "Many scholars read 2 Kings 2:23–25 as a didactic story intended for a youthful audience. [The Old Testament scholar] John Gray suggests that this tale recalled a bygone disaster and was told by the locals 'to awe their children.'"[599]

But let's suppose that the bears were actually sent by God to attack the boys. Are there elements in the text that modern readers may be missing, things that show it isn't as harsh as they think? There are several.

First, they weren't a bunch of small children harmlessly teasing Elisha; they were a large, threatening group of young men. The Hebrew words often translated as "small boys" is *hunearim qetannim*.[600] *Qetannim* comes from *qatan* and means "small, young, least"; it doesn't specifically designate the boy's ages. *Hunearim* is derived from the Hebrew *na'ar*, which means "boy, lad, or youth."[601] In Scripture this word is predominantly used of young men who are over the age of twelve, like Isaac (Gen. 22:12) or Joseph (Gen. 37:2). 1 Kings 20:15 says Ahab "mustered all the sons (*na-a-re*) of Israel," and 1 Kings 11:14–17 refers to Hadad the Edomite as a *qatan na'ar*. It's hard to say that Hadad was a small child when he was old enough to flee to Egypt and find "great favor in the sight of the Pharaoh" (1 Kings 11:19).

It's also important to ask, "Why were there forty-two boys gathered in one place to confront Elisha?" In ancient Israel you wouldn't find dozens of very small children hanging out on the outskirts of town. They'd be with their parents or relatives. The only group of this size would be adolescents who had more freedom to wander (think of how Jesus made his way back to the temple in Jerusalem at age twelve, and no one in his family noticed for a while).

Now, imagine if over forty adolescents started making fun of you as you walked by yourself across a desolate area. You might become nervous, knowing that such a large group could cause you serious harm. In countries like Peru, gangs of children as young as eleven habitually rob and even kill people in broad daylight.[602] The boys may even have foolishly attacked the bears in order to get a delicious meal or prove their valor. After all, how could two bears kill over forty humans? The text doesn't attribute the bears with miraculous speed or agility.

Lastly, the boys weren't merely making fun of Elisha's lack of hair in the way a comedienne might make a joke about receding hairlines. Elisha was probably a young man himself in the story, because after this incident he went on to live for at least fifty years, through the reign of four kings. Elisha may have been bald, not from age, but from a vow he took to serve the Lord (Acts 21:24 refers to a similar vow and corresponding head shaving).

Therefore, the boys' taunts about his baldness may have been directed toward his decision to serve the God of Israel. It also could have been an epithet on par with calling someone an "idiot" regardless of his actual intelligence. Either way, the boys demonstrated profound lack of respect both for God and the prophets he sent.

Keep in mind that before this incident Elisha had just miraculously cleansed Jericho's water supply and now began an approximately ten-mile walk uphill to Bethel. If the boys came from Jericho, they saw firsthand that Elisha was a prophet of God, and they still chose to mock him. If they came from Bethel (which means "house of God"), then they probably represented the pagan elements of that city. 1 Kings 12:29 tells us that Jeroboam set up idolatrous golden calves in Bethel and the prophet Hosea referred to the city as *beth-aven* or "house of trouble" (Hos. 4:15).

According to *The Bible Knowledge Commentary*, "That 42 men were mauled by the two bears suggests that a mass demonstration had been organized against God and Elisha."[603] The boy's taunt to "go up" was almost certainly a reference to Elijah's assumption into heaven. It represented a desire for Elisha and his God to "get out of here" and disappear in a similar way. Rachelle Gilmour, in her study of the Elisha narratives, wrote, "It is no longer just an insult to Elisha, it is an insult to the Lord, and the bears appear only after a curse in his name . . . The stories of the water at Jericho and the bears on the road to Bethel resonate with an emphasis on the fulfillment of the prophetic word, bringing both life and death."[604]

THE SIN FACTOR

Notice that the episodes involving Nadab and Abihu, Uzzah, and the youths who taunted Elisha all share a common element. In each case, a person or persons deliberately refuse to recognize God's supreme holiness and give him the worship he deserves. As a result, they lose the lives God has given them. As we've already seen, this is not an act of evil, because God alone has the right to end the lives of human beings as he sees fit.

Modern people balk at the violence and loss of life in these stories, but what is usually absent from their criticisms is a concern about the sins these individuals and groups were guilty of committing. If we recognize that avoiding sin and seeking God with our heart, mind, and strength is what our focus in life should be, then we can understand why gruesome stories that treat sin with a heavy hand are included in Scripture. They serve as grim warnings not to follow the path that leads to death but the path that leads to eternal life.

23

Campaigns of Genocide? Part I

The Claim: What sane person could worship a God who
ordered believers to exterminate entire races of people? This
is undeniable proof that the Bible is not the word of God
but is instead the product of ancient, war-mongering barbarians.

What do you think of the following ancient Chinese account of
a warlord named General Lin?

> The General's army came to some great cities with high walls
> and strong fortresses. The Great Spirit appeared to General
> Lin in his dream and promised him victory, ordering him to
> kill all the living souls in the cities because those people did
> not worship the Great Spirit. So, General Lin and his soldiers
> took the towns and devoted to destruction all that was in
> the cities, both men and women, young and old, and ox and
> sheep and ass, with the edge of the sword.

If you're like most people, you probably disapprove of General Lin's actions. You might even think they were barbaric.
But what you may not know is that there was no General Lin.
He was the invention of a psychologist named George Tamarin,
who used the story in a study of Israeli children in the 1960s.[605]
Tamarin asked the children what they thought of General Lin's
actions as well as what they thought of the biblical hero Joshua.
The catch was that Joshua's battle commands served as the basis
for the story about General Lin. The Bible describes Joshua conquering the Canaanite city of Jericho this way:

> Joshua said to the people, "Shout! For the Lord has given you
> the city. And the city and all that is in it shall be devoted to

the Lord for destruction" . . . they utterly destroyed all in the city, both men and women, young and old, oxen, sheep, and donkeys, with the edge of the sword (Josh. 6:16–17, 21).

The children in Tamarin's study disagreed with what General Lin did but supported what Joshua did, even though the two men did almost exactly the same thing. But if we are morally repulsed when non-Christians "kill infidels," then shouldn't we be repulsed when God commands believers to do the same thing?

We have now come to what for many people is the most difficult problem in Scripture—passages that seem to record God ordering human beings to kill other innocent human beings. Let's examine these passages and see what moral and historical lessons we can draw from them in order to answer the charge that God is a "genocidal maniac."

The Problem of the Canaanites

In ancient times the land of Canaan covered an area that roughly corresponds to modern-day Israel, Lebanon, and parts of Jordan and Syria. In the Late Bronze Age (1500–1000 B.C.), this land was inhabited by a group of tribes that came to be known as the Canaanites. Before we discuss the conflict involving the Canaanites and the Israelites, we should examine some relevant background information about both groups.

In the book of Genesis, God told Abraham that his descendants would be "sojourners in a land that is not theirs, and will be slaves there, and they will be oppressed for four hundred years; but I will bring judgment on the nation which they serve, and afterward they shall come out with great possessions" (Gen. 15:13–14). This, of course, corresponds to the centuries of slavery the Hebrews endured in Egypt and their liberation through the Exodus.

God then told Abraham that he would "be buried in a good old age. And they [Abraham's descendants] shall come back here [the land of Canaan] in the fourth generation; for the iniquity of the Amorites is not yet complete" (Gen. 15:15–16). The Amorites were a group of mountain-dwelling Canaanites, but the iniquity God referred to was also present in the other Canaanites who inhabited the land. This includes worship of deities that committed murder, incest, and even bestiality.

God forbade the Israelites to worship these gods, not because of petty jealously, but out of concern that his children would imitate the destructive behavior of these deities. In Exodus 23:32–33, God explicitly says of the Canaanites, "You shall make no covenant with them or with their gods. They shall not dwell in your land, lest they make you sin against me; for if you serve their gods, it will surely be a snare to you."

When it comes to moral behavior, the Canaanite deities were certainly snares for their own people. For example, in Canaanite culture incest was punished only with a fine; it was not considered an abomination because their deities frequently engaged in it.[606] This probably explains why Lot's daughters, who had been raised in the Canaanite city of Sodom, thought it was acceptable to have intercourse with their father.

Other sexual sins among the Canaanites included adultery, homosexuality, and temple prostitution and bestiality.[607] Of course, these sexual sins were practiced in Israel, but whereas the Canaanites tolerated or even exalted these behaviors, the Israelites denounced them legally and socially.[608]

Perhaps the most heinous sin the Canaanites practiced was child sacrifice. Leviticus 18:21 forbade the Israelites from sacrificing their children to the Canaanite deity Molech, and Leviticus 20:2 requires that anyone who sacrifices to Molech be stoned. Jephthah's sacrifice of his daughter, which we discussed earlier, demonstrates the poisonous effects of Canaanite culture and why God was trying to protect the Israelites from it.

2 Kings 23:10 tells us that the righteous reformer King Josiah destroyed the sites in Israel where these sacrifices took place so that "no one might burn his son or his daughter as an offering to Molech." By the time of Christ, the place Josiah razed, the Valley of Hinnom, became known as *Gehenna*. This evil place had

become synonymous with the fires of hell that would consume evildoers (Mark 9:43–47).

Some people might claim that these descriptions of the Canaanites were exaggerated in order to justify the Israelites conquering their land. However, ancient historical and archaeological evidence have corroborated the Bible's testimony. The third century B.C. Greek historian Cleitarchus describes one such ceremony practiced by the descendants of the Canaanites who settled in the city of Carthage:

> There stands in their midst a bronze statue of Kronos, its hands extended over a bronze brazier, the flames of which engulf the child. When the flames fall upon the body, the limbs contract and the open mouth seems almost to be laughing, until the contracted [body] clips quietly into the brazier.[609]

The ancient Roman historian Plutarch adds this detail, "The whole area before the statue was filled with a loud noise of flutes and drums [so that] the cries of wailing should not reach the ears of the people."[610]

Archaeologists have also uncovered a site under the neighborhood of Salammbo in modern Carthage that contains vast deposits of small animal and human bones. The soil is infused with ash and charcoal, which shows that this was not just a burial site. It was instead a place where fire sacrifices were made.[611] Sometimes the bones of unborn children and two-year-olds were found next to one another, leading investigators to the conclusion that the next youngest child was sacrificed along with his stillborn brother or sister in case the latter was not sufficient to appease the deity.

Some critics try to downplay this evidence, but the ancient Near East scholar Christopher B. Hays bluntly said, "Efforts to show that the Bible does not portray actual child sacrifice in the Molek cult, but rather dedication to the god by fire, have been convincingly disproved. Child sacrifice is well attested in the ancient world, especially in times of crisis."[612]

Israelite Child Sacrifice?

Some critics object to the condemnation heaped on the Canaan-ites for their practice of child sacrifice by claiming the *Israel-ites* practiced child sacrifice as well. Isn't it hypocritical to say that the Canaanites were wicked for offering their children to Molech when the Israelites routinely offered their own children to Yahweh?

Critics who defend this view usually cite just a few texts to justify their position, some of which we have already discussed. They say, for example, that the story of Jephthah is evidence of child sacrifice being practiced in Israel. But as we've already seen, the book of Judges contains examples of pagan moral decay in Israel—not of accepted Israelite practices. Jephthah's story is tragic precisely because child sacrifice was so outside the norm for the Israelites, not because it was commonplace.

The closest critics come to showing the Bible sanctions child sacrifice is an appeal to Ezekiel 20:25–26. Through his prophet, God says of Israel, "I gave them statutes that were not good and ordinances by which they could not have life; and I defiled them through their very gifts in making them offer by fire all their first-born, that I might horrify them; I did it that they might know that I am the Lord."

But according to Scott Hahn and John Bergsma's analysis of this passage, Ezekiel is criticizing the accommodations found in Deuteronomy's law codes. He was trying to show that they were inferior to God's earlier standards for his people—which included standards for proper animal sacrifices. Hahn and Bergs-ma elaborate:

Many scholars recognize that the phrase is a reference to Ex-odus 13:12, since Ezekiel 20:26 uses virtually the same dic-tion. Notably, Exodus 13 goes on to refer specifically to "every first-born of man," only to exclude them from the consecrated "firstlings" mentioned in the previous verse. In other words, Exodus 13:13 distinguishes human firstborn from "every open-er of the womb" in order to exclude them from being offered.

Thus, in the closest biblical parallel to Ezekiel 20:26, the context makes clear that human sacrifice is not the referent. This supports our reading of Ezekiel 20:26 as referring to the sacrifice of animal firstlings, not humans.[613]

It's true some Israelites may have practiced child sacrifice just like Jephthah did, but it is not the case that the Bible approves of this behavior. Leviticus 18:21 specifically bans offering children in fire to molech and one of the evil things King Manasseh did in the sight of the Lord was burning his son as an offering (2 Kings 21:6). God also denounced those who, "built the high places of Baal to burn their sons in the fire as burnt offerings to Baal, which I did not command or decree, nor did it come into my mind" (Jer. 19:5).

Micah 6:7 even describes how an Israelite might rhetorically ask God, "Shall I give my first-born for my transgression, the fruit of my body for the sin of my soul?" in imitation of the Canaanites wicked behavior. The next verse gives the answer to this question—No. Specifically, it says that God "has showed you, O man, what is good; and what does the Lord require of you but to do justice, and to love kindness, and to walk humbly with your God?"

CRUEL TIMES

Genesis 15:13–16 tells us that God waited 400 years, until the sin of the Canaanites was so great that God "vomited" them out of the land (Lev. 18:25). This was accomplished when the Israelites conquered Canaan, or the "promised land," through a series of military campaigns that are described in the books of Joshua and Judges. It's important to remember that God said in Deuteronomy 9:5 that it was not Israel's righteousness that warranted them receiving the promised land (they too had been guilty of idolatry and other grave sins), but "because of the wickedness of these nations the Lord your God is driving them out from before you."

In other words, Israel wasn't perfect, but they weren't as depraved as other cultures of the time.

Deuteronomy 20 records how Israel was supposed to deal with the Canaanites in the promised land, as well as those who lived outside Canaan. Concerning the latter, the Israelites were told that they must offer peace terms to enemy cities in those regions. If the terms were accepted, then the inhabitants of those cities would be subjected to forced labor and would not be killed. If the terms were not accepted, then war was declared and the men of the city would be killed while the remaining women, children, and property would be confiscated. Old Testament scholar Joe Sprinkle, though, argues that the original Hebrew actually says that the victorious Israelites were *permitted* to kill the males of the conquered cities. God did not necessarily *command* them to do this.[614]

For most modern readers this may seem very cruel. Why couldn't the Israelites have found a nice, unoccupied plot of land and made it their own without engaging in war with other tribes? Why did they have to fight and enslave those they defeated? This seems awful because we in the Western world live in a different and generally more peaceful time than the ancient Israelites. Steven Pinker put it this way:

> The Bible depicts a world that, seen through modern eyes, is staggering in its savagery. People enslave, rape, and murder members of their immediate families. Warlords slaughter civilians indiscriminately, including the children. Women are bought, sold, and plundered like sex toys.[615]

People in undeveloped nations today still face these threats when warlords or terrorist groups like ISIS and Boko Haram attack their villages. People in developed nations, on the other hand, have a hard time understanding that threat until modern conveniences like electricity and a reliable police force no longer function. Consider, for example, the lawlessness that was rampant in the city of New Orleans just days after Hurricane

Katrina flooded it in 2005. One survivor recounts how he feared roving gangs bent on looting and murdering those who stood in their way. He says, "There was no electricity, no police, no nothing. We were like sitting ducks. I slept with a butcher knife and a hatchet under my pillow."[616]

In disaster situations safety in numbers can be more valuable than being alone, even when well supplied. That's why in the ancient world, where goods were scarce and often taken by force, people lived in tribes that provided them with some degree of protection. It was probably the case that other tribes occupied all the habitable areas of the land, so the Israelites would inevitably have come to blows with these people in competition for resources like water and food.

In his study of ethics in ancient Israel, John Barton showed that some ancient tribes, such as the Assyrians, believed that aggressive wars of expansion glorified their deities and so they could be launched for any reason or no reason at all. But Barton said that Israel did not share this attitude toward war: "No such motivation is to be found in Israelite warfare and what [the prophet] Amos says about the nations who ill-treat not only Israel but also each other implies that war is subject to strict limits."[617]

Israel's combat was primarily defensive in nature as the Israelites were trying to survive in a hostile world—they were not trying to conquer it. Indeed, Israel had a reputation for dealing honorably with their enemies. According to Roland de Vaux, "[T]he massacre of prisoners was never a general rule, nor were the tortures of which Assyrian texts and monuments offer only too many examples . . . the kings of Israel had a reputation for mercy (1 Kings 20:31): they did not kill their prisoners of war."[618]

Besides, even if the Israelites had kept to themselves, trouble would have eventually found them. Exodus 17:8 records how the Canaanite tribe of Amalek attacked Israel's weakest members after they left Egypt. Deuteronomy 25:17–19 provides a recollection of that event: "Remember what Amalek did to you on the way as you came out of Egypt, how he attacked you on the way, when you were faint and weary, and cut off at your rear all who lagged behind you . . . you shall blot out the remembrance of Amalek from under heaven; you shall not forget."

Leave Nothing That Breathes

The combat instructions recorded in Deuteronomy 20:1–15 reflected the harsh living conditions and cultural norms of the Bronze Age. They were not a mandate for Israel to conquer the known world and, in fact, on several occasions God prohibited the Israelites from going to war with other nations (Deut. 2:9, 19). But God's instructions for dealing with the Canaanites were different. Deuteronomy 20:16–18 says,

> In the cities of these peoples that the Lord your God gives you for an inheritance, you shall save alive nothing that breathes, but you shall utterly destroy them, the Hittites and the Amorites, the Canaanites and the Perizzites, the Hivites and the Jebusites, as the Lord your God has commanded; that they may not teach you to do according to all their abominable practices which they have done in the service of their gods, and so to sin against the Lord your God."

This is what the ancient Israelites called *herem* (also spelled *charam*), which means "the ban." This word can be found in passages like Numbers 21:2, which says that "Israel vowed a vow to the Lord, and said, 'If you will indeed give this people into my hand, then I will utterly destroy (*wehaharamti*) their cities.'"

Herem refers to the practice of taking what would normally have been the spoils of war like livestock, precious metals, and even prisoners, and devoting them to the Lord through their complete destruction. This seems to be what God required when it came to dealing with the Canaanites. They were simply so wicked that they had to be purged from the land and given back to God. The *herem* involving the Canaanites first took place under the leadership of Joshua. Joshua 10:40 says that he "defeated the whole land, the hill country and the Negeb and the lowland and the slopes, and all their kings; he left none remaining, but utterly destroyed all that breathed, as the Lord God of Israel commanded."

But even after Israel settled in Canaan, the Canaanite threat still loomed. This is why 1 Samuel 15:3 records God telling King Saul, "Now go and strike Amalek, and utterly destroy all that they have; do not spare them, but kill both man and woman, infant and suckling, ox and sheep, camel and donkey."

Now that we have more background on the relationship between the Israelites and the Canaanites, as well as the threat the Canaanites posed to the social order and God's plan for his people, we are in a position to examine different interpretive approaches for these texts.

24

Campaigns of Genocide? Part II

One common approach to interpreting the *herem* texts is to say they represent literal commands that God gave the Israelites and that were carried out within a historical context. The biggest objection to this view is that, if it's true, then the Bible records God commanding Israel to wipe out an entire people group in order to possess their land, or what many today would call genocide. How could God order his people to slaughter women, children, and even babies who had done nothing but live in a culture that differed from their own?

Interpretive Approach #1:
Literal Commands, Literal History

The literal approach is usually defended with the following rationale: as we saw in the previous chapter, God has the right to take any human being's life, regardless of age or moral character. If God has the right to end our lives with a plague or a natural disaster, then he has the right to end our lives through the use of human mediators. In the case of the Canaanites, this took the form of the Israelite soldiers. St. Thomas Aquinas put it this way:

> All men alike, both guilty and innocent, die the death of nature: which death of nature is inflicted by the power of God on account of original sin, according to 1 Samuel 2:6: "The Lord killeth and maketh alive." Consequently, by the command of God, death can be inflicted on any man, guilty or innocent, without any injustice whatever.[619]

This means that it is not always wrong for human beings to kill other, innocent human beings. Since God is morally permitted

315

to end the lives of human beings, it follows that someone who is acting under God's authority would be permitted to do the same thing. But why would God use such a violent means to end the lives of the Canaanites?

Anyone who has studied the philosophical problem of evil knows that God can allow human beings to suffer as long as God has a good reason for allowing the suffering. So let's consider the reasons God could have for commanding these killings as well as the context in which he issued these commands.

Commands in Context

First, God was committed to shepherding a chosen people from whom would come the Messiah, who would atone for the sins of all people, including the Canaanites. But this chosen people had to be protected from idolatry and other sins that would cause them to turn away from the one, true God. Since the habitable areas around God's chosen people were already occupied, God had to forcibly remove some people from these lands so that his chosen people could prosper and eventually bring their knowledge of him to the entire world.

Therefore, God used Israel as the means to remove the Canaanites from what would become the promised land. God did this because the Canaanites had already rejected him as the sovereign Lord and as a result had become exceedingly wicked. The author of the Book of Wisdom gave the following reminder to later Israelites:

> Those who dwelt of old in your holy land you hated for their detestable practices, their works of sorcery and unholy rites, their merciless slaughter of children, and their sacrificial feasting on human flesh and blood . . . but judging them little by little you gave them a chance to repent, though you were not unaware that their origin was evil and their wickedness inborn, and that their way of thinking would never change (Wis. 12:3–5, 10).

They would have been a disastrous influence upon not just Israel, but civilization as a whole. In his commentary on Deuteronomy, Fr. Raymond Brown wrote,

> Canaanite worship was socially destructive. Its religious acts were pornographic and sick, seriously damaging to children, creating early impressions of deities with no interest in moral behavior. It tried to dignify, by the use of religious labels, depraved acts of bestiality and corruption. It had a low estimate of human life. It suggested that anything was permissible, promiscuity, murder or anything else, in order to guarantee a good crop at harvest. It ignored the highest values both in the family and in the wider community—love, loyalty, purity, peace and security—and encouraged the view that all these things were inferior to material prosperity, physical satisfaction and human pleasure. A society where those things matter most is self-destructive.[620]

TOTAL WAR

What about the commands to slaughter not just the sinful Canaanites, but also the innocents among them? Here is where context is important. The Israelites were not on a mission to kill every single Canaanite. The Bible records, for example, how Israel spared Canaanites like Rahab and employed the skills of others, like Caleb, to spy on the land for them.[621] But when Israel's soldiers were in battle they acted in accordance with the prevailing cultural norms that espoused tribal warfare and its nondistinction between combatants and noncombatants. This concept of "total war" was common not only in the ancient Near East but also in ancient America, even up to the time of the Civil War. Historian Mark van de Logt provides a vivid example:

> Although military historians tend to reserve the concept of "total war" for conflicts between modern industrial nations, the term nevertheless most closely approaches the state of affairs

between the Pawnees and the Sioux and Cheyennes. Both sides directed their actions not solely against warrior-combatants but against the people as a whole. Noncombatants were legitimate targets. Indeed, the taking of a scalp of a woman or child was considered honorable because it signified that the scalp taker had dared to enter the very heart of the enemy's territory.[622]

As Catholic apologist Jimmy Akin put it, when it comes to ancient tribes in the Bible, "God was dealing with blunt instruments."[623] Just as God allowed the ancient Israelites to exist without a modern understanding of the physical world, he allowed them to exist without a modern understanding of warfare. According to Roland de Vaux, "The laws of war were crude. The annals of the kings of Assyria have a constant refrain of towns destroyed, dismantled or burnt, leveled as if by a hurricane, or reduced to a heap of rubble."[624]

Because of the cultural framework in which they lived, God's people practiced total war in spite of that fact that the Church now rejects this kind of military engagement. In fact, the practice of *herem* may have been another example of divine accommodation, or God giving imperfect laws that would limit evils committed by his hardhearted people. In this case, the command to not retain plunder from the conquests but to consecrate it to the Lord could be an example of limiting the reasons the Israelites might choose to go to war with a rival nation.

At this point a critic could object that if God is all-powerful, why couldn't he transform these "blunt instruments" into surgically sharp ones? Why couldn't God make the Israelites "ahead of their time" and cause them to reject total warfare? God could have done that, but then again, why couldn't God just have made the Canaanites not be wicked? Why couldn't God make us all morally perfect? Why didn't God create a world without any evil in it at all?

Part of the problem of evil, or the mystery of why a perfect God allows evil to exist, is something we can't fully comprehend in this life (CCC 309). But that doesn't mean we can only respond to this problem with the answer, "God works in mysterious ways." Instead, we can say that God is infinitely good and infinitely powerful, so he can always bring a greater good from any evil. There will certainly be evils we don't understand, but that doesn't mean that God has no good reasons for allowing them to exist. As long as there are some *possible* good reasons for allowing the suffering that comes from things like the *herem* commands, then these texts are not intractable problems.

So what should we think of God's command resulting in an ancient Israelite soldier slaughtering the family of a four-year-old Canaanite child and then turning his blade on her? Akin offers a helpful analysis:

> From a purely human perspective, that is *horrendous*. My heart is *sickened* at the thought of what such a child would go through. But is God—who is infinitely powerful—*incapable* of making it up to this child? No, he is not incapable of making up to her the sufferings that she experienced on earth, however horrible they were. If he gives her an *infinite* amount of happiness (natural or supernatural) then that more than makes up for the *finite* amount of unhappiness that he allowed her to suffer in this life. And if he assigns her a positive destiny in the afterlife, an infinite amount of happiness will be hers.
>
> I know that if *I myself* were in her situation—if I experienced a horrible, devastating, but still finite amount of suffering in this life—and then God gave me an *infinite* amount of happiness in the next that I would count myself fortunate. I would say with St. Paul that—no matter how horrible they were—"the sufferings of this present time are not worth comparing with the glory that [has been] revealed to [me]."[625]

ABRAHAM AND ISAAC

What about Abraham? Should we really praise someone who was willing to kill his own son just because God told him to? As we've already seen, God has the right to end human life and can

even delegate his authority to end human life to other humans.
But when we examine the context of this story in light of Abraham's life as a whole, we understand why modern people who
kill in the name of God are not justified in their actions, even
though Abraham was justified in his.

A major theme of the book of Genesis is Abraham's faith in
God's promise that he would be the father of many nations. In
Genesis 15, God said Abraham's descendants would be as numerous as the stars in the sky (Gen. 15:5) but Abram, as he was
called at this point in the narrative, faltered in his faith because
he was certain that his wife was infertile. If Abram couldn't have
even one child, then how could he ever spawn an entire galaxy
worth of offspring? Abram decided instead to have a son with
his maidservant Hagar, a son whom he later named Ishmael. But
this was not a part of God's plan, because God had intended that
Abram's offspring would come from him *and* his wife, Sarai.

In Genesis 17, God changed Abram's name to Abraham,
which literally means "a father of many nations," and changed
Sarai's name to Sarah as a sign of the covenant he was making
with them. God also made it clear that Abraham had to be obe-
dient in order to keep the covenant (something that would be
expected of all of Abraham's descendants as well). God promised
that Ishmael would have descendants, but his main promise was
that Abraham's lineage would be through his and Sarah's son
Isaac, or the "son of the promise." This brings us to the sacrifice
of Isaac in chapter 22.

Faith Put to the Test

Genesis 22:1 says that God was testing Abraham, but the test
wasn't for God's sake since he's all-knowing.[626] It was for
Abraham's sake, because Abraham didn't know he had the ability
to completely trust God. In order to demonstrate Abraham's
faith, God gave him a command unlike any other. In Genesis
22:2 God even directs Abraham to take his son, his only son
whom he loves, to be sacrificed. Abraham had other biological

children, like Ishmael, but Isaac was the only son through whom God promised to give Abraham a multitude of descendants.

As we've already seen, child sacrifice was abhorred to ancient Israel. This directive, therefore, was an extraordinary command meant to inaugurate a very extraordinary covenant. But why did God command human sacrifice to take place at all? Remember that Abraham was unfaithful in chapter 15 because he didn't know how God could give him a son in his old age. Now, as Abraham stood in front of his son, who was bound on the sacrificial altar, he would really have to trust God, because it seemed impossible that God could give Abraham descendants through a sacrificed son.

In fact, the most plausible explanation of why Abraham went through with the sacrifice is because Abraham knew God would not go back on his promise. In order to fulfill his promise of descendants through Isaac, God could bring Isaac back to life. Genesis even gives us clues that Abraham anticipated some outcome that did not result in Isaac's permanent death.

For example, Genesis 22:5 records Abraham saying to his servants, "I and the lad will go yonder and worship, and come again to you." Other translations, like the New International Version, explicitly bring out the plural form of the verb "come again" and read, "*we* will come again." In verse 8, Abraham explains to Isaac that God will provide a lamb that they failed to bring for the sacrifice. While this can be taken as an oblique reference to Isaac being the lamb, it's quite possible that Abraham hoped that an actual lamb would be substituted at some point—which of course it was, as verse 13 records.

Abraham knew that, whatever happened, Isaac would return with him to the camp and become the father of his descendants, even if God had to raise him from the dead. Hebrews 11:17–19 reaches this same conclusion and says, "By faith Abraham, when he was tested, offered up Isaac, and he who had received the promises was ready to offer up his only-begotten son, of whom it was said, 'Through Isaac shall your descendants be named.' He considered that God was able to raise men even from the dead; hence he did receive him back and this was a symbol."

Another crucial element of this story we must take into consideration is not just Abraham's faith, but Isaac's. Isaac was not a small child given that he was able to carry the heavy firewood needed for the sacrifice (Gen. 22:6). Various interpretations of this story place his age somewhere between fourteen and thirty-nine.[627] Even if he were a teenager, Isaac could probably have overpowered his elderly father if he did not want to go along with the sacrifice. But since Isaac, too, believed this was for the best, he agreed to the sacrifice.

This means that what Abraham did was very different from modern cases of child killing that are allegedly done out of obedience to divine commands. Abraham had evidence that the commands he was given came from God. The evidence was so strong that even his own child was willing to go along with the sacrifice—a detail that is not found in contemporary accounts of parents killing their children "in the name of God."

It does not follow that because some people mistakenly attribute their actions to divine commands (instead of something like mental illness), that God does not have the right to take human life and the right to deputize other humans to do this under his authority.

Light for Dark Passages

So far we've reviewed one possible approach to the issue of the slaughter of the Canaanites. God really issued these commands, and the Israelites really carried them out. Since the actions God commanded the Israelites to perform were not intrinsically evil, they do not contradict God's goodness. The Israelites had been lawfully deputized by God to exact his judgment on the Canaanites for their centuries of violent and wicked behavior.

I suspect, however, that some people will still feel uncomfortable about God commanding the Israelite soldiers to hack women and children, including babies, to death—although just because something makes us uncomfortable doesn't mean it's not true. If God decrees the death of any human being, regardless of age or moral character, then we have to acquiesce to the fact that it is that human being's appointed time to die.

But suppose God did not decree these people's deaths? Perhaps modern critics are misreading the genre of these texts, in the same way they misread other genres found in Scripture? In fact, a nonliteral approach to the problem of the Canaanites can be found as far back as the third-century, when ecclesial writer Origen said in his commentary on Joshua, "Within us, indeed, are all those breeds of vices that continually and incessantly attack the soul. Within us are the Canaanites; within us are the Perizzites; here are the Jebusites."[628]

Origen also said that when Joshua "destroyed the enemies, [he was] not teaching cruelty through this, as the heretics think, but representing the future sacraments in these affairs."[629] According to Old Testament scholar Jerome Creach, Origen believed that "the order to place under the ban all the residents of the land is not an injunction to kill other human beings. Rather, it is a figurative way of saying that the Christian must purge the self of all that would hinder pure devotion to God."[630]

Although not everyone would agree with Origen's allegorical approach to the biblical texts, this does not mean that the texts he analyzes are not nonliteral in nature. Is there a good reason to support a nonliteral view besides our own discomfort with the actions a literal view seems to endorse? Actually, there are several reasons to support this approach.

INTERPRETIVE APPROACH #2: NONLITERAL COMMANDS, LITERAL HISTORY

A second interpretive approach to these texts holds that they describe historical events (that is, the killing of Canaanite noncombatants really happened), but that God did not command that they be killed. Instead, God issued different commands, which Israel's leaders or prophets misunderstood. How could that happen?

St. Thomas Aquinas once said, "Whatever is received is received according to the mode of the receiver." Just as liquid water becomes cylindrical if it is received according to the mode of a glass, God's nuanced commands may have become "blunt" when they were received by the Israelites, who acted according to the "mode" of the culture in which they lived. When the sacred author of Scripture recounted the battles that took place, he attributed everything Israel did, including killing women and children, to God's commands. He may have done this because of the widespread belief that God is sovereign over all things.

You may recall that this commitment to divine sovereignty on the part of the ancient author explains other difficult texts that attribute evil acts to God, such as the hardening of Pharaoh's heart or God motivating David's disastrous census. It also explains passages in Scripture that say humans lie because God sends them "a lying spirit."[631] Since God doesn't cause people to sin (James 1:13), the sacred author of these texts must be using nonliteral language to communicate how God anticipates and orders all that we do, both good and evil, to his providential ends.

Just as we take into account an ancient author's use of anthropomorphic language to describe God, or his use of phenomenological language to describe the natural world, we must take into account the author's use of "divine command language" to describe the relationship between God's commands and the behavior of his chosen people. According to Matthew Ramage, "If it seemed clear [to the ancient writer] that God wanted a certain battle won, and the tactics employed therein were successful, then God must have sanctioned or even directly willed these tactics."[632]

This explanation avoids the charge of commanding genocide, but critics may still respond by saying that God was an awful communicator and that he allowed genocide to occur. But this objection simply takes us back to the mystery of why God allows people to sin and why he allows people to misunderstand what he has revealed (for example, why does God allows people to think the Bible is pro-abortion or pro-homosexual behavior?). The burden of proof falls on the critic to show that God could not have a good reason for allowing humans to sin or to misunderstand him. Since God is all-knowing and all-powerful, it is impossible to show that God could not bring a greater good from any kind of evil he allows to exist.

A more troubling objection is that this explanation calls into question the inerrancy of Scripture. After all, how can we trust Scripture if some parts represent that God's people did not receive his message correctly? To this charge Ramage said that parts of Scripture that exhibit mistaken human worldviews should not be seen as truths a writer was asserting but as details that expressed parts of the sacred author's worldview. This would be similar to the physical details asserted about the Creation or the firmament (such as the latter being a solid, domelike structure in the sky) that we discussed in chapter 2. According to Ramage,

> Any imperfect perception of reality on the part of the sacred author is not being taught for its own sake. It may be the result of an "environmental glitch" that causes him to draw an invalid conclusion about some aspect of the faith or another. For example, if the environment of the authors discussed above assumed that Yahweh's omnipotence meant that he directly caused evil, then these authors would be epistemically justified in concluding that Yahweh did what we today would recognize as evil. This does not mean that imperfect statements conform to reality. It simply offers one avenue by which to explain that scripture does not contain error in the sense that Catholic magisterial teaching understands it.[633]

But some critics say this nonliteral approach doesn't explain all of the *herem* commands. After all, Saul was instructed hundreds of years after Joshua in first Samuel to "utterly destroy the Amalekites." This language can't be a case of Saul misinterpreting God due to an "environmental glitch," because God was angry at Saul for allowing some Amalekites to live, thus contradicting his command to utterly destroy them (1 Sam. 15:9).

However, Samuel makes no mention of God being displeased that Saul chose not to kill women and children. Instead, God was displeased that Saul kept alive Amalek's king Agag and Agag's best cattle, presumably as a kind of trophy. It was this act of pride, and not a failure to kill noncombatants, that displeased God. Therefore, God's anger in this text is not evidence that the *herem* commands always have a literal meaning.

The book of Samuel even provides evidence that the language describing the utter destruction of the Amalekites is not literal. If the Amalekites had all been destroyed save for Agag in chapter 15, then why does chapter 27 record David still having to fight lots of Amalekites? As you'll recall from our discussion of alleged Bible contradictions, 2 Samuel 1 even records David having an Amalekite executed because he took credit for killing Saul. This brings us to our next and last possible interpretive approach—one that resolves how Scripture can speak of a group's "total destruction" and its "not total destruction" at the same time.

INTERPRETIVE APPROACH #3:
NONLITERAL COMMANDS, NONLITERAL HISTORY

The previous interpretations both assumed that the commands to slaughter Canaanite noncombatants were carried out in a historical context; they just disagreed about the ultimate source of these commands. The first explanation grounded them in God's will, while the second grounded them in Israel's culturally conditioned understanding of God's will. But another nonliteral explanation of these texts proposes that God never issued these commands *and* that they were never carried out. In effect, there simply was no wholesale destruction of the Canaanites.

Instead, the language used in these texts is exaggerated, nonliteral "warfare rhetoric." This kind of language is akin to saying your favorite sports team "destroyed" or "massacred" its opponents. Granted, there would still have been civilian casualties when Israel fought the Canaanites, just as there are civilian casualties in modern wars, but those noncombatants would not have been Israel's main targets, nor was it the case that Israel "wiped out" these peoples.

Even Joshua 6:21's reference to the slaughter of "men and women" (in Hebrew "from man (and) unto woman") and "young and old" may involve expressions equivalent to "everyone" or "all the people." They may not literally refer to the killing of non-combatant women and children. Richard Hess has argued that Jericho and many other conquered cities described in Joshua were primarily military forts and so there would have been few civilian casualties. Most non-combatants would have resided in the countryside surrounding the fort and fled when the battle began.[634]

In fact, many details in Scripture assume the total destruction of Israel's enemies did not take place. For example, Joshua 11:22 says, "There was none of the Anakim left in the land of the sons of Israel," even though four chapters later Caleb is described as still driving the Anakim out of the land (Josh. 15:13–14). The book of Judges records Israel's conquest of Canaan, but it differs significantly from the account we find in the book of Joshua. Instead of recounting the utter destruction of the Canaanites, Judges only records the Israelites destroying Canaanite idols (Judg. 6:25–27)—not the people as a whole. Judges 1:28 even says, "When Israel grew strong, they put the Canaanites to forced labor, but did not utterly drive them out."

Other relevant passages in Exodus, Leviticus, Numbers, and Deuteronomy speak of "driving out" or causing the land to "vomit out" the Canaanites.[635] They don't speak of the Canaanite's total destruction or even their complete displacement.

A simple way to resolve this apparent contradiction is to assume that passages describing the total destruction of the Canaanites are not literal. Phrases like "all were struck down with the edge of the sword," repeated over and over again in these passages are typical of the hyperbole used in ancient battle accounts. For example, the Egyptian Merneptah Stele discussed in chapter 6 says that Israel was "laid waste and his seed is not," even though the nation of Israel continued to exist for several centuries after the stele was erected. Other ancient Syrian and Egyptian texts describe how opposing armies were "completely

destroyed," even instantaneously, but those same texts also refer
to the continued existence of the supposedly decimated forces.[636]

Therefore, the purpose of Joshua and Samuel's bombastic
rhetoric may not have been to provide a strictly historical chronicle of Israel's confrontations with the Canaanites. It may instead
have been used to describe in grandiose language the battles Israel faced, without denying the literal threat these groups posed
even after these military engagements were over.

This language could have come from the people who first told
the stories or from Israelite historians who transformed the oral
traditions into written accounts. A later chronicler in Israel's history may even have used this hyperbolic language to underscore
to his audience the importance of making a complete break with
neighboring pagan religions. This is similar to the hypothesis we
discussed earlier about later editors of the Pentateuch composing
nonliteral accounts of the patriarchs or the Exodus in order to
teach lessons to audiences in their own times.

At this point, some people, even faithful Catholics, may say
that questioning the literal nature of these stories is indicative
of a view of Scripture that denies its divine inspiration. To that
charge I would point to the words of the Pope Benedict XVI,
who can scarcely be accused of having an unorthodox view on
this matter. In a conversation with journalist Peter Seewald,
Benedict was asked about the supposed contradiction between
God issuing the fifth commandment ("Thou shall not kill") in
Exodus 20:13 and then, just a few chapters later, ordering the
Israelites to kill three thousand of their brethren as punishment
for idolatry. Here is part of Benedict's reply:

> The story that follows does sound terribly bloodthirsty, and
> for us it is scarcely comprehensible. There too we have to look
> forward, toward Christ. He does the opposite. He takes death
> upon himself and does not kill others. But in this moment
> of the Sinai story, Moses, as it were, puts into effect what is
> already present: the other people have perverted their own
> lives. *How far we should take this story literally is another question*

[emphasis added]. The people of Israel stay in existence. What happens expresses the truth that anyone who turns from god not only departs from the Covenant but from the sphere of life: they ruin their own life and, in doing so, enter into the realm of death.[637]

In sum, the Church has not definitively taught how we should interpret these "dark passages" of Scripture. They might be literal accounts of the past that challenge our moral intuitions, or they might be nonliteral accounts that challenge our understanding of ancient genres and literary forms. Or they may be a blend of the literal and the nonliteral. The fact that these texts are challenging does not mean that they are intractable; as we've seen, there are several plausible ways to explain them without sacrificing God's goodness or the inerrancy of his sacred word.

Bible-Reading Rules Recap

Now that we've come to the end of our journey through the most common Bible difficulties, it might be helpful to quickly review the rules we learned that help us explain these passages.

Rule 1: *The Bible's human authors were not divine stenographers.* Everything asserted in Scripture is asserted by the Holy Spirit, but God allowed the human authors of Scripture to incorporate their own words, ideas, and worldviews into the sacred texts.

Rule 2: *The Bible's human authors were not writing scientific textbooks.* Scripture does not assert a scientific description of the world, so details in the Bible that utilize "the language of appearances" are not erroneous.

Rule 3: *The Bible contains many different literary styles.* The Bible contains many different genres, some of which communicate true, historical facts through the use of poetic, nonliteral language.

Rule 4: *Check the original language.* Some Scripture passages are only difficult because they have been mistranslated. Examining the original language can help us better understand the sacred author's intended meaning.

Rule 5: *The Bible is allowed to be a sole witness to history.* Ancient nonbiblical historians could make mistakes or fail to record events. Therefore, it is not necessary to require biblical events to be corroborated by nonbiblical sources.

Rule 6: *Read it in context!* Sometimes biblical passages only sound bad because they are isolated from their original context. Find the context, and you'll usually find the explanation of the passage.

Rule 7: *Consult a reliable commentary.* Commentaries provide details or facts not found in Scripture that can help explain Bible difficulties.

Rule 8: *Evaluate Scripture against the whole of divine revelation.* Interpret Scripture in light of what God has revealed in natural law as well as through his Church in the form of Sacred Tradition and the teaching office of the magisterium.

Rule 9: *Differing descriptions do not equal contradictions.* The authors of Scripture may have differed in their descriptions of an event's details, but not in the essential truths they were asserting about those events.

Rule 10: *Incomplete is not inaccurate.* Just because the sacred author did not record something another author recorded does not mean his text is in error.

Rule 11: *Only the original texts are inspired, not their copies.* Errors that came about through the copying process do not fall under the doctrine of inerrancy and can usually be located and corrected with ease.

Rule 12: *The burden of proof is on the critic, not the believer.* If a critic alleges that Scripture is in error, he has the burden of proving that is the case. If the believer even shows a *possible* way of resolving the text, then the critic's objection that there is an intractable contradiction is refuted.

Rule 13: *When the Bible talks about God, it does so in a nonliteral way.* Because God is so unlike us, Scripture must speak about him with anthropomorphic language that should not be taken literally.

Rule 14: *Just because the Bible records it doesn't mean God recommends it.* The Bible is not an instruction book for how we should live, though sometimes it teaches us life lessons through stories that show us what *not* to do.

Rule 15: *Just because the Bible regulates it doesn't mean God recommends it.* God progressively revealed himself to mankind over several centuries. During this progression, the authors of Scripture regulated sinful practices in order to help God's people eventually reject them in the future.

Rule 16: *Life is a gift from God, and he has complete authority over it.* It is not morally impermissible for God to take away the mortal life he freely gave us.

As our discussion draws to a close, I'd like to leave you with one last rule: *Give God's word the benefit of the doubt.*

In chapter nine we learned that even if we can't resolve a difficulty at the present moment, it doesn't mean that the Bible is in error or that it is uninspired. It just means *we* don't know how to resolve the difficulty in question. This attitude is seen in early Church Fathers like Justin Martyr, who told critics in the second century, "[Since] I am entirely convinced that no Scripture contradicts another, I shall admit rather that I do not understand what is recorded, and shall strive to persuade those who imagine that the Scriptures are contradictory, to be rather of the same opinion as myself."[638]

Maybe someone else has already resolved the difficulty but we aren't aware of it, or perhaps an explanation will arise when additional evidence is discovered in the future. The bottom line is that the truth of what God has revealed to us does not depend on our ability to defend that revelation in discussions or debates with nonbelievers. The *Catechism* teaches, "Faith is certain. It is more certain than all human knowledge because it is founded on the very word of God who cannot lie. To be sure, revealed truths can seem obscure to human reason and experience, but 'the certainty that the divine light gives is greater than that which the light of natural reason gives'" (CCC 157).

But this does not mean that we accept the truth of what Scripture teaches by faith alone (or what some call *fideism*). Throughout this book we've seen that the historical and literary evidence

supports what the Bible teaches. We've also seen that objections
to God's word can be answered in a clear and compelling way.
If we don't share this evidence with others, then countless souls
could be deprived of the treasure that is God's word just because
of a critic's misinformed objection. The words penned by Pope
Leo XIII over a century ago still ring true for us today:

> It is deplorable to see these attacks [on Scripture] growing ev-
> ery day more numerous and more severe. It is sometimes men
> of learning and judgment who are assailed; but these have lit-
> tle difficulty in defending themselves from evil consequences.
>
> The efforts and the arts of the enemy are chiefly directed
> against the more ignorant masses of the people. They diffuse
> their deadly poison by means of books, pamphlets, and news-
> papers; they spread it by addresses and by conversation; they
> are found everywhere; and they are in possession of numerous
> schools, taken by violence from the Church, in which, by ridi-
> cule and scurrilous jesting, they pervert the credulous and un-
> formed minds of the young to the contempt of Holy Scripture.
>
> Should not these things, Venerable Brethren, stir up and
> set on fire the heart of every Pastor, so that to this "knowl-
> edge, falsely so called," may be opposed the ancient and true
> science which the Church, through the Apostles, has received
> from Christ, and that Holy Scripture may find the champions
> that are needed in so momentous a battle?[639]

I hope you, dear reader, will take what you've learned here,
reinforce it with study and prayer, and consider the call to be
a champion for our Faith, a faith rooted in the inspiration and
inerrancy of God's sacred word.

Appendix

Has the Bible Been Corrupted?

Have you ever played the children's game of telephone? It's not so much a game as it is an excuse for a chain of people to quickly whisper a message from one person to the next. By the time the message reaches the last person, it has been transformed into something that is almost unrecognizable from the original.

Of course, telephone is fun when the message doesn't matter, but what if a person's eternal destiny relied on it being transmitted correctly? What if the Bible's message was distorted through a copying process that produced the same effects as the game of telephone? New Testament scholar Bart Ehrman thinks it has been corrupted and presented this grim diagnosis of the situation:

> Not only do we not have the originals, we don't have the first copies of the originals, we don't even have the copies of the copies of the originals, or copies of the copies of the copies of the originals. What we have are copies made later—much later. In most instances they are copies made many centuries later. And these copies all differ from one another, in many thousands of places . . . possibly it is easiest to put it in comparative terms: there are more differences among our manuscripts than there are words in the New Testament.[640]

Ehrman is correct that we no longer possess the original manuscripts of the Bible. For example, we do not have the original scroll upon which Paul wrote his letter to the Galatians. In fact, we don't have any of the original copies of any of the books and letters found in the Bible. This may worry you, but keep in mind that we do not possess the original manuscripts of *any* work that was composed in the ancient world.

We do not possess Plato's original *Republic* nor do we possess the original Jewish histories of Josephus, the Roman histories of Tacitus, or the Greek histories of Thucydides. Those books were written on dried leaves or animal skins that were lost, destroyed, or decayed over time. Fortunately, modern scholars can reconstruct the original manuscripts of these works by comparing all the surviving copies, or by a process called *textual criticism*. How does it work?

Aunt Mildred's Recipe

Imagine your Aunt Mildred showed you the recipe for her delicious chocolate chip cookies while you were visiting her cabin up in the mountains. Since there's no electricity at this cabin (and hence no scanner or computer), you decide to make a handwritten copy of the recipe. Perhaps a few weeks later you baked Mildred's cookies for a dinner party, and now your guests are begging you for the recipe. You oblige them by quickly copying the recipe you had affixed to the refrigerator.

Now, imagine fifty years have passed and someone wants to find out what the exact ingredients were in Aunt Mildred's original secret recipe. Unfortunately, Aunt Mildred passed away several decades earlier and her cabin where the original recipe was kept burned down.

Fortunately, the original recipe isn't really lost, because there are lots of copies of it in the possession of Mildred's family members. These copies not only include the ones you gave away to your friends and family, but also the copies that Mildred herself sent to her other nieces and nephews. Of course, some of the recipes will differ slightly from one another. Maybe Uncle Bob was lactose intolerant and left the milk out of his recipe. Maybe cousin Suzy didn't realize that vanilla is spelled with two l's and not one. But if you have enough copies of the original recipe then it's easy to sift through the minor differences in each copy and reconstruct the original.

What worked for Mildred's recipe also works for books written in the ancient world. As long as we have enough copies, we can compare them and reconstruct the original manuscripts. For example, although we do not have any of Plato's original writings, we do have over 250 ancient manuscripts that help us reconstruct what Plato originally said. For many other ancient writers we have only a handful of manuscripts, and sometimes only a single copy of the original that was written centuries or even millennia later. But this does not deter scholars from study-ing these writings and, at the very least, it does not deter them from knowing what these texts originally said.

What makes the New Testament unique, different from all these other ancient works, is both the sheer number of copies we have and the reverence people paid to these copies.

COPY FOR GOD IN THE HIGHEST

There currently exist over 5500 copies of New Testament man-uscripts written in Greek, as well as 15,000 manuscripts writ-ten in other languages like Latin, Coptic, and Syriac. Fifty of the Greek manuscripts can be dated to within 250 years of the original copies. The first complete copy of the New Testament, called Codex Sinaiticus (because it was discovered in a mon-astery at the foot of Mount Sinai), can be dated to within 300 years of the original documents.

Now, compare this to Homer's *Iliad*, which was written in the eighth century B.C. Although a few fragments of the *Iliad* can be dated to within 500 years of Homer, the oldest complete copy of the *Iliad* (a manuscript scholars refer to as Venetus A) was written in the tenth century A.D., or 1,800 years later! Biblical scholar F. F. Bruce put it bluntly: "There is no body of ancient literature in the world which enjoys such a wealth of good tex-tual attestation as the New Testament."[641]

The reason we have so many copies of the New Testament is that as new Church communities sprang up in Europe and Asia, they wanted one for their public liturgies as well as for private reading. During this time, Christianity was illegal within the Roman Empire, so Christians who copied the New Testament,

HARD SAYINGS

or scribes, endured monotonous hours of writing by hand and risked painful deaths just so others could have a copy of Scripture. As modern readers we should feel very spoiled every time we encounter a free Bible in a hotel room or on the Internet.

Although some of these copies have been lost, many others survived due in large part to the idea that scribal copying was a way to glorify God. The products of this divine service were then revered and protected for centuries. In the sixth century, the monk Cassiodorus, who was a contemporary of St. Benedict, said, "What happy application, what praiseworthy industry, to preach unto men by means of the hand, to untie the tongue by means of the fingers, to bring quiet salvation to mortals, and to fight the Devil's insidious wiles with pen and ink!"[642]

You might have taken some liberties while casually copying Aunt Mildred's secret recipe, but these scribes saw it as their sacred duty before God to make sure their copies of the New Testament were as accurate as possible.

Along with faithful scribes, we also have the testimony of faithful Church Fathers, who glorified God by teaching and commenting on the Bible. Even though the Bible manuscripts they consulted no longer exist, they have survived as quotations in the Fathers' commentaries on Scripture. Ehrman even admitted that this is a resource for textual critics: "so extensive are these citations that if all other sources for our knowledge of the text of the New Testament were destroyed, they would be sufficient alone *for the reconstruction of practically the entire New Testament.*"[643]

The huge number of ancient manuscripts as well as quotations in the writings of the Church Fathers helps disprove a common conspiracy about the Bible. Popular novels like *The Da Vinci Code* sometimes assert that the Church hid the "truth" about Jesus by destroying all the early copies of the Gospels and replacing them with ones that better fit their man-made doctrines. But the problem with this theory is that no one was ever in a position to gather up *all* the manuscripts and replace or destroy them.

The fact that we've only discovered fifty manuscripts from the first few centuries implies that there were hundreds or even thousands more in circulation at the time that, like most manuscripts in the ancient world, were later lost. Moreover, Christians who had heard the traditional readings of Scripture their entire life would have vigorously challenged any later group who tried to change the biblical text. St. Augustine once told St. Jerome that the people of Tripoli rioted in the streets because Jerome's new translation of the book of Jonah was so unfamiliar to them.[644] Imagine what these people would do if a completely new story about Christ were presented to them!

The sheer number of manuscripts that existed, spread over hundreds of thousands of square miles in an area hostile to Christian activity, kept in the custody of Christians who opposed the slightest change to the text, makes any claim that a conspiracy in the early Church to alter the Bible only tenable in the realm of fiction.

Scribal Appreciation Day

"Okay, maybe the Bible wasn't changed as part of some elaborate conspiracy," says the critic. "Maybe it was changed unintentionally as scribes introduced errors into the texts as they copied them."

Given the circumstances that ancient scribes faced it's understandable how errors crept into the copying process. For example, scribes would not sit at desks but would sit down on the floor with some dried leaves or an animal skin in their laps. They often complained about how work that only involved "three fingers" was able to put their entire body in pain from being hunched over for hours at a time. Discomforts like this could have caused a mental lapse and allowed an error to enter their copies.

There were also hazards associated with the various copying methods a scribe might use. If a text was read aloud to him, the scribe might miss something that was said due to a distraction in the room (like another scribe coughing). Even if he heard the words read aloud, he might write down the wrong word if two words sounded the same. On the other hand, if he was reading a text instead of listening to it, the scribe might look away to dip his pen in ink before returning to the page. During that motion he might return to the wrong word and either miss a word or accidentally duplicate one.

Another circumstance that affected the scribal process was the environment. Even modern people make mistakes when they copy documents in air-conditioned, well-lit office buildings. Imagine the challenges a scribe faced when he copied under the light of an oil lantern, without reading glasses, and without adequate climate control. In some conditions the scribe's inkwells would freeze along with the scribe's fingers!

If the scribe made a mistake on a scroll he would have to start all over again if he could not correct the mistake in the margin. It's no wonder that some scribes finished their manuscripts with the line, "The end of the book; thanks be to God!"[645]

Variants: Much Ado About Nothing

We now see how unintentional variants crept into the copies of New Testament manuscripts. And it's true, as Ehrman says, that, "there are more differences among our manuscripts than there are words in the New Testament." In fact, scholars believe that there are about 200 thousand–400 thousand differences among all New Testament manuscripts and, like snowflakes, that no two manuscripts are exactly alike.[646] But although that sounds like an imposing obstacle to reconstructing the New Testament texts, it actually isn't. In fact, the huge number of variants should give us *hope* that we can reconstruct the original manuscripts.

The reason there are so many variants is because there are so many manuscripts in general. For example, suppose that each of the 20,000 manuscripts of the New Testament we possess has twenty variants in it. This adds up to 400 thousand variants but, as you see, when this huge number of variants is distributed across a huge number of manuscripts. we are left with individual manuscripts that contain only a few dozen variants.

In contrast to the New Testament, consider the first six books of the annals of the Roman historian Tacitus, one of our primary historical sources about ancient Rome. There exists only one copy of this section of the *Annals*, and it was written about a thousand years after the original. It has no variants, but that's only because there are no other copies for the text to differ with! This is actually a very bad thing, because we have no way to know if this manuscript represents what Tacitus originally wrote.

A New Testament with many variants distributed across lots of manuscripts is *more* reliable than a New Testament with few variants that are distributed across only a few manuscripts, especially since the variants between the manuscripts are almost always trivial and easily fixed. For example, a name or a word might be misspelled but can be corrected by anyone who knows there's only one "n" in John.

Other times, the context makes the correct reading clear, as in 1 Thessalonians 2:7, where Paul says, "But we were gentle (*nepioi*) among you, like a nurse taking care of her children." Alternative readings use the Greek word *hepioi*—"we were little children among you"—which doesn't really change the meaning. But one manuscript uses *hippoi*, which changes the passage to read: "we were horses among you."[647] This is no doubt a scribal error and any competent critic would not be confused about what the original text said, provided he had not been raised by a horse.

A textual variant could also arise because the order of the words in a passage might be transposed. What reads "Christ Jesus" in one manuscript might say "Jesus Christ" in another. This is counted as a "variant," but the original text's meaning hasn't changed. In languages like ancient Greek, the location of the words within a sentence don't matter as much as they do in English. The phrase "Jesus loves Peter" and the phrase "Peter loves Jesus" have two different meanings in English because the word order has been switched. But in Greek the meaning of a sentence can remain the same even if the word order is switched. That's because the indicator of which word is the subject and which word is the object is typically found in the spelling of the word and not in the word's location within the sentence. This is just one of the ways that ancient manuscripts can differ from each other but still possess the exact same meaning.

When Meaning Matters

When these minor variants are corrected we see that there are not 400 thousand important variants in the New Testament texts, that is, variants that change what the text means. The United Bible Societies' fourth edition of the Greek New Testament, the premiere version that is used in modern translations, lists about 1,400 disputed passages that are relevant to translating the text.[648] However, most Bible translations only include a few hundred of the most important of these variants in footnotes or in brackets within the text itself. You've probably come across these during personal Bible study and dismissed them as academic minutiae.

For example, in some manuscripts Jesus says in Matthew 11:23 that Capernaum will be "*brought* down" to Hades, while in other manuscripts Jesus says Capernaum will be "*driven* down" to Hades. In some manuscripts Paul says in 1 Corinthians 1:4, "I thank God always for you," while in others he says, "I thank *my* God always for you." Although it's true that these are variants in the texts, it's more accurate to call them "differences without a distinction." The vast majority of them don't change the meaning of the sacred text and so they should not cause us to doubt our reconstruction of what the original authors intended to communicate.

Even in cases in which the meaning could be altered, we can see which tradition behind the variants is stronger and, as a result, show which variant is more closely related to the original text. For example, when Luke 3:22 describes what the Father says at Jesus' baptism, the text can be rendered as "You are my beloved son; with you I am well pleased," or it can be rendered as "You are my beloved son; today I have begotten you."

The latter rendering would seem to support the view that the Son of God was begotten on earth and that the Father did not eternally beget him. However, there is only one Latin manuscript, dating from the sixth century, that has the second rendering, while every other manuscript, including the early Greek ones, has the traditional rendering. This gives us good reason to accept the traditional rendering of Luke 3:22 that does not mention begetting.

Most of the several hundred variants that remain in the biblical text involve minor issues like these.[649] Craig Blomberg put it this way:

> Only about a tenth of 1 percent are interesting enough to make their way into footnotes in most English translations. It cannot be emphasized strongly enough that *no orthodox doctrine or ethical practice of Christianity depends solely on any disputed wording* [emphasis in the original]. There are always undisputed passages one can consult that teach the same truths. Tellingly, in the appendix to the paperback edition of *Misquoting Jesus*, Ehrman himself concedes that, "essential Christian beliefs are not affected by textual variants in the manuscript tradition of the New Testament." It is too bad that this admission appears in an appendix and comes only after repeated criticism![650]

Critics might object that the vast majority of manuscripts we have come from hundreds or over a thousand years later than the originals, and so they don't show us what the New Testament looked like during the crucial first centuries of the copying process. However, we can compare early manuscripts like P75, which contains large portions of Luke's and John's Gospels and has been dated to the late second century, and Codex Vaticanus, which has been dated to the early fourth century and contains the whole Bible. Even though there is a 100– to 150–year difference, both manuscripts have, in the words of Greek scholar Daniel Wallace, "an incredibly high agreement."[651]

This is even more remarkable given that Vaticanus was not copied from P75. Both manuscripts share an even earlier "common ancestor." In fact, New Testament scholar Craig Evans has recently shown that the original texts of the New Testament may have survived much longer than we think:

Autographs and first copies may well have remained in circulation until the end of the second century, even the beginning of the third century . . . The longevity of these manuscripts in effect forms a bridge linking the first-century autographs and first copies to the great codices, via the early papyrus copies we possess.[652]

This shows that the first centuries of Christian history were not textual "black holes," but that the original documents survived for a long time on their own, and then survived even longer through multiple, independent lines of transmission.

WHAT ABOUT THE OLD TESTAMENT?

Currently, the oldest complete copy of the Hebrew Bible is the Codex Leningrad, a medieval bound copy of the Old Testament housed, as its name would suggest, in Leningrad, or what is now called St. Petersburg, in Russia. It has been dated to the early eleventh century and is believed to have come from a group of Jews called the Mazorites, who diligently copied and preserved Old Testament manuscripts between the seventh and tenth centuries. These scribes had a reputation for painstaking accuracy, but the opportunity to test that accuracy did not present itself until the discovery of the Dead Sea Scrolls in the twentieth century.

In 1946, three shepherd boys were throwing rocks into caves near Qumran, an area adjacent to the Dead Sea in southern Israel, when to their surprise they heard something shatter. The boys discovered jars containing writings from the first century B.C. They were eventually determined to include, among other apocryphal works, the Hebrew Bible. Textual critics now had the opportunity to compare portions of the Hebrew Bible written one thousand years before the Codex Leningrad with medieval Jewish manuscripts that were the basis for modern Old Testament scholarship. The results were extraordinary in that very little of the text had changed and what did change was minor. Bible scholar Norman Geisler wrote of one example,

Of the 166 words in Isaiah 53, there are only 17 letters in question. Ten of these letters are simply a matter of spelling, which does not affect the sense. Four more letters are minor stylistic changes, such as conjunctions. The three remaining letters comprise the word LIGHT, which is added in verse 11 and which does not affect the meaning greatly. Furthermore, this word is supported by the Septuagint (LXX). Thus, in one chapter of 166 words, there is only one word (three letters) in question after a thousand years of transmission—and this word does not significantly change the meaning of the passage.[653]

THE FINAL VERDICT

The New Testament unquestionably surpasses all other ancient literature in both the quantity and quality of manuscript evidence, and the Old Testament also fares well when compared to other ancient works. In order to be consistent, critics who say we can't trust the Bible because it was written a long time ago must also reject the trustworthiness of ancient works that describe people like Socrates, Julius Caesar, or any other figure in ancient history. If critics are willing to trust copies of texts that refer to these people, despite the fact that the originals were lost thousands of years ago, then they should be willing to place that same trust in the better-attested records of the Bible.

Select Bibliography

Avalos, Hector. *Slavery, Abolitionism, and the Ethics of Biblical Scholarship*. Sheffield: Sheffield Phoenix Press, 2013.

Avalos, Hector. *The End of Biblical Studies*. Amherst, NY: Prometheus Books, 2007.

Baker, Brian. *Nonsense from the Bible*. FastPencil, 2012.

Barker, Dan. *Godless: How an Evangelical Preacher Became One of America's Leading Atheists*. Berkeley, CA: Ulysses Press, 2008.

Bauckham, Richard. *God and the Crisis of Freedom: Biblical and Contemporary Perspectives*. Louisville, KY: Westminster John Knox Press, 2002.

Bertman, Stephen. *Handbook to Life in Ancient Mesopotamia*. New York: Oxford University Press, 2003.

Bienkowski, Piotr, and Alan Millard, eds. *Dictionary of the Ancient Near East*. Philadelphia: University of Pennsylvania Press, 2010.

Block, Daniel I. *Judges, Ruth: An Exegetical and Theological Exposition of Holy Scripture*. Nashville, TN: Broadman and Holman, 1999.

Blomberg, Craig L. *Can We Still Believe in the Bible?: An Evangelical Engagement with Contemporary Questions*. Grand Rapids, MI: Brazos Press, 2014.

Blomberg, Craig L. *The Historical Reliability of the Gospels,* second edition. Downer's Grove, IL: InterVarsity Academic, 2007.

Blomberg, Craig L. *The Historical Reliability of John's Gospel*. Downer's Grove, IL: InterVarsity Press, 2001.

Broshi, Magen. *Bread, Wine, Walls and Scrolls.* New York: Sheffield Academic Press, 2001.

Brown, Raymond E. *The Birth of the Messiah: A Commentary on the Infancy Narratives in the Gospels of Matthew and Luke.* New York: Doubleday, 1993.

Brown, Raymond. *The Message of Deuteronomy.* Downer's Grove, IL: InterVarsity Press, 1993.

Brown, William P. *The Oxford Handbook of Psalms.* New York: Oxford University Press, 2014.

Burnside, Jonathan. *God, Justice, and Society: Aspects of Law and Legality in the Bible.* New York: Oxford University Press, 2011.

Burridge, Richard. *What Are the Gospels? A Comparison with Graeco-Roman Biography,* second edition. Grand Rapids, MI: William B. Eerdmans, 2004.

Chisholm Jr., Robert B. *A Commentary on Judges and Ruth.* Grand Rapids, MI: Kregel Publications, 2013.

Chirichigno, Gregory C. *Debt Slavery in Israel and the Ancient Near East.* Sheffield: Sheffield Academic Press, 1993.

Collins, Raymond F. *These Things Have Been Written: Studies on the Fourth Gospel.* Louvain: Peeters, 1990.

Copan, Paul. *Is God a Moral Monster? Making Sense of the Old Testament God.* Grand Rapids, MI: Baker Books, 2011.

Copan, Paul, and Matt Flanagan. *Did God Really Command Genocide?: Coming to Terms with the Justice of God.* Grand Rapids, MI:, Baker Books, 2014.

Coogan, Michael D. *A Brief Introduction to the Old Testament: The Hebrew Bible in Its Context*. New York: Oxford University Press, 2008.

Creach, Jerome F.D. *Violence in Scripture: Interpretation: Resources for the Use of Scripture in the Church*. Louisville, KY: Westminster John Knox Press, 2013.

Dawkins, Richard. *The God Delusion*. New York: Houghton-Mifflin, 2008.

Day, John. *Yahweh and the Gods and Goddesses of Canaan*. New York: Sheffield Academic Press, 2002.

De Vaux, Roland. *Ancient Israel: Its Life and Instructions*. Grand Rapids, MI: Wm. B. Eerdmans, 1997.

Dever, William G. *Who Were the Early Israelites and Where Did They Come From?* Grand Rapids, MI: Wm. B. Eerdmans, 2006.

Dever, William G. *What Did the Biblical Writers Know and When Did They Know It?* Grand Rapids, MI: Wm. B. Eerdmans, 2001.

Dozeman, Thomas B. *Exodus*. Grands Rapids, MI: Wm. B. Eerdmans, 2009.

Dunn, James D.G. *Jesus Remembered: Christianity in the Making,* Vol. 1. Grand Rapids, MI: Wm. B. Eerdmans, 2003.

Dunn, James D.G. *The Theology of Paul the Apostle*. Grand Rapids, MI: Wm. B. Eerdmans, 1998.

Eddy, Paul Rhodes, and Greg A. Boyd. *The Jesus Legend: A Case for the Historical Reliability of the Synoptic Jesus Tradition*. Grand Rapids, MI: Baker Academic, 2007.

Ehrman, Bart. *Jesus, Interrupted: Revealing the Hidden Contradictions in the Bible (and Why We Don't Know About Them)*. New York: HarperOne, 2009.

Ehrman, Bart. *Misquoting Jesus: The Story Behind Who Changed the Bible and Why*. New York: HarperCollins, 2005.

Evans, Craig A. *Matthew*. New York: Cambridge University Press, 2012.

Finegan, Jack. *Handbook of Biblical Chronology*. Peabody, MA: Hendrickson Publishers, 1998.

Gagnon, Robert A.J. *The Bible and Homosexual Practice: Texts and Hermeneutics*. Nashville, TN: Abingdon Press, 2001.

Gardiner, Alan. *Egypt of the Pharaohs*. New York: Oxford University Press, 1961.

Geisler, Norman, and Thomas Howe. *When Critics Ask: A Popular Handbook on Bible Difficulties*. Grand Rapids, MI: Baker Books, 1992.

Geisler, Norman L., and William E. Nix. *A General Introduction to the Bible*. Chicago: Moody Press, 1986.

Gilmour, Rachelle. *Juxtaposition and the Elisha Cycle*. London: Bloomsbury T&T Clark, 2014.

Glancy, Jennifer A. *Slavery as Moral Problem: In the Early Church and Today*. Minneapolis, MN: Fortress Press, 2011.

Goldingay, John. "Daniel." *Word Biblical Commentary*, Vol. 30. New York: Thomas Nelson, 1989.

Goldingay, John. *Exodus and Leviticus for Everyone*. Louisville, KY: Westminster John Knox Press, 2010.

Green, Ruth Hurmence. *Born Again Skeptic's Guide to the Bible.* Madison, WI: Freedom From Religion Foundation, 1979.

Greenlee, J. Harold. *The Text of the New Testament: From Manuscript to Modern Edition.* Peabody, MA: Hendrickson Publishers, 2008.

Grethlein, Jonas. *Experience and Teleology in Ancient Historiography: "Futures Past" from Herodotus to Augustine.* Cambridge: Cambridge University Press, 2014.

Hahn, Scott, and Curtis Mitch. *The Ignatius Catholic Study Bible: Genesis,* second edition. San Francisco: Ignatius Press, 2010.

Hahn, Scott, and Curtis Mitch. *The Ignatius Catholic Study Bible: Daniel,* second edition. San Francisco: Ignatius Press, 2013.

Hahn, Scott, and Curtis Mitch. *The Ignatius Catholic Study Bible: New Testament,* second edition. San Francisco: Ignatius Press, 2010.

Hahn, Scott, and David Scott. *Letter and Spirit Vol. 6: For the Sake of Our Salvation.* Steubenville, OH: Emmaus Road Publishing, 2010.

Hamilton, Victor P. *Handbook on the Pentateuch: Genesis, Exodus, Leviticus, Numbers, Deuteronomy.* Grand Rapids, MI: Baker Academic, 2005.

Hamilton, Victor P. *Handbook on the Historical Books: Joshua, Judges, Ruth, Samuel, Kings, Chronicles.* Grand Rapids, MI: Baker Academic, 2001.

Hasel, Michael G. *Domination and Resistance: Egyptian Military Activity in the Southern Levant, Ca. 1300–1185 B.C.* Leiden: Brill Academic Publishers, 1998.

Hiers, Richard H. *Justice and Compassion in Biblical Law.* New York: Continuum International Publishing, 2009.

Hoffmeier, James K. *Akhenaten and the Origins of Monotheism.* New York: Oxford University Press, 2015.

Hoffmeier, James K. *The Archaeology of the Bible.* London: Lion, 2008.

Hoffmeier, James K. *The Immigration Crisis: Immigrants, Aliens, and the Bible.* Wheaton: Crossway, 2009.

Hoffmeier, James K. *Ancient Israel in Sinai: The Evidence for the Authenticity of the Wilderness Tradition.* New York: Oxford University Press, 2005.

Hoffmeier, James K. *Israel in Egypt: The Evidence for the Authenticity of the Exodus Tradition.* New York: Oxford University Press, 1996.

Jenkins, Philip. *Laying Down the Sword: Why We Can't Ignore the Bible's Violent Verses.* New York: HarperOne, 2011.

Jones, Arthur W. Walker. *Hebrew for Biblical Interpretation.* Atlanta: Society of Biblical Literature, 2003.

Jordan, James. *Judges: A Practical and Theological Commentary.* Eugene, OR: Wipf and Stock, 1999.

Joshel, Sandra R. *Slavery in the Roman World.* New York: Cambridge University Press, 2010.

Keating, Daniel A. *First and Second Peter, Jude.* Grand Rapids, MI: Baker Academic, 2011.

Keating, Karl. *Catholicism and Fundamentalism: The Attack on Romanism by Bible Christians.* San Francisco: Ignatius Press, 1988.

Keating, Karl. *What Catholics Really Believe: Answers to Common Misconceptions About the Faith.* San Francisco: Ignatius Press, 1992.

Keener, Craig. *The Historical Jesus of the Gospels*. Grand Rapids, MI: Wm. B. Eerdmans, 2009.

Kitchen, K.A. *On the Reliability of the Old Testament*. Grand Rapids, MI: Wm. B Eerdmans, 2003.

Kochler, Hans. *The Concept of Monotheism in Islam and Christianity*. International Progress Association, 1982.

Lamb, David. *God Behaving Badly: Is the God of the Old Testament Angry, Sexist, and Racist?* Downer's Grove, IL: InterVarsity Press, 2011.

Licona, Michael. *The Resurrection of Jesus: A New Historiographical Approach*. Downer's Grove, IL: InterVarsity Press, 2010.

Loftus, John. *The Christian Delusion: Why Faith Fails*. Amherst, NY: Prometheus Books, 2010.

Loftus, John. *The End of Christianity*. Amherst, NY: Prometheus Books, 2011.

Long, Jason. *Biblical Nonsense: A Review of the Bible for Doubting Christians*. iUniverse, 2005.

Matthews, K.A. *Genesis 11:27–50:26: An Exegetical And Theological Exposition of Holy Scripture*. Nashville, TN: Broadman and Holman, 2005.

Mayor, Adrienne. *The First Fossil Hunters: Paleontology in Greek and Roman Times*. Princeton: Princeton University Press, 2000.

Maier, Paul. *Chronos, Kairos, Christos II*. Macon, GA: Mercer University Press, 1998.

McCann, J. Clinton. *Judges: Interpretation: A Bible Commentary for Teaching and Preaching*. Louisville: Westminster John Knox Press, 2011.

McGrath, Alister. *Reformation Thought: An Introduction*, fourth edition. West Sussex: Wiley Blackwell, 2012.

McKinsey, Dennis. *The Encyclopedia of Biblical Errancy*. Amherst, NY: Prometheus Books, 1995.

Metzger, Bruce M., and Bart D. Ehrman. *The Text of the New Testament: Its Transmission, Corruption, and Restoration*. New York: Oxford University Press, 2005.

Mills, David. *Atheist Universe: The Thinking Person's Answer to Christian Fundamentalism*. Berkeley, CA: Ulysses Press, 2006.

Most, Fr. William G. *The Consciousness of Christ*. Front Royal, VA: Christendom College Press, 1980.

Most, Fr. William G. *Free from All Error: Authorship Inerrancy Historicity of Scripture, Church Teaching, and Modern Scripture Scholars*. Libertyville, IL: Franciscan Marytown Press, 1985.

Mullen Jr., E. Theodore. *The Assembly of the Gods: The Divine Council in Canaanite and Early Hebrew Literature*. Chico, CA: Scholar's Press, 1986.

Nelson, Richard D. *Joshua: A Commentary*. Louisville, KY: Westminster John Knox Press, 1997.

Orchard, B., and E.F. Sutcliffe. *A Catholic Commentary on Holy Scripture*. New York: Thomas Nelson, 1953.

Oswalt, John N. *The Bible Among the Myths: Unique Revelation or Just Ancient Literature?* Grand Rapids, MI: Zondervan, 2009.

Parker, Julie Faith. *Valuable and Vulnerable: Children in the Hebrew Bible, Especially the Elisha Cycle*. Providence, RI: Brown University, 2013.

Pinker, Steven. *The Better Angels of Our Nature: Why Violence Has Declined.* Great Britain: Allen Lane, 2011.

Pontifical Biblical Commission. *The Inspiration and Truth of Sacred Scripture.* Collegeville, MN: Liturgical Press, 2014.

Pope Benedict XVI. *Jesus of Nazareth: The Infancy Narratives.* San Francisco: Image, 2012.

Pressler, Carolyn. *The View of Women Found in the Deuteronomic Family Laws.* Berlin: de Gruyter, 1993.

Ramage, Matthew. *Dark Passages of the Bible: Engaging Scripture with Benedict XVI and Thomas Aquinas.* Washington, DC: The Catholic University of America Press, 2013.

Ratzinger, Joseph and Peter Seewald. *God and the World: Believing and Living in Our Time.* San Francisco: Ignatius, 2000.

Ratzinger, Joseph. *Eschatology: Death and Eternal Life,* second edition. Washington, DC, The Catholic University of America, 2007.

Ratzinger, Joseph. *Jesus of Nazareth: From the Baptism in the Jordan to the Transfiguration.* San Francisco: Ignatius Press, 2008.

Ray, Jasper James. *God Wrote Only One Bible.* Junction City, KS: The Eye Opener Publishers, 1955.

Rooker, Mark F. *Leviticus: An Exegetical and Theological Exposition of Holy Scripture.* Nashville, TN: Broadman and Holman, 2000.

Shectman, Sarah. *Women in the Pentateuch: A Feminist and Source-Critical Analysis.* Sheffield: Sheffield Phoenix Press, 2009.

Simpson, William Kelly. *The Literature of Ancient Egypt: An Anthology of Stories, Instructions, Stelae, Autobiographies, and Poetry.*

New Haven: Yale University Press, 2003.

Smith, Ken. *Ken's Guide to the Bible*. New York: Blast Books, 1995.

Smith, Mark S. *The Origins of Biblical Monotheism: Israel's Polytheistic Background and the Ugaritic Texts*. New York: Oxford University Press, 2001.

Smith, Mark S. *The Early History of God: Yahweh and the Other Deities in Ancient Israel*. Grand Rapids, MI: Wm. B. Eerdmans, 2002.

Snell, Daniel C. *Life in the Ancient Near East*. New York: Yale University Press, 1997.

Sommer, Benjamin D. *The Bodies of God and the World of Ancient Israel*. Cambridge: Cambridge University Press, 2009.

Spong, John Shelby. *The Sins of Scripture: Exposing the Bible's Texts of Hate to Reveal the God of Love*. New York: HarperOne, 2006.

Sproul, R.C. *What Is Reformed Theology? Understanding the Basics*. Grand Rapids, MI: Baker Books, 2005.

Stark, Thom. *The Human Faces of God: What Scripture Reveals When It Gets God Wrong (and Why Inerrancy Tries to Hide It)*. Eugene, OR: Wipf and Stock: 2011.

Stein, Robert A. *Luke: An Exegetical and Theological Exposition of Holy Scripture*. Nashville, TN: Broadman and Holman, 1993.

Stein, Robert H. *Mark*. Grand Rapids, MI: Baker Academic, 2008.

Steinmann, Andrew E. *From Abraham to Paul: A Biblical Chronology*. St. Louis, MO: Concordia Publishing, 2011.

Stewart, Robert, ed. *The Reliability of the New Testament: Bart D. Ehrman and Daniel B. Wallace in Dialogue.* Minneapolis: Fortress Press, 2011.

Stuart, Douglas K. *Exodus: An Exegetical and Theological Exposition of Holy Scripture.* Nashville, TN: B&H Publishing, 2006.

Sungenis, Robert. *Not by Scripture Alone: A Catholic Critique of the Protestant Doctrine of Sola Scriptura.* Santa Barbara, CA: Queenship Publishing, 1997.

University of Navarre, *Saint Paul's Letters to the Romans & Galatians.* New York: Four Courts Press, 2005.

Walton, John H. *Ancient Near Eastern Thought and the Old Testament.* Grand Rapids, MI: Baker Academic, 2006.

Warren, Sam. *The Bible Naked.* San Diego, CA: Warren Communications, 2010.

Wells, Steve. *The Skeptic's Annotated Bible.* SAB Books, 2012.

Wells, Steve. *Drunk with Blood: God's Killings in the Bible.* SAB Books, 2013.

Westbrook, Raymond, and Bruce Wells. *Everyday Law in Biblical Israel: An Introduction.* Louisville, KY: Westminster John Knox Press, 2009.

Westbrook, Raymond. *A History of Ancient Near Eastern Law,* Vol 1. Leiden: Brill, 2003.

Werleman, C.J. *God Hates You, Hate Him Back: Making Sense of the Bible.* Great Britain: Dangerous Little Books, 2009.

Witherington, Ben. *Conflict and Community in Corinth: A Socio-*

Rhetorical Commentary on 1 and 2 Corinthians. Grand Rapids, MI: Wm. B. Eerdmans, 1995.

Witherington, Ben. *The Acts of the Apostles: A Socio-Rhetorical Commentary.* Grand Rapids, MI: Wm. B. Eerdmans, 1998.

Wright, Christopher J.H. *Old Testament Ethics for the People of God.* Downer's Grove, IL: InterVarsity Press, 2004.

Wright, Christopher J.H. *Knowing the Holy Spirit Through the Old Testament.* Downer's Grove, IL: InterVarsity Press, 2006.

Wright, Christopher J.H. *Knowing God the Father Through the Old Testament.* Downer's Grove, IL: InterVarsity Press, 2007.

Wright, N.T. *The Resurrection of the Son of God.* Minneapolis, MN: Fortress Press, 2003.

Wright, N.T. *Who Was Jesus?* Grand Rapids, MI: Wm. B. Eerdmans, 1992.

Younger Jr., K. Lawson. *Ancient Conquest Accounts: A Study in Ancient Near Eastern and Biblical History Writing.* Sheffield: Sheffield Academic Press, 1990.

Zuck, Roy B., and John F. Walvoord. *The Bible Knowledge Commentary: Old Testament.* Wheaton, IL: Victor Books, 1985.

About the Author

Trent Horn is an apologist and speaker for Catholic Answers. He specializes in pro-life issues as well as outreach to atheists and agnostics. He holds a master's degree in theology from Franciscan University of Steubenville.

Index

Endnotes

Introduction

1   "Reading the Bible (or the Koran) Will Make You an Atheist," Penn Jillette, interview by Paul Hoffman, June 8, 2010, bigthink.com/videos/reading-the-bible-or-the-koran-or-the-torah-will-make-you-an-atheist.

2   Laurie Goodstein, "Basic Religion Test Stumps Many Americans," *New York Times,* September 28, 2010, www.nytimes.com/2010/09/28/us/28religion.html?_r=0.

3   Richard Carrier, "From Taoist to Infidel," *The Secular Web,* 2001, infidels.org/library/modern/testimonials/carrier.html.

4   Richard Dawkins, *The God Delusion* (New York: Houghton-Mifflin, 2008), 51.

5   *Verbum Domini,* 42.

6   Norman Geisler and Thomas Howe, *When Critics Ask: A Popular Handbook on Bible Difficulties* (Grand Rapids, MI: Baker Books, 1992), 350–51.

7   *Verbum Domini,* 42.

8   This comes from an endorsement McLaren gave for Kenton L. Sparks's book *Sacred Word, Broken Word: Biblical Authority & the Dark Side of Scripture* (2012), found on the book's back cover.

Chapter 1: The Catholic View of Scripture

9   Karl Keating, *Catholicism and Fundamentalism: The Attack on Romanism by Bible Christians* (San Francisco: Ignatius Press, 1988), 126.

10 St. Augustine, *Against the Fundamental Epistle of Manichaeus* 5.

11 Protestants claim there are only sixty-six books in the canon of Scripture and omit the books of Tobit, Judith, Wisdom, Sirach, Baruch, 1 and 2 Maccabees, along with portions of Daniel and Esther. In addition, some descriptions of the canon say there are seventy-two books instead of seventy-three, because they combine Jeremiah and Lamentations (which are attributed to the same author) into one book.

12 Eusebius, *Church History* 4:23:11.

13 R.C. Sproul, *What Is Reformed Theology? Understanding the Basics*

(Grand Rapids, MI: Baker Books, 2005), 54.

14 Luther called James "an epistle of straw" and placed it with Jude and
Hebrews in the back of the Bible. Luther did not want to reject these
books as Scripture, but he also did not want to give them the same
authority as other writings in the Bible he was more fond of, like
Romans. See Timothy George, *Theology of the Reformers* (Nashville,
TN: Broadman and Holman Publishing, 2013), 84–85.

15 For a defense of the inspiration of the deuterocanonical books see
Gary Michuta, *The Case for the Deuterocanon: Evidence and Arguments*
(Livonia, MI: Nikaria Press, 2015).

16 *Dei Verbum*, 10.

17 Patrick Madrid, "Sola Scriptura: A Blueprint for Anarchy," in *Not
by Scripture Alone: A Catholic Critique of the Protestant Doctrine of Sola
Scriptura,* ed. Robert Sungenis (Santa Barbara, CA: Queenship Publishing, 1997).

18 *Dei Verbum*, 10. Pope Benedict XVI also said, "The Holy Spirit, who
gives life to the Church, enables us to interpret the scriptures authoritatively. The Bible is the Church's book, and its essential place
in the Church's life gives rise to its genuine interpretation" (*Verbum
Domini*, 29).

19 Sam Warren, *The Bible Naked: The Greatest Fraud Ever Told* (San Diego, CA: Warren Communications, 2010), preface.

20 Ruth Hurmence Green, *The Born Again Skeptic's Guide to the Bible*
(Madison, WI: Freedom From Religion Foundation, 1979), 14–15.

21 Dan Barker, *Godless: How an Evangelical Preacher Became One of America's Leading Atheists* (Berkeley, CA: Ulysses Press, 2008), 241.

22 *Lumen Gentium*, 16.

23 Alister McGrath, *Reformation Thought: An Introduction,* fourth edition
(West Sussex: Wiley Blackwell, 2012), 111.

24 J.I. Packer and O.R. Johnston, trans., *The Bondage of the Will* (Peabody, MA: Hendrickson Publishers, 2008), 82.

25 For example, the Westminster Confession says, "All things in Scripture are not alike plain in themselves, nor alike clear unto all: yet
those things *which are necessary to be known, believed, and observed for
salvation* [emphasis added] are so clearly propounded, and opened in
some place of Scripture or other, that not only the learned, but the

unlearned, in a due use of the ordinary means, may attain unto a sufficient understanding of them" (1.8). Modern Protestants tend to summarize it this way: "The main things are the plain things, and the plain things are the main things."

26 Theologians refer to the principle that all that is needed for salvation is located within Scripture as the "material sufficiency" of Scripture. But even though the truths necessary for salvation may all be found in Scripture, that doesn't mean the reader will correctly assemble those truths into one theological framework. The idea that this latter framework can be found in Scripture alone is called the "formal sufficiency" of Scripture. This is analogous to how a junkyard may be materially sufficient for the task of constructing a car, but if a person lacks mechanical know-how, then the junkyard becomes formally insufficient for that task. For more on the distinction between the material and formal sufficiency of Scripture, see,Mark Shea, "What is the Relationship Between Scripture and Tradition?," in *Not by Scripture Alone*, 181–82.

27 St. Vincent of Lerins, *Commonitory*, 2.5

28 *Verbum Domini*, 7, quoting CCC 108.

29 For a theological explanation, see the Second Vatican Council's Dogmatic Constitution on Divine Revelation, *Dei Verbum*. For a defense of this view see Mark Shea, *By What Authority? An Evangelical Discovers Catholic Tradition* (San Francisco: Ignatius Press, 2013).

30 St. Basil the Great, *Moralia, Regula* LXXX, XXII: PG 31, 867. Cited in *Verbum Domini*, 48.

31 *Providentissimus Deus,* 20.

32 Pontifical Biblical Commission, *The Inspiration and Truth of Sacred Scripture* (Collegeville, MN: Liturgical Press, 2014), 70.

33 *Dei Verbum*, 11.

34 For an in-depth treatment of this issue see *Letter and Spirit, Vol. 6: For the Sake of Our Salvation: The Truth and Humility of God's Word,* eds. Scott Hahn and David Scott (Steubenville, OH: Emmaus Road Publishing, 2010), especially the entries by Hahn, Pitre, and Fr. Harrison.

35 *Divino Afflante Spiritu*, 1.

36 *Dei Verbum*, 11.

37 Ibid.

38 *Divino Afflante Spiritu,* 35–36.

374   HARD SAYINGS

39   *Dei Verbum*, 12.

40   Steve Wells, *The Skeptic's Annotated Bible* (SAB Books, 2012), 1209.

41   Hadley Arkes, *Constitutional Illusions and Anchoring Truths: The Touchstones of Natural Law* (Cambridge: Cambridge University Press, 2010), 60.

42   *Verbum Domini*, 42.

43   Brant Pitre, "The Mystery of God's Word: Inspiration, Inerrancy, and the Inspiration of Scripture," in *Letter and Spirit, Vol. 6: For the Sake of Our Salvation: The Truth and Humility of God's Word* eds. Scott Hahn and David Scott (Steubenville, OH: Emmaus Road Publishing, 2010), Kindle edition.

Chapter 2: Unscientific Nonsense?

44   The ancient Roman historians Polybius and Livy describe Hannibal's trek across the Alps, and the ancient Egyptian writer Manetho chronicled the life of King Tutankhamen.

45   Diana Fishlock, "Atheist Group's Slave Billboard in Allison Hill Neighborhood Called Racist, Ineffective," *The Patriot-News*, March 06, 2012, www.pennlive.com/midstate/index.ssf/2012/03/athiests_slave_billboard_might.html.

46   It is possible some biblical authors were illiterate but had secretaries who assisted them. One example would be Peter, whose epistles may have been penned entirely by Silvanus (1 Pet. 5:12) since Peter was "unlettered" (cf. Acts 4:13). However, this passage in Acts is not proof Peter was illiterate, since it could just refer to a lack of traditional, rabbinic schooling and not necessarily to illiteracy in general.

47   Though I disagree with his pessimistic view of the historicity of biblical events, I agree with Gunkel that "Genesis contains the final sublimation into writing of a body of oral traditions." Hermann Gunkel, *The Legends of Genesis: The Biblical Saga & History* (Eugene, OR: Wipf and Stock, 2003), 3.

48   For a good treatment of this subject, see Douglas Geivett and Gary Habermas, *In Defense of Miracles: A Comprehensive Case for God's Action in History* (Downer's Grove, IL: InterVarsity Press, 1997).

49   *Verbum Domini*, 35.

50   John Shelby Spong, *The Sins of Scripture: Exposing the Bible's Texts of Hate to Reveal the God of Love* (New York: HarperOne, 2006), 21.

51 For a more in-depth defense of this miracle in comparison to other ancient stories, see Michael Licona, *The Resurrection of Jesus: A New Historiographical Approach* (Downer's Grove, IL: InterVarsity Press, 2010).

52 See for example 1 Corinthians 15:3–7. For a detailed analysis of this creed see Michael Licona, *The Resurrection of Jesus: A New Historiographical Approach* (Downer's Grove, IL: InterVarsity Press, 2010), 223–235.

53 Ibid., 343–75.

54 Buddha is recorded as saying in Sutta 11.5 of the *Digha Nikaya*, "Seeing the danger of such miracles, I dislike, reject and despise them." Sura 13:7 of the Qu'ran says, "Those who disbelieved say, 'Why has a sign not been sent down to him from his Lord?' You are only a warner, and for every people is a guide." Muhammad's role was simply to preach about Allah, not to perform any miracles.

55 The stories about Buddha were recorded in the Pali canon about 400 years after his death. The accounts describing Muhammad's miracles are found in a compilation of Islamic traditions called the hadith, written a century after his death.

56 See Paul Rhodes Eddy and Gregory A. Boyd, *The Jesus Legend: A Case for the Historical Reliability of the Synoptic Jesus Tradition* (Grand Rapids, MI: Baker Academic, 2007), 113–16.

57 Pope St. Clement, a disciple of St. Peter, wrote in his letter to the Corinthians that Peter, "through unrighteous envy, endured not one or two, but numerous labors, and when he had finally suffered martyrdom, departed to the place of glory due to him. Owing to envy, Paul also obtained the reward of patient endurance . . . and suffered martyrdom under the prefects" (*First Clement* 5:4–5). St. Polycarp of Smyrna, who was a disciple of St. John, describes Jesus' endurance till death and similarly exhorts believers to "practice all endurance, which also you saw with your own eyes in the blessed Ignatius and Zosimus and Rufus, and in others also who came from among yourselves, as well as in Paul himself and the rest of the apostles" (*Letter to the Philippians* 9.1). Because Clement and Polycarp personally knew the apostles, we can have a high degree of confidence in their testimony that at least some of the apostles were martyred. Finally, the Jewish historian Josephus records that the high priest Caiaphas

stoned James, whom Josephus describes as "the brother of Jesus," for transgressing the law (*Antiquities of the Jews* 20.9.1).

58 Gary Habermas, "My Pilgrimage from Atheism to Theism: An Exclusive Interview with Former British Atheist Professor Antony Flew," *Faculty Publications and Presentations of Liberty University* Paper, 2004, 333.

59 Jasper James Ray, *God Wrote Only One Bible* (Junction City, KS: The Eye Opener Publishers, 1955), 118.

60 The Pontifical Biblical Commission, *The Interpretation of the Bible in the Church* (Washington, DC: USCCB Publishing, 1993), 19.

61 *Dei Verbum*, 11.

62 *Gaudium et Spes*, 22.

63 The *Catechism* teaches us that Christ is God's single Word revealed to us: "Through all the words of Sacred Scripture, God speaks only one single Word, his one Utterance in whom he expresses himself completely. For this reason, the Church has always venerated the scriptures as she venerates the Lord's Body. She never ceases to present to the faithful the bread of life, taken from the one table of God's Word and Christ's Body" (CCC 102–03).

64 *Dei Verbum*, 13

65 "Address of Pope John Paul II to Pontifical Biblical Commission," April 23, 1993, in *The Scripture Documents: An Anthology of Official Catholic Teachings*, ed. Dean P. Bechard (Collegeville, MN: The Order of Saint Benedict, 2002), 174.

66 Scott Hahn, "For the Sake of Our Salvation: The Truth and Humility of God's Word," in *Letter and Spirit, Vol. 6: For the Sake of Our Salvation*, eds. Scott Hahn and David Scott (Steubenville, OH: Emmaus Road Publishing, 2010), 37.

67 *Providentissimus Deus*, 18.

68 Another example of an idiom that should not be taken literally is Judges 5:20: "From heaven fought the stars, from their courses they fought against Sisera."

69 Jason Long, *Biblical Nonsense: A Review of the Bible for Doubting Christians* (np: iUniverse, 2005), 43.

70 "The hegemony of heart over brain was the prevailing view in the Ancient Near and Far East, and advocates of this opinion can be

found in Europe into the 17th century." Charles C. Gross, "Neuro-science, Early History of" in *Encyclopedia of Neuroscience,* ed. G. Adelman (Boston: Birkhauser, 1987) 843.

71 Another example is the King James Version's use of the word "reins" in passages like Revelation 2:23, where Jesus says, "all the churches shall know that I am he which searcheth the reins and hearts: and I will give unto every one of you according to your works." Skeptics say "reins" is an archaic word for "kidneys," so the Bible teaches that Jesus will search our kidneys. The Greek word used in this verse, or *nephrous,* does mean "kidneys," but this should be considered a popular description and not a scientific one. It is on par with a modern person saying, "My gut is telling me this is wrong."

72 St. Thomas Aquinas, *Summa Theologicae* 1.68.3.

73 Scott Hahn and Curtis Mitch, *The Ignatius Catholic Study Bible: Genesis,* second edition (San Francisco: Ignatius Press, 2010), 18.

74 St. Augustine, *De Acts cum Felice Manichaeo* I.10. Cited in Jerome J. Langford, *Galileo, Science, and the Church* (Ann Arbor, MI: University of Michigan Press, 1992), 65. In the ancient world astronomy and mathematics were closely related because mathematical formulas were used to calculate the movement of celestial bodies.

75 Pope John Paul II, "Cosmology and Fundamental Physics," October 3, 1981, www.ewtn.com/library/PAPALDOC/JP2COSM.HTM.

Chapter 3: Darwin Refutes Genesis?

76 Michael Shermer. "Science and Religion: Natural Adversaries?," *Los Angeles Times,* July 30, 2009, www.latimes.com/news/opinion/opinionla/la-oew-ayala-shermer30-2009jul30-story.html#page=1.

77 James Ussher, et al., *The Annals of the World* (Green Forest, AR: New Leaf Publishing Group, 2003), 9.

78 While it does not constitute magisterial teaching on this subject, a 2004 document released by the International Theological Commission—which at the time was headed by the future pope, Cardinal Joseph Ratzinger—did say, "According to the widely accepted scientific account, the universe erupted 15 billion years ago in an explosion called the 'Big Bang' and has been expanding and cooling ever since . . . Since it has been demonstrated that all living organisms on earth

are genetically related, it is virtually certain that all living organisms have descended from this first organism. Converging evidence from many studies in the physical and biological sciences furnishes mounting support for some theory of evolution to account for the development and diversification of life on earth, while controversy continues over the pace and mechanisms of evolution." "Communion and Stewardship: Human Persons Created in the Image and Likeness of God," *International Theological Commission,* 2004.

79 *Decrees of the First Vatican Council,* 1.5.

80 For evidence for the theory of evolution that does not come from authors with an atheistic worldview, see Francis Collins, *The Language of God: A Scientist Presents Evidence for Belief* (New York: Free Press, 2007), and Kenneth Miller, *Finding Darwin's God: A Scientist's Search for Common Ground Between God and Evolution* (New York: Harper Perennial, 2007).

81 Origen, *Against Celsus* 6.60.

82 St. Augustine, *The Literal Meaning of Genesis* 1.14.

83 Origen, *De Principiis* 4.16.

84 St. Augustine, *The Literal Meaning of Genesis* 15.29.

85 According to Alister McGrath, "God brought everything into existence in a single moment of creation. Yet the created order is not static. God endowed it with the capacity to develop. Augustine uses the image of a dormant seed to help his readers grasp the point. God creates seeds, which will grow and develop at the right time. Using more technical language, Augustine asks his readers to think of the created order as containing divinely embedded causalities that emerge or evolve at a later stage." Alister McGrath, *The Passionate Intellect: Christian Faith and the Discipleship of the Mind* (Downer's Grove, IL: InterVarsity Press, 2010), 140.

86 For a defense of a nonchronological perspective of Genesis that is similar to the framework view, see John H. Walton, *The Lost World of Genesis One: Ancient Cosmology and the Origins Debate* (Downer's Grove, IL: InterVarsity Press, 2009).

87 "These works are recorded to have been completed in six days (the same day being six times repeated), because six is a perfect number—not because God required a protracted time, as if he could not at once

create all things, which then should mark the course of time by the movements proper to them, but because the perfection of the works was signified by the number six." St. Augustine, *City of God* 11.30.

88 John Henry Newman, "Letter to J. Walker of Scarbourugh on Darwin's Theory of Evolution," Birmingham, May 22, 1868. *Interdisciplinary Encyclopedia of Religion & Science,* www.inters.org/Newman-Scarborough-Darwin-Evolution.

89 St. Thomas Aquinas, *Summa Theologica* 1.96.1.

90 See also my treatment of natural evil in Trent Horn, *Answering Atheism: Making the Case for God with Logic and Charity* (El Cajon, CA: Catholic Answers Press, 2013).

91 Pontifical Biblical Commission, *The Inspiration and Truth of Sacred Scripture,* 120.

92 "The Light of Revelation in the Old Testament," Wednesday Audience, May 8, 1985. Regarding the book of Tobit, the Pontifical Biblical Commission writes, "We have here, then, a popular religious fable with a didactic and edifying purpose which, by its nature, places it in the sphere of the wisdom tradition" (*The Inspiration and Truth of Sacred Scripture,* 129). The same can be said for the book of Judith, which is often accused by critics of having historical inaccuracies. According to one Protestant commentary, "[Judith's] original author was an ironist who knew, as did many in his ancient audience, that he was writing fiction rather than fact." Carey A. Moore, *Judith, The Anchor Yale Bible Commentaries* (New York: Doubleday, 1985), 85.

93 Karl Keating, *Catholicism and Fundamentalism: The Attack on Romanism by Bible Christians* (San Francisco: Ignatius Press, 1988), 129–30.

94 Craig Blomberg, *Can We Still Believe in the Bible?: An Evangelical Engagement with Contemporary Questions* (Grand Rapids, MI: Brazos Press, 2014), 156.

95 This view is common among critics like John Shelby Spong, Marcus Borg, and John Dominic Crossan. For a refutation of their claims, I recommend watching William Lane Craig's debates with each of these scholars at his Web site, www.reasonablefaith.org. The debate with Crossan is available in book form under the title *Will the Real Jesus Please Stand Up? A Debate Between William Lane Craig and John Dominic Crossan,* ed. Paul Copan (Grand Rapids, MI: Baker Academic, 1999).

96 See N.T. Wright, *The Resurrection of the Son of God* (Minneapolis: Fortress Press, 2003).

97 Pope Benedict XVI, "Meeting of the Holy Father Benedict XVI with the Clergy of the Diocese of Belluno-Feltre and Treviso," July 24, 2007. www.vatican.va/holy_father/benedict_xvi/speeches/2007/july/documents/hf_ben-xvi_spe_20070724_clero-cadorc_en.html.

98 *Humani Generis*, 38.

99 Pope John Paul II, "General Audience," November 7, 1979, www.vatican.va/holy_father/john_paul_ii/audiences/catechesis_genesis/documents/hf_jp-ii_aud_19791107_en.html.

100 *Dominum et Vivificantem*, 36. See also CCC 396.

101 See canons 1-5 of the First Vatican Council (1870), and Pope Pius XII's encyclical *Humani Generis* (1950).

Chapter 4: Bronze Age Ignorance?

102 C. Dennis McKinsey, *The Encyclopedia of Biblical Errancy* (Amherst, NY: Prometheus Books, 1995), 214.

103 Llewelyn Lloyd, *The Field Sports of the North of Europe: A Narrative of Angling, Hunting, and Shooting in Sweden and Norway* (London: Hamilton, Adams and Co., 1885), 366.

104 Steve Wells, *The Skeptic's Annotated Bible* (SAB Books, 2012), 153.

105 "flying creatures, i.e. birds or insects," R. Laird Harris, Gleason L Archer, Bruce K. Waltke. *Theological Wordbook of the Old Testament* (Chicago: Moody Publishers, 1980), 654.

106 Farrell Till, "Bible Biology," *The Skeptical Review* 2, no. 2 (April/May/June 1991).

107 Jason Long, *Biblical Nonsense: A Review of the Bible for Doubting Christians* (np: iUniverse, 2005), 41.

108 Scott Hahn and Curtis Mitch, *The Ignatius Catholic Study Bible: Genesis*, second edition (San Francisco: Ignatius Press, 2010), 56-57.

109 Some people say 2 Chronicles 16:12–13 condemns medicine and encourages faith healing. It says, "In the thirty-ninth year of his reign Asa was diseased in his feet, and his disease became severe; yet even in his disease he did not seek the Lord, but sought help from physicians. And Asa slept with his fathers, dying in the forty-first year of his reign." But this passage comes at the end of the Chronicler's description of how

Asa continually ignored the Lord and put his trust instead in human authorities like the king of Syria. Asa's trust in doctors to save him instead of the Lord was the last sign of his reluctance to trust in God. The text does not condemn Asa for relying on doctors, but for his decision not to seek after the Lord during any part of his ordeal.

110 According to *The Lexham Bible Dictionary,* "This medical description of [modern] leprosy is strikingly different than the description given of (*tsara'ath*) in the Old Testament. Biblical symptoms include swelling, crusty or scabby rash, or bright inflamed areas. Furthermore, the Old Testament description lacks the very obvious symptoms of leprosy (e.g., numbness, depressed nose, problems with extremities) . . . Already in 1919, it was becoming the general consensus that the word for leprosy (*tsara'ath*) actually related to general skin diseases. B. Heyink, "Leprosy" in *The Lexham Bible Dictionary,* eds. D. R. Brown et al. (Bellingham, WA: Lexham Press, 2012).

111 Steve Wells, *The Skeptic's Annotated Bible* (SAB Books, 2012), 158.

112 P.P. Saydon, "Leviticus" in *A Catholic Commentary on Holy Scripture,* eds. B. Orchard & E. F. Sutcliffe (New York: Thomas Nelson, 1953), 237.

113 Jason Long, *Biblical Nonsense: A Review of the Bible for Doubting Christians* (np: iUniverse, 2005), 160

114 A critic could object that while demons cannot be located directly, science could detect them in an indirect way by studying demonic effects on the physical world. But even this approach would be unable to test the phenomena in question in a way that precludes demonic interaction and shows the effect has natural rather than supernatural causes.

115 See, for example, Matt Baglio, *The Rite: The Making of a Modern Exorcist* (New York: Doubleday, 2010).

116 The Church's new guidelines are, at this time, only available in Latin under the title *De Exorcismus et Supplicationibus Quibusdam* (*Of Exorcisms and Certain Supplications*). For a helpful lay approach to the issue, see also Jean Lhermitte, *True or False Possession: How to Distinguish the Demonic from the Demented* (Manchester, NH: Sophia Institute Press, 2013).

117 C. Dennis McKinsey, *The Encyclopedia of Biblical Errancy* (Amherst, NY: Prometheus Books, 1995), 211, and Steve Wells, *The Skeptic's Annotated Bible* (SAB Books, 2012), 599.

118 See "Technical Characteristics—Boeing 747-400ER," www.boeing. com/boeing/commercial/747family/pf/pf_400er_prod.page.

Chapter 5: Legendary Biblical Creatures?

119 See Dwight Young, "A Mathematical Approach to Certain Dynastic Spans in the Sumerian King List," *Journal of Near Eastern Studies* 47, no. 2 (1988), 123–29. The number of years a person was said to have lived may also have had a symbolic meaning of which we are now ignorant. This may be the case, for example, with Enoch, whose life span was equivalent to the number of days in a year, or 365.

120 "Sumerian Kings List," www.livius.org/k/kinglist/sumerian.html. For the historical record of the two kings listed here, see Kathleen Kuiper, *Mesopotamia: The World's Earliest Civilization* (New York: Britannica Educational Publishing, 2011), 48.

121 Scott Hahn and Curtis Mitch, *The Ignatius Catholic Study Bible: Genesis*, second edition (San Francisco: Ignatius Press, 2010), 25.

122 See St. Thomas Aquinas, *Summa Theologica* 1.50.4, and Matthew 22:30.

123 For example, the fifth century rabbinic commentary *Genesis Rabbah* says about the Nephilim that the first-century rabbi Simeon ben Yohai "called them the sons of nobles; [furthermore], Rabbi Simeon ben Yohai cursed all who called them the sons of God" (26.5). In *City of God*, Augustine refers to an incident when he discovered that what he thought was a molar of an ancient human that was a hundred times larger than a normal tooth (15.9). He goes on to explain the nonangelic origin of these giants: "Giants therefore might well be born, even before the sons of God, who are also called angels of God, formed a connection with the daughters of men, or of those living according to men, that is to say, *before the sons of Seth formed a connection with the daughters of Cain* [emphasis added]."(15.23). See also Scott Hahn and Curtis Mitch, *The Ignatius Catholic Study Bible: Genesis*, second edition (San Francisco: Ignatius Press, 2010), 26.

124 See *Antiquities* 1.3.1 and Justin Martyr *Second Apology* 5.

125 Numbers 13:23 says that the scouts "cut down from there a branch with a single cluster of grapes, and they carried it on a pole between two of them." This may be hyperbolic or it could just be a description of the large grapes that still grow in Israel today. They may have

needed to be carried on a pole because it would be awkward to carry such a large cluster by hand.

126 See "Human Height," Wikipedia.org, en.wikipedia.org/wiki/Human_height.

127 Jason Long, *Biblical Nonsense: A Review of the Bible for Doubting Christians* (np: iUniverse, 2005), 159.

128 G. Johannes Botterweck and Helmer Ringgren, *Theological Dictionary of the Old Testament,* Vol. 13 (Grand Rapids, MI: Wm. B. Eerdmans, 2004), 243.

129 Pliny the Elder. *Natural History* 8.31.

130 Jason Long, *Biblical Nonsense: A Review of the Bible for Doubting Christians* (np: iUniverse, 2005), 159.

131 Laurence A. Breiner. "The Career of the Cockatrice," *Isis* 70, no. 1 (1979), 30.

132 R. Laird Harris, Gleason L Archer, Bruce K. Waltke. *Theological Wordbook of the Old Testament* (Chicago: Moody Publishers, 1980), 775.

133 R. Dennis Cole, *Numbers: An Exegetical and Theological Exposition of Holy Scripture* (Nashville, TN: Holman Reference, 2000), 347.

134 David Mills, *Atheist Universe: The Thinking Person's Answer to Christian Fundamentalism* (Berkeley, CA: Ulysses Press, 2006), 150.

135 Ironically, Mills makes the same mistake as the extreme fundamentalists he argues against in his book. These fundamentalists, or so-called "King-James Only" advocates like Peter Ruckman, believe that the King James Version of the Bible is the only inspired word of God, even more so than the original Hebrew and Greek manuscripts of the Bible. For a good treatment of this issue see D. A. Caron, *The King James Version Debate: A Plea for Realism* (Grand Rapids, MI: Baker Books, 1979).

136 Notice that the satyr is mentioned alongside other wild animals, and the Hebrew word for "dance" used in this passage usually means "to skip" or "frolic" when used of animals. It only means "to dance" when it is used of humans. See F. Brown, S. Driver, and C Briggs, *The Brown-Driver-Briggs Hebrew and English Lexicon* (Peabody, MA: Hendrickson Publishers, 2006), 955.

137 Ibid., 1072.

138 Mark S. Smith, *The Origins of Biblical Monotheism: Israel's Polytheis-

tic Background and the Ugaritic Texts (New York: Oxford University Press, 2001), 36–37.

139 John N. Oswalt, *The Bible Among the Myths: Unique Revelation or Just Ancient Literature?* (Grand Rapids, MI: Zondervan, 2009), 93.

140 See Adrienne Mayor, *The First Fossil Hunters: Paleontology in Greek and Roman Times* (Princeton: Princeton University Press, 2000).

Chapter 6: The Mythical Patriarchs?

141 William G. Dever, *Who Were the Early Israelites and Where Did They Come From?* (Grand Rapids, MI: Wm. B. Eerdmans), 202.

142 Avalos claims this is not proof a group related to the patriarch Israel existed because the Egyptians could have erroneously imposed the name "Israel" on the group they defeated, just as Columbus imposed the name "Indians" upon Native Americans. Hector Avalos, *The End of Biblical Studies* (Amherst NY: Prometheus Books, 2007), 122. But this seems unlikely given the Hebrew roots of the name Israel and the antipathy ancient Jews would have had toward fashioning an origin story based on a foreign power's misunderstanding of their heritage.

143 James K. Hoffmeier, *The Archaeology of the Bible* (London: Lion, 2008), 40.

144 Modern critiques of the historicity of the patriarchs are drawn largely from arguments found in Thomas L. Thompson's 1974 work, *The Historicity of the Patriarchal Narratives: The Quest for the Historical Abraham* (Berlin: Walter de Gruyter, 1974). For a reply from a conservative scholar, see K.A. Kitchen, *On the Reliability of the Old Testament* (Grand Rapids, MI: Wm. B Eerdmans, 2003), especially chapters 7 and 10. For a reply from a moderate scholar, see William G. Dever, *What Did the Biblical Writers Know and When Did They Know It?* (Grand Rapids, MI: Wm. B Eerdmans, 2001).

145 Paul Tobin, "The Bible and Modern Scholarship," in *The Christian Delusion: Why Faith Fails,* ed. John Loftus (Amherst, NY: Prometheus Books, 2010), 153.

146 Lidar Sapir-Hen and Erez Ben-Yosef, "The Introduction of Domestic Camels to the Southern Levant: Evidence from the Aravah Valley," *Tel Aviv* 40 (2013), 277–85.

147 Michael Ripinsky, "The Camel in Dynastic Egypt," *Journal of Egyp-*

tian Archaeology 71 (1985), 134–41.

148 Martin Heide, "The Domestication of the Camel: Biological, Archaeological and Inscriptional Evidence from Mesopotamia, Egypt, Israel and Arabia, and Literary Evidence from the Hebrew Bible," *Ugarit-Forschungen* 42 (2011), 367–68.

149 David Jobling and Catherine Rose, "Reading as a Philistine," in *Ethnicity and the Bible*, ed. Mark G. Brett (Leiden: Brill Academic, 1997), 404.

150 Robert Drews, "Canaanites and Philistines," *Journal for the Study of the Old Testament* 81 (1998), 39–61.

151 Brian Haughton, *Hidden History: Lost Civilizations, Secret Knowledge, and Ancient Mysteries* (Franklin Lakes, NJ: New Page Books, 2007), 113.

152 A similar issue arises in passages like Genesis 14:14, which refers to Abram pursuing his enemies to the city of Dan. This city was named after the tribe of Dan, whose progenitor was Abram's great-grandson, who had not been born at this point in the story. The name, therefore, is probably a helpful designation for the reader to understand the story's geography. It would be like saying Lewis and Clark reached Oregon in 1805 even though the state of Oregon did not yet exist.

153 William Kelly Simpson, *The Literature of Ancient Egypt: An Anthology of Stories, Instructions, Stelae, Autobiographies, and Poetry* (New Haven: Yale University Press, 2003), 161.

154 Kenneth Kitchen, "Genesis 12–50 in the Near Eastern World," in *He Swore an Oath: Biblical Themes from Genesis 12–50*, ed. R.S. Hess (Cambridge: Tyndale House, 1993), 79–80.

155 J.M.A. Janssen, "*On the Ideal Lifetime of the Egyptians*," OMRO 31 (1950), 33–43. See also 2 Samuel 19:32–35 and Psalm 90:10.

156 Alan Gardiner, *Egypt of the Pharaohs* (New York: Oxford University Press, 1961), 277.

157 "The story of Moses' birth . . . parallels closely the nativity story of the legendary Akkadian king Sargon." Paul Tobin, "The Bible and Modern Scholarship," in *The Christian Delusion: Why Faith Fails,* ed. John Loftus (Amherst, NY: Prometheus Books, 2010), 154.

158 Clarence O. Cheney, "The Psychology of Mythology," in *Psychology and Myth,* ed. Robert Segal (New York: Routledge, 1995) 136.

159 James K. Hoffmeier, *Israel in Egypt: The Evidence for the Authenticity of the Exodus Tradition* (New York: Oxford University Press, 1996), 137.

160 James K. Hoffmeier, *The Immigration Crisis: Immigrants, Aliens, and the Bible* (Wheaton: Crossway, 2009), 64.

161 Cited in Hoffmeier, *Israel in Egypt: The Evidence for the Authenticity of the Exodus Tradition* (New York: Oxford University Press, 1996), 112.

162 Some critics claim the sixth plague contains supernatural "fire" mixed with hail. The KJV translates Exodus 9:24, "So there was hail, and fire mingled with the hail, very grievous, such as there was none like it in all the land of Egypt since it became a nation." But this is probably just a reference to lightning, which often occurs in hailstorms. The RSV translates this passage as "There was hail, and fire flashing continually in the midst of the hail, very heavy hail, such as had never been in all the land of Egypt since it became a nation."

163 Michael G. Hasel, *Domination and Resistance: Egyptian Military Activity in the Southern Levant, Ca. 1300–1185 B.C.* (Leiden: Brill Academic, 1998), 155.

164 The Bible names neither the Pharaoh who oppressed the Israelites nor the one who reigned during the Exodus. Scholars who favor an earlier date for the Exodus generally prefer to identify the Pharaoh with Thutmose III or Amenhotep II, while scholars who favor a later date prefer Ramses II. For a discussion of this issue, see Scott Hahn and Curtis Mitch, *The Ignatius Catholic Study Bible: Exodus*, second edition (San Francisco: Ignatius Press, 2010), 30–31.

165 Paul Tobin, "The Bible and Modern Scholarship," in *The Christian Delusion: Why Faith Fails,* ed. John Loftus (Amherst, NY: Prometheus Books, 2010), 155.

166 Joel Greenberg, *A Feathered River Across the Sky: The Passenger Pigeon's Flight and Extinction* (New York: Bloomsbury, 2014), 5–6.

167 David E. Blockstein, "Passenger Pigeon *Ectopistes migratorius,*" in *The Birds of North America,* eds. Alan Poole and Frank Gill, no. 611 (Philadelphia: The Birds of North America, Inc., 2002), 3.

168 Israel Finkelstein and Avi Perevolotsky, "Processes of Sedentarization and Nomadization in the History of Sinai and the Negev," *Bulletin of the American Schools of Oriental Research,* no. 279 (August 1990), 67–88. Cited in James K. Hoffmeier, *Ancient Israel in Sinai: The Evidence for the Authenticity of the Wilderness Tradition* (New York: Oxford University Press, 2005), 150.

169 Michael D. Coogan, *A Brief Introduction to the Old Testament: The Hebrew Bible in Its Context* (New York: Oxford University Press, 2008), 116.

170 See Douglas K. Stuart, *Exodus: An Exegetical and Theological Exposition of Holy Scripture* (Nashville, TN: B&H Publishing, 2006), 297–303, for an in-depth defense of this view.

171 David Foust, "A Defense of the Hyperbolic Interpretation of Large Numbers in the Old Testament," *Journal of the Evangelical Theological Society* 40/3 (Sept 1997), 386.

172 Victor P. Hamilton, *Handbook on the Pentateuch: Genesis, Exodus, Leviticus, Numbers, Deuteronomy* (Grand Rapids, MI: Baker Academic, 2005), 170. For U.S. military statistics, see "By the Numbers: Today's Military," NPR, July 3, 2011, www.npr.org/2011/07/03/137536111/by-the-numbers-todays-military.

173 Paul Tobin, "The Bible and Modern Scholarship," in *The Christian Delusion: Why Faith Fails,* ed. John Loftus (Amherst, NY: Prometheus Books, 2010), 155.

174 K.A. Kitchen, *On the Reliability of the Old Testament* (Grand Rapids, MI: Wm. B. Eerdmans, 2003), 188.

175 Ibid., 187. In addition, if Joshua is not a strict historical account, then charges of it being nonhistorical make a category error. See chapter 24 for an in-depth examination of this claim.

176 For example, an 1882 article in the *British Quarterly Review* says, "In 1857 Professor F.W. Newman, fellow of Balliol College, Oxford, in his *History of the Hebrew Monarchy* [178–79] speaks of the Bible references to the Hittites as 'unhistorical,' and as 'not exhibiting the writer's acquaintance with the times in a very favourable light,' and the Rev. T.K. Cheyne, fellow of the same college, writing on the Hittites, in the *Encyclopaedia Britannica,* last year, treats the Bible statements regarding the Hittites as unhistorical and unworthy of credence." "The Hittites and the Bible," *British Quarterly Review* (July and October 1882), 54.

177 Horst Klengel, "Problems in Hittite History, Solved and Unsolved," in *Recent Developments in Hittite Archaeology and History: Papers in Memory of Hans G. Guterbock,* eds. K Aslihan Yener, Harry A. Hoffner, and Simrit Dhesi (Winona Lake, IN: Eisenbrauns, 2002), 101.

Chapter 7: Bungled History?

178 William Sierichs Jr., "Daniel in the Historians' Den," *The Skeptical Review* (July-August 1996), www.theskepticalreview.com/tsrmag/4danie96.html.

179 Steve Wells, *The Skeptic's Annotated Bible* (SAB Books, 2012), 1118.

180 Andrew E. Steinmann, *From Abraham to Paul: A Biblical Chronology* (St. Louis, MO: Concordia Publishing, 2011), 158.

181 *Chronicle Concerning the Early Years of Nebuchadnezzar II,* obverse side, 12–13. "Although this taking of Jerusalem and first deportation of some of its people to Babylon is otherwise unknown, the event must have taken place in the time soon after the battle of Carchemish, when Nebuchadnezzar accomplished his other victories in Syria Palestine." Cited in Jack Finegan, *Handbook of Biblical Chronology* (Peabody, MA: Hendrickson, 1998), 254. See also Scott Hahn and Curtis Mitch, *The Ignatius Catholic Study Bible: Daniel*, second edition (San Francisco: Ignatius Press, 2013), Kindle edition.

182 Josephus, *Against Apion* 1.19.

183 It is as accurate to say "King Nebuchadnezzar" besieged Jerusalem before he was crowned in Babylon as it would be to say the president of the United States lived in a certain state before he moved into the White House. Obviously he wasn't the president wherever he lived prior to taking up residence in the White House, but it would not be strange to refer either to him or a ruler like Nebuchadnezzar by a later, better-known title.

184 "The Verse Account of Nabonidus," translation available online at www.livius.org/ct-cz/cyrus_I/babylon03.html.

185 "The Nabonidus Cylinder from Ur" translation available online at www.livius.org/na-nd/nabonidus/cylinder-ur.html.

186 Scott Hahn and Curtis Mitch, *The Ignatius Catholic Study Bible: Daniel*, second edition (San Francisco: Ignatius Press, 2013), Kindle edition.

187 John Goldingay "Daniel," *Word Biblical Commentary*, Vol. 30 (New York: Thomas Nelson, 1989), 109.

188 Herodotus, *The Persian Wars* I.188. "The expedition of Cyrus was undertaken against the son of this princess, who bore the same name as his father Labynetus [the Greek spelling of Nabonidus], and was king of the Assyrians." Translation available online at mcadams.posc.

mu.edu/txt/ah/Herodotus/Herodotus1.html.

189 Andrew E. Steinmann, *From Abraham to Paul: A Biblical Chronology* (St. Louis, MO: Concordia Publishing, 2011), 177.

190 Scott Hahn and Curtis Mitch, *The Ignatius Catholic Study Bible: Daniel*, second edition (San Francisco: Ignatius Press, 2013), Kindle edition.

191 The *Chronicle* calls this man Ugbaru (or possibly Gubaru), while Greek writings refer to him as Gobyras. Translators of the *Nabonidus Chronicle* often consider Ugbaru and Gobryas to be the same person.

192 Fr. William G. Most, *Free from All Error: Authorship Inerrancy Historicity of Scripture, Church Teaching, and Modern Scripture Scholars* (Libertyville, IL: Franciscan Marytown Press, 1985), 53.

193 U.S. Department of the Interior, "Fatalities at Hoover Dam: www. usbr.gov/lc/hooverdam/History/essays/fatal.html.

194 Pontifical Biblical Commission, *The Inspiration and Truth of Sacred Scripture*, 120.

195 For an analysis of a similar thesis, see Brevard S. Childs. *The Book of Exodus: A Critical, Theological Commentary* (Louisville, KY: Westminster John Knox Press, 2004), 142–49.

196 Ibid., 127.

197 Raymond E. Brown, *The Birth of the Messiah: A Commentary on the Infancy Narratives in the Gospels of Matthew and Luke* (New York: Doubleday, 1993), 36.

198 Pope Benedict XVI, *Jesus of Nazareth: The Infancy Narratives* (San Francisco: Image, 2012), 17.

199 "Apographe: a register, inventory, registration, enrollment Lk. 2:2, Acts 5:37," William D. Mounce, *Mounce's Complete Expository Dictionary of the Old and New Testament Words* (Grand Rapids, MI: Zondervan, 2006), 1091.

200 Josephus, *Antiquities* 17.2.4.

201 Augustus, *Res Gestae Divi Augusti* 35. Cited in Robert K. Sherk, *The Roman Empire: Augustus to Hadrian* (New York: Cambridge University Press, 1988), 26.

202 Jack Finegan, *Handbook of Biblical Chronology* (Peabody, MA: Hendrickson, 1998), 291. Thanks to Jimmy Akin for this reference.

203 A.E. Steinmann, "When Did Herod the Great Reign?," *Novum Testamentum* 51, Issue 1 (2009), 1–29.

204 Josephus, *Antiquities* 18.1.

205 Ibid., 17.5.2 and 9.3.

206 Tacitus, *Annals* 3.48. See also Erich S. Gruen, "The Expansion of the Empire under Augustus," in *The Cambridge Ancient History, Vol. 10: The Augustan Empire, 43 BC-AD 69*, ed. Alan K. Bowman, et al. (Cambridge: Cambridge University Press, 1996), 650.

207 N.T. Wright, *Who Was Jesus?* (Grand Rapids, MI: Wm. B. Eerdmans, 1992), 89. Carrier argues in reply, "the basic rules of Greek ensure that there is absolutely no way this [prote] can mean 'before' Quirinius in this construction." Richard Carrier, "The Date of the Nativity in Luke," *The Secular Web*, 2011, infidels.org/library/modern/richard_carrier/quirinius.html. For a critique of grammatical arguments made against interpretations like Wright's, see Stanley Porter, "The Reasons for the Lukan Census," *Paul, Luke and the Graeco-Roman World: Essays in Honour of Alexander J.M. Wedderburn* (New York: Sheffield Academic Press, 2002).

208 C.J. Werleman, *God Hates You, Hate Him Back: Making Sense of the Bible* (Great Britain: Dangerous Little Books, 2009), 190.

209 Josephus, *Antiquities* 15.7.5–6 and 16.11.7.

210 Aryeh Kasher and Eliezer Witztum, *King Herod: A Persecuted Persecutor: A Case Study in Psychohistory and Psychobiography* (Berlin: Walter de Gruyter, 2007). Augustus is reported to have quipped, "It is better to be Herod's pig than son" (Macrobius, *Saturnalia* 2:4:11). As a Jew, Herod would have not eaten pork even if he would have killed his own family members.

211 Paul Maier, *Chronos, Kairos, Christos II* (Macon, GA: Mercer University Press, 1998), 178.

212 Suetonius, *The Twelve Caesars,* "Life of Claudius" 25, and Acts 18:2.

213 Philo, *Embassy to Gaius,* 38.

214 *Providentissimus Deus,* 20.

215 For good resources on this see K.A. Kitchen's *On the Reliability of the Old Testament* (2006), Craig Blomberg's *The Historical Reliability of the Gospels* (2007), and Craig Keener's four-volume commentary on the Acts of Apostles (2012–14).

Chapter 8: Over-the-Top Miracles?

216 Christians who identify as Young Earth Creationists and believe the earth was created 6,000–10,000 years ago in six literal days also tend to believe that there was a global flood that covered the surface of the entire earth about 4,000 years ago. However, the overwhelming consensus among geologists and other scientists who study the history of the earth is that no such flood ever took place. For an in-depth treatment of the issue, see David R. Montgomery, *The Rocks Don't Lie: A Geologist Investigates Noah's Flood* (New York: W.W. Norton, 2012).

217 Montgomery writes, "I now believe that there is no way to tell whether Noah's flood was the Black Sea flood or a major Mesopotamian flood. No matter how intriguing either idea may sound, both offer seemingly reasonable explanations" (ibid., *The Rocks Don't Lie*, 223). For a defense of Noah's flood being a local Black Sea flood, see William Ryan and Walter Pitman, *Noah's Flood: The New Scientific Discoveries about the Event that Changed History* (New York: Simon & Schuster, 2000).

218 "Even the gods were terrified at the flood, they fled to the highest heaven, the firmament of Ann; they crouched against the walls, cowering like curs." N.K. Sandars, trans., *The Epic of Gilgamesh* (London: Penguin Books, 1972), 110.

219 In fact, Isaac M. Kikawada and Arthur Quinn show in their book *Before Abraham Was: The Unity of Genesis 1–11* that this theme permeates the entire Genesis story and demonstrates a unity within the Pentateuch that counts against the so-called JEDP hypothesis, or the claim that parts of the first five books of the Old Testament were a very late compilation of four different ancient sources.

220 *Humani Generis*, 38.

221 For example, the Sumerian legend *Enmerkar and the Lord of Aratta* contains language confusion/multiplication themes that are similar to the ones found in Genesis 11. Modern readers who lack knowledge of the ANE may be tempted to misinterpret the Babel story as a myth about humans trying to reach God rather than as a polemic against Mesopotamian urbanism. See John H. Walton, *Ancient Near Eastern Thought and the Old Testament* (Grand Rapids, MI: Baker Academic, 2006), 119–23.

222 Julius Africanus noted this impossibility in A.D. 220. Martin Wallraff, trans., *Iulius Africanus: Chronographiae: The Extant Fragments [Die*

Griechischen Christlichen Schriftsteller Der Ersten Jahr] (Berlin: Walter de Gruyter, 2007), 277.

223 See St. Thomas Aquinas, *Summa Theologica* 3.44.2. Thomas seems to endorse the view that a supernatural eclipse occurred (possibly only affecting the immediate area) because he knew that the Jewish lunar calendar prohibited a natural eclipse from occurring.

224 Richard D. Nelson, *Joshua: A Commentary* (Louisville, KY: Westminster John Knox Press, 1997), 144.

225 K. Lawson Younger Jr., *Ancient Conquest Accounts: A Study in Ancient Near Eastern and Biblical History Writing* (Sheffield: Sheffield Academic Press, 1990), 219.

226 John H. Walton, "Joshua 10:12–15 and Mesopotamian Celestial Omen Texts," in *Faith, Tradition, and History: Old Testament Historiography in its Near Eastern Context,* eds. A.R. Millard, J.K. Hoffmeier, and D.W. Baker (Winona Lake, IN: Eisenbrauns, 1994), 188.

227 "The Book of Jashar was apparently a collection of archaic poetry that, though well known in ancient Israel, has not survived." D. L. Christensen, "Jashar, Book of" in *The HarperCollins Bible Dictionary,* ed. M. A. Powell (New York: HarperCollins. 2011), 430.

228 An alternative explanation comes from St. John Chrysostom in his seventh homily on Matthew's Gospel. Chrysostom said the star led the Magi to the general vicinity of the child and then God allowed for the absence of direction in order to fulfill Herod's role in the search. The star then returned to guide the Magi to Jesus.

229 The most in-depth treatment of the star from a skeptical perspective is probably Aaron Adair's *The Star of Bethlehem: A Skeptical View* (np: Onus Books, 2013). For a response to Adair, see Jimmy Akin, "Responding to the 'Go To' Skeptic on the Star of Bethlehem," *National Catholic Register,* February 26, 2014, www.ncregister.com/blog/jimmy-akin/responding-to-the-go-to-skeptic-on-the-star-of-bethlehem.

230 Brian Baker, *Nonsense from the Bible* (np: FastPencil, 2012), Kindle edition.

231 Pontifical Biblical Commission, *The Inspiration and Truth of Sacred Scripture,* 140. For an evangelical perspective, see Michael Licona's paper, "When the Saints Go Marching In," which was presented to the Evangelical Philosophical Society in San Francisco on No-

vember 18, 2011. Available online at http://www.risenjesus.com/
wp-content/uploads/2011-eps-saints-paper.pdf.

232 N.T. Wright, *The Resurrection of the Son of God* (Minneapolis: Fortress
     Press, 2003), 636.

233 Fr. William G. Most, *The Consciousness of Christ* (Front Royal, VA:
     Christendom College Press, 1980), 60.

234 Joseph Ratzinger, *Jesus of Nazareth: From the Baptism in the Jordan to the
     Transfiguration* (San Francisco: Ignatius Press, 2008), 317.

Chapter 9: "1001 Bible Contradictions"?

235 See the Web site at www.1001biblecontradictions.com/.

236 D.A. Carson, *Exegetical Fallacies* (Grand Rapids, MI: Baker Academ-
     ic, 1996), 115.

237 Steve Wells, *The Skeptic's Annotated Bible* (SAB Books, 2012), 1602.

238 In response to this argument, some people claim the wine Jesus cre-
     ated was not alcoholic. It's true that wine in the ancient world was
     often mixed with water in order to make it weaker, but the resulting
     wine was still alcoholic. For example, the Roman author Pliny the
     Elder described how you could set Falernian wine on fire, which
     means it contained at least 30 percent alcohol (*Natural History* 14.8).
     Even if you diluted such a drink with three parts water it would still
     be more alcoholic than most beer. Moreover, the steward at the wed-
     ding said the wine Jesus made was "good wine," which should have
     been served first (John 2:10). That's because the guests were now too
     inebriated from the inferior wine to notice the superior quality of
     Jesus' wine—a quality that would have been greatly diminished if it
     were not alcoholic.

239 Steve Wells, *The Skeptic's Annotated Bible* (SAB Books, 2012), 1619.

240 Dan Barker, *Godless: How an Evangelical Preacher Became One of Amer-
     ica's Leading Atheists* (Berkeley, CA: Ulysses Press, 2008), 230–31.

241 Martin Luther King Jr., *Stride Toward Freedom: The Montgomery Story*
     (New York: Harper and Brothers, 1958), 217.

242 These include: the damage inflicted by the aggressor on the nation or
     community of nations must be lasting, grave, and certain; all other
     means of putting an end to it must have been shown to be impractical
     or ineffective; there must be serious prospects of success; and the use

of arms must not produce evils and disorders graver than the evil to
be eliminated.

243 Jim Meritt, "A List of Biblical Contradictions" (1992), infidels.org/
library/modern/jim_meritt/bible-contradictions.html#fool.

244 Jason Long, *Biblical Nonsense: A Review of the Bible for Doubting Christians*
(np: iUniverse, 2005), 152. Long also says there are two other accounts
of Saul's death that seem to contradict these verses: "death by a Philistine (2 Sam. 21:12), and struck down by God (1 Chron. 10:13–14)."
However, the former verse merely associates Saul's death with the Philistines, which is correct because if the Philistines had not been fighting
Saul, then Saul would have lived. This is similar to describing a soldier
who commits suicide in order to avoid being captured as having been
"killed by the enemy." The latter verse simply tells the same story as
1 Samuel, but attributes Saul's demise to God. Since he has ultimate
providence over Creation, God orchestrated the events that led to Saul's
death because Saul had been unfaithful to the Lord.

245 Deuteronomy 25:17–19 reminds the Israelites, "Remember what
Amalek did to you on the way as you came out of Egypt, how he
attacked you on the way, when you were faint and weary, and cut
off at your rear all who lagged behind you; and he did not fear God.
Therefore when the Lord your God has given you rest from all your
enemies round about, in the land which the Lord your God gives you
for an inheritance to possess, you shall blot out the remembrance of
Amalek from under heaven; you shall not forget."

246 "The messenger is offering him a self-serving fiction, or at best an
embroidered version of the truth." Graeme Auld, "1 and 2 Samuel" in
Eerdmans Commentary on the Bible, ed. James Dunn (Grand Rapids, MI:
Wm. B. Eerdmans, 2003), 230. "Standing before David, the Amalekite offers what we know to be a fabrication." Paul Borgman, *David,
Saul and God: Rediscovering an Ancient Story* (New York: Oxford University Press, 2008), 154. "The Amalekites claim in 2 Samuel 1:6 that
he just happened to be on the battlefield when Saul was killed does not
make much sense; and the reader is probably expected to understand
that he is lying." Steven L. McKenzie, "Saul in the Deuteronomistic
History," in *Saul in Story and Tradition,* eds. Carl S. Ehrlich and Marsha
C. White (Tubingen: Mohr Siebeck, 2006), 67.

247 Or, at the least, David suspected him of lying and concluded that his testimony was enough to convict him. This conclusion is reached in Yong Ho Jeon, *Impeccable Solomon? A Study of Solomon's Faults in Chronicles* (Eugene, OR: Wipf and Stock, 2013), 52. Borgman says, "The audaciousness of such a claim proves sufficient grounds for death" (*David, Saul and God*, 154).

248 "The events described in 1 Samuel 31 and 2 Samuel 1 are historically consistent if it is assumed that the Amalekite messenger was attempting to deceive David. This conviction is supported by the nature of the Amalekite's report, David's assumption that he was an opportunist (2 Sam. 4:10), and the lack of references to the royal insignia in 1 Samuel 31. Finally, we have suggested that deception was an important motif in the Samuel materials and that the author's presentation of the deceptive Amalekite is consistent with the book as a whole." Bill T. Arnold, "The Amalekite's Report of Saul's Death: Political Intrigue or Incompatible Sources?," *Journal of the Evangelical Theological Society* 32, no. 3 (September 1989), 298.

249 As of this publishing, the New Testament *Ignatius Catholic Study Bible* is complete and several books of the Old Testament *Ignatius Catholic Study Bible* have also been released. The latter series may be compiled into one or two volumes in the future.

250 It's true that some German Christians invoked Romans 13 in order to justify their lack of opposition to Hitler, but Bonhoeffer, the Lutheran pastor who lost his life for opposing the Nazis, exposed their erroneous view of Scripture. According to Eric Metaxas in his popular biography of Bonhoeffer, "As far as he was concerned, to dare to sing to God when his chosen people were being beaten and murdered meant that one must also speak out against their suffering. If one was unwilling to do this, God was not interested in one's worship. The willingness of Lutherans to keep the church out of the world reflected an unbiblical overemphasis on Romans 13:1–5, which they had inherited from Luther. They had never been forced to deal with the boundary of this scriptural idea of obedience to worldly authorities. The early Christians stood up against Caesar and the Romans. Surely the Nuremberg Laws would force the Confessing Church to take a stand against the Nazis." Eric Metaxas, *Bonheoffer: Pastor Mar-*

tyr, Prophet, Spy (Nashville, TN: Thomas Nelson, 2010), 281.

251 *Dei Verbum*, 12.

252 Dan Barker, *Godless: How an Evangelical Preacher Became One of America's Leading Atheists* (Berkeley, CA: Ulysses Press, 2008), 222.

253 "Instability, a state of disorder, disturbance, confusion." Joseph Henry Thayer, *A Greek English Lexicon of the New Testament* (Grand Rapids, MI: Baker Book House, 1977), 21.

254 St. Augustine, *Contra Faustum* 11.5.

Chapter 10: Gospels That Can't Agree?

255 Even Tatian the Syrian, who authored the earliest known attempt to harmonize the four Gospels in the *Diatessaron*, says that God only spoke once and said, "This is my beloved Son, in whom I am well pleased" (4.28).

256 H.W. Fowler and F.G. Fowler, trans., *The Works of Lucian of Samosata,* Vol. II (Oxford: Clarendon Press, 1905), 129–31.

257 "Inasmuch as many have undertaken to compile a narrative of the things which have been accomplished among us, just as they were delivered to us by those who from the beginning were eyewitnesses and ministers of the word, it seemed good to me also, having followed all things closely for some time past, to write an orderly account for you, most excellent Theophilus, that you may know the truth concerning the things of which you have been informed" (Luke 1:1–4).

258 H.W. Fowler and F.G. Fowler, trans., *The Works of Lucian of Samosata,* Vol. II (Oxford: Clarendon Press, 1905), 130.

259 Ibid., 134.

260 Thucydides, *History of the Peloponnesian War* 1.22.1. Cited in Brant Pitre, *The Case for Jesus: The Biblical and Historical Evidence for Christ* (New York: Doubleday, 2016), 79–81.

261 Jonas Grethlein, *Experience and Teleology in Ancient Historiography: "Futures Past" from Herodotus to Augustine* (Cambridge: Cambridge University Press, 2014), 64.

262 Craig Keener, *The Historical Jesus of the Gospels* (Grand Rapids, MI: Wm. B. Eerdmans, 2009), 110.

263 Craig Blomberg, *The Historical Reliability of the Gospels,* second edition (Downer's Grove, IL: IVP Academic, 2007), 176.

264 Here's another example: "Who asked Jesus to sit beside him in his kingdom? Was it James and John as Mark 10:35–37 describes, or was it their mother as Matthew 20:20–21 describes?" The answer is: "It could be both." Their mother could have approached Jesus at one time and her sons approached him with the same question at another. Or James and John may have approached Jesus and made the request through their mother, a detail Matthew included but Mark did not.

265 Bart Ehrman, *Jesus, Interrupted: Revealing the Hidden Contradictions in the Bible (and Why We Don't Know About Them)*, (New York: Harper-One, 2009), 48.

266 Pontifical Biblical Commission, *The Inspiration and Truth of Sacred Scripture*, 141.

267 Barker complains of responses like this to Mark 2:26: "[I]f this defense is allowed, then there could be no possible contradiction anywhere, inside or outside of the bible. We can simply claim metaphor where we don't like what the actual text says." Dan Barker, *Godless: How an Evangelical Preacher Became One of America's Leading Atheists* (Berkeley, CA: Ulysses Press, 2008), 231. But sound reasons to justify this translation can be gleaned from the text, which shows that it is not an ad hoc explanation. For example, Lane notes that in Mark 12:26 Jesus uses *epi* to mean "in the part" of the book of Moses that refers to Exodus 3:14. Mark 2:26's use of *epi* could, therefore, be a similar reference by Jesus or Mark to the scroll that contained the story of David taking the bread. See William L. Lane, *The Gospel of Mark* (Grand Rapids, MI: Eerdmans, 1974), 115–16. This is all the more pertinent when we realize that the majority of the times when Mark uses the Greek preposition *epi* he means "where," opposed to "when." A similar construction is found in Luke 3:2, *epi archiereos Hanna kai Kaiapha*, which could be taken to mean "in the days or general time period when Annas and Caiaphas each served as high priest." Edwards agrees with this construction and says it "seems to better capture Mark's intention, for the event under consideration appears to have been associated in popular memory with the high priesthood of Abiathar." James Edwards, *The Gospel According to Mark* (Grand Rapids, MI: Wm. B. Eerdmans, 2002), 95.

268 It's also possible that the name Abiathar is a copyist error based on an

original Aramaic source that read *abba Abiathar,* or "father of Abia-thar." The copyist simply combined the two words that both began with "ab." See James A. Brooks, *Mark: An Exegetical and Theological Exposition of Holy Scripture* (Nashville, TN: B&H Publishing Group, 1991), 65. Another explanation comes from Aramaic scholar Maurice Casey, who says the Aramaic phrase "in the day of Abiathar the high priest" may have been mistranslated into the Greek text. Maurice Casey, *Aramaic Sources of Mark's Gospel* (Cambridge: Cambridge University Press, 1998), 151–52.

269 Scott Hahn and Curtis Mitch, *The Ignatius Catholic Study Bible: Daniel,* second edition (San Francisco: Ignatius Press, 2013), 70. Gundry makes a similar argument from the flexibility inherent in rabbinic speech. He writes, "Jesus not only adds a number of features [to the account in 1 Samuel]. He also replaces Ahimelech with Abiathar the son of Ahimelech for a link with the added house of God, which for Jesus and his audience stands in Jerusalem." Robert Gundry, *Mark: A Commentary on His Apology for the Cross* (Grand Rapids, MI: Wm. B. Eerdmans, 1993), 141.

270 Suetonius, *Life of Augustus* 9.

271 Quoted in Eusebius, *Ecclesiastical History* 3.39.15.

272 Origen, *Commentary on John*, 10. 4.

273 St. Augustine, *Harmony of the Gospels,* 2.21.51.

274 I owe this observation to Jimmy Akin, from his unpublished commentary on Mark's Gospel.

275 Bart Ehrman, *Jesus, Interrupted: Revealing the Hidden Contradictions in the Bible (and Why We Don't Know About Them),* (New York: HarperOne, 2009), 40.

276 One commentary says of this usage, "This characteristic of Mark's rapid and popular style frequently has a temporal function, often serves to focus the reader's attention, and may require different translations according to the context." Daniel J. Harrington, *The Gospel of Mark* (Collegeville, MN: The Liturgical Press, 2002), 65.

277 Fr. William G. Most, *Free from All Error: Authorship Inerrancy Historicity of Scripture, Church Teaching, and Modern Scripture Scholars* (Libertyville, IL: Franciscan Marytown Press, 1985), 54.

278 A similar explanation can be found in the differing accounts of Jesus

healing the blind men in Jericho. According to Karl Keating, "Bartimaeus called out to Jesus as he and the crowd entered Jericho, but in the commotion Bartimaeus was not heard. By the time Jesus left the city, Bartimaeus had been joined by another blind man. Only Bartimaeus's name is recorded, perhaps because of his persistence, perhaps because he later became well-known in the Christian community. Bartimaeus calls out again and this time is heard because the crowd is now subdued. Jesus cures him and the other man." Karl Keating, *What Catholics Really Believe: Answers to Common Misconceptions About the Faith* (San Francisco: Ignatius Press, 1992), 35.

279 The penitent criminal or as he is sometimes referred to, "the good thief," is known through an ancient tradition as Dismas. The impenitent criminal, or "the bad thief," is traditionally known as Gestas.

280 See, for example, E. Mary Smallwood, *The Jews under Roman Rule: From Pompey to Diocletian: A Study in Political Relations* (Leiden: Brill Academic, 1997).

281 Bart Ehrman, *Jesus, Interrupted: Revealing the Hidden Contradictions in the Bible (and Why We Don't Know About Them)*, (New York: HarperOne, 2009), 45–47. See also Kenton L. Sparks, *Sacred Word, Broken Word: Biblical Authority and the Dark Side of Scripture* (Grand Rapids, MI: Wm. B. Eerdmans, 2012), 33.

282 Ehrman says, "Ingenious interpreters, wanting to splice the two accounts together into one true account, have a field day here" (ibid., *Jesus, Interrupted*, 47). But this is not a bad explanation if it has more explanatory power than either account alone and does not resort to ad hoc elements. The fact that it can better explain why Judas burst open and does not rely on the Jewish authorities or anyone else acting in an unusual way makes this a plausible account.

283 Paul Rhodes Eddy and Gregory A. Boyd, *The Jesus Legend: A Case for the Historical Reliability of the Synoptic Jesus Tradition* (Grand Rapids, MI: Baker Academic, 2007), 424.

284 "It has become much clearer that the Gospels are in fact very similar in type to ancient biographies (Greek, *bioi*; Latin, *vitae*)." James D.G. Dunn, *Jesus Remembered: Christianity in the Making,* Vol. 1 (Grand Rapids, MI: William B. Eerdmans, 2003), 185.

285 Richard Burridge, *What Are the Gospels?: A Comparison with Graeco-*

   Roman Biography, second edition (Grand Rapids, MI: William B. Eerdmans, 2004), 67.

286 Ibid., 249.

287 Our main sources for the fire are Tacitus, Suetonius, and Cassius Dio.
   All three of these ancient Roman historians agree there was a fire
   in Rome, but they disagree about the actions of the emperor, who
   many believed had started the fire in order to free up space for the
   construction of a future palace. Was Nero not responsible and away
   in the city of Antium during the fire as Tacitus says (*Annals* 15.44)?
   Did Nero send men to burn the city and watch from the tower of
   Maecenas as Suetonius says (*Life of Nero* 38)? Or did Nero start the
   fire himself and watch from the rooftop of the imperial palace as
   Dio Cassius says (*Roman History* 62.16–17)? See also Michael Licona,
   The Resurrection of Jesus: A New Historiographical Approach (Downer's
   Grove, IL: InterVarsity Press, 2010), 570.

Chapter 11: Contradictory Names and Numbers?

288 "Other details add to our doubt regarding the historicity of the story. We
   have at least three names for Moses' father-in-law." Paul Tobin, "The Bible and Modern Scholarship," in *The Christian Delusion: Why Faith Fails,*
   ed. John Loftus (Amherst, NY: Prometheus Books, 2010), 154.

289 Steve Wells, *The Skeptic's Annotated Bible* (SAB Books, 2012), 1620.

290 Other contradictions can be resolved when we remember that just because two people share the same name it doesn't follow that they are
   the same person. For example, Genesis 36 describes someone named
   Anah, who appears to be the daughter, brother, and son of Zibeon.
   The most likely explanation of these passages is that this chapter is describing three different individuals named Anah, one female and two
   male, from two entirely different families. The woman in Genesis 36:2
   is the wife of Esau and daughter of Zibeon, the Anah in Genesis 36:20
   is a brother of another Zibeon, and the Anah in Genesis 36:24–25 is
   the nephew of the previous Anah and a son of Zibeon.

291 "Jethro," *Jewish Encyclopedia* (1906), www.jewishencyclopedia.com/
   articles/8620-jethro.

292 Josephus endorsed the former view, saying, "Moses, when he had obtained the favor of Jethro, for that was one of the names of Raguel

[Reuel], staid there and fed his flock" (*Antiquities* II.12.1). The difficulty with this view is that it seems to contradict Judges 4:11, which refers to "the descendants of Hobab the father-in-law of Moses." It could be the case that in this passage "father-in-law" is an error that arose in a later manuscript or even a mistranslation. This is plausible because the Hebrew word for "father-in-law" (*hoten*) can also refer to a generic male in-law (though it is predominantly used for father-in-law). However, Judges 4:11 could also be correct, and Hobab was indeed Moses' father-in-law and Reuel was Moses' grandfather-in-law. This does not contradict Exodus 2's reference to Reuel being the father of Moses' wife, Zipporah, because the Hebrew word for father (*ab*) can refer to grandfathers (Gen. 28:13). As Zipporah's grandfather, Reuel would have contracted the marriage arrangement with Moses since he would have been a higher-ranking member within his clan.

293 Steve Wells, *The Skeptic's Annotated Bible* (SAB Books, 2012), 1602.
294 Ibid., 1605–6.
295 "The Biblical text, indeed, seems to indicate that this last was its proper name, while 'Sinai' was applied to the desert." "Sinai, Mount" *Jewish Encyclopedia* (1906), www.jewishencyclopedia.com/articles/13766-sinai-mount.
296 James K. Hoffmeier, *Ancient Israel in Sinai: The Evidence for the Authenticity of the Wilderness Tradition* (New York: Oxford University Press, 2005), 115. He also writes, "Only once is 'Mount Horeb' used, in Exodus 33:6. This lone reference might not actually name the mountain, but *har horeb* in this case might be a genitive of association, which could be translated 'mountain of Horeb,' that is, a mountain located in Horeb, rather than a mountain named Horeb," 114–15.
297 Steve Wells, *The Skeptic's Annotated Bible* (SAB Books, 2012), 1604.
298 Richard Dawkins, *The God Delusion* (New York: Houghton-Mifflin, 2008), 94–95.
299 The letters are d-w-d, or in Hebrew, daleth-vav-daleth. Daleth has the value of 4 and vav has the value of 6.
300 Some critics claim that the Bible contradicts itself when it lists genealogies, because Paul says to "avoid foolish controversies and genealogies" (1 Tim. 1:3–4, Titus 3:9). But Paul was admonishing Christians who retained the Jewish practice of using genealogies in order

to prove their Jewish identity or to claim certain birthrights based on their tribal affiliation. Paul did not condemn all genealogies and even traced Jesus' lineage back to David (Rom. 1:1–3).

301 "By Estha then (for this was the woman's name according to tradition) Matthan, a descendant of Solomon, first begot Jacob. And when Matthan was dead, Melchi, who traced his descent back to Nathan, being of the same tribe but of another family, married her as before said, and begot a son [Heli]. Thus we shall find the two, Jacob and [Heli], although belonging to different families, yet brethren by the same mother. Eusebius, *Ecclesiastical History*, I.7.8–9.

302 Steve Wells, *The Skeptic's Annotated Bible* (SAB Books, 2012), 51.

303 Ibid., 1621.

304 Ibid., 1625.

305 Ibid., 1626.

306 Raymond F. Collins, *These Things Have Been Written: Studies on the Fourth Gospel* (Louvain: Peeters, 1990), 91.

307 See Craig Blomberg, *The Historical Reliability of the Gospels,* second edition (Downer's Grove, IL: IVP Academic, 2007), 216–219, for arguments for and against both theories.

308 Taken from personal correspondence on February 1, 2015.

309 Michael Licona, *The Resurrection of Jesus: A New Historiographical Approach* (Downer's Grove, IL: InterVarsity Press, 2010), 596.

310 "Luke presupposes a familiarity with the saving story. Their familiarity allows Luke occasionally to telescope a given narrative . . ." James R. Edwards, *The Hebrew Gospel and the Development of the Synoptic Tradition* (Grand Rapids, MI: Wm. B. Eerdmans, 2009), 150. This is also true for events in the Old Testament, which are not always arranged in chronological order either.

311 "John was not speaking of the practice of Jesus and the apostles; he was speaking of the practice of the Sadducees, who had a large number of priests in their camp and great influence in the culture at the time. This fact explains why John calls Friday the "day of preparation" instead of Thursday. The Sadducees, who moved the Passover to Saturday, celebrated the day of preparation on Friday, rather than on Thursday as Jesus and the apostles did." Tim Staples, "How do we explain the Passover 'discrepancy'?," *Catholic Answers Magazine*

18, no. 5 (May 2007). For other proposals see Craig Blomberg, *The Historical Reliability of the Gospels,* second edition (Downer's Grove, IL: InterVarsity Academic, 2007), 221–29, and Craig Keener, *The Historical Jesus of the Gospels* (Grand Rapids, MI: Wm. B. Eerdmans, 2009), 372–374.

312 Craig L. Blomberg, *The Historical Reliability of John's Gospel* (Downer's Grove, IL: InterVarsity Press, 2001), 247.

313 *Providentissimus Deus,* 20.

314 Brant Pitre, "The Mystery of God's Word: Inspiration, Inerrancy, and the Inspiration of Scripture," in *Letter and Spirit, Vol. 6: For the Sake of Our Salvation,* eds. Scott Hahn and David Scott (Steubenville OH: Emmaus Road Publishing, 2010), Kindle edition.

315 J. Harold Greenlee, *The Text of the New Testament: From Manuscript to Modern Edition* (Peabody, MA: Hendrickson Publishers, 2008), 76.

316 C. Dennis McKinsey, *The Encyclopedia of Biblical Errancy* (Amherst, NY: Prometheus Books, 1995), 65, and Dan Barker, *Godless: How an Evangelical Preacher Became One of America's Leading Atheists* (Berkeley, CA: Ulysses Press, 2008), 238.

317 Stables located at Tell-Megiddo in Israel could house almost 500 horses. If Solomon had a series of these stables, then the amount of four thousand is plausible. See Graham Davies, "King Solomon's Stables," *Biblical Archaeology Review* 20.1 (1994), 44–49.

318 Steve McRoberts, *The Cure for Fundamentalism: Why the Bible Cannot Be the Word of God,* second edition (np: CreateSpace, 2014), 27.

319 Arthur W. Walker Jones, *Hebrew for Biblical Interpretation* (Atlanta: Society of Biblical Literature, 2003), 97.

320 Hector Avalos, *The End of Biblical Studies* (Amherst NY: Prometheus Books, 2007), Kindle edition.

321 Jason Long, *Biblical Nonsense: A Review of the Bible for Doubting Christians* (np: iUniverse, 2005), 152. McKinsey feels this alleged contradiction is so significant that it deserves the following anecdote: "I can remember debating this very issue with a Church of Christ minister on a Cincinnati radio station years ago. He thumbed through his book; we cut to a commercial; he still had no answer when we returned. The minister said he would have to look that one up and get back with me later. The host of the program said that was pretty

good and asked for another one. In effect, the minister conceded the point. There was no answer and that's why it should be used by all rational people." C. Dennis McKinsey, *The Encyclopedia of Biblical Errancy* (Amherst, NY: Prometheus Books, 1995), 63.

322 Jim Meritt, "A List of Biblical Contradictions" (1992), infidels.org/library/modern/jim_meritt/bible-contradictions.html#baasha.

323 "There remains therefore no alternative but to regard the text as erroneous,—the letters [*lamed*] (30) and [*yodh*] (10), which are somewhat similar in the ancient Hebrew characters, having been interchanged by a copyist; and hence the numbers 35 and 36 have arisen out of the original 15 and 16." C.F. Keil and F. Delitzsch, *Commentary on the Old Testament,* Vol. 3 (Peabody, MA: Hendrickson Publishers, 1989), 367.

324 "Elhanan got the shaft when it comes to fame and fortune as no one remembers him as the slayer of the giant." Mark Roncace, *Raw Revelation: The Bible They Never Tell You About* (np: CreateSpace, 2012), 35. See also Hector Avalos, *The End of Biblical Studies* (Amherst NY: Prometheus Books, 2007), Kindle edition.

325 Kaiser ably summarizes the issue: "The copyist of 2 Samuel 21:19 made three mistakes: (1) he read the direct object sign (*'et*) that came just in front of the name of the giant Elhanan killed, named Lahmi, as if it were the word 'beth,' thereby getting 'the Bethlehemite,' when the 'Beth' was put with 'Lahmi.' (2) The copyist also misread the word for 'brother' (Hebrew *'ah*) as the direct object sign before Goliath, thus making Goliath the one that was killed, instead of what it should have been— 'the brother of Goliath.' (3) The copyist misplaced the word *Oregim* meaning 'weavers,' so that it yielded 'Elhnan son of Jaare-Oregim,' a most improbable reading for anyone: Elhanan the son of the forest of weavers! Instead, the word for 'weavers' should have come as it does in 1 Chronicles 20:5 as the spear being a 'beam/shaft like a weaver's rod.'" Walter C. Kaiser, *A History of Israel: From the Bronze Age Through the Jewish Wars* (Nashville, TN: Broadman and Holman, 1998), 234.

326 Steve Wells, *The Skeptic's Annotated Bible* (SAB Books, 2012), 184.

327 Karl Keating, *What Catholics Really Believe: Answers to Common Misconceptions About the Faith* (San Francisco: Ignatius Press, 1992), 37.

328 Dan Barker, *Godless: How an Evangelical Preacher Became One of Amer-*

ica's Leading Atheists (Berkeley, CA: Ulysses Press, 2008), 235.

329 Hector Avalos, *The End of Biblical Studies* (Amherst NY: Prometheus Books, 2007), Kindle edition.

330 Magen Broshi, *Bread, Wine, Walls And Scrolls* (New York: Sheffield Academic Press, 2001), 72.

331 Cornelius Tacitus. *The Agricola and the Germania*, trans. Edward Brooks Jr. (Stilwell: Digireads Publishing, 2008), 43.

Chapter 12: Conflicting Advice?

332 www.yourpersonalizedbible.com/frequently-asked-questions/.

333 The different senses of Scripture (literal, spiritual, moral, and anagogical) are described in CCC 115–19.

334 Steve Wells, *The Skeptic's Annotated Bible* (SAB Books, 2012), 1617.

335 Ibid., 1616.

336 Ibid., 1617.

337 Peter Kreeft. *Socratic Logic: A Logic Text Using Socratic Method, Platonic Questions, and Aristotelian Principles* (South Bend, IN: St. Augustine's Press, 2004), 173.

338 Steve Wells, *The Skeptic's Annotated Bible* (SAB Books, 2012), 203.

339 Pliny the Elder, *The Natural History*, 10.33.

340 Another likely example of hyperbole is the description of Nineveh being a city that took three days to cross (Jon. 3:3), which would make it approximately sixty miles wide. This is about the size of modern-day Los Angeles.

341 Steve Wells, *The Skeptic's Annotated Bible* (SAB Books, 2012), 1599.

342 This includes Mary, who said she rejoiced in God her savior (Luke 1:47). Unlike other humans, however, Mary was preserved from original sin by having the saving effects of Christ's sacrifice applied retroactively to her, which is possible in light of God's omnipotence and timeless existence.

343 University of Navarre, *Saint Paul's Letters to the Romans & Galatians* (New York: Four Courts Press, 2005), 78.

344 Quoted in Fr. William G. Most, *Free from All Error: Authorship Inerrancy Historicity of Scripture, Church Teaching, and Modern Scripture Scholars* (Libertyville, IL: Franciscan Marytown Press, 1985), 39.

345 Ibid., 40.

346 Joseph Ratzinger, *Eschatology: Death and Eternal Life*, second edition (Washington, DC: Catholic University of America, 2007), 82–83.

347 For a good treatment of subjects related to the Protestant/Catholic debate over salvation, see Jimmy Akin, *The Drama of Salvation* (El Cajon, CA: Catholic Answers Press, 2014).

348 "What must you do to be saved?," available online at skepticsanno-tatedbible.com/contra/saved.html.

349 One example would be number 22, which Wells describes as "Get lost." The verses listed here (e.g., Matt. 18:11, Luke 19:10) just mean that God comes to save those who need to be saved from their sins (or everyone). It's not a reference to anything a person must do to be saved.

350 This is true in the Western or Latin rite of the Church. In Eastern rites a child may receive the Eucharist immediately after baptism, even if he is an infant.

351 The concept of merit in Catholic theology is basically one of un-earned reward. The *Catechism* says, "The merit of man before God in the Christian life arises from the fact that God has freely chosen to associate man with the work of his grace. The fatherly action of God is first on his own initiative, and then follows man's free acting through his collaboration, so that the merit of good works is to be attributed in the first place to the grace of God, then to the faithful. Man's merit, moreover, itself is due to God, for his good actions proceed in Christ, from the predispositions and assistance given by the Holy Spirit" (2008).

Chapter 13: An All-Too Human God?

352 See Arthur Fairbanks, *The First Philosophers of Greece* (London: Paternoster House, 1898), 78, and James Lesher, "Xenophanes," *The Stanford Encyclopedia of Philosophy* (Fall 2011 edition), ed. Edward N. Zalta, plato.stanford.edu/archives/fall2011/entries/xenophanes/. Quoted in Trent Horn, *Answering Atheism: Making the Case for God with Logic and Charity* (El Cajon, CA: Catholic Answers Press, 2013), 53.

353 Ludwig Feuerbach, *Lectures on the Essence of Religion* (New York: Harper and Row, 1967), 187.

354 First Vatican Council, Session III, Chapter 2.

355 St. Thomas Aquinas, *Summa Contra Gentiles*, 1.22.

356 St. Thomas Aquinas, *Summa Theologica*, 1.2.3.

357 This is also called divine simplicity. For a modern treatment, see James Dolezal's *God Without Parts: Divine Simplicity and the Metaphysics of God's Absoluteness* (Eugene, OR: Pickwick, 2011).

358 Tim Gray, "Apparent Bible Contradictions," *Catholic Answers Live*, March 18, 2013. Available online at www.catholic.com/radio/shows/apparent-contradictions-in-the-bible-8124.

359 St. Thomas Aquinas, *Summa Theologica,* 2.2.2.3.

360 *Verbum Domini*, 42.

361 Perfect being theology has its roots in the eleventh-century writings of St. Anselm of Canterbury. According to Morris, "Most contemporary philosophers have taken Anselm's basic idea here to be best interpreted to mean that God is to be thought of as the greatest possible being, an individual exhibiting maximal perfection." Thomas V. Morris, *Our Idea of God* (Downer's Grove, IL: InterVarsity Press, 1991), 35–40. For another perspective see Brian Davies, *An Introduction to the Philosophy of Religion,* third edition (Oxford: Oxford University Press, 2004), 1–47.

362 Mark Roncace, *Raw Revelation: The Bible They Never Tell You About* (np: CreateSpace, 2012), 43–44.

363 St. John Chrysostom, *On the Incomprehensibility of God*, 3.3. Cited in Stephen D. Benin, *The Footprints of God: Divine Accommodation in Jewish and Christian Thought* (Albany, NY: SUNY Press, 1993), 68.

364 Valerie Tarico, "God's Emotions?," in *The End of Christianity,* ed. John Loftus (Amherst, NY: Prometheus Books, 2011), 176–77.

365 This stands in contrast to the so-called "process theology" of Alfred North Whitehead, which says that God changes along with Creation and is not perfect or all-powerful. For a rebuttal of this view, see Winifred Corduan, *Handmaid to Theology: An Essay in Philosophical Prolegomena* (Eugene, OR: Wipf and Stock, 2009), 129–47.

366 See *Summa Theologica* 1.29.3. Thomas said the word *person* "is fittingly applied to God; not, however, as it is applied to creatures, but in a more excellent way."

367 "They are called three persons, or three substances, not in order that any difference of essence may be understood, but that we may be able to answer by some one word, should any one ask what three, or what

three things?" St. Augustine, *On the Trinity* 8.1.

368 According to Catholic philosopher Patrick Lee, "[C]an one truly and literally, not just in an improper or metaphorical sense, say that God is pleased with us or is angry with us? The answer is, yes, in the relational sense . . . That is, it is true to say that we are related to God as one who pleases is related to the one who is pleased, and that God has what is necessary to be related to in this way. We are related to God as one who elicits anger is related to the one who is angry, and God is in his own being what is necessary to be the term of this relation. Each of these predications indirectly tells us something about God." Patrick Lee, "Does God Have Emotions?," in *God Under Fire,* eds. Douglas S. Huffman and Eric L. Johnson (Grand Rapids, MI: Zondervan, 2002), 229–30.

369 Joseph Cardinal Ratzinger and Peter Seewald, *God and the World: Believing and Living in Our Time* (San Francisco: Ignatius, 2000), 104.

370 Or they outright reject it. Gerike says, "None of these divine psychological characteristics were in their biblical contexts understood as being mere metaphorical descriptions or the result of any supposed divine accommodation." Jaco Gerike, "Can God Exist if Yahweh Doesn't?," in *The End of Christianity,* ed. John Loftus (Amherst, NY: Prometheus Books, 2011), 121. But the whole point of divine accommodation is that God lowered himself to a level for the biblical authors to understand him. Just as these authors would not have considered their descriptions of the physical world to be "popular descriptions accommodated to ancient sensibilities," but rather "how the world appeared," they would have thought the same of the descriptions of God they penned in the Bible. Those descriptions are true, but not if we read them as modern, theological treatises.

371 Gerike, ibid., 142.

372 Gerike takes aim in particular at the elaborate instructions for constructing the Ark of the Covenant in Exodus 25–40, but fails to see that these instructions were for the Israelite's benefit, not God's (ibid., 133). Human beings require custom and ritual in order to form their identities, and these rituals foster proper reverence for God. Just because they were tailored for what a resident of the ancient Near East would expect for pious worship does not make them evidence

of God's "narcissism."

373 St. Athanasius makes the same point in his work *On the Incarnation*, writing, "If he is not himself the cause of the material, but makes things only of previously existing material, he proves to be weak, because unable to produce anything he makes without the material; just as it is without doubt a weakness of the carpenter not to be able to make anything required without his timbe" (2).

374 St. Irenaeus, *Against Heresies* 2:13:3.

375 Joseph Smith, the founder of Mormonism, said, "The Father has a body of flesh and bones as tangible as man's." *Doctrines and Covenants*, 130:22.

376 Jaco Gerike, "Can God Exist if Yahweh Doesn't?," 137.

377 Scott Hahn and Curtis Mitch, *The Ignatius Catholic Study Bible: Genesis*, second edition (San Francisco: Ignatius Press, 2010), 19.

378 Stephen Bertman, *Handbook to Life in Ancient Mesopotamia* (New York: Oxford University Press, 2003), 66.

379 This is not to say that the ancient Jews thought of God as being immaterial in the same way as later Jews and Christians. Benjamin Sommer has made the case that the ancient Israelites thought of God as having "more than one body," by way of a concept Sommer calls "divine fluidity." If this were the case, then it would simply represent one progressive step in the Israelite's understanding that God is a transcendent being. See Benjamin D. Sommer, *The Bodies of God and the World of Ancient Israel* (Cambridge: Cambridge University Press, 2009).

380 Cardinal Ratzinger also said, "Christianity is not 'our' work; it is a Revelation; it is a message that has been consigned to us, and we have no right to reconstruct it as we like or choose. Consequently, we are not authorized to change the Our Father into an Our Mother: the symbolism employed by Jesus is irreversible; it is based on the same Man-God relationship he came to reveal to us." Joseph Cardinal Ratzinger and Vittorio Messori, *The Ratzinger Report: An Exclusive Interview on the State of the Church* (San Francisco: Ignatius Press, 1985), 97.

381 Peter J. Kreeft and Ronald K. Tacelli, *Handbook of Catholic Apologetics: Reasoned Answers to Questions of Faith* (San Francisco: Ignatius Press, 2009), 104.

382 Dan Barker, *Godless: How an Evangelical Preacher Became One of Amer-*

ica's Leading Atheists (Berkeley, CA: Ulysses Press, 2008), 233.

383 St. Irenaeus, *Against Heresies* 3.4.2.

Chapter 14: An Imperfect God?

384 There is a debate among theologians and philosophers over whether God knows all that *could be*, or counterfactuals. I am inclined to say he does, but such a discussion is beyond the scope of this present volume.

385 Steve Wells, *The Skeptic's Annotated Bible* (SAB Books, 2012), 1138.

386 Ibid., 1597.

387 C. Dennis McKinsey, *The Encyclopedia of Biblical Errancy* (Amherst, NY: Prometheus Books, 1995), 176.

388 St. Thomas Aquinas, *Summa Theologica* 1.19.7.

389 Gunkel and Biddle makes this point in their commentary on Genesis 6:6: "How should we evaluate such anthropomorphisms? One need not be ashamed of them nor should one chide them or scoff at them. They demonstrate not only that religion of the time was in its childhood, but also that is was vital and powerful . . . Even the most extreme anthropomorphisms in the OT are by far more gentle than say, the manner in which the Babylonian speaks of his gods. Our religion, too—although we realize quite clearly the insufficiency of such modes of expression—will never transcend anthropomorphisms." Hermann Gunkel and Mark E. Biddle, *Genesis* (Macon, GA: Mercer University Press, 1997), 61.

390 *Reformation Commentary on Scripture: Genesis 1–11*, ed. John L. Thompson (Downer's Grove, IL, InterVarsity Press, 2012), 239.

391 The Greek word for almighty, *pantokrator*, means "one who prevails over all." The Hebrew word *shaddai* is less clear and could refer to *shadad* ("power, destroy") or *shadaim* ("breasts"), the latter term referring to God's ability to completely nourish his people.

392 See Thomas Flint and Alfred Freddoso's essay "Maximal Power," in *Philosophy of Religion: A Reader and Guide,* ed. William Lane Craig (New Brunswick, NJ: Rutgers University Press, 2002).

393 St. Augustine, *City of God* 5.10.

394 The Web site this verse inspired is wiki.ironchariots.org. See also Jason Long, *Biblical Nonsense: A Review of the Bible for Doubting Christians* (np: iUniverse, 2005), 166.

395 James B. Jordan, *Judges: A Practical and Theological Commentary* (Eugene, OR: Wipf and Stock, 1999), 13. Other commentaries reach a similar conclusion: "So why was Judah unable to drive the people from the plains? Not because the Philistines had iron chariots, but because of spiritual factors that will be explained later (Judg. 2:1–3, 10–15). J. Gordon Harris, Cheryl A. Brown, and Michael S. Moore, *Joshua, Judges, Ruth* (Peabody, MA: Hendrickson Publishers, 2000), 144–45. "The Judahites failed to take an area that was far beyond their own borders, hardly a damning indictment." Victor P. Hamilton, *Handbook on the Historical Books: Joshua, Judges, Ruth, Samuel, Kings, Chronicles* (Grand Rapids, MI: Baker Academic, 2001), 102.

396 St. Thomas Aquinas, *Summa Theologica* 1.49.1.

397 Ibid.

398 "[W]ith infinite wisdom and goodness God freely willed to create a world 'in a state of journeying' towards its ultimate perfection. In God's plan this process of becoming involves the appearance of certain beings and the disappearance of others, the existence of the more perfect alongside the less perfect, both constructive and destructive forces of nature. With physical good there exists also *physical evil* as long as Creation has not reached perfection" (CCC 310).

399 C.S. Lewis, *The Problem of Pain* (New York: HarperOne, 2001), 93.

400 Dan Barker, *Godless: How an Evangelical Preacher Became One of America's Leading Atheists* (Berkeley, CA: Ulysses Press, 2008), 230.

401 K. Smyth, "3 and 4 Kings," in *A Catholic Commentary on Holy Scripture,* eds. B. Orchard and E. F. Sutcliffe (New York: Thomas Nelson, 1953), 338.

402 John H. Walton, *The Lost World of Genesis One: Ancient Cosmology and the Origins Debate* (Downer's Grove, IL: InterVarsity Press, 2009), 20.

403 See also St. Thomas Aquinas, *Summa Theologica* 1.11.3.

404 Thom Stark, *The Human Faces of God: What Scripture Reveals When It Gets God Wrong (and Why Inerrancy Tries to Hide It)* (Eugene, OR: Wipf and Stock, 2011).

405 Joseph Ratzinger, *Eschatology: Death and Eternal Life,* second edition (Washington, DC: Catholic University of America, 2007), 83.

406 For an extended treatment see James K. Hoffmeier, *Akhenaten and the Origins of Monotheism* (New York: Oxford University Press, 2015).

Hoffmeier claims, "this Egyptian evidence seems to support the view that this is the very region [i.e., northeastern Sinai] where the Bible suggests Moses encountered Yahweh and where the Israelites encamped in the wilderness during the period 1350–1250 B.C." (263).

407 See Benjamin D. Sommer, *The Bodies of God and the World of Ancient Israel* (Cambridge: Cambridge University Press, 2009), 172.

408 Mark S. Smith, *The Early History of God: Yahweh and the Other Deities in Ancient Israel* (Grand Rapids, MI: Wm. B. Eerdmans, 2002), 33. See also Matthew Ramage, *Dark Passages of the Bible: Engaging Scripture with Benedict XVI and Thomas Aquinas* (Washington, DC: Catholic University of America Press, 2013), 165–67 and John Day, *Yahweh and the Gods and Goddesses of Canaan* (New York: Sheffield Academic Press, 2002), 14–17. In his monograph on the divine council, Mullen Jr. says, "It is clear, however, that within biblical tradition 'Elyon was regarded as a suitable appellative for Yahweh . . . If our interpretation that 'Elyon = Yahweh is correct, then Deuteronomy 32 becomes a conceptual unity." E. Theodore Mullen Jr., *The Assembly of the Gods: The Divine Council in Canaanite and Early Hebrew Literature* (Chico, CA: Scholar's Press, 1986), 204.

409 John Day, *Yahweh and the Gods and Goddesses of Canaan* (New York: Sheffield Academic Press, 2002),16.

410 Mark S. Smith, *The Early History of God: Yahweh and the Other Deities in Ancient Israel* (Grand Rapids, MI: Wm. B. Eerdmans, 2002), 49.

411 Matthew Ramage, *Dark Passages of the Bible: Engaging Scripture with Benedict XVI and Thomas Aquinas* (Washington, DC: Catholic University of America Press, 2013), 166.

412 Joseph Ratzinger, *Eschatology: Death and Eternal Life*, second edition (Washington, DC: Catholic University of America, 2007), 80.

413 St. Clement of Alexandria quotes Xenophanes in *Miscellanies* 5.14.

414 *Metaphysics* Book XII.

Chapter 15: A Dysfunctional God?

415 Mark Roncace, *Raw Revelation: The Bible They Never Tell You About* (np: CreateSpace, 2012), 52.

416 Christopher J.H. Wright, *Knowing God the Father Through the Old Testament* (Downer's Grove: InterVarsity Press, 2007), 71.

417 St. Augustine, *On Grace and Free Will* 45.

418 "To say God hardened Pharaoh's heart means that God's sovereignty permeates the whole of life." Arnold Rhodes and W. Eugene March, *The Mighty Acts of God* (Louisville, KY: Geneva Press, 2000), 65.

419 "North Korean Prisoner Escaped After Twenty-Three Brutal Years," *CBS News,* May 19, 2013, www.cbsnews.com/news/north-korean-prisoner-escaped-after-23-brutal-years-19-05-2013.

420 A difficult case to understand in light of this passage is the punishment of Achan, who retained war booty in violation of the command given in Joshua 6:18–19. According to Joshua 7:24–25, "Joshua and all Israel with him took Achan the son of Zerah, and the silver and the mantle and the bar of gold, and his sons and daughters, and his oxen and asses and sheep, and his tent, and all that he had; and they brought them up to the Valley of Achor. And Joshua said, 'Why did you bring trouble on us? The Lord brings trouble on you today.' And all Israel stoned him with stones; they burned them with fire, and stoned them with stones." It may be the case that Achan's children were older and complicit in his crime, thus warranting their punishment. Or this may be an example of Israel failing to live up to the Deuteronomic law as they sought to preserve tribal unity. Finally, the whole story may be an example of didactic fiction whose purpose was to warn later generations about the hazards of breaking God's covenants. Regardless, it was certainly not the norm for Israel to execute entire families, as can be seen in Numbers 26:11, which says that even though God caused the earth to swallow up and kill the rebellious Korah, "the sons of Korah did not die."

421 St. Augustine, *Enchiridion* VIII.

422 David Lamb, *God Behaving Badly: Is the God of the Old Testament Angry, Sexist, and Racist?* (Downer's Grove, IL: InterVarsity Press, 2011), 9.

423 Tertullian refers to Marcion as a shipmaster from Pontus (a narrow strip of land on the southern coast of the Black Sea) and says he went "with the two hundred sesterces which he had brought into the church, and, when banished at last to a permanent excommunication, they scattered abroad the poisons of their doctrines." *Prescription Against Heresies* 30.

424 This idea is rooted in the early heresy of Gnosticism. For a survey of

this belief system see John Arendzen, "Gnosticism," in *The Catholic Encyclopedia*, Vol. 6. (New York: Robert Appleton Company, 1909), 20, www.newadvent.org/cathen/06592a.htm.

425 Pope John Paul II, "Old Testament Essential to Know Jesus," Address to the Pontifical Biblical Commission, *L'Osservatore Romano*, April 23, 1997, 2.

426 Karl Keating, *What Catholics Really Believe: Answers to Common Misconceptions About the Faith* (San Francisco: Ignatius Press, 1992), 37–38. Cardinal Ratzinger also said, "It is because faith is not set before us as a complete and finished system that the Bible contains contradictory texts, or at least ones that stand in tension to each other." Joseph Cardinal Ratzinger and Peter Seewald, *God and the World: Believing and Living in Our Time* (San Francisco: Ignatius, 2000), 152.

Chapter 16: An Evil Bible?

427 "Hot List 2005," *Rolling Stone*, Issue 984, October 6, 2005, 98.

428 Thomas Paine, *Age of Reason*, 1.4.

429 The adulterous affair with Bathsheba could also be described as a "power rape," in which David abused his royalty authority, and so Bathsheba would have been helpless to refuse his sexual advances.

430 "Rape in the Bible," www.evilbible.com/Rape.htm.

431 Steve Wells, *The Skeptic's Annotated Bible* (SAB Books, 2012), 1603.

432 C. Dennis McKinsey, *The Encyclopedia of Biblical Errancy* (Amherst, NY: Prometheus Books, 1995), 255.

433 It is fair to ask whether this story is literal in nature or a retelling of the Sodom story that was meant to portray how wicked Israel had become. In any case, since most critics balk at the moral elements in this story, I will not focus on questions related to the historical nature of this account.

434 Luke Muehlhauser, "Top 20 Evil Bible Stories," *Common Sense Atheism*, December 4, 2008, commonsenseatheism.com/?p=21.

435 "By the end of the book Israel's moral decline is transparently clear. Though we see a society giving lip service to hospitality and justice, its conduct was, as Webb observes, 'debased because of the moral blindness and/or perversity of its citizens (including Levites and elders).'" Robert B. Chisholm Jr., *A Commentary on Judges and Ruth* (Grand Rapids, MI: Kregel Publications, 2013), 510.

436 "[T]he Levite's dismembering of the concubine's corpse also seems unnecessarily brutal. This impression is intensified when the Levite's action is read in the light of Saul's dismemberment of oxen in 1 Samuel 11:6–11 . . . Judges 19 seems to be an intentional parody of 1 Samuel 11:6–11 with the object of communicating "the perversity of the events described in Judges 19–21." J. Clinton McCann, *Judges* (Louisville, KY: Westminster John Knox Press, 2011), 133.

437 "Rape in the Bible," www.evilbible.com/Rape.htm.

438 John Loftus, "What We Have Here Is a Failure to Communicate," in *The Christian Delusion: Why Faith Fails*, ed. John Loftus (Amherst, NY: Prometheus Books, 2010), 189.

439 "[T]he narrator invites the reader to interpret this episode as an illustration of the principle explicitly declared in 17:7 and 21:25: 'everyone (lit. "a man") did what was right in his own eyes.' Israel did not need a king to lead them into these depths of depravity. The inhabitants of Gibeah are determined to sink this low on their own." Daniel I. Block, *Judges, Ruth: An Exegetical and Theological Exposition of Holy Scripture* (Nashville, TN: Broadman and Holman, 1999), 538.

440 *Mit Brennender Sorge*, 15.

441 Or morally obligatory, as in it's wrong if we don't do it. For example, taking care of one's infant and not letting him starve to death is not just morally right, it's morally obligatory. One is evil for not performing this act.

442 J.L. Mackie, *The Miracle of Theism: Arguments for and against the Existence of God* (Oxford: Oxford University Press, 1982), 115.

443 Two other examples that are cited include Judith's deception of Holofernes (Jth. 10:11–13; 11:5–6) and the angel Azarias's description of himself in Tobit 5:17–18. St. Thomas Aquinas says, "Judith is praised, not for lying to Holofernes, but for her desire to save the people, to which end she exposed herself to danger. And yet one might also say that her words contain truth in some mystical sense." *Summa Theologica* II.2.110.3. This also applies to the allegation of divinely approved lying in the book of Tobit. *A Catholic Commentary on Holy Scripture* says, "The language is vague and involved, but it is not false. That Tobias senior was deceived does not enter into the question of the veracity of the Angel's statement. He had no obligation to make

known his full identity." C.F. Devine, "Tobit," in *A Catholic Commentary on Holy Scripture,* eds. B. Orchard and E. F. Sutcliffe (New York: Thomas Nelson, 1953), 399.

444 It could also be the case that these women did not tell lies but used "mental reservations" or some other kind of speech that hid the truth in a non-sinful way. For more on this see Cardinal John Henry Newman's essay "Lying and Equivocation" in his *Apologia Pro Vita Sua.*

445 Dan Barker, *Godless: How an Evangelical Preacher Became One of America's Leading Atheists* (Berkeley, CA: Ulysses Press, 2008), 224.

446 Edmée Kingsmill, "The Psalms: A Monastic Perspective," in *The Oxford Handbook of the Psalms,* ed. William P. Brown (New York: Oxford University Press, 2014), 602.

447 Scott Hahn, *Catholic Bible Dictionary* (New York: Doubleday, 2009), 743.

448 Ophelia Benson and Jeremy Stangroom, *Does God Hate Women?* (New York: Bloomsbury Academic, 2009), 127.

449 St. Augustine, *Exposition on Psalm 137.*

450 Rebecca Ong, "Policing Obscenity in Hong Kong," *Journal of International Commercial Law and Technology* 4, Issue 2 (2009), 158.

451 Jim Walker, "Sex, Obscenities, Filth," *The Dark Bible* (2006), www.nobeliefs.com/DarkBible/darkbible4.htm.

452 *Jacobellis v. Ohio* (1964).

453 Dan Barker, *Godless: How an Evangelical Preacher Became One of America's Leading Atheists* (Berkeley, CA: Ulysses Press, 2008), 176–77.

Chapter 17: Bad Role Models?

454 *Verbum Domini,* 42.

455 Jason Long, *Biblical Nonsense: A Review of the Bible for Doubting Christians* (np: iUniverse, 2005), 113

456 K.A. Mathews, *Genesis 11:27–50:26: An Exegetical And Theological Exposition of Holy Scripture* (Nashville, TN: Broadman and Holman, 2005), 234.

457 Francis X.E. Albert, "Lot," in *The Catholic Encyclopedia*, Vol. 9 (New York: Robert Appleton Company, 1910), www.newadvent.org/cathen/09366a.htm.

458 The Hebrew word for righteous (*tam*) refers to moral completion or fulfilling one's duties. R. Laird Harris, Gleason L Archer, Bruce K.

Waltke. *Theological Wordbook of the Old Testament* (Chicago: Moody Publishers, 1980), 973.

459 Brian Baker, *Nonsense from the Bible* (np: FastPencil, 2012), Kindle edition.

460 Steve McRoberts, *The Cure for Fundamentalism: Why the Bible Cannot Be the Word of God,* second edition (np: CreateSpace, 2014), 38–39.

461 "The idea was to deceive their father into thinking it was Joseph's blood and wild animals had killed him. Ironically, Jacob had fooled his father Isaac using a goat skin years earlier (Genesis 27:16)." John MacArthur, *Twelve Unlikely Heroes: How God Commissioned Unexpected People in the Bible and What He Wants to Do with You* (Nashville, TN: Nelson Books, 2014), 27.

462 [S]ubsequent exegetes, particularly Protestant ones, argue that Jephthah did not kill his daughter but consecrated her virginity to God . . ." Debora Shuger, *The Renaissance Bible: Scholarship, Sacrifice, and Subjectivity* (Berkeley, CA: University of California Press, 1998), 137.

463 Thom Stark, *The Human Faces of God: What Scripture Reveals When It Gets God Wrong (and Why Inerrancy Tries to Hide It)* (Eugene, OR: Wipf and Stock: 2011), 90.

464 Mark Roncace, *Raw Revelation: The Bible They Never Tell You About* (np: CreateSpace, 2012), 61.

465 The Hebrew word in question is *asher,* that means "who" or "which." It's essentially an article of relation or conjunction. R. Laird Harris, Gleason L. Archer, Bruce K. Waltke. *Theological Wordbook of the Old Testament* (Chicago: Moody Publishers, 1980), 82.

466 J. David Schloen, *The House of the Father as Fact and Symbol: Patrimonialism in Ugarit and the Ancient Near East* (Winona Lake, IN: Eisenbrauns, 2001), 138. Cited in Mark Giszczak, *Light on the Dark Passages of Scripture* (Huntington, IN: Our Sunday Visitor, 2015), 91.

467 David Grimm, *Citizen Canine: Our Evolving Relationship with Cats and Dogs* (Philadelphia: Public Affairs, 2014), 30.

468 One example of this occurred when King Mesha of Moab sacrificed his oldest son to the deity Chemosh on the city wall in view of the Israelites (2 Kings 3:27). This caused a "great wrath" to come upon Israel, which was followed by the Moabites repelling them in battle. It is doubtful, however, that the narrator literally attributes the wrath to Chemosh since he describes Chemosh as being a detestable idol (1

HARD SAYINGS

Kings 11:7). The author also describes humans as being full of wrath
(*qatsaph*) in 2 Kings 5:11. (The word used for wrath in 2 Kings 3:27,
qetseph, is derived from *qatsaph*.) Paul Copan and Matt Flanagan, *Did
God Really Command Genocide?: Coming to Terms with the Justice of God*
(Grand Rapids, MI: Baker Books, 2014), 325. But what does "the
great wrath" refer to? It might refer to the Moabites being driven
to a frenzied rage after seeing what their king had done. Or it could
refer to some superstitious Israelites who believed the wrath of Chemosh had actually come upon them because of this sacrifice. Paul R.
House, *1, 2 Kings: An Exegetical and Theological Exposition of Holy Scripture* (Nashville, TN: Broadman and Holman, 1995), 264. Goldingay
says the narrator is being ambiguous and that he wasn't sure what the
source of the "wrath" was. He therefore left this open to the reader
to interpret for himself. John Goldingay, *1 and 2 Kings for Everyone*
(Louisville, KY: Westminster John Knox Press, 2011), 117.

469 F. Duane Lindsey, "Judges," in *The Bible Knowledge Commentary: Old
Testament*, eds. Roy B. Zuck and John F. Walvoord (Wheaton, IL:
Victor Books, 1985), 402.

470 Christopher J.H. Wright, *Knowing the Holy Spirit Through the Old
Testament* (Downer's Grove, IL: InterVarsity Press, 2006), 40.

471 Ibid., 41.

472 Thom Stark, *The Human Faces of God: What Scripture Reveals When
It Gets God Wrong (and Why Inerrancy Tries to Hide It)* (Eugene, OR:
Wipf and Stock: 2011), 90–91.

473 Steven Pinker, *The Better Angels of Our Nature: Why Violence Has
Declined* (Great Britain: Allen Lane, 2011), 8.

474 Philip Jenkins, *Laying Down the Sword: Why We Can't Ignore the Bible's
Violent Verses* (New York: HarperOne, 2011), 6–7.

475 University of Navarre, *Joshua–Kings* (New York: Four Courts Press,
2005), 163–64.

476 Matthew Ramage, *Dark Passages of the Bible: Engaging Scripture with
Benedict XVI and Thomas Aquinas* (Washington, DC: Catholic University of America Press, 2013), 149.

477 Robert A. Stein, *Luke: An Exegetical and Theological Exposition of Holy
Scripture* (Nashville, TN: Broadman and Holman, 1993), 396. See
also the Old Testament expression "the wife he hates," which only

refers to a wife in a polygamous relationship who is loved less (Gen. 29:31, Deut. 21:15).

478 Craig A. Evans, *Matthew* (New York: Cambridge University Press, 2012), 229. Jerome and Epiphanius even say that since the beginning of the Church's history synagogues prayed an anathema or curse upon Christians three times a day. However, other scholars dispute whether this evidence is reliable or if it can be dated all the way back to the first century. See Ruth Langer, *Cursing the Christians? A History of the Birkat HaMinim* (New York: Oxford University Press, 2011).

479 Dan Barker, *Godless: How an Evangelical Preacher Became One of America's Leading Atheists* (Berkeley, CA: Ulysses Press, 2008), 233, and Jason Long, *Biblical Nonsense: A Review of the Bible for Doubting Christians* (np: iUniverse, 2005), 164.

480 "The lesson of the fig tree involves the fall of Jerusalem, not the Parousia." Robert H. Stein, *Mark* (Grand Rapids, MI: Baker Academic, 2008), 618.

481 "Like Father, Like Clown," *The Simpsons,* original airdate October 24, 1991.

482 "Tractate Baba Mezi'a 59a," *Babylonian Talmud.* Available online at www.come-and-hear.com/babamezia/babamezia_59.html.

483 Bruce J. Malina, *The New Testament World: Insights from Cultural Anthropology* (Louisville, KY: Westminster John Knox Press, 1993), 104–5.

484 See "Tractate Berakoth 64a," *Babylonian Talmud.* Available online at www.come-and-hear.com/berakoth/berakoth_64.html.

485 This thinking comes from the seventeenth-century philosopher Blaise Pascal, who said that God "instituted prayer in order to lend to his creatures the dignity of causality." Quoted and expanded upon by C.S. Lewis in "The World's Last Night" in *The Essential C.S. Lewis,* ed. Lyle Dorsett (New York: Touchstone, 1988), 381.

Chapter 18: Anti-Woman?

486 R. Laird Harris, Gleason L. Archer, Bruce K. Waltke. *Theological Wordbook of the Old Testament* (Chicago: Moody Publishers, 1980), 661.

487 David Lamb, *God Behaving Badly: Is the God of the Old Testament Angry, Sexist, and Racist?* (Downer's Grove, IL: InterVarsity Press, 2011), 52.

488 *Mulieris Dignitatem*, 10.

489 The meaning of verse 15 is difficult to discern. It says, "Yet woman will be saved through bearing children, if she continues in faith and love and holiness, with modesty." This may refer to gnostic heretics who condemned sexual relations and childbearing as sinful (1 Tim. 4:3). See also George T. Montague, *First and Second Timothy, Titus* (Grand Rapids, MI: Baker Academic, 2008), 69.

490 Ibid., 67.

491 Brian Baker, *Nonsense from the Bible* (np: FastPencil, 2012), Kindle edition.

492 Mark F. Rooker, *Leviticus: An Exegetical and Theological Exposition of Holy Scripture* (Nashville, TN: Broadman and Holman, 2000), 183.

493 Iain Lonie, *The Hippocratic Treatises, "On Generation," "On the Nature of the Child," "Diseases IV": A Commentary* (Berlin: Walter de Gruyter, 1981), 192.

494 I. Brosens, J. Brosens, G. Benagiano, "Neonatal Uterine Bleeding as Antecedent of Pelvic Endometriosis," *Human Reproduction,* no. 11 (November 28, 2013), www.ncbi.nlm.nih.gov/pubmed/24048011.

495 Mark F. Rooker, *Leviticus: An Exegetical and Theological Exposition of Holy Scripture* (Nashville, TN: Broadman and Holman, 2000), 185.

496 Montague says that this is probably the correct interpretation for 1 Timothy 3:2. George T. Montague, *First and Second Timothy, Titus* (Grand Rapids, MI: Baker Academic, 2008), 74–75. Redford notes the connection to 1 Timothy 5 but he considers this to be a less likely interpretation and opts for the view that Paul is speaking about marital infidelity, although he agrees that a ban on polygamy is an "extremely unlikely" reading of the text. Shawn B. Redford, *Missiological Hermeneutics: Biblical Interpretations for a Global Church* (Eugene, OR: Wipf and Stock, 2012), 177–78.

497 Long misses this point when he writes, "[D]ivinely inspired biblical authors wholeheartedly claim that God looks upon these men favorably. Would we expect God to view these individuals in a positive light if this lifestyle was displeasing to the almighty?" (112). But as we've seen, God can have favor toward people in spite of their sins. Just because the Bible records good people doing bad things does not mean that the Bible endorses those bad actions.

498 "The bill of divorce was permitted in the Law, not indeed for the sake of obtaining a greater good, as was the dispensation to have several wives, but for the sake of preventing a greater evil, namely wife-murder, to which the Jews were prone on account of the corruption of their irascible appetite." St. Thomas Aquinas, *Summa Theologica* 3.3.67.3.

499 See also Jimmy Akin, "Is It Okay to Force a Woman You've Captured to Marry You?," *National Catholic Register* (November 14, 2012), www.ncregister.com/blog/jimmy-akin/is-it-okay-to-force-a-woman-youve-captured-to-marry-you.

500 Carolyn Pressler, *The View of Women Found in the Deuteronomic Family Laws* (Berlin: Walter de Gruyter, 1993), 11.

501 Ibid., 15.

502 Sarah Shechtman, *Women in the Pentateuch: A Feminist and Source-Critical Analysis* (Sheffield: Sheffield Phoenix Press, 2009), 166.

503 It is beyond the scope of this book to address the issue of Pauline authorship of the disputed letters in the New Testament. I will simply use the canonical approach and refer to Paul as the author of letters that have been commonly attributed to him throughout Church history.

504 Robert A.J. Gagnon, *The Bible and Homosexual Practice: Texts and Hermeneutics* (Nashville, TN: Abingdon Press, 2001), 368.

505 Daniel A. Keating, *First and Second Peter, Jude* (Grand Rapids, MI: Baker Academic, 2011), 76.

506 Pope Benedict XVI, General Audience, February 14, 2007, w2.vatican.va/content/benedict-xvi/en/audiences/2007/documents/hf_ben-xvi_aud_20070214.html.

507 See also Jimmy Akin, "Should Women Keep Silence in Church?," *National Catholic Register* (September 9, 2012), www.ncregister.com/blog/jimmy-akin/should-women-keep-silence-in-church#ixzz3UobGd8CH.

508 This naturally leads to the question of why women can't be priests, which is beyond the scope of this book and has been addressed by several other authors. See, for example, Manfred Hauke and David Kipp, *Women in the Priesthood: A Systematic Analysis in the Light of the Order of Creation and Redemption* (San Francisco: Ignatius Press, 1988), and Sara Butler, *The Catholic Priesthood and Women: A Guide to the*

Teaching of the Church (Mundelein, IL: Hillenbrand, 2007).

509 Ben Witherington, *Conflict and Community in Corinth: A Socio-rhetorical Commentary on 1 and 2 Corinthians* (Grand Rapids, MI: Wm. B. Eerdmans, 1995), 276.

510 *Mulieris Dignitatem*, 24.

Chapter 19: Bizarre Laws and Cruel Punishments?

512 J. Kent Ashcraft, "An Open Letter to Dr. Laura," www-users.cs.york. ac.uk/~susan/joke/laura.htm.

512 The exception being, of course, orthodox and ultra-orthodox Jews as well as some Christians who call themselves "Messianic Jews." These believers adhere to most or even all of the Old Testament laws, including the dietary restrictions and restrictions on working during the Sabbath.

513 "Among the Greeks and Romans the name was applied to trustworthy slaves who were charged with the duty of supervising the life and morals of boys belonging to the better class. The boys were not allowed to so much as step out of the house without them before arriving at the age of manhood." Joseph Henry Thayer, *A Greek English Lexicon of the New Testament* (Grand Rapids, MI: Baker Book House, 1977), 472.

514 John Goldingay, *Exodus and Leviticus for Everyone* (Louisville, KY: Westminster John Knox Press, 2010), 147.

515 "The terms *holy sacrifice of the Mass, "sacrifice of praise," spiritual sacrifice, pure and holy sacrifice* are also used, since it completes and surpasses all the sacrifices of the Old Covenant" (CCC 1330).

516 Paul Copan, *Is God a Moral Monster? Making Sense of the Old Testament God* (Grand Rapids, MI: Baker Books, 2011), 78.

517 Cate Lineberry, "Tattoos: The Ancient and Mysterious History," Smithsonian.com, January 1, 2007, www.smithsonianmag.com/ist/?next=/history-archaeology/tattoo.html?c=y&page=2.

518 P.P. Saydon, "Leviticus," in *A Catholic Commentary on Holy Scripture,* eds. B. Orchard and E. F. Sutcliffe (New York: Thomas Nelson, 1953), 241.

519 Mark Giszczak, *Light on the Dark Passages of Scripture* (Huntington, IN: Our Sunday Visitor, 2015), 144.

520 *Dei Verbum*, 15. Cited in CCC 122.

521 Mark Giszczak, *Light on the Dark Passages of Scripture* (Huntington, IN: Our Sunday Visitor, 2015), 40.

522 See also St. Thomas Aquinas, *Summa Theologica* 1.2.103.3.

523 It's true that verse 19 refers to a ceremonial law related to menstruation, but this prohibition merely forbids sex during menstruation. It is not like the other verses in this section that describe moral evils as being "defilements," "profane," "perverted," and, in the case of same-sex behavior, "abominations." Even before the time of Moses the Bible forbade the drinking of blood (Gen. 9:4), and the Mosaic Law contained several prescriptions that dealt with how to be cleansed from contact with bodily fluids. As we learned in our previous discussion of leprosy, the Israelites considered bodily fluids to be sacred. They knew blood had something to do with death, or that when you lose enough blood you die, so "life" must be in the blood. Similarly, semen carried with it the "seed" that brings forth new life, so it too was sacred. As a result, spilling semen on the ground, touching blood from a dead body, or mixing semen and blood (in the case of sex with a menstruating woman) literally involved matters of "life and death," and so they were forbidden.

524 Violating the command to honor the Sabbath was punishable by death, but this was and still is a moral law that is binding upon believers even if nonbelievers cannot know it through the natural law. Christians do not celebrate the Sabbath, but they do keep holy the day of the week that Christ rose from the dead, and so the fourth commandment is still upheld. According to the *Catechism*, "for Christians [Sunday's] ceremonial observance replaces that of the sabbath. In Christ's Passover, Sunday fulfills the spiritual truth of the Jewish sabbath and announces man's eternal rest in God. For worship under the Law prepared for the mystery of Christ, and what was done there prefigured some aspects of Christ" (CCC 2175).

525 John Shelby Spong, *The Sins of Scripture: Exposing the Bible's Texts of Hate to Reveal the God of Love* (New York: HarperOne, 2006), 19.

526 The Supreme Court rejected the use of capital punishment for the crime of child rape in *Kennedy v. Louisiana* (2008).

527 St. John Chrysostom, *Homilies on Matthew* 39.3.

528 "The story is deliberately located in the book of Numbers as an ex-

ample of the offence that is committed 'with upraised hand' (Num. 15:30). The 'upraised hand' (which functions visually as a sign of protest) contrasts with the 'mighty hand' (e.g., Exod. 32:11) with which God delivered Israel out of Egypt. The Sabbath breaker's behavior thus signifies a desire to return to Egypt. In this sense it thematically repeats the earlier spy-story which includes a statement of the Israelites' desire to return to Egypt (Num. 14:4)." Jonathan Burnside, "'What Shall We Do with the Sabbath-Gatherer?' A Narrative Approach to a 'Hard Case' in Biblical Law (Numbers 15:32–36)," *Vetus Testamentum,* Vol. 60 (2010), 59.

529 Mark Giszczak, *Light on the Dark Passages of Scripture* (Huntington, IN: Our Sunday Visitor, 2015), 38.

530 "The cognitive structures that go into reading the biblical Sabbath laws are narrative and visual, rather than semantic and literal." Burnside, "'What Shall We Do with the Sabbath-Gatherer?,'" *Vetus Testamentum,* Vol. 60 (2010), 60.

531 Raymond Westbrook, "The Character of Ancient Near Eastern Law," in *A History of Ancient Near Eastern Law,* Vol. 1, ed. Raymond Westbrook (Leiden: Brill Academic, 2003), 70–71.

532 Paul Copan, *Is God a Moral Monster? Making Sense of the Old Testament God* (Grand Rapids, MI: Baker Books, 2011), 95–96.

533 It's also possible a later editor of the text added these punishments to the law in order to communicate how severe these crimes were to his audience. Stories about stoning unruly children, for example, may belong to a nonliteral, didactic genre instead of a literal, historical one.

534 Richard H. Hiers, *Justice and Compassion in Biblical Law* (New York: Continuum International Publishing, 2009), 94.

535 By "married" I include the state of being betrothed, which was legally on par with marriage in ancient Israel.

536 Pascale Harter, "Libya Rape Victims 'Face Honor Killings,'" BBC News, June 14, 2011, www.bbc.com/news/world-africa-13760895.

537 Law of Hammurabi 132. See also Sophie Démare-Lafont, "Judicial Decision-making: Judges and Arbitrators," in *The Oxford Handbook of Cuneiform Culture,* ed. Karen Radner et al. (Oxford: Oxford University Press, 2011), 354.

538 See Raymond Westbrook, "The Character of Ancient Near Eastern

Law," in *A History of Ancient Near Eastern Law,* Vol. 1, ed. Raymond Westbrook (Leiden: Brill Academic, 2003), 80–81, for a concurrence with this interpretation.

539 R. Laird Harris, Gleason L. Archer, Bruce K. Waltke. *Theological Wordbook of the Old Testament* (Chicago: Moody Publishers, 1980), 742–43. The word is associated with the idea of simpletons, being made silly, or being deceived. For example, the Philistines tell Delilah to *entice* Samson so that he will reveal the secret behind his strength (Judg. 14:15).

540 This would have also been the case if the rape were statutory in nature or even if the encounter were consensual.

541 J. Clinton McCann, *Judges* (Louisville, KY: Westminster John Knox Press, 2011), 133.

542 Kenton L. Sparks, *Sacred Word, Broken Word: Biblical Authority and the Dark Side of Scripture* (Grand Rapids, MI: Wm. B. Eerdmans, 2012), 40.

Chapter 20: Endorsement of Slavery? Part I

543 Dan Gilgoff, "Columnist Dan Savage Stands by Comments on 'Bulls★★t in the Bible,'" *CNN Belief Blog,* April 30, 2012, religion. blogs.cnn.com/2012/04/30/columnist-dan-savage-stands-by-comments-on-bullst-in-the-bible/?hpt=hp_c2.

544 Dan Savage, "On 'Bullshit' and 'Pansy-Assed,'" *The Slog,* April 29, 2012, slog.thestranger.com/slog/archives/2012/04/29/on-bullshit-and-pansy-assed.

545 Hector Avalos, *Slavery, Abolitionism, and the Ethics of Biblical Scholarship* (Sheffield: Sheffield Phoenix Press, 2013), 7.

546 "Prison Labor: Perspectives on Paying the Federal Minimum Wage," Report to the Honorable Harry Reid, U.S. Senate, Government Accounting Office (May 1993), 4. Available online at www.gao.gov/assets/220/217999.pdf. In fact, the Thirteenth Amendment to the U.S. Constitution says, "Neither slavery nor involuntary servitude, *except as a punishment for crime whereof the party shall have been duly convicted* [emphasis added], shall exist within the United States."

547 St. Thomas Aquinas, *Summa Theologica* 2.2.57.3.

548 *Dictionary of the Ancient Near East,* eds. Piotr Bienkowski and Alan Millard (Philadelphia: University of Pennsylvania Press, 2010), 100.

549 Daniel C. Snell, *Life in the Ancient Near East* (New York: Yale University Press, 1997), 125.

550 Gregory C. Chirichigno, *Debt Slavery in Israel and the Ancient Near East* (Sheffield: Sheffield Academic Press, 1993), 51.

551 Avalos suggests that the Athenian lawgiver Solon surpassed biblical ethics in his laws because he outlawed all debt slavery in Greece (*Slavery, Abolitionism, and the Ethics of Biblical Scholarship*, 48). However, Avalos overlooks the fact that Solon's reforms may have had the unintended consequence of making the Greek economy worse by depriving borrowers of the only collateral they had for making loans—themselves. This shows that abolishing debt slavery in ancient Israel would have been just as impractical or even maleficent to subsistence farmers. According to Sagsetter, the elaborate debt-avoidance scheme in Aristophanes' *Clouds* is an example of negative Athenian reaction to Solon's reforms. See Kelcy Sagstetter, "Solon of Athens: The Man, the Myth, the Tyrant?," (2013), Publicly Accessible Penn Dissertations, Paper 923, 163.

552 David Galenson, "The Rise and Fall of Indentured Servitude in the Americas: An Economic Analysis," *Journal of Economic History* 44:1 (1984).

553 Avalos attempts to show that other ANE slave laws were just as progressive as Israel's, but fails to make his case. For example, he cites the Laws of Eshnunna that inflict the death penalty upon kidnappers whose victims die, and Law of Hammurabi 14 that makes stealing children a capital offense. However, Exodus 21:16 does not limit its punishment to only when the kidnapped victim dies or is a child, thus making it more wide-reaching and humane. Avalos then tries to use a translation from Raymond Westbrook to argue that Exodus 21:16 only punishes the person who buys a stolen man, not the person who originally kidnapped him, but this contradicts the vast majority of scholars who hold that the act of kidnapping itself was treated as a capital offense. See Jonathan Burnside, *God, Justice, and Society: Aspects of Law and Legality in the Bible* (New York: Oxford University Press, 2011), 288–89, and Douglas K. Stuart, *Exodus: An Exegetical and Theological Exposition of Holy Scripture* (Nashville, TN: B&H Publishing, 2006), 488. Westbrook himself says, "Two types of aggravated theft

are mentioned: kidnapping and stealing sacral property. Kidnapping meant the stealing of a person for sale into slavery. It was punishable by death (Exod. 21:16)." Raymond Westbrook and Bruce Wells, *Everyday Law in Biblical Israel: An Introduction* (Louisville, KY: Westminster John Knox Press, Louisville, 2009), 84. Finally, Avalos argues that this law would only have applied to stealing Israelites and not to anyone who happened to live in the land (e.g., resident aliens). But Old Testament scholar Thomas Dozeman notes that this law "does not distinguish between an Israelite and a foreigner." Dozeman also contradicts Avalos's contention that Westbrook believes Exodus 21:16 only punishes slave buyers and not slave kidnappers as well. See Thomas B. Dozeman, *Exodus* (Grand Rapids, MI: Wm. B. Eerdmans, 2009), 533.

554 *Verbum Domini*, 42.

555 Richard Bauckham, *God and the Crisis of Freedom: Biblical and Contemporary Perspectives* (Louisville, KY: Westminster John Knox Press, 2002), 12.

556 Avalos objects, "The inhumanity of this biblical law is even more apparent when one compares it to the law of Athens. In regard to violence against slaves at Athens Xenophon says, 'You can't hit them there'" (*Slavery, Abolitionism, and the Ethics of Biblical Scholarship*, 81). But Avalos has pulled this quote out of context. Xenophon is only saying that it is a matter of *custom* and not a matter of law that one can't hit a slave in Athens. That's because in Athens you're likely to hit a freeman due to the fact that it is difficult to distinguish between slaves and freemen. Xenophon writes, "Now among the slaves and metics [resident aliens] at Athens there is the greatest uncontrolled wantonness; you can't hit them there, and a slave will not stand aside for you. I shall point out why this is their native practice: if it were customary for a slave (or metic or freedman) to be struck by one who is free, you would often hit an Athenian citizen by mistake on the assumption that he was a slave. For the people there are no better dressed than the slaves and metics, nor are they any more handsome." *The Athenians* 1.10. Available online at www.perseus.tufts.edu/hopper/text?doc=Perseus:text:1999.01.0158#note-link2.

557 "If any one receive into his house a runaway male or female slave of the court, or of a freedman, and does not bring it out at the pub-

lic proclamation of the major domus, the master of the house shall be put to death." Law of Hammurabi 8. Translated by L.W. King. Available online at avalon.law.yale.edu/ancient/hamframe.asp. Avalos tries to reinterpret this passage as a reference to punishing the crime of stealing slaves instead of just failing to return fugitive slaves, but this interpretation is untenable. Mesopotamian scholar Dominique Charpin only mentions laws 17–20 as being related to stealing fugitive slaves and leaves law 16 in the context of failing to return fugitives. See Dominique Charpin, *Writing, Law, and Kingship in Old Babylonian Mesopotamia* (London: University of Chicago Press, 2010), 75–76.

558 Christopher J.H. Wright, *Old Testament Ethics for the People of God* (Downer's Grove, IL: InterVarsity Press, 2004), 292. Avalos cites Westbrook as saying that kings could grant asylum to fugitive slaves when not forbidden by a treaty, and so Israel's law is not unique (*Slavery, Abolitionism, and the Ethics of Biblical Scholarship*, 90). This is true but irrelevant since we are talking about the absence of laws that allowed average people to refuse to return slaves, not kings who had royal authority that allowed them to dispense with certain laws or customs.

559 Jonathan Burnside, *God, Justice, and Society: Aspects of Law and Legality in the Bible* (New York: Oxford University Press, 2011), 325.

560 "If any one steal cattle or sheep, or an ass, or a pig or a goat, if it belong to a god or to the court, the thief shall pay thirtyfold therefore; if they belonged to a freed man of the king he shall pay tenfold; if the thief has nothing with which to pay he shall be put to death." Law of Hammurabi 8. Translated by L.W. King. Available online at avalon. law.yale.edu/ancient/hamframe.asp.

561 Likewise, Numbers 35:22–28 says that if a man kills another man by accident and without enmity (or he lacks premeditation), then he is allowed to be exiled to a city of refuge and the family of the man he killed is prohibited from killing him.

562 Gregory C. Chirichigno, *Debt Slavery in Israel and the Ancient Near East* (Sheffield: Sheffield Academic Press, 1993), 169.

563 G. Johannes Botterweck and Helmer Ringgren, *Theological Dictionary of the Old Testament*, Vol. 10 (Grand Rapids, MI: Wm. B. Eerdmans, 2010). 9. See also Genesis 4:15, Leviticus 26:25, and Numbers 31:2.

564 "Generally, the interpretation of bride-price as a straight purchase

transaction overlooks the subtleties within a society. In Indonesian society, [for example,] divorce can be obtained, and if the fault lies with the man, he loses the bride-price paid to the family. If the fault is on the woman's part, the bride-price is repaid." George P. Monger, *Marriage Customs of the World: From Henna to Honeymoons* (Santa Barbara: ABC-CLIO, 2004), 40.

565 Gregory C. Chirichigno, *Debt Slavery in Israel and the Ancient Near East* (Sheffield: Sheffield Academic Press, 1993), 253.

Chapter 21: Endorsement of Slavery? Part II

566 Compare with Law of Hammurabi 196, 199, and 201.

567 Gregory C. Chirichigno, *Debt Slavery in Israel and the Ancient Near East* (Sheffield: Sheffield Academic Press, 1993), 176–77.

568 Raymond Westbrook, "Slave and Master in Ancient Near Eastern Law," *Chicago-Kent Law Review* 70, no. 4 (June 1995), 1673.

569 Roland De Vaux, *Ancient Israel: Its Life and Institutions* (Grand Rapids, MI: Wm. B. Eerdmans, 1997), 75. Leviticus 25:35 says, "if your brother becomes poor, and cannot maintain himself with you, you shall maintain him; as a stranger and a sojourner he shall live with you." This implies that an Israelite who could not sustain himself became a transient who did not own land, a status shared with foreigners and resident aliens. After being relegated to this status the impoverished Israelite would probably have tried to make ends meet by selling himself as a hired laborer in the same manner as a foreigner or resident alien.

570 Gregory C. Chirichigno, *Debt Slavery in Israel and the Ancient Near East* (Sheffield: Sheffield Academic Press, 1993), 229.

571 Pope John Paul II said this is morally licit in his 1995 encyclical *Evangelium Vitae*. He writes, "When it is not possible to overturn or completely abrogate a pro-abortion law, an elected official, whose absolute personal opposition to procured abortion was well known, could licitly support proposals aimed at limiting the harm done by such a law and at lessening its negative consequences at the level of general opinion and public morality. This does not in fact represent an illicit cooperation with an unjust law, but rather a legitimate and proper attempt to limit its evil aspects" (73).

572 Siu Fung Wu, *Suffering in Romans* (Eugene, OR: Wipf and Stock, 2015), 234.

573 Sandra R. Joshel, *Slavery in the Roman World* (New York: Cambridge University Press, 2010), 38, 41.

574 Ibid., 71–72.

575 Jennifer A. Glancy, *Slavery as Moral Problem: In the Early Church and Today* (Minneapolis, MN: Fortress Press, 2011), 27.

576 Origen, *Against Celsus,* 3.59.

577 The primary source for this claim is found in Appian's *Civil Wars* I.120, which was written in the mid-second century after Christ.

578 A major point of contention in this verse is the Greek clause *mallon chresai,* or "use instead." It can be read as saying the slave should use instead his slavery in order to build up the kingdom (and thus remain a slave), or he should use instead his freedom if he can gain it (and thus refrain from being a slave). The passage is covered in book-length treatments by Scott Bartchy, *First Century Slavery and 1 Corinthians 7:21* (Eugene, OR: Wipf and Stock, 1973) and J. Albert Harrill, *The Manumission of Slaves in Early Christianity* (Tubingen: Mohr Siebeck, 1995), both of whom accept the latter interpretation of "use instead freedom." The issue can become quite technical, but one point should be mentioned against the idea that Paul is encouraging slaves to remain as they are. Witherington says that since slaves were not persons they could not legally choose freedom, but could instead only make a plea to their masters for freedom. He then writes, "Bartchy argues that the slave was not free to reject manumission either, if the owner was determined to be rid of the slave. The slave could only plead against it. This means that 1 Cor. 7:21 certainly cannot mean 'if you have the option to become free, do not avail yourself of it.' The slave had no such options." Ben Witherington, *Conflict and Community in Corinth: A Socio-rhetorical Commentary on 1 and 2 Corinthians* (Grand Rapids, MI: Wm. B. Eerdmans, 1995), 184. Avalos says in reply that Paul could be referring to any form of manumission (*Slavery, Abolitionism, and the Ethics of Biblical Scholarship,* 107–8), but Avalos does not provide evidence that a slave could anymore refuse manumission by testament in a will or a census decree than he could refuse manumission provided by the master directly. Paul's

message in 1 Corinthians 7:20–21 is summarized well in Wright's commentary: "If you were a slave when you became a Christian, you shouldn't be constantly seeking to become free as though everything depends on it. (But, as he says in 7:21, if you can gain your freedom, grab it with both hands.) Likewise, if you were free, you shouldn't enslave yourself to someone." N.T. Wright, *1 Corinthians* (Downer's Grove, IL: InterVarsity Press, 2009), 35.

579 One example of this is the philosopher Seneca who, although he discouraged merciless corporal punishment, compared slaves to valuable property like jewels one must constantly worry about. According to Joshel, "Seneca sees slaves as inferiors who can never rise above the level of humble friends." Sandra R. Joshel, *Slavery in the Roman World* (New York: Cambridge University Press, 2010), 127.

580 *Institutes of the Civil Law* 6.

581 Stephen Wilson, *The Means of Naming: A Social History* (London: UCL Press, 1998), 30.

582 Sandra R. Joshel, *Slavery in the Roman World* (New York: Cambridge University Press, 2010), 122.

583 Ignatius of Antioch, *Letter to the Ephesians* 1.

584 James D.G. Dunn, *The Theology of Paul the Apostle* (Grand Rapids, MI: Wm. B. Eerdmans, 1998), 699, 701.

Chapter 22: Drunk with Blood?

585 Mark Twain, *The Mysterious Stranger and Other Stories* (Mineola, NY: Dover, 1992), 64.

586 Steve Wells, *Drunk with Blood: God's Killings in the Bible* (SAB Books, 2013), 10.

587 Ibid.

588 Dan Barker, *Godless: How an Evangelical Preacher Became One of America's Leading Atheists* (Berkeley, CA: Ulysses Press, 2008), 204.

589 Lakshmi Gandhi, "The History Behind the Phrase 'Don't Be an Indian Giver,'" NPR, September 2, 2013, www.npr.org/sections/codeswitch/2013/09/02/217295339/the-history-behind-the-phrase-dont-be-an-indian-giver.

590 CCC 402–3, 1008.

591 See Trent Horn, *Answering Atheism: Making the Case for God with Logic*

and *Charity* (El Cajon, CA: Catholic Answers Press, 2013), 177–216.

592 A variant of this objection can be found in Dan Barker, *Godless: How an Evangelical Preacher Became One of America's Leading Atheists* (Berkeley, CA: Ulysses Press, 2008), 202.

593 "Direct abortion, that is, abortion willed as an end or as a means, always constitutes a grave moral disorder, since it is the deliberate killing of an innocent human being." *Evangelium Vitae*, 62.

594 Jason Long, *Biblical Nonsense: A Review of the Bible for Doubting Christians* (np: iUniverse, 2005), 88.

595 Richard Hess, "Leviticus 10:1: Strange Fire and an Odd Name," *Bulletin for Biblical Research*, 12.2 (2002), 198.

596 "While the Jews were in no doubt whatsoever about the oneness of God, they still needed something to represent God among themselves in order to feel his presence. That need was satisfied in the Ark of the Covenant: an inanimate object which represented God to the Jews as their national savior." Hans Kochler, *The Concept of Monotheism in Islam and Christianity* (np: International Progress Association, 1982), 73.

597 Sir William Robertson Nicoll, *The Expositor's Bible*, Vol. 11, 27.

598 Eric J. Ziolkowski, "The Bad Boys of Bethel: Origin and Development of a Sacrilegious Type," *History of Religions* 30 (1991).

599 Julie Faith Parker, *Valuable and Vulnerable: Children in the Hebrew Bible, Especially the Elisha Cycle* (Providence, RI: Brown University, 2013), 97.

600 The word comes from *qatan,* which is a relative term. For example, Genesis 19:11 describes how the angels blinded the mob that wanted to rape them at Lot's house. The verse says that men "both great and small" (*gadowl* and *miq-qa-ton*) were blinded. Certainly the small members of the mob would have been nearly as dangerous as the larger members.

601 Lamentations 5:13 is the only other place in Scripture where the exact form of *hunearim* is used, and in that passage it refers to boys who are forced to engage in menial labor alongside young male captives in Babylon. The text probably describes the fate of adolescents who were not old enough to be numbered among the captured male soldiers but were still old enough to be useful as prisoners of war.

602 G.K. Lieten and Talinay Strehl, *Child Street Life: An Inside View of Hazards and Expectations of Street Children in Peru* (New York: Springer, 2015), 22.

603 John F. Walvoord, *The Bible Knowledge Commentary: Old Testament* (Wheaton, IL: Victor Books, 1985), 542.

604 Rachelle Gilmour, *Juxtaposition and the Elisha Cycle* (London: Bloomsbury T&T Clark, 2014), 102–3.

Chapter 23: Campaigns of Genocide? Part I

605 Cited in Richard Dawkins, *The God Delusion* (New York: Houghton-Mifflin, 2008), 289.

606 The Canaanite deity Baal, for example, engaged in bestiality and incestuous relationships with his mother and sister. See Clay Jones, "We Don't Hate Sin So We Don't Understand What Happened to the Canaanites: An Addendum to 'Divine Genocide' Arguments," *Philosophia Christi* 11, no. 1 (2009).

607 Ibid. See also Harry Hoffner, "Incest, Sodomy, and Bestiality in the Ancient Near East," in *Orient and Occident: Essays Presented to Cyrus H. Gordon on the Sixty-fifth Birthday*, ed. H.A. Hoffner, *Alter Orient And Altes Testament 22* (Neukirchen-Vluyn: Neukirchener, 1973), 82. Some ANE cultures prohibited kinds of bestiality while tolerating others. For example, the law code of the Hittites said, "If anyone have intercourse with a pig or a dog, he shall die. If a man have intercourse with a horse or a mule, there is no punishment" (The Code of the Nesilim, 199).

608 "You shall not lie with any beast and defile yourself with it, neither shall any woman give herself to a beast to lie with it: it is perversion" (Lev. 18:23).

609 Jeffrey H. Schwartz, *What the Bones Tell Us* (New York: Henry Holt, 2015), 29–30.

610 Cleitarchus, *On Superstition*, 13.

611 Paolo Xella, et. al., "Phoenician Bones of Contention," *Antiquity* 87 (2013), 1–9.

612 Christopher B. Hays, *Death in the Iron Age II and in First Isaiah* (Tubingen: Mohr Siebeck, 2011), 181.

613 Scott Hahn and John Bergsma, "What Laws Were 'Not Good'? A Canonical Approach to the Theological Problem of Ezekiel 20:25–26," *Journal of Biblical Literature* 123/2 (2004), 212.

614 Joe Sprinkle, *Biblical Law and Its Relevance: A Christian Understanding*

and Ethical Application for Today of the Mosaic Regulations (Lanham, MD: University Press of America, 2006), 176–78. Cited in Paul Copan and Matt Flanagan, *Did God Really Command Genocide: Coming to Terms with the Justice of God* (Grand Rapids, MI: Baker Books, 2014), 58.

615 Steven Pinker, *The Better Angels of Our Nature: Why Violence Has Declined* (Great Britain: Allen Lane, 2011), 10. Pinker, no fan of religion, also adds this detail: "And Yahweh tortures and massacres people by the hundreds of thousands for trivial reasons, or for no reason at all."

616 Trymaine Lee, "Rumors to Fact in Tales of Post-Katrina Violence," *The New York Times,* August 26, 2010. Available online at www.nytimes.com/2010/08/27/us/27racial.html?_r=0.

617 John Barton, *Ethics in Ancient Israel* (Oxford: Oxford University Press, 2014), 104.

618 Roland De Vaux, *Ancient Israel: Its Life and Institutions* (Grand Rapids, MI: Wm. B. Eerdmans, 1997), 256.

Chapter 24: Campaigns of Genocide? Part II

619 St. Thomas Aquinas, *Summa Theologica* I–II.94.5.

620 Raymond Brown, *The Message of Deuteronomy* (Downer's Grove, IL: InterVarsity Press, 1993), 146.

621 Caleb was the biological son of the Kenezite Jephunneh (Num. 32:12) but was later adopted by Hezron and incorporated into the tribe of Judah (1 Chron. 2:9).

622 Mark van de Logt, *War Party in Blue: Pawnee Scouts in the U.S. Army* (Norman, OK: University of Oklahoma Press, 2010).

623 Jimmy Akin, "Blunt Commands in the Old Testament," jimmyakin.com, August 2005.

624 Roland De Vaux, *Ancient Israel: Its Life and Institutions* (Grand Rapids, MI: Wm. B. Eerdmans, 1997), 255.

625 Jimmy Akin, "Hard Sayings of the Old Testament," jimmyakin.com, February 2007.

626 St. Augustine seems to endorse the view that these passages refer to human rather than divine knowledge by saying, "It is said, Now I know, that is, Now I have made to be known; for God was not previously ignorant of this." *City of God* 16.32.

627 For example, Josephus said Isaac was twenty-five years old (*Antiqui-*

ties 1.13.2) whereas the Talmud said he was thirty-seven (*Seder Olam Rabbah*).

628 Origen, *Homilies on Joshua*, trans. Barbara J. Bruce, ed. Cynthia White (Washington, DC: The Catholic University of America Press, 2002), 34.

629 Ibid., 119.

630 Jerome F.D. Creach. *Violence in Scripture: Interpretation: Resources for the Use of Scripture in the Church* (Louisville, KY: Westminster John Knox Press, 2013), 102.

631 In 1 Kings 22:22, God says, "I will go forth, and will be a lying spirit in the mouth of all his prophets." According to the Navarre Bible, "The prophet's anthropomorphic language helps explain that everything is part of God's plan—even the fact that there are those who consciously or unconsciously let themselves be guided by a lying spirit, and particularly the fact that the king lets himself be deceived by those false prophets." University of Navarre, *Joshua–Kings* (New York: Four Courts Press, 2005), 511. This also applies to 2 Thessalonians 2:10–12, where the author says that God "sends upon them a strong delusion, to make them believe what is false, so that all may be condemned who did not believe the truth but had pleasure in unrighteousness." In this context, God allows those who have rejected the truth and accepted the anti-Christ's message to be given over to his deception.

632 Matthew Ramage, *Dark Passages of the Bible: Engaging Scripture with Benedict XVI and Thomas Aquinas* (Washington, DC: Catholic University of America Press, 2013), 188.

633 Ibid., 192.

634 Richard Hess, "The Jericho and Ai of the Book of Joshua," in *Critical Issues in Early Israelite History*, ed. Richard Hess et al. (Winona Lake, IN: Eisenbrauns, 2008), 34.

635 Exodus 23:27–31; 33:2; Leviticus 18:26–28; Numbers 21:32; 33:50–53; Deuteronomy 7:17–19.

636 Lawson Younger Jr., *Ancient Conquest Accounts*, 227–228. Cited in Paul Copan and Matt Flanagan, *Did God Really Command Genocide: Coming to Terms with the Justice of God* (Grand Rapids, MI: Baker Books, 2014), 104.

637 Matthew Ramage, *Dark Passages of the Bible: Engaging Scripture with*

Benedict XVI and Thomas Aquinas (Washington, DC: Catholic University of America Press, 2013), 168.

638 Justin Martyr, *Dialogue with Trypho*, 65.

639 *Providentissimus Deus*, 10.

Appendix: Has the Bible Been Corrupted?

640 Bart D. Ehrman, *Misquoting Jesus: The Story Behind Who Changed the Bible and Why* (New York: HarperCollins, 2005), 10.

641 F.F. Bruce, *The Books and the Parchments: How We Got Our English Bible* (Grand Rapids, MI: Fleming H. Revell Co., 1984), 78.

642 Bruce M. Metzger and Bart D. Ehrman, *The Text of the New Testament: Its Transmission, Corruption, and Restoration* (New York: Oxford University Press, 2005), 29.

643 Ibid., 126.

644 "When the bishop of Oea (modern Tripoli) introduced Jerome's recent rendering into his community service, Augustine worriedly related, the congregation nearly rioted. (At issue, perhaps, was the identity of the vine under which the prophet Jonah had rested—a 'gourd' so the traditional version, or an 'ivy' so Jerome; *Letter 75.7*, 22; Jonah 4:6)." Paula Fredriksen, *Augustine and the Jews: A Christian Defense of Jews and Judaism* (New Haven, CT: Yale University Press, 2010), 289.

645 Bruce M. Metzger and Bart D. Ehrman, *The Text of the New Testament: Its Transmission, Corruption, and Restoration* (New York: Oxford University Press, 2005), 18.

646 Bart D. Ehrman, *Misquoting Jesus: The Story Behind Who Changed the Bible and Why* (New York: HarperCollins, 2005), 89.

647 Daniel Wallace, "The Textual Reliability of the New Testament: A Dialogue," in *The Reliability of the New Testament: Bart D. Ehrman and Daniel B. Wallace in Dialogue*, ed. Robert Stewart (Minneapolis, MN: Fortress Press, 2011), 39.

648 Craig Blomberg, *Can We Still Believe in the Bible?: An Evangelical Engagement with Contemporary Questions* (Grand Rapids, MI: Brazos Press, 2014), 17.

649 The exceptions that include many verses would be the story about the woman caught in adultery (John 7:53–8:11) and the long ending of Mark (Mark 16:9–20), but scholars have known about these

variants for a long time. For a recent defense of the claim that the story of the woman caught in adultery was taken from one of Luke's sources and later added to John's Gospel (thus preserving the story's canonicity), see Kyle R. Hughes, "The Lukan Special Material and the Tradition History of the Pericope Adulterae," *Novum Testamentum* 55 (2013), 232–51. For a treatment of the longer ending in Mark see Daniel J. Harrington, *The Gospel of Mark* (Collegeville, MN: The Liturgical Press, 2002), 462–64.

650 Craig Blomberg, *Can We Still Believe in the Bible?: An Evangelical Engagement with Contemporary Questions* (Grand Rapids, MI: Brazos Press, 2014), 27–28.

651 Wallace, "The Textual Reliability of the New Testament: A Dialogue," 36.

652 Craig A. Evans, "How Long Were Late Antique Books in Use? Possible Implications for New Testament Textual Criticism," *Bulletin for Biblical Research* 25.1 (2015), 35.

653 Norman L. Geisler and William E. Nix, *A General Introduction to the Bible* (Chicago: Moody Press, 1986), 382.